MAYOR
AN AUTOBIOGRAPHY

EDWARD I. KOCH

WITH
WILLIAM RAUCH

WARNER BOOKS

A Warner Communications Company

DAN WOLF,
THE WISEST MAN I KNOW.

Contents

FOREWORD
Why This Book?

December 1983

EARLY IN MY ADMINISTRATION AS MAYOR, I began keeping notes on matters I perceived as important or interesting. I never taped for these notes, either with or without permission, any conversations that I had with anyone. All the conversations recorded in this book are my recollections jotted down immediately after the meeting, or on the following weekend. There is only one exception—a verbatim report of what took place at a town hall meeting. And that is because a recording by WNYC, the City's municipal radio station, was taken of the event, and that recording was made available to me.

I am sure that when I recalled the conversations, I have sometimes missed nuances or misinterpreted the intent, and perhaps even misquoted. But I did my best to recall what was said, and I never intentionally added to or changed any comment or fact. Nevertheless, I am certain that there will be people who will find fault with my recollection of what they said or did. If I was incorrect in recalling the details of an incident, I am sorry. But it was the best of my recollection, and we are all human and subject to error.

I had originally meant to keep these recollections for historical purposes, because I believe that events are best recorded fresh. When I decided to publish them while still in office, I told my intention to a reporter, who found it surprising. I'm not sure that at the time I really meant it. But my resolve to do it became firm in the fourth year of my first term.

When I discussed my final decision with advisers and

friends, all of them, without exception, urged me not to do it. And their comment was always the same. They said, "It has never been done. It will make new enemies for you, who will be outraged by what you say about them. It will make it more difficult for you to deal with others in public office. It will give your enemies things you wrote to use against you, in or out of context, when you run for reelection."

My response is I believe that the government of the City of New York is very important and that far too few people outside government understand what takes place. I want the people who live in this City—and those elsewhere in America—to know what City Hall is like, and how it functions. I believe that no matter how interesting books on public life are, if they are published long after the events occurred and when the individual who was in the eye of the hurricane is no longer in office and gone from the scene, those books are purchased and placed on coffee tables and read by very few and have no major impact. I want this book to be read, because I think it will have an impact on government and on people's attitudes toward government.

Finally, I want my recollections to be published without the benefit of hindsight revision.

My equanimity in office comes from the fact that I have always tried to tell the whole story, warts and all. I believe in the common sense of the ordinary person—and of the reader. In this book, as it relates to particular episodes over a twenty-six-year period, I have tried in every case to recount them faithfully. If I have failed, I am solely responsible.

I

Running for Mayor

1

A Child of the City

IN MARCH OF 1975, when I was a U.S. Congressman from New York, I received a call from Jac Friedgut, an executive at Citibank, asking for an opportunity to brief New York City's Congressional delegation on the state of the City. I told the caller that in all probability there would not be a large turnout, because the delegation did not like to give special opportunities to particular groups to come in and brief it, since there were so many requests. I was told that it was urgent and very important to the City, so in my capacity as secretary of the New York delegation I arranged the briefing.

In the whole delegation, perhaps six of the forty-one House members came, and neither Senator. In all, there were about twenty people in the room. Jac Friedgut, whom I had never met, was the spokesman. His briefing took about twenty minutes. The thrust of it was that the City was on the edge of bankruptcy, that it could no longer borrow money and that no one knew what ought to be done. The banks wanted to be sure that the Congressional delegation was informed.

No one, myself included, appreciated the urgency of the message. It didn't seem possible that Friedgut's assessment could be true. It sounded alarmist and ridiculous that the City of New York had run out of money and no one would lend it any and, while there were a couple of questions asked, it was a rather desultory meeting.

That was the first indication that those of us in Washington had of how terrible things really were. Months later, after all the bad news had become public and we had been briefed by the Governor, all the fiscal savants, who had remained quiet throughout the previous ten years, surfaced and began to wail.

I cannot say that the fiscal crisis was the beginning of my desire to be Mayor of New York, because New Yorkers with long memories and a taste for the obscure will recall that I ran briefly and unsuccessfully in the Democratic primary in 1973. But I can say honestly that the challenge of saving the City from financial ruin or worse was the kind of challenge I like. It was at that moment that I knew I was going to run again for Mayor.

The story of my public life really begins in Greenwich Village, and it was Greenwich Village that was for many years my political base.

I was born in 1924 in the Bronx. My family moved to Newark, New Jersey, in 1931, and to Brooklyn in 1941. I went to war, took an accelerated course through New York University Law School, practiced law in a tiny office on Wall Street and continued to live with my parents on Ocean Parkway in Brooklyn. I found along the way that I enjoyed the give-and-take of politics, and finally, in 1956, I scraped together enough money to move into my own apartment on Bedford Street in Greenwich Village.

At that time, Greenwich Village politics was controlled from a second-story loft at 88 Seventh Avenue South. One flight up, above the barbershop, was the headquarters of the Tamawa Club. The Tamawa was the regular Democratic club that had controlled Village politics since before anyone could remember. In 1956 the Tamawa's standard-bearer was Carmine G. DeSapio, the male Democratic district leader for Greenwich Village and the New York County leader. DeSapio was the boss of bosses, a backroom man, a cutter of deals. He was exactly the kind of politician who was unacceptable to my generation, who for a decade had been changing the face of Greenwich Village. They fancied themselves to be intellectually and morally honest. In Carmine DeSapio they had a leader in whom they did not perceive either quality.

In 1956 the Democrats ran Adlai Stevenson for the Presidency. The Republican Party's candidate was Dwight D. Eisenhower.

The match-up was a rerun of the 1952 race. Stevenson was an intellectual, a man whose speeches were of a high order. Eisenhower was the general who had engineered the Allies' victory in Europe. He was a product of West Point and the Army. In 1952 I had read Stevenson's speeches in the newspapers. I was not discouraged by the Governor's underdog status. For me that choice had been a clear one: Stevenson. And it still was in '56.

I had supported Stevenson in 1952 as a street speaker, or as they used to say, "on a soapbox." And I did so again, to an even greater extent, in 1956. I would take my U.S. flag and walk around, speaking wherever I could find anyone who would listen. (The State Democratic Committee provided American flags, which the law required be displayed by all speakers.) It was very exciting.

So I joined the Village Independent Democrats. The Stevenson committee—which later was to become the VID—had opened up because, while Carmine DeSapio didn't come out against Stevenson, he was not supporting him either. He didn't do anything. So the Stevenson people had caused this committee to come into being, and I joined.

I became a reasonably good street speaker. I appeared every night in Sheridan Square or at 8th Street and Sixth Avenue. I happen to like street speaking. A lot of people don't, but I like the give-and-take of the crowd and the heckler. If you know how to handle a heckler, he can be very good for you. You can really make great points when there are hecklers in the audience. The only kind of heckler you can't use is the drunk. The others, the ones who want to debate, are terrific. I love them. I became politically active then and there.

After Stevenson lost, there was a meeting to decide whether or not this group of Stevenson volunteers should stay in existence. There were two people running the club at this time, and I was put off by the way they were running it. It was a clique-type operation, and I wasn't one of the clique.

In 1957, in frustration, I went to DeSapio's club and joined it. But that affiliation didn't turn out any better than the other. The problem was that I was the only person at the meetings who was wearing a three-button Brooks Brothers suit. The club officers wouldn't talk to me and they wouldn't let me do anything. They thought I was a spy. Most of the others were old-line politicians. They didn't trust me. It was just as simple as that. And so I left.

After that I was again inactive for a while—I just practiced law. And I missed being involved in politics. I thought again about the VID, and one night I went to one of its regular Thursday-night meetings. And I'm sitting there and one of the older members comes over to me and says, "Why don't you come back?"

I say, "Well, I really would like to. But you know, I opposed you earlier?"

And he said, "Forget it."

It was very nice, and I said I'd love to come back.

In 1961, the VID ran James Lanigan against DeSapio for male district leader and won. It thus became the official Democratic club for Greenwich Village. But Lanigan quickly made an ass of himself. Two weeks after he won, he went on a TV program and announced he was going to run for county leader. That was the beginning of the end for him, and a sort of beginning for me.

In 1962, I ran for the 63rd District seat in the New York State Assembly. My opponent in the Democratic primary was the incumbent, William F. Passannante. The race was my first experience in party politics, and with the exception of Eleanor Roosevelt, the party elite lined up against me. Governor Herbert Lehman, Mayor Robert F. Wagner and Manhattan County Leader Edward N. Costikyan orchestrated the regulars' support of Passannante. Carmine DeSapio supplied the local machine.

As the campaign progressed through the summer of 1962, the regulars leaned harder and harder on Lanigan. Their interest was not only the reelection of Passannante but the appointment of James A. Farley, the 74-year-old onetime Postmaster General, as a delegate to the 1962 Democratic State Convention—a move we opposed as basically the old regulars' nothing-for-nothing politics.

It was a fascinating campaign. I was hurt beyond telling when the Citizens Union endorsed Passannante. In retrospect, it certainly makes sense that they would. He wasn't a bad guy—he had a good record; except I just knew I was much better. Still, he won.

In December of 1962, however, I had recouped my losses, and I won a very close race for the presidency of the VID. By June 1963 *The Village Voice* was proclaiming, "He [Koch] has healed the wounds of a badly divided club during his tenure as president," and our fight against bossism in the Village was on again. This time I grabbed the banner to run for male district leader.

And I had others in my corner this time. Eddie Costikyan recognized the necessity of blocking DeSapio's political comeback. Costikyan was now the New York County leader—a position DeSapio had held for twelve years. It was not inconceivable that DeSapio could unseat Costikyan if he were once again to sit on the County Democratic Executive Committee. That committee—sometimes called Tammany Hall—was composed solely of the county's district leaders. So now it was in Costikyan's interest to stop DeSapio, even if it meant cooperating with the reformers at the VID.

This time I won by an eyelash—41 votes out of 9,000 cast.

In 1965, John Lindsay was running for Mayor. A Republican, Lindsay also had the Liberal Party's backing. His major opponent, the Democrat, was City Comptroller Abraham Beame. Beame was the status-quo candidate, the candidate of the clubhouses. Nonetheless, he was the Democrat, and I was a Democratic district leader—a party post.

In the Village, most of my constituents were for Lindsay. I had stayed out of endorsing anyone up until the last weekend. As a reformer, I could hardly campaign for Beame; and as a Democrat, I was in a difficult position to support Lindsay.

Finally I decided to announce my support for Lindsay. And it got a lot of attention.

November 2, 1965

DAILY NEWS

IT'S THE DAY
LBJ and Humphrey Push Beame;
Reform Dem Koch Backs Lindsay

The night he won, Lindsay called me up. We had never before had a conversation other than a hello. "Ed," he said, "I'll never forget what you did." He sounded very grave. He sounded like Frank Costello. I said, "It was nothing, Mr. Mayor."

When John Lindsay was sworn in as Mayor on January 2, 1966, he vacated his Congressional seat. At that time Theodore Kupferman, a Republican, resigned his 2nd Councilmanic District seat to run for the "silk stocking"* Congressional seat just vacated by Lindsay. Following Kupferman's resignation from the City Council, the Council appointed Woodward Kingman to fill Kupferman's seat in an interim designation. The following November, in a special election, I opposed Kingman, the Republican incumbent, who had Lindsay's support.

Lindsay's problem—that he was ideologically more Democrat than Republican—was already becoming sticky. In the Kingman–Koch race, Lindsay's problem was compounded by my problem—that I had crossed party lines to endorse him. I expected Lindsay to endorse me, or at least to stay neutral, but he went ahead and endorsed the Republican. Our relationship had begun to cool.

The 2nd Councilmanic District is made up of most of Manhattan's East Side and some of Greenwich Village on the Lower West Side. It had been a Republican seat since the 1920s. I was strong in parts of it because I had built up a record on community issues, but only in the area of my district leadership, not uptown. It was in that area, the Upper East Side, that Lindsay would have been helpful. Nevertheless, always the optimist, I went to work at the subway stops uptown. Early on in the race it became evident I would be able to count on my unlikely downtown coalition of the early-rising Italians in the South Village and the late-sleeping liberals of the West Village.

Under the leadership of Dina Nolan, a storefront was opened on MacDougal Street as headquarters for Independent

---

*So-called because the voters there were among the wealthiest in the nation, and therefore the women wore silk stockings.

Citizens for Koch. From that South Village base the word of my effectiveness in solving community problems was spread among the Italian families who lived in the area. On Election Day I carried all ten of those crucial South Village election districts.

Throughout the campaign I received regular coverage from *The Village Voice*. Its page 1 Election Day endorsement indicates the extent to which the late sleepers' journal supported me. It read:

> Koch is something else. He has had more effect on the government of this city while out of office than most men have had while in office. Today, the City no longer moves in and freely shaves off sidewalks to make room for more cars. Koch is responsible for that. Today, clubhouse politics is in retreat. He, as much as anyone, is responsible for that too. He has been in dozens of battles as a front-line urban fighter, and in a sense is the best example of the new, effective urban politician.

In the end, I beat Kingman without Lindsay's endorsement, and was elected to the City Council. On January 1, 1967, the day of my installation as Councilman, which was to take place at 1:45, people arrived about 1:30 and the City Council chamber in City Hall was filled by 2 o'clock. Percy Sutton* came in at just about 2 to preside at the ceremony. He used the notes that I'd given him, including the soon-famous line "I got my job through *The Village Voice*."

Donald Szantho Harrington† gave an invocation in which he talked about the cities' being the most important level of government, and then Emanuel Popolizio‡ spoke and talked about how I had worked in the South Village and had reached the community. Then Thomas Hoving, Lindsay's Parks Commissioner, spoke and said that I should be a "rebel with reason" and that I was a very strong but sensitive person and he thought of me as his favorite Councilman.

Then I spoke in turn and said that I had wondered as I got

*The Manhattan Borough President.
†A politically active Unitarian minister in New York.
‡A community activist and lawyer in Greenwich Village; an early Koch supporter.

up what it was that had brought us all together. "There is Percy Sutton, whose family came out of bondage, and because he is personally able, he has risen to the top; and there is Donald Harrington, a fighting minister, who is not content just to sermonize; and there is Wally Popolizio, who is the son of immigrant parents, who delivered ice in the neighborhood with his father and who has become a prominent attorney, and who in this past election climbed those same staircases and said, 'Hi, remember me—Wally Popolizio? I used to deliver ice to you, and now I want you to vote for my friend Ed Koch.' And me, also the son of immigrant parents; and of course, Tom Hoving, son of Tiffany." (Walter Hoving was then president of Tiffany and Company.) I talked about my family and how proud they were, how proud I was of them. Everybody enjoyed the ceremony, and there were those who were laughing so hard they were crying.

John Lindsay's progress foreshadowed my own in another way. By yielding his Congressional seat to a less popular Republican, he'd created an opportunity for a Democrat, namely me. The New York 17th Congressional District is one of the most coveted and best-known Congressional seats in the United States. Politically, it is perhaps the best-organized territory in the country. Ethnically, it is probably the most diverse. It includes the immigrant neighborhoods of the Lower East Side, most of Greenwich Village, middle-class Murray Hill, international Turtle Bay, upwardly mobile Yorkville and the richest neighborhood in the world: the Upper East Side.

By defeating S. William Green in the Republican primary, Whitney North Seymour, Jr., Republican State Senator for the Upper East Side, had gained the inside track, and the opportunity to contest the November race with me.*

---

*One morning in October of 1968 I was standing at the corner of 14th Street and First Avenue. It's 8:30 in the morning and Seymour drives by in his big campaign station wagon. He sees me standing on the corner giving out literature to people going into the subway. That was by no means the biggest subway stop in the district. So he stops the car, gets out and approaches me.

In the course of the campaign, Seymour relied heavily on his WASP/Wall Street credentials. On one occasion, I was interviewed by a *Daily News* reporter who wanted to do a profile on both of us. The reporter called me up and said, "I've just been to see Senator Seymour, and I'd like to come over and talk to you."

I said, "Fine."

So he came over and talked to me, and he said, "You know, I've been to his office. It's a very posh law office. All the clerks and interns walk around in blue blazers. . . ." And here's my little law office, three partners and myself—very modest—and I'm probably in shirt sleeves. But it's clear this *Daily News* reporter didn't really like the pomposity of Seymour's Wall Street law office and in my judgment he's already on my side, just simply because he comes from the same milieu that I come from and not from Seymour's. And what really annoyed him was: He had said to Seymour—and he repeated it to me—"Tell me something about your background."

And Seymour had responded, "Well, when my mother was *enceinte* (pregnant) with me, she went back to the family estates in Virginia so that I could be born there, and I trace my lineage back to the Revolutionary War."

So the *Daily News* reporter says to me, "How far can you trace your lineage?"

I say, "Well, I think the best I could do is back to Ellis Island." And since that was also as far back as he could trace his, the reporter loved it. That was really the nature of the campaign, always between Seymour and me. I structured it that way because it *was* me and it *was* him. It wasn't a phony operation.

"What time did you start this morning?" asks Seymour.

I say, "Seven o'clock."

Seymour says, "And how long have you been doing this?"

I say, "Oh, about a year." At that moment I saw the look on Seymour's face. And it was clear that there was a significant change in his perception of what that campaign was going to be like.

After the election was over, I said, "Nobody thought I could win. After all, how could a guy with two names beat a guy with four names?"

I took him to the cleaners.

2

Picking My Fights

I WAS A MAVERICK CONGRESSMAN from the beginning; what I call a hair shirt.

A hair shirt is someone who is constantly in a state of agitation, someone who is itching, who is never at ease. A hair shirt is an activist. As I said, I was a hair shirt.

The organization man does not trust the hair shirt. The party politician cannot trust the hair shirt beyond his next itch. The hair shirt is owned by no one. He lives by his wits.

Jimmy Carter used to say that dissent within an organization is healthy—but once policy is established, the organization has the right to expect from its members loyalty and an enthusiastic implementation of policy.

I was always proud of being Jewish, but I had never been a Jewish activist. In my district in 1968 or 1969 a lot of people did not know I was Jewish. My name is not particularly Jewish. K-o-c-h for many people is more German than Jewish, though in fact it can be either. I had been an activist, to be sure, and in Congress I was soon involved in every civil rights issue for the blacks and Hispanics and women, and worked for every oppressed group in the country—except the Jews. Well, I changed that, and made the Jews one of my priorities.

I came up with the idea that I should introduce legislation which would allow—and encourage—Soviet Jews to come to the United States. At that time Congress was very supportive of getting Jews out of the Soviet Union. But assuming Soviet Jews got out of the Soviet Union, there was no automatic way they could come to the United States. So I said we ought to allocate 25,000 refugee visas for Soviet Jews who might be allowed to emigrate from the Soviet Union. And I began my campaign.

It was very highly regarded by the Jewish public, but the Jewish organizations disliked it intensely for several reasons, and although most could not do so publicly, they tried to subvert it. The Zionist Organization of America attacked me in its paper, maintaining that I was proposing to lure Jews to the United States when those Jews should be encouraged to go to Israel.

I said in response to that, "I think they should be given an option. I hope they go to Israel, but what bothers me is this: it's on the record that in World War II, when Jews could have been rescued from Nazi Germany, the United States took only a small number. I have never forgotten that, and that's why I want to provide that opportunity, whether they use it or they don't use it."

Other groups, such as the American Jewish Congress, were distressed that I was raising an issue they regarded as their own. Who, after all, was I, a first-term Congressman, to get so involved in their parade? Moreover, they didn't think we could win on it; and they felt it would be a terrible, terrible mistake to take on a major Jewish issue that had to come before the Congress and would probably lose.

I didn't care. I have a very stick-to-it kind of personality. If I undertake something, I can't be intimidated, and I move ahead. I'm really very good at getting things done. I'm a very pragmatic guy. I was getting hundreds, maybe thousands, of letters on this from Jews, and also many Members of Congress loved it, because it was a no-lose way of getting their names down on a pro-Jewish issue.

So I pursued it, and Emanuel Celler,* who was then chairman of the Judiciary Committee, said to me, "We'll never get this out of committee. We can't win this thing."

I said, "Manny, I think it's something that we need. We should be able to get it out."

---

*A Democratic Representative from Brooklyn.

He said, "I can only tell you that we're not going to be able to get it out. The pressure is against us. But if you want to do something, why don't you talk to [Gerald] Ford?* It doesn't have to be done legislatively. It can be done through the Administration under a section of the immigration law in which they say that they're exercising what's called the parole authority, as they did for Cuba and Hungary and other countries—not by legislation. We simply say a group is a refugee group and we'll take them without regard to quota restrictions."

So that's what I did. I went to see Jerry Ford and explained it to him.

He said, "Yes, these people are very good people," talking about the Jews who had come out of the Soviet Union. "I will help you. If these people were to come here, they would never go on welfare."

And he did help. John Mitchell, then the Attorney General, issued a letter. Manny Celler immediately brought me into the issue, and we had a press conference on it. The letter said that anybody (while there was a reference to Jews, the parole authority was for anybody) permitted to leave the Soviet Union could come here without regard to quota restrictions, and that is still the rule today.

Now, let me tell you about the climate that public officials who were Jewish lived in. The Jewish groups took Congressmen who were Jewish for granted. They made no attempt to honor them, to try to place them in the spotlight. They loved it when a non-Jewish Congressman did something in the Jewish interest; he was given accolades. Jewish Congressmen, not so. I'll give you an illustration of what I mean.

When I became a Congressman, I went to the Salute to Israel parade, which is held every year, like the Saint Patrick's Day parade. I go to all the parades, and that year, my first as a Congressman, I hoped to be invited to march in this one; but the sponsors did not issue individual invitations.

I got to Fifth Avenue around 59th Street, and I saw a guy

---

*Then leader of the Republicans in the House.

with a walkie-talkie who was wearing a sash that read
MARSHAL. I walked over to him and said, "I'm Congressman
Koch."

He said, "I know who you are. How are you?"

"I'd like to be in the parade," I said. "Where are the
dignitaries and officials going to march from?"

He said, "We don't do that. Everybody has to find his own
group. They march with Hadassah and the Flatbush Jewish
Center and that sort of thing."

"I don't have a group to march with," I said. "Could you
suggest one?"

"No, Congressman, you have to find your own group."

So I said to myself: This guy is a number one dope. How
many Congressmen does he meet at Fifth Avenue and 59th
Street who want to march in the parade? I'm the only one
here. But I'm not going to fight with him.

So I walked down to 56th Street, where I saw a car with a
banner reading MARSHAL. I walked over to it and I said, "I'm
Congressman Koch."

The two guys in the car replied, "Oh, of course, we know
you. How are you, Congressman?"

I said, "You know, I'd like to be in the parade," and their
faces lit up. "Where can I get into the parade?"

So they said, "We'll take care of that." And they took out
their walkie-talkie and the conversation went something like
this: "This is Rover Two; come in Rover One."

At the other end: "Rover One speaking."

"Rover One, I have Congressman Koch here, and he'd like
to march in the parade. Where shall I send him?"

Rover One: "I told Congressman Koch he's got to find his
own group." It was the guy I'd just left!

So these two guys say, "Sorry, he's in charge."

I said to myself, My God, what a wonderful way to make
friends. So I stood there thinking: How am I going to get into
this parade? And suddenly along comes Herman Badillo*
leading the American Jewish War Veterans of the Bronx, so I

*A Puerto Rican–born Democratic Congressman from the Bronx, whose wife
is Jewish.

ran over to Herman and said, "Herman, can I march with you?" And Herman Badillo got me into the parade.

One of the first things I did after I took my seat in Congress was ascertain who was supporting the Vietnam War. Most Members didn't really want to support the war, but many of them were stuck with it. They had supported it from the beginning—I had actively opposed it from the beginning— and they didn't know how to change their public position.

I ate lunch every day in the private Members' dining room. I thought it was very important to do so. I got to know many of the Congressmen, and they in turn got to know me. I enjoyed their company. So it became evident to me that Bob Giaimo*—a very powerful guy—had turned against the war, but he didn't know how to declare his position. As he put it to me, "If I came out against the war now it would look like I was getting on the bandwagon." That is the way he put it, which is kind of ridiculous when we were talking about 1969–70.

So I said, "You know what we should do? The two of us should introduce a resolution saying that whether we are for or against the war, the fact is we cannot win the war, and without expressing a moral judgment, we the undersigned believe it is now in the best interests of the United States to withdraw." I don't know how many names we got on that resolution—maybe 50. But it was unique because it was me against the war and Bob Giaimo for the war both saying Let's get out. I thought that was helpful.

There were two fights I ended up walking away from:
As a member of the Small Business Committee, which was part of the Banking and Currency Committee, I proposed legislation saying that in the distribution of Small Business Administration loans there was no longer to be discrimination, either for or against, on the basis of race, national origin, sex and so forth. The vote was 10 to 2 in favor. But when the bill got into the full Committee, the blacks, who were one of six preferred groups under existing SBA rules (the others being

*Robert N. Giaimo, a moderate Democrat from Connecticut.

Spanish-surname, Orientals, American Indians, Eskimos and Aleuts), sought to reverse me. They went to work, and I got a lot of letters from blacks. I got no letters from Jews or any other white group. They either couldn't have cared less, weren't interested, didn't want to stand up on it or took it for granted that there was no discrimination. I fought for my bill in the full Committee, and I lost. I remember Henry Reuss,* who was the chairman, saying to me, "Shame, shame, shame, Ed."

I thought, He must be crazy. What is this "shame, shame, shame"? I want to end discrimination. I don't want to create new discrimination. These grants should be made on the basis of economic need, not race. But the Committee reversed me.

Then I went to lunch and talked to Ben Rosenthal, Sid Yates and others,† and they all agreed with me. I said, "Why don't we take it to the floor and try to reverse the Committee? I believe that the House of Representatives is not for racial set-asides."

Sid Yates agreed, but suggested, "Before we do anything, why don't we talk to Joe Rauh?"‡

So, we are at a party at Governor Harriman's§ house in Georgetown—this huge estate, one block square—and there is Joe Rauh. I know Joe: Mr. Liberal. So Sid and I went over to him.

"Joe," Yates said, "Ed here has a question and I think he ought to get your point of view. Ed, tell him what your story is."

I then proceeded to explain, and I asked Rauh whether or not he thought it advisable to bring the matter up on the floor and try to reverse the Committee.

Rauh simply became enraged. "We will fight you in the

---

*A Democrat from Wisconsin.

†Benjamin Rosenthal was a Democratic Congressman from Queens; Sidney Yates, a Democrat from Chicago, was Celler's successor as dean of the Jewish Congressional Caucus.

‡Joseph L. Rauh, Jr., an attorney and former chairman of Americans for Democratic Action.

§Averell Harriman, diplomat, former Democratic Governor of New York (1951–59) and party elder.

streets!'' he cried. ''We will fight you in the cities! ...'' It was like a speech by Churchill! If I dared to do as I proposed, they, the liberal Establishment, would crush me.

Well, I was shocked. I wasn't terrified, because I didn't think the liberal Establishment could defeat me in my Congressional district. But my district was liberal, and it was filled with ideologues. So it wasn't very pleasant.

I decided I wouldn't do it. I wasn't getting any support. The Members of Congress I talked to who agreed with me weren't going to stand up and say what had to be said. I knew it, just judging by the way they were running away from the issue. I decided I wouldn't fight that battle.

The other fight I sized up and decided not to take on was over the issue of investigating the poverty programs. These were the brainchildren of the Great Society, brought to pass by Lyndon Johnson and the 89th Congress in 1964-65. Then, in the flush of victory, and with the threat of the Vietnam War still only on the horizon, Lyndon Johnson had caused breathtaking amounts of legislation to be passed into law. In the heady days of the '60s boom, federal largesse had seemed limitless. But a decade later, I and others in Washington and New York wondered if all these poverty programs, with their huge budgets that ended up God-only-knew-where, should be continued without review every year.

In 1975, the Federal Government refused to fund a New York City drug program on the ground that the program was incompetently run and hugely wasteful. The City drug programs were then administered by Jerome Hornblass. Hornblass came down to see Charlie Rangel* and me to try to get the Feds to restore the dollars that they said they were going to take away because of incompetency. (The Feds said they would give money to the State but they wouldn't give it to the City.)

Charlie's response was ''Well, the Feds may be right, but we still have to get this money for the drug programs.''

I said to him, ''Look there are a lot of allegations relating to these programs and other programs that the Federal Govern-

---

*Charles B. Rangel, the Democratic Congressman from Harlem.

ment finances. Why don't we do a study on them? If they are bad, let's end them. Or change them.''

Rangel said, ''No, we don't want them to do any study of our programs and possibly lose us the funding. If they're going to do a study, let them study the whole country. Maybe some programs are bad in the whole country, but we have to get our share of the funds.''

His attitude was startling to me at the time. But I thought: Well, I am not able to take on all of these battles.

3

The 1977 Campaign

THE BIGGEST FIGHT I picked during my years in Congress was the one I picked on March 4, 1977, with New York's Mayor Abraham Beame—for the Democratic and Liberal Party nominations for his office. Nor was I the only challenger—there were five other Democrats opposing Beame in the primary: Bella Abzug, Herman Badillo, Mario Cuomo, Joel Harnett and Percy Sutton.

After my withdrawal from the '73 race, there had appeared on the editorial page of *The New York Times* a brief commendation of my efforts. In part, it said:

> To his credit U.S. Representative Edward I. Koch of Manhattan refrained from name-calling and campaigned instead from sunrise to sunset and often later at subway stops, introducing himself to the voters and asking for their support. Mr. Koch has now abandoned his long-shot quest with typical grace and good humor.

Now on March 4, three and a half years later, I was back—still, I hope, with the grace and good humor, but now with a few more guns to display. In a hallway of the Hilton Hotel, just prior to my announcement press conference, I was asked how Governor Hugh Carey's recent veto of a June primary would affect my campaign. I replied, "I expect them [the voters] to love me in September as they would have in June."

Once under the lights, I previewed some of my favorite campaign issues: "I do not hold the [Emergency Financial

21

Control Board] in low regard," I said. "It was because of their presence and their pressures that the present Mayor has been dragged—kicking and screaming—into every decision that's been helpful to this city since the crisis."

Asked what my number one priority would be, were I to be elected 105th Mayor of the City of New York, I replied, "Getting the hacks off the payroll."

On the state of the City, I declared, "New York City may be facing its darkest hour—the continued threat of bankruptcy, the loss of more and more jobs and the steadily increasing crime rate . . . ."

The *Post*'s headline summed up the tenor of the announcement: "KOCH LAUNCHES DRIVE BY JUMPING ON BEAME." And throughout the campaign I never let up on the three Cs. My slogan was "After eight years of charisma [Lindsay] and four years of the clubhouse [Beame], let's try competence."

Right after my announcement, Governor Carey said he was for me. He told me that. At that time he said to several of the Liberal Party leaders—Edward Morrison and Alex Rose's son, Herbert—that if the Liberal Party designated me, even if I lost on the Democratic line, he would support me on the Liberal line.

I thought that was rather bizarre. I didn't really believe it; but it was nice that he said it. The fact is that when he switched to Cuomo he said the same thing, and then he didn't do it. He said he would support Cuomo on the Liberal Party line even if Cuomo lost the Democratic primary. It is not possible, of course, for a Governor to do anything of the kind, nor should anyone expect him to do anything of the kind. A Democratic Governor has to endorse the Democratic candidate, although it is all right for him to say he might not in the course of negotiations to get the Liberal Party's support.

Cuomo had been the early favorite of a lot of people, but he had decided he was not going to run. It was then that media consultant David Garth had agreed to take on my campaign, and Carey had agreed to be supportive. Then, somewhere along the line, there was a change of heart.

I heard about the change of heart in the following way. I was in my Congressional office in the City, and I received a call about 3 o'clock in the afternoon. It was from the Governor. And the call went very much like this: "Ed, would you indulge me by coming over to Bob Wagner, Senior's, house?* I would like to talk with you. Could you get here by four o'clock?"

I said, "Of course, Governor. I'll be right over."

I called David Garth before I left. I asked him if he knew why the Governor was calling. He said, "Yes, I had lunch with him today and he asked me to leave your campaign and take over Cuomo's campaign. I said that I wouldn't do it."

So I went to the Wagner brownstone. It was just Wagner, the Governor and me. Wagner was very quiet. Carey was very edgy.

Before Carey started, I said to him, "Governor, before you tell me whatever it is you want to tell me, I just want you to know that whatever it is you are going to tell me, I will be supporting you next year. Now, what is it you want to tell me?"

Then the Governor sort of gulped and said, "You know, Ed, I really think that you are probably the best. If I had my way, you would be the Mayor—but I don't think you can win. Mario wants to run and I think he *can* win. We have to stop Bella or Beame from winning. I hope you understand."

This conversation took about twenty minutes. I didn't say a word. I let him talk. And that is not my style. I hear something and I want to respond to it. I kept myself under very good control, and let him talk until he seemed to be exhausted.

I said, "Have you finished?"

He said, "Yes."

Then I said, "Governor, I won nine times in fourteen years. Mario did not support you in 1974. And now let me ask you a couple of questions. What makes you think that Mario Cuomo can win? The last time he ran for anything he was beaten. When he ran for Lieutenant Governor in '74, Mary Anne Krupsak creamed him. She was nothing, and she beat him up. Can't we get together on this? Cuomo can run with me for City Council President."

---

*Robert F. Wagner, Mayor of the City of New York, 1954–1965.

And then Carey said, "I was thinking about it the other way around."

I said, "Governor, I represent the most prestigious district in the Congress. For me, City Council President would be a step down. For Mario it would be a step up. And let me tell you one more thing: he will not be elected Mayor. I will. And so I just want you to know that I am not withdrawing." And that was the last I heard from him until he endorsed me after the runoff.

After the meeting at Wagner's brownstone, everyone discounted me. I became sixth in a field of seven—Joel Harnett being seventh, and nobody had ever heard of him. The other Democratic candidates, as I said, were Beame, Cuomo, Abzug, Badillo and Sutton—and briefly, Richard Ravitch.

I had known Ravitch for some five years. He was not too fond of me when I was in the Congress. That would be true of most of the rich and powerful people in my district. Maybe I was in the streets too much. Maybe it's my Polish-Jewish antecedents. Who knows? Anyway, most of them now appear to have forgotten that they used to not like me very much.

The story with Ravitch was kind of funny. Early on in the 1977 campaign Ravitch was a serious candidate. He thought he had Carey's support (so did half the people in the race) because he had been a member of the Carey team and had saved the UDC* from bankruptcy. Besides that, he was the candidate of the rich. Ravitch thought he was going to be the next Mayor. But it developed that Carey pulled the rug out from under him and supported Cuomo.

To make a long story short, by September Ravitch was long gone. I had topped the primary and was in a runoff with Cuomo. I went to see Ravitch at his home. I was looking for his support. I walk in. He is so upset he keeps saying, "The Governor screwed me. How could the Governor do that? It's awful."

Well, I didn't have patience for that at that time. He was talking about something that had happened six months earlier.

*The New York State Urban Development Corporation.

And I had to go out the next week and win the runoff and then the general election. And there I was listening to someone complaining that someone had screwed him in politics, and that the Governor owed him something. It was as if he were shocked that that could happen. It happens all the time. It had happened to *me* with the Governor—that year. It is regrettable, but you don't sit around moping about it.

I said to him: "Dick, politics is not for you. You should stay home. Just worry about Diane and the kids and have a good time. Politics is definitely not for you." Well, he was a little stunned that I would say that. Then I said, "What I need now is support. The runoff is next week. Dick, I need your support."

He would not give it. He couldn't get off the Governor thing. So I left. It was dumb on his part. I think he regrets it now. But he certainly remembers my comment. It wasn't intended to be malicious, just a straightforward statement. Ultimately, of course, Governor Carey appointed Ravitch Chairman of the Metropolitan Transportation Authority (MTA) and Ravitch performed in that capacity brilliantly.

In the course of the 1977 campaign, it became clear that people around Cuomo were going to stoop to an attack alleging that I was homosexual. It was one of those undercover attacks. And it was clear that Mario was going to be doing nothing toward disciplining or dismissing those of his aides who participated in the smear. The way in which he did that was so clear and so heavy-handed that there can be no doubt of his complicity.

Throughout the campaign both Mario and I had said that we supported the Gay Rights Bill that had been proposed to the City Council. It was a bill that prohibited discrimination based on sexual orientation in the fields of employment, housing and places of public accommodation. We had appeared on numerous platforms, and upon this issue we had agreed.

Then, however, his campaign aides must have decided that it wasn't any longer politically advantageous for Mario to be for the Gay Rights legislation, because in two debates toward the end of the campaign he began to back away from supporting the legislation and then sought to portray me as someone who favored what he called "proselytization": the teaching in schools of homosexuality by homosexuals. The bill did not advocate any such thing, and no one in that race, and certainly not I, supported such an idea.

In the Channel 13 *Round Table* debate that was held on November 4, for example, Mario said: "I have repeatedly, before every gay group—particularly the gay group that endorsed you and condemned me—made the point that I am opposed to proselytization." That is a very difficult sort of attack to defend yourself against in a debate. He didn't name the group, and in the City of New York there are maybe ten major gay political groups. It was what these things always are. It was innuendo. And innuendo, to me, is the low road.

Moreover, this was clearly not a question of naiveté. It may be that in 1977 Mario Cuomo had never held elective office, but in this instance he knew exactly what he was doing. He put it out there clearly for all of us to read.

On November 7, *The Village Voice* ran a story by Geoffrey Stokes entitled "Smear News Is No News." The story was about a guy named Michael Dowd, who was Mario Cuomo's campaign manager during the primary and the runoff. As the story was told in the *Voice*, Dowd had hired a private eye, Roger Horan, who was to conduct an investigation into my sex life. Meanwhile, according to this article, Cuomo's Brooklyn coordinator, Thomas Chardavoyne, had hired another guy, Bruce Romanoff,* a "security consultant," to see if "there was a chance Koch had a few boyfriends."

So what does Mario Cuomo say when Geoffrey Stokes of the *Voice* asks him about all these guys and their activities? According to the article, he said: "Oh, Christ. Holy Mother

---

*In 1979, as a result of an incident unrelated to his employment by Chardavoyne, Bruce Romanoff pleaded guilty in Queens County Supreme Court to tampering with a witness. He paid a $500 fine and was placed on three years probation. On September 7, 1984 the *Daily News* reported that Romanoff had again been arrested, this time in Philadelphia, the *News* said, and for accepting $60,000 from a Rose Owens Reese in exchange for Romanoff's furnishing "two hit men from New York" who then allegedly murdered Reese's husband, John Reese. At this writing that case is still pending before Philadelphia Common Pleas Court.

of God. I'm so . . . I'm so . . . disappointed. . . . Asking questions like that about someone can injure his reputation. What if you hurt this fellow and he wins? What you've done is you've scarred the reputation of the Mayor of the greatest city in the world."

And that was it. Mario Cuomo walked away from the whole episode, one that Stokes described as "particularly vicious," without even an admonishment for Dowd or Chardavoyne, whereas the ethical thing would have been to fire these people on the spot.

Then, adding insult to injury, Jack Newfield of the *Voice* wrote an article commending both me and Mario for our position on the Gay Rights Bill.* But the way he did it had the effect of doing me a disservice and hyping Mario. The gist was that Koch is to be commended because he is a bachelor and is therefore subject to suspicion, and Cuomo because he is a Catholic and therefore doing something his constituency wouldn't like. Such a man of courage!

I have said: "I hold Mario Cuomo responsible for what happened." I also hold him responsible for the same thing happening in 1982, but we'll get to that later.

Cuomo's response was that I should apologize to him because my campaign made attacks on him to the effect that he was part of the Mafia. He alleged that his son had said he'd heard a truck with a loudspeaker say, "A vote for Cuomo is a vote for the Mafia." I don't believe that ever happened. And if it did happen—which I don't believe—it was an isolated incident (someone obviously doing it on his own and whose name I never heard), as opposed to a campaign with photocopied posters;† with Cuomo campaign people engaging in attacks and hiring detectives; with Cuomo himself raising the homosexuality issue on television and radio programs.

In the midst of all this, we were informed by a couple of reporters that Cuomo's people were hiring a renegade cop to perjure himself. He was apparently either someone who was

---

*See *Village Voice*, July 18, 1977.

†Someone who had an interest in Mario Cuomo's victory put up flyers around the city that read, "VOTE FOR CUOMO, NOT THE HOMO." We never knew who it was, but there were a lot of flyers up during that campaign.

on the force and no good, or someone who had been thrown off the force. Anyway, he was going to swear to having arrested me as a result of an alleged fight in my apartment. He was also going to swear to having arrested me for soliciting male prostitutes on the street. He was going to perjure himself. The allegations were inherently unbelievable; but, of course, when that sort of story gets out on the weekend of an election, what can you do? By the time you catch up to this guy the election is over. The story got so far as to be "on hold" on the AP wire, which means that it had been written and was in the AP's computer, waiting to be transmitted.

David Garth was very good about this. Before the story got on the AP wire, Samuel DeMilia, the president of the Patrolmen's Benevolent Association, had come up to Garth's office. Now, according to Garth, who told me later what took place, DeMilia had said he had an affidavit from this cop who swore he had arrested me on two occasions: once after a fight in my apartment and once with a male prostitute. DeMilia said it would be terrible to have a Mayor who was subject to blackmail and that the story had to come out before the election.

So Garth said, "Listen, Sam, I know Ed Koch, and I know that this is not true. But if it is true, then what you should do is tell it to the world." Then he picks up the phone and calls Frank Lynn, who writes about politics for *The New York Times*. Lynn gets on the phone and Garth says, "Frank, I have Sam DeMilia here and he has a story for you."

And DeMilia is shaking his head, No, no, no.

And Garth says, "Here, Sam, tell him what you just told me."

And DeMilia wouldn't talk to Lynn.

We thought maybe that had stopped it, but a day or two later it shows up, as I said, "on hold" on the AP wire. So Garth calls the people at AP and he puts me on the phone, and I say, "Look, this never happened, and if it did it would be reported by the cops in their daybooks." Well, the newspeople couldn't get confirmation, so then they stopped the story; but by that time some of Cuomo's people had copied it from the wire and passed it around to some reporters, so that after the election it did appear in some of the papers.*

In the ten days between the primary and the runoff, the two Democratic finalists divided up 61 percent of the vote. In those ten days Mario Cuomo showed what an inexperienced politician he was—and it hurt him. He stormed at his staff. He sulked to his family. He could not keep to his schedule, enabling me to portray his operation as amateurish and flawed.

For all his errors, Cuomo might still have managed a victory had he not needlessly alienated the losers. Carey had handpicked Cuomo to beat Beame; thus Beame would never have thrown his 18 percent to Cuomo. Abzug had made a career of feuding with me; thus she could never have supported me. Abzug for Cuomo; Beame for Koch: a standoff.

Assuming this was the case, the black and Puerto Rican votes, about 25 percent of the total vote, would become a substantial factor. Now, Percy Sutton was so crushed by his poor showing that he, as he put it, "went fishing." In his place at the head of the black leadership appeared Charlie Rangel, my former colleague in Congress. He became a major figure by default. And there to share the podium with him was Herman Badillo, with his Hispanic 11 percent.

Earlier, Abzug and Badillo and Rangel and Sutton had joined forces to decide what they were going to do. They lasted about twenty-four hours together. Herman said he had gone to see Cuomo and Cuomo had treated him very high-handedly. As he put it, "Cuomo didn't even ask me to have a cup of coffee." And so Herman came to see me.

He agreed to take an active role in my campaign. At the time, I really didn't think in terms of his eventually being one of my deputy mayors. I never would have thought he'd want to leave Congress. But I was delighted later on when he said

---

*In March of 1980, DeMilia resigned as president of the PBA. Although his power within the association had diminished to a point at which no one thought he could win another term as president, the reason DeMilia gave for his resignation was cancer of the eye. On that occasion I said privately, "I never liked him. I have no respect for him. He was a creep. But I never wished cancer on him. Other things maybe—but not cancer."

he was interested. Herman is a terrific campaigner: no follow-through, but a terrific campaigner.

In that same period, I met with Bella. I wouldn't do anything for her, and she came out for Cuomo. It was bizarre when you think about it. She is so radical. I would have seemed the more likely person, but on the other hand, I understand why. She and I have never gotten along, and I don't hold it against her. There are so many other things I hold against her, I don't need that one to add to it.

I first met Bella when I ran for Congress in 1968. She was then the leader of the 17th Peace Action Coalition, basically a front group for Women Strike for Peace—far left. In seeking endorsements, I went to see her. She then lived in a brown-stone on 16th or 17th Street on the East Side. I was interviewed by Bella and Douglas Ireland, a journalist friend of hers. The thrust of their questioning was: What was my position on jets for Israel (which was then very controversial on the radical left)? The radical left position was No jets for Israel.

I said, "I am for doubling whatever President Johnson is for. I don't think we're giving them enough."

That was terrible, terrible, terrible, according to Bella.

Their second question was: Would I support our terminating the NATO alliance?

I said, "Well, when they terminate the Warsaw alliance, then we'll terminate the NATO alliance, but not before. I happen to think the Soviet Union is a threat."

Well, that crossed off those two—because they didn't. And from that point on we were never, ever unaware of where I stood and where she stood.

Now, one day when Bella was in the Congress and running for the Senate in 1976, I got a copy of a letter from one of the women's groups that had originally been organized to oppose the war in Vietnam. It was directed to the 76 Senators who had sent a letter to President Ford urging jets for Israel, deploring their position and urging the Senators to reverse it. Bella's name was on the letterhead as one of the directors. So I sent a letter back to the woman who had signed it saying that I thought her position was outrageous, a terrible thing, and that I was for jets. And, urging the Senators to stand fast.

I put the whole correspondence into the *Congressional Record*. Then I sent copies to every Jewish group I knew. The letter was there with Bella's name on it. I didn't say a word about her.

Then all these rabbis and Jewish groups started to call Bella: "What are you doing, arrh . . ."—really incredible; calling her in the middle of the night, screaming at her.

How do I know? Because two or three days after that she sees me and says, "What are you trying to do, destroy me?"

I say, "What's up, Bella?"

"What are you trying to do sending out those letters?"

I said, "Isn't that your organization?"

"You know where I stand."

Well, she was fit to be tied. So she sent Sid Yates, the dean of the Jewish delegation in Congress, to see me. He says, "Bella says you're trying to destroy her, and she wants me to call a meeting of all the members of the Jewish delegation. I told her," he said, "that the last Sanhedrin met in the year 70 C.E.* But," he said, "what's going on?"

I said, "Nothing—I'm just telling the truth. It was just this correspondence. I haven't added anything. Her name is on it."

He said, "Well, she wants me to get a list of the people to whom you sent all of this." (You have to understand that, as a Congressman, I had the frank—a free mailing privilege. I had sent out maybe a hundred copies of that extract from the *Congressional Record*.) "Well, how many did you send out?" he asked.

"Oh, hundreds of thousands," I said.

He said, "Hundreds of thousands?"

"Yes."

"Well, she wants the list."

So I said, "I cannot give her the list because I will not permit her to use the frank on this matter; that's a political statement that she wants to send. But if she wants to, I'll prepare the envelopes and she can stamp them with her own money."

*C.E. (Common Era) is the Jewish term that corresponds to A.D. (Anno Domini). The Sanhedrin was a Jewish tribunal in ancient Israel that exercised religious, civil and criminal authority.

*   *   *

I'm not the type to get ulcers. I give them.

Another time, in 1972, she was running against William Fitts Ryan, my fellow Congressman from the West Side of Manhattan. And I was for Bill. I helped him as much as I could—suggesting positions he might take; whatever I could do. But I didn't come out for him. Since it was two Congressional incumbents opposing each other, I didn't endorse either one.

The night of the primary, I said to my staff, "I can't stay away. I'm going to go up there. I've got to go up to cheer Bill Ryan in."

They said, "All right, but don't get there before the polls are closed." The polls in the primary close at 10 o'clock. I got there at 10:01.

Ryan couldn't speak well at the time; his face was twice the size it should have been because he was taking cortisone. He was dying of cancer. But he had worked like a horse.

The first return to come in was from Bella's home election district, and she'd lost. That was really startling. The press came running over to me, the *Times* and the *News*—I was the only public-office holder in the room; even Ryan wasn't there—and they asked, "Congressman, isn't this unusual? How do you explain this? Isn't it surprising that Mrs. Abzug would lose in her own home election district? Why do you think that happened?"

I thought for a moment. There was a pregnant pause, and I said, "Her neighbors know her," and that was carried in the *News* and in the *Times*. She never got over it.

On later occasions, whenever we attempted rapprochements—you know, goodwill and forget about the past—she'd say, "Why did you have to say, 'Her neighbors know her'?"

But through it all, Bella's husband, Martin Abzug, was always very friendly to me, and I liked him. One time I saw him by the elevators in the Capitol and we stopped and spoke for a while. And then when he got on the elevator his parting words were "I won't tell Bella I saw you." I always loved that.

*   *   *

At any rate, to get back to the runoff election, Sutton felt that in the primary, he had been a victim of white bigotry. He had expected the whites to vote for him simply because he was black and because, as he saw it, he was the great hope of the City. It is nutty to think that if large numbers of whites don't vote for you, that makes them anti-black. Maybe they liked me better—particularly since large numbers of blacks didn't vote for him.*

Well, after Sutton pulled out, Rangel became the leader of the blacks, and he brought the black leadership to Garth's office. We were there for two hours or more, and I was very eloquent.

I recapitulated the history of my activities in behalf of civil rights—how I had gone to Mississippi in 1964 to help with black-voter registration; how I had marched into Montgomery, Alabama, with the Reverend Martin Luther King, Jr. I made the point that I was not for racial quotas or for preferential treatment and had never been and never could be. I said that the City administration should reflect the diversity of the public and I believed in reaching out and finding people on their merits. I said that I believed in putting money where it was needed; I said that I would strike down discrimination; and I said that I would appoint more blacks to high positions in the administration than had held office in the last three administrations combined: those of Wagner, Lindsay and Beame.†

Well, after I had spoken, Rangel came over and joined me, because he knew me and I think he genuinely liked me; and I

*In the primary, Sutton, the only black in the race, and for many years the Borough President of Manhattan, garnered only 53 percent of the Harlem vote.

†At that time I didn't know how many blacks those administrations had had. The number was very high—much higher than I realized. When I ultimately looked at the figures, they broke down something like this. of the 135 top management positions in the government, Wagner had named blacks to 5 percent, Lindsay 10 percent and Beame 12 percent. I never would have believed it. I must say that both Lindsay and Beame, in my judgment, had appointed second-raters. Nevertheless, if you put the figures together, that is 27 percent. I didn't say it would all be done in the first year. The pledge was in fact met in December 1983.

genuinely liked him. There was a quality of Congressional collegiality. He knew me; Herman knew me; and it was important.

I also actively pursued the Jewish vote at this time. Between the primary and the runoff we solicited the support of the different Orthodox groups. Rabbi Jacob Bronner, who is a good friend of mine, set up the meetings. And I must say they were fun. We invited the representatives of each group to meet with me at my apartment at 14 Washington Place—all within about two hours. Now, you have to understand that my apartment is only three rooms and a terrace. And of the three, one is a kitchen that is quite small—perhaps big enough for three people to stand in at once.

Well, these groups start showing up, and of course each one dislikes the others, so Rabbi Bronner has to start putting them into different rooms. I am seeing one group on the terrace and he is putting another group into the living room. Then another group shows up and they are put into the bedroom. Then another. He puts them into the bathroom.

I told them all the same thing. I said, "Other than decency, fairness and equity, you will get nothing from me. I will not discriminate against you because you are Jewish and I am Jewish—never. On the other hand, you won't get anything special." I always said that, and they always applauded. I said, "All the Jews want is equality. They don't want more. If they get equality they are getting more than they have, because they have been discriminated against."

In the runoff, I received 76 percent of the Jewish vote, and an overall majority of the votes in all boroughs except Staten Island.

Cuomo still had the Liberal line, however, and the number one question after the runoff was who would receive Carey's endorsement for the November election—a dubious prize in view of Cuomo's experience in the primary, which perhaps I should explain.

Carey and Cuomo really didn't like each other; but be that as it may, the worst albatross Cuomo had was Carey. For example, they were both against the death penalty, which became a rather important issue in the race. If Cuomo had been against the death penalty and Carey for it, then Carey would have been an asset. But as it was, Carey simply reinforced Cuomo's position on that issue, which was not popular.

Carey's animosity also hurt. Each would say something about the other that was sort of silly. I can't even remember what was said, but it was clear they didn't like each other. I kept saying throughout the campaign, "The Governor is a good Governor but a terrible politician. Thank God he's not my campaign manager."

Still, after the runoff there was a period when the question was What will Carey do? Would I want his endorsement? I said repeatedly, "I accept the endorsement of any Democrat." But that is not what you say about the Governor if the Governor means anything, right? And when he endorsed me it wasn't because I asked for it. He called me up while I was attending a meeting in Brooklyn. He said he was going to endorse me that night. I said, with no great enthusiasm, "Fine. Thanks so much, Governor."

Who needed his endorsement? It hadn't helped Cuomo, had it?

II

Confronting New York's Problems

4

Mayor-Elect

THE NIGHT I WON the general election for Mayor, the Governor called up as we were watching the returns and asked me if he could come over. I was at the Hilton. He comes over. He is very tense, because he knows my supporters don't like him for the shabby way he treated me. There was a crowd of maybe 2,000 out in the ballroom. He came on stage along with Abe Beame, who had been helpful in the general-election campaign.

So what I did—the crowd was cheering, and I knew that when I introduced the Governor he was going to be in for a tough time. I gave this no prior thought; it was very spontaneous on my part—I said, "Ladies and gentlemen, please give me a couple of moments of your attention. I have something to say." Then I went back to Carey, took him by the hand and brought him to the microphone, threw my arm over his shoulders and said, "Governor, I forgive you." And the place just erupted in pandemonium. It broke the ice. It put an end to that problem.

Then, the next year Carey had to run for reelection. And I helped him. I went with him every time he asked me to. I told people he had saved the City. He could not have won without me. Most people believe I acted in an extraordinary way. And I made both Wagner Senior and Carey ashamed of themselves—as much as those two guys ever could be embarrassed.

My first decision as Mayor-elect involved housing. I decided that I would keep my apartment. I wanted to keep it because I like it. There is no question that it is a bargain. I pay the highest rental in the building for that apartment and it is still very cheap. When rent control ends—and it is being phased out—I may give up my apartment, but not so long as it is under rent control. That would be ridiculous. So I said I would live at Gracie Mansion during the week and live in my apartment on weekends. The apartment is helpful. It is a break in my routine. Other people go out of town. I go to my apartment.

The New York Times didn't like that. It ran an editorial denouncing me for keeping my apartment. I thought, Who are these editors to say that? They probably each have six different houses all around the country. Or maybe it is only two. Probably one is in Connecticut. Here I have this little apartment that makes me happy, on which I pay the rent, and they are resentful. "So," I said, "I am not leaving. I am not giving up this apartment," and it became a sort of *cause célèbre*.

I was interviewed on the phone by Lee Dembart, the *Times* City Hall bureau chief in 1978, who called and asked me to describe my apartment. "I have a nice apartment," I said. "Two real bona fide, genuine Barcelona chairs, which are rather nice. A magnificent leather couch, which I really like. I have my brass bed, which is extraordinary and cost only nine dollars because it was bought at a farm auction. I have a terrace where I sit in the spring and summer. I like my apartment."

Well, the story was a good story, but the headline gave the impression that I didn't live at Gracie Mansion, that I lived only in this apartment. And that myth remained: most people somehow believed I didn't live at Gracie Mansion. So then, when asked or when it seemed appropriate, I would point out that I live at Gracie Mansion from Monday to Friday and then I would always add, "I would have to be a nut not to live there. It is a terrific place to live. But on the weekends, I go to my own apartment. What's wrong with that?"

After the election I called Abe Beame and asked him if I could come see him sometime at Gracie Mansion and he said, "Of course."

I arrived and we had breakfast, which was very formal—in

the dining room, not in the kitchen. We had Nova Scotia lox—a very fancy Jewish breakfast.

Anyway, it was a nice breakfast—very sociable and chatty. After breakfast, we went into the big living room and sat down again and talked. We were sitting across from the fireplace. I asked Abe if it was a working fireplace; he said he didn't know. Now, that is amazing to me. Living in a house for four years and never having tried the fireplace!

Then he points to the piano and says, "That piano was here when we came, so Mrs. Beame took lessons." I could hear "Tinkle, tinkle, tinkle" in my head.

The next day, there was a call from Mary Beame. She said, "Ed, Mr. Beame told me not to ask." (Imagine that—she calls me "Ed" and refers to him as "Mr. Beame"!) She went on, "But I must ask you, if we can't get out at the end of the month, could we stay over?"

Well, what do you say? Of course, you say "Yes." But in my head I was saying, They will never leave! So I called a reporter and told him the Beames had called, they were having problems getting settled in their new place and Mrs. Beame had asked if they could stay over after January 1, and I, of course, had said yes. "But," I said, "I am also moving in on January first, and I don't know who is going to be whose guest. I will be there with or without them."

They made a special effort to get out.

5

Choosing a Staff

In ONE OF MY FIRST MOVES as Mayor-elect, I set up ten "search panels" to seek out qualified candidates to fill the key commissionerships. The idea seemed like a good one, but I wouldn't do it again. I wouldn't urge anyone to do it. I would say if you are going to do anything like that, appoint one person in whom you have total confidence and have that person make the search of the field. Once you put together a panel with representation from blacks and whites and women and Hispanics, you find that you have created a group of people who in their own eyes become more important than they really are. And then you have a problem: they forget they are serving at your pleasure.

Of the ten search panels I set up, two really went sour. The transportation search panel ended up attacking me and my choice for Commissioner of Transportation, Anthony R. Ameruso. And the panel that was set up to assist in the search for a Police Commissioner wasn't too cooperative.

Robert J. McGuire had been recommended to me by Robert M. Morgenthau, Manhattan District Attorney. There were in addition six or seven people recommended by the search panel.

The panel came to see me after they were given the mission of finding a Police Commissioner. They said that they would like to limit their search to people who either were in the Police Department or had come out of the Department.

I said, "No, anyone in law enforcement can be considered." That would include DAs and U.S. Attorneys as well.

They didn't like that, but I said I wanted them to do it anyway. I said to them, "I got this name from Bob Morgenthau and would you please interview Bob McGuire." There was no fix or anything. I did know him, but it was Bob Morgenthau who had asked that he be interviewed.

Well, there had been another fellow—Maurice Nadjari's successor as special prosecutor, John Keenan. He had been recommended and I held him in very high regard. So I sent his name over too. One member of the search panel was Richard Gelb, who is a member of the Board of Directors of *The New York Times*. I believe he didn't want John because John didn't come out of the Police Department. So I believe it was Dick who leaked an adverse statement to the *Times*, which ran editorials denouncing John. It was dumb. Those editorials didn't mean anything to me anyway, but they were destructive to John. That wasn't nice of *The New York Times* or of those who leaked the statement.

Then the panel gave me their list. At the top of the list they had Donald Cawley, who had been Police Commissioner for nine months under Lindsay. And then there were a number of other people, and Dick Gelb said, "Now, these are the people we prefer." And they named three or four who either were in the Police Department or had come out of the Police Department, and he said, "We don't believe these others should be considered in the same way, but if you do, then the one that we think is best is Bob McGuire."

Well, David Garth is a police buff, and at that time he wanted to take a very active role in the selection process. He wanted to sit in on the interviews, and he did. These were held at my campaign headquarters sometime in December. And I interviewed all the candidates. And when we had finished, Garth said that he thought we should take Cawley.

And I said, "No, I think we should take McGuire; he's the best."

So I in fact took McGuire.

I should say that when I told that to Garth, he said, "Well, your judgment should prevail. I would prefer Cawley, but use your judgment." He didn't fight it, in short. I trust I would have resisted his fighting, but I didn't have that problem. I having made the choice, Garth was very supportive.

So I called my first press conference. Bob McGuire and his wife, Joan, and little boy, Brendon, were there. Bob looks like a Jesuit priest. He has this high domed forehead and long locks and is just very ascetic-looking. And I said, "Ladies and gentlemen, I want to announce my first appointment, Police Commissioner: Robert McGuire."

And one of the reporters says, "Mr. Mayor, isn't this just a continuation of the old Irish Mafia syndrome?" meaning police commissioners are always Irish.

So I looked shocked and I put my right hand on Bob's shoulder and I said, "Bob, you told me you were Jewish!"

And McGuire put his left hand on my shoulder and said, "No, I didn't, Mr. Mayor—I just told you I *looked* Jewish."

We have a very good relationship. In the six years he was Police Commissioner I never told him what to do except to do it on the merits. And he appreciated that, and so did the cops. Everybody said it was a very unusual relationship. Mutual respect.

A year or so later Dick Gelb came down and said he had been wrong and I was right. It is always nice to hear that.

In late November I had gone to Cambridge, Massachusetts, to a Harvard seminar on "Transition and Leadership." It was a weekend conference of Mayors on some of the aspects of being a chief executive. Of the participants I was the one about to embark on the most difficult mission. And, of course, I was becoming a Mayor after having been a Congressman. Congressmen can pick their fights while Mayors have to deal with whatever fights are handed to them.

There were incessant phone calls to New York, where the appointments process was being conducted. There was the financial plan to be fashioned. And, in Cambridge, there was Victor Gotbaum,* the lecturer.

The Harvard people had brought in a lot of experts to

*Executive Director of the Municipal Employees Union, District Council 37. One of the most thoughtful, and toughest, of the labor leaders in the City of New York, Victor Gotbaum had established himself as a major player in the fiscal affairs of the City when in 1975 he led the group that per-

lecture to the seventeen Mayors. One of their experts was
Victor Gotbaum. In his talk Gotbaum said something that I
will always remember. He said to these Mayors: "You know,
you are going to be involved in collective bargaining and you
are going to meet a lot of labor leaders. Never, ever become
friends with them. They are not your friends. You can be
friendly, but they are not your friends."

Well, you know—he was absolutely right.*

Another person I came to have a bit of difficulty with was
Edward Costikyan. Eddie Costikyan is a very smart Manhattan lawyer, politician and teacher. He was for a brief time the
New York County Democratic leader, the first reformer to
hold that position. It was he who had figured prominently in
my successful campaign against Carmine DeSapio for Greenwich
Village district leader in 1963. Costikyan had since then
continued to aspire to high elective office, but he somehow
always failed to excite the electorate.

Eddie Costikyan's was not a public constituency. It was an
editorial constituency. The *New York Post* publisher, Rupert
Murdoch, liked him very much—Murdoch had expressed
great support for Eddie Costikyan. He considered Costikyan
to be very tough on labor excesses. Costikyan is no tougher
on labor excesses than I am, although Murdoch didn't know
me at that time. But Murdoch knew Costikyan, and he
wanted to be sure that if he supported me he would be
supporting someone who had tough people around him.

Now, when Eddie dropped out of the race he agreed to
support me, and I hoped that he would bring Murdoch and

---

suaded the unions to accept reduced benefits as a result of the City's reduced
ability to pay.

*In the course of the seminar weekend, I asked Gotbaum to come to a party
at Mary Nichols' house—formerly city editor of *The Village Voice*, Mary was
Director of Communications for Boston Mayor Kevin White—and then go
out to dinner with me. He said, "No, I have a tennis game."

Here is a guy, I thought, that Gotbaum is going to have to be dealing
with over the course of the next four years who is asking him to go to
dinner, and he thinks a tennis game is more important? You wonder: Where
are the superb trade unionists of the past?

I mentioned this to Harry Van Arsdale a few years later, and he said,
"Well, Victor takes his tennis very seriously."

the *Post* along with him. Well, then Murdoch wasn't sure.

He thought maybe he would come out for Cuomo. I had several lunches with Garth and Costikyan and Murdoch, and I know Murdoch had several lunches with Cuomo. I was looking for editorial support, and at one of those lunches Murdoch had said that I should take Costikyan as a deputy mayor. Garth also had said at that time that I should take Costikyan; and so prior to one of those lunches I made the decision that Eddie should come into the administration—should there be a Koch administration, because this was all before the primary—and that he would be the First Deputy Mayor.

Frankly, when I said I was going to make him my First Deputy Mayor, I did so without really understanding what the word "First" meant.

After I made the announcement that Costikyan would be the First Deputy Mayor, I began to get glimpses of the monster I'd created. As Costikyan and later Herman Badillo and Donald Kummerfeld* and the City Hall reporters viewed it, the First Deputy Mayor automatically has the following prerogatives: nobody sees the Mayor except through the First Deputy Mayor; he controls the Mayor's calendar; Commissioners cannot come independently to the Mayor.

For some people, the First Deputy Mayor has more power than the Mayor. So, I resolved, as long as I am at City Hall I am going to be the Mayor *and* the First Deputy Mayor, because apparently the second job is more powerful than the first.

It was clear that what Costikyan wanted and what I wanted were not the same thing. The fact is that on at least one occasion prior to the general election he had indicated to me that if he couldn't be the First Deputy Mayor in the traditional sense, he would withdraw his backing from me. And I knew it would cause an uproar if he quit and then went around denouncing me. The week before the election, I had to sort of go along with it a little—and I did.

It became very complicated after the election, when I asked

*First Deputy Mayor under Beame.

Herman Badillo to serve. Herman said he would never serve if there was a First Deputy Mayor. He wanted all the deputy mayors to be equal. In fact, Herman rejected the position of deputy mayor and took off for London. He was friendly, but he said, "So long as there is a First Deputy Mayor, I won't come in."

I said to Herman, "I told Costikyan that he could have it and now I can't withdraw it. I'd like to, but there really isn't anything I can do." I was getting telegrams from Hispanic groups urging me to make Herman my First Deputy. He went to England; I started looking around for some more people.

I wanted Don Kummerfeld. He said no, that he would come into the cabinet only if he were the First Deputy Mayor, because he had been the First Deputy Mayor under Beame and therefore it would be a step down to be just another deputy mayor—one among equals.* I wanted him to be the Deputy Mayor for Finance. I tried to bring him together with Costikyan. We met at my apartment on Washington Place. When they left, I thought that we would be able to find a way to resolve the problem. And then Kummerfeld called up and said he would not be coming into the administration.

So I called up Eddie and told him about my conversation with Kummerfeld—tried to explain the situation. And he said, "You know, if you had asked me to give up the title, I would have, if that was what was necessary."

I thought: I had to go through all this agony . . . he didn't know?

So then I called Eddie back and I said, "Eddie, you asked me to ask you; now I'm asking you: give up the title so at least I can bring in Herman."

And he sort of gulps and says, "Okay."

Now it's my option. So I get on the phone to Herman in London and I say, "Herman, we are not going to have a First Deputy Mayor and I would like you to be a part of my administration, and I would like you to come back from England . . . ."

---

*In fact, Kummerfeld had exercised considerable power under the politically wounded Mayor Beame.

And he said, "Sure." And that is how Herman Badillo ended up in the administration, and how, ultimately, Costikyan did not.

For my other deputies there are other stories; but suffice it to say that on January 1, 1978, I had seven deputy mayors. Two years later, I was down to three.

6

Administration:
Governing the City

MY FIRST CLEAR SIGNAL to the municipal workers occurred in an interesting way. It was two weeks after I had taken office. I was at Gracie Mansion, and it was January 15 at 3 in the morning, when the phone rings. I answer the phone, "Yes?"

At the other end of the phone I hear the voice of Thomas Roche, who was at the time the Personnel Director, and he says, "Mr. Mayor, it's snowing outside."

I say to myself, What a novel way to bring the news.

He says, "Shall I declare a snow day?"

Being somewhat suspicious, I say, "What does it mean to declare a snow day?"

He says, "Well, Mr. Mayor, when you declare a snow day, the people who don't come in get paid and those who do come in get time-and-a-half."

I say, "Tom, from this day forth there are no snow days in the City of New York." That simple exercise of reasonable judgment saved the City of New York, in the three days that could have been snow days in the month of January 1978, $8.5 million.

I was determined to get the biggest bang for the bucks we were spending. I had said during my campaign that I would do that, and I had meant it. But that was a big promise and one that required a lot of resolve to keep.

There are very few people in government who are capable of firing. And there are especially few who are capable of firing their friends. The usual move is the lateral promotion.

But I am one of those who will get rid of people. Once I decide someone has to go, I will psych myself up so that I won't retreat. I will just fire. It is very hard to do. And it is often messy. But in the first year or so, as I tried to tighten my administration, it was not unusual.

When I arrived on the City Hall scene, I was championing what I called "the commissioner form of government." This meant that there would be no intermediaries in the chain of command between the Mayor and his Commissioners. The Commissioners were to report directly to me. I would have time to keep track of them, I said. Moreover, "the commissioner form of government" meant that I would not be imposing political appointees on the Commissioners. As I often said: I pick the Commissioners and they pick their own people. That way, when the job isn't done they can't blame it on the incompetents that City Hall made them hire.

I said I didn't want to run a patronage operation out of City Hall and I didn't. I was so strict about this that Daniel Wolf* later said to me, "You know, Ed, the only person in the city government who doesn't control jobs is you." By "jobs" Dan meant, of course, low-level patronage-type positions. Early in the administration, John LoCicero, my 1977 campaign manager, was dubbed "Koch's patronage dispenser" by City Hall reporters. LoCicero laughed when he heard himself referred to in that way. "I don't think I control three jobs," he said.

I refer to patronage as "the glue of politics," and yet I gave it to my Commissioners. What, then, did I get from them in return?

It wasn't long before the Commissioner stories began to circulate. And they continued. I was driving them hard. I instigated a biweekly system in which the Commissioners reported on their activities and I responded with follow-up memos. Additionally, various Commissioners were asked to attend my monthly "town hall" meetings and constituent hours. There their work was held up to public scrutiny.

*A trusted adviser and longtime friend, Dan was the original editor, 1956–74, of *The Village Voice*.

Moreover, I constantly referred to them problems I had encountered in traveling around the City.

I was always devising ways to get more work out of the agencies. For example, at one town hall meeting, a concessionaire who held a contract with the City stood up and confessed that because the City was so slow in paying its bills, the concessionaires were in the habit of building additional charges into their invoices. I asked the budget people to study how quickly the agencies were paying their bills. The study showed that more than 50 percent of the City's bills were not being paid within thirty days, and some were not being paid within eighteen months. The effect of that over the long term was that most suppliers didn't wish to do business with the City. Who would want to provide goods or services when the prospect of timely payment was remote? The City was left to deal with second- and third-rate businesses, which came into the bidding process with bids that had nine months to a year of the cost of money built in. The budget study indicated that ten agencies did more than 80 percent of the City's purchasing of supplies. I called in the ten Commissioners.

First, the Commissioner of Purchasing at General Services said that this was what we should do: all bills should be sent to her, and she would make sure they got paid on time.

The Budget Director, James Brigham, said, "No, that's crazy. There are thousands of slips of paper out there. You could never keep track of them. What we need is a computer."

I said, "How long do you think that will take?"

"Well," Brigham said, "we'll have to get the computer and then someone will have to program it. I guess at least a year."

I said, "No. I'll tell you what we're going to do. I'm giving the City agencies sixty days to get their shops in order. Then at the end of the third month I'm going to publish a list of your names in rank order, one through ten, with ten being the worst—the slowest. And I'll do that every month."

The Commissioners said, "No, no, no. You can't do that. It will embarrass us."

"Watch me," I said.

And so at the end of the following ninety days Brigham

brings in the list, and without even informing the Commissioners, we turn it over to Maureen Connelly, my first press secretary, who takes it down to the reporters' room, Room 9. The following day, the list appears in all the papers. In midmorning, Gordon Davis, the Parks Commissioner, comes into my office, and he is in great distress because he has seen the papers and his name is at the bottom of the list as the worst. He says, "Mr. Mayor, I am beside myself. I have called in my comptroller and I have said to him, 'If my name is at the bottom of that list next month, it's your ass!' "

Well, it worked. A little competition is always healthy. Davis was not at the bottom of the list again, and very soon thereafter the City was paying 85 percent of its bills within thirty days and taking the cash discount, and it was paying another 10 percent of its bills within sixty days, and the remaining 5 percent were not being paid because there was litigation or some other claim involved. We are saving millions of dollars in both cash discounts and more competitive bidding.

But to return to the business of accountability, and firing, let me give several examples.

Robert Milano had been recommended to me as the Deputy Mayor for Economic Development by a search committee I had set up because I wasn't able to find anyone who could do the job. The committee members interviewed a lot of people, and he was their recommendation. I knew Bob Milano. I knew him through David Margolis.* He is not a close friend of David's, but both Margolis and I had been to his home in the Hamptons and to his hunting lodge in Upstate New York. The lodge is a very beautiful place. He is a multimillionaire and is retired. He wanted to work as a $1-a-year guy, and I said okay.

---

*One of my close friends—not in government, but once a member of the Emergency Financial Control Board. David and I go back to a very boring dinner in Queens in 1967. It was for a retiring guard or warden. And I was seated at a table with David and Bobbie Margolis. I didn't know them then. Mario Biaggi—then a lawyer in private practice; now a Bronx Congressman—was the speaker, and the dinner just went on and on. So David and I started talking. He said, "What do you do?"

I said, "I'm a City Councilman. What about you?"

Right from the start I knew it was a mistake. His vision of the Office of Economic Development was three hundred, four hundred, God-knew-how-many staff people doing God-knew-what. My idea was to have a dozen hungry dealmakers working out ways to lure business into the City. He was constantly asking for new furniture, new carpets and so on for his offices and the offices of his deputies. In my conversations with Bob Milano I could never get a straight answer from him. It would take him fifteen minutes to get to the point; he talked in circles. Even then I was usually embarrassed by his presentations before the cabinet and before businessmen's groups. He would get up and make a fool of himself. I decided he had to go.

I called him in. He had no idea what the appointment was about. I was told he also wanted to see me about his plans to add people to the payroll. He was rather exuberant as he walked in the door. Before he sat down, I said, "Bob, it is not working and we have to end it. Let's figure out the best way for you." You could almost hear the pain that had struck him when he realized he was being fired. That is what I mean by saying it isn't easy.

He said, "I can't believe it. What's wrong?"

"Bob," I said, "we don't agree. I believe there should be twelve people who are lean and hungry. You believe there should be two hundred or four hundred people. That is a bureaucracy, and I don't want it. I have been telling you and telling you that. And you continue to take a tack that is not what I want."

He said, "I'm a businessman." And so we talked about business and politics.

And I remember I said, "You know, the level of honesty in public life is just so low it's disgusting."

And he said, "It's higher than it is in business."

So there we were with Mario Biaggi droning on in the background, each of us dumping on his respective profession, trying to fend off the boredom.

Thereafter we became friends. Later, Margolis was one of the three private members of the EFCB when I was an observer. He always supported me in my campaigns. And I should be paying rent for all the summer weekends I've stayed with David and Bobbie at their home in Quogue. We don't do much except eat, drink and talk. We rarely go out. I really enjoy it.

"Well, can't we change it?" he said. "Can't we do what you want?"

I said, "No. If something doesn't work, you have to end it. It won't do any good now to decide you are going to do what I want. Because you won't. It doesn't work that way. We don't look at things the same way, so let's end it. And let's end it in a nice way so that you are not embarrassed."

And then he broke into tears. I was very much distressed. It is very hard for me to see an adult cry. Then he said, "You have disgratadadoed me!"

I said to myself, I've what? Apparently what he was saying was I had disgraced him in Italian. I asked myself, Jesus Christ, what am I in for?

But that was a passing moment. He composed himself and said he was sorry he had broken down, that it had never happened to him before. Then he said, "Fine. I understand now, and I agree. I will leave."

But it rarely works out that way. He left and then he held a press conference denouncing me and saying that I knew nothing about economic development and how he knew everything and how I was standing in the way. It was just foolish. And of course, the reporters came running over to me, as they always will in such a case, and asked that I respond to his denunciation.

My response was "I will not add to his agony."

The next one was the most bizarre—and the messiest. Patria O. Nieto Ortiz. The question really was: Is it possible, regardless of her poor record, to fire a Hispanic woman from the post of Chairperson of the Human Rights Commission? Well, I took the position that it was. My position is: if you can hire them, you can fire them. And that applies to everyone except judges, who are a separate entity under the law.

Once again, she had been proposed to me by a panel. She seemed okay; but after she got into the job we discovered ours had not been a good choice. In one situation, a community group in Laurelton had written to her complaining that her Commission was not doing enough to keep a bank in their area. And she wrote back to them a rather convoluted letter which was at best impolitic.

Then she started in on the Commissioners. She sent them all letters saying she was going to subpoena them if they didn't provide her with their hiring records. That's not the way you deal with your peers. You ask them to do it voluntarily, and if they don't comply, then you come to see the Mayor about it. Then she writes *me* a letter. She wants to subpoena me. At that point it is clear to me that this woman has to go.

So we have a little meeting with Herman Badillo. Herman says, "Get rid of her. She will only cause more trouble."

Then she comes in with her lawyer demanding that she and her agency not be represented by the Corporation Counsel, which is the law, but that we furnish her with independent counsel. And she starts threatening Allen G. Schwartz, the Corporation Counsel, saying that she is going to take her complaints about him to the Bar Association.

Ultimately, Herman sat down with her lawyer, and between the two of them they were able to persuade her to resign.

The next one to go was Andrew Jenkins, Deputy Commissioner of Buildings, because he had refused to bring up on charges, with a view toward removing them from the payroll, several buildings inspectors who had pleaded guilty to taking bribes. His position was that they should not be removed, just fined a month's pay or something. I said, "Anybody who takes that position can't stay on the payroll himself."

So he had to resign. And because he was running for the State Assembly, he sent me a letter of resignation—a letter which was denunciatory and which he clearly intended to use in his campaign. He was told that he'd better withdraw the letter or I would start telling people why he was resigning. So then he sent me another letter, which was more conciliatory. It said he wanted to resign because he wanted to devote more time to running for public office. That was better, and I let it stand.

Perhaps the most distressing adjustment I had to make was the dismissal of Bernard Rome in January 1979. Rome, my 1977 campaign treasurer, had made a small fortune publishing reports on various statistics. Chubby, middle-aged, balding and bespectacled, he looks like the competent store manager that he is.

Rome and I were friends. I trusted him. He had helped raise money. He had even lent his own money to the campaign when we were short. He had been a great source of comfort during the 1977 campaign.

After the campaign, I had asked him to be Commissioner of General Services. He didn't think that was sufficiently important. He wanted to be Deputy Mayor for Economic Development. He is a very good businessman, but I did not want him to be a deputy mayor. I appointed him instead chairman of the search panel for the Department of General Services head, and then ultimately I appointed him chairman of the Off-Track Betting board, and as a result he became its president—a paying position. He was the executive officer.

Now, prior to January 1979, Rome was doing quite well at OTB. He was increasing the "handle"—the amount of money bet. He hadn't known anything about horse racing before. He quickly became knowledgeable about it and sought to increase the business even more by various changes of a substantive nature, all of which I supported, and some of which required the assistance of the State Legislature. But then Bernie started to attack the integrity of the Governor and other elected officials, all of whom I have to work with. He began alleging that they were in bed with the New York Racing Association and that they were not honest. That is what he kept saying in the papers.

In addition, he expressed opposition to casino gambling because it would reduce the OTB "handle." I happen to be for casino gambling and had said so before I was elected. It was part of my campaign. After weeks of his obstructiveness I decided I could not continue working with Bernie Rome.

First Philip Toia, the Deputy Mayor for Finance, spoke with him. Phil told him to stop insulting the legislators and the Governor. He also told him that I had established a policy favoring casino gambling and that was it. Then I wrote Bernie a note to this effect: "You are the Chairman of OTB and I have appointed you. Once a policy is established you have to carry it out."

Bernie knew then that I was cutting him off in a personal way, and he asked Allen Schwartz to arrange a short meeting with me. He came in with charts and an easel. The meeting took about a half-hour, and the charts showed how the City, in his judgment, didn't have to have casino gambling. We could increase the take of OTB, even though we would have to remove the surcharge,* and get the State Legislature to authorize live telecasting of horse racing into OTB parlors.

I agreed with all of that. I responded by saying, "I don't think it is inconsistent to have OTB *and* casino gambling. Anyway, that is the subject of a referendum—let the people decide; but I happen to be for it."

He said, "I have said publicly that I am against casino gambling."

I said, "You shouldn't have done that, Bernie. I don't want you to oppose it."

"Well, what should I do?" he said.

I said, "I never want you to say anything that you don't believe. So you really have two options. One is to say simply, 'The Mayor has established a policy in favor of casino gambling and I support the Mayor's policy.' Or if you cannot say that, as apparently you cannot, then you have to say, 'The Mayor has established a policy in favor of casino gambling. I support the mayor.' "

He says, "Well, what if I can't say *that*, morally or philosophically?"

I said, "It's easy. You resign."

He says "Well, then you better start looking for a businessman to take my place." And he leaves.

Well, for the next week he held press conferences every day in which he attacked me as arrogant, saying that I was trying to shut him up, and that I was taking my orders from the Governor. He was really attacking my integrity.

This was one case in which I decided I was going to avoid harsh rhetoric. So I responded by simply saying, "He is a very good businessman, but he does not agree with me on policy. I will have to remove him because he will not resign. I am now looking for someone to take his place."

Since then I have been asked a number of times: Was there nothing unusual in his performance as treasurer of the campaign?

---

*A 5-percent payment, over and above taxes, that the City collects from winners at its Off-Track Betting parlors.

No clues? Well, I never thought so. Others did not like him. But the nice part about this whole business is that I never did anything wrong in my campaign. There isn't anything that he can use; and I think that is unique—because, regrettably, for whatever reasons, either because people are stupid or corrupt or because the laws are so arcane, there is generally something that a campaign treasurer would know that would not be helpful to the candidate. That doesn't exist here. With my former campaign treasurer out there beating the bushes against me, I slept easy.

My apparent inflexibility on this question of loyalty had to do directly with my own doctrine of personal accountability. And the question of accountability also arose in connection with the so-called "covered" agencies, the semipublic corporations providing public services in the City.

These so-called covered agencies are interesting. Earlier Mayors had disassociated themselves from the public school system, the public transportation system and the public hospital system. Most people think this was done so that Mayors would not be able to play politics with these services. That's what the Mayors told the people: that they were doing them a favor getting politics out of the schools. Not true. They were playing politics, all right. They were disassociating themselves from the flak. When they gave away their power and allowed the Board of Education and the Metropolitan Transportation Authority and the Health and Hospitals Corporation to be formed, they weren't doing a favor for anyone but themselves and the respective unions. They were setting up fall guys: Let these entrenched boards take the heat for lousy schools or broken buses or crummy doctors, they were thinking. Lindsay's apologists will say he formed the Health and Hospitals Corporation in order to be able to install a modern management system, but I believe nonaccountability is why John Lindsay formed the Corporation: so that he would be able to say, "Don't blame me. I don't have anything to do with hospitals."

I didn't want that. I didn't want to have an authority between the services and me—so that when there were complaints I could blame the authority. I'm not interested in passing the blame onto some committee. I'd said during the campaign that I would be happy to accept the blame if it could be arranged that the Mayor could get the power back from these authorities, to do what has to be done—specifically with the Board of Ed and HHC—to deliver the services in a responsible and efficient and fair way. That's what I'd said and I meant every word of it.

When I took office, HHC was a zero. The people on the board were for the most part second-rate. It was losing money like a hemorrhage. I went to Albany and tried to get control of it—but couldn't. We finally managed to get rid of its president, just by persistence, and despite the fact that we didn't have a majority on the HHC board—they were mostly holdover appointments, and the majority of the board represented an ideology that was basically "Who cares what it costs? We are going to provide full medical benefits to the poor, no matter what the cost," and they were going to use HHC for political jobs and appointments, regardless of the competency of the appointees. And it showed. The heads of many of the seventeen municipal hospitals had been chosen on the basis of political criteria. They weren't necessarily medical experts or management experts. The choices had been dictated basically by racial politics.

I went to Albany and I said, "I want to change that. I want New York's hospitals to be run by first-rate people." But I found that it was impossible. HHC was considered to be the province of the black and Hispanic caucuses. They didn't want HHC changed, and so I could never hope to get reform legislation through. I recognized reality.

So then we began to change the membership of the board. And we did, slowly—so that after two years in office we were getting votes of 7-6 or 8-6.*

Now, regarding the Board of Education: the City provides it with its budget, but we don't have control over the Board in the absolute sense. The members of the Board of Education are not like my Commissioners, in the sense that I can hire and fire them at will. So right after I took office, I went to Albany with a plan that would have abolished the Board of Ed. But here too, I found that it would be impossible to get

*The HHC board, when without vacancies, has sixteen members.

the legislation through. We considered one compromise. The State Board of Regents had proposed that the Board of Education be increased from a committee of seven who serve four-year terms (Mayor appoints two, Borough Presidents appoint one each), to a committee of fifteen, of whom I would appoint ten. That would have given me a majority and I could have gotten some things done. I said I would take that, but it wouldn't fly. The union* and the parents didn't want it.

The fact is I had tremendous difficulty just getting Frank Macchiarola appointed as Chancellor of the Board of Ed. It was only after great effort that I was able to get four of the seven to support him.

In December 1977, Abe Beame, in his last month in office, had appointed Louis Rivera to the Board of Ed. I'd called up Beame and said, "Please, don't appoint him. If you appoint him I will have no control over him."

Beame said, "No, I am going to appoint him." Beame was actually satisfying Albert Shanker, who heads the local teachers' union, because Shanker and his United Federation of Teachers had supported Beame's reelection.

Then I talked to Rivera and I could not get him to support Macchiarola; I didn't control a single person on that board. Rivera wouldn't work with me, and the other Mayoral appointee, Amelia Ashe, although she was considered a very able person, was subject to a great deal of pressure by Shanker because her husband was a lawyer who did a lot of work for the unions.

Shanker had his own candidate, a guy named Theodore Wiesenthal. So Shanker comes to see me and he says, "Your candidate, Macchiarola, can't win. I have five votes of the seven."

I mean it's incredible when you think about it—his power. First he stops me in Albany from restructuring the Board, and then he comes into my office and tells me he's going to pick the next Chancellor; the teachers' boss is going to be picked by the teachers' union boss. It's an outrage to the people whose kids are trying to get an education.

*The United Federation of Teachers (UFT).

I went to work on all seven of them. We knew we had two votes for Macchiarola. One was Steven Aiello, who comes from Brooklyn and is of Italian descent and who knew Macchiarola. And Macchiarola knew the Kings County (Brooklyn) Democratic leader, Meade Esposito, and I'm sure Meade leaned on Aiello. Then there was Joseph Barkan, who comes from Queens. Meade talked to Queens Borough President Donald Manes, and Manes talked to Barkan, and Barkan decided he was for Macchiarola. So those were our two, courtesy of two friendly county leaders.

Shanker had the two Mayoral appointments because Beame had given them away, and Shanker had three of the Borough Presidents' people as well. I started to call them in.

When I reached Rivera, he said, no, he couldn't help.

I asked him then, "Please, don't vote for the UFT. Vote a standoff. Vote for yourself. Then we would need only three votes."

"You have only two," he said.

"If we get three," I rejoined, "would you please not vote—just stay neutral or something?"

"Okay," he said, "I'll stay neutral if you get the third vote."

But he called up the next Monday and said he wouldn't do it. Undoubtedly he'd been pressured by Shanker.

Then I was told by the City's chief lobbyist in Albany, Peter Piscitelli, that Isaiah Robinson, a member of the Board whom I had never met, had said he would vote for Macchiarola. Robinson was former Manhattan Borough President Percy Sutton's appointment. But people said that I could not count on him because he had been offered a deputy secretary position with HEW in Washington and he would probably take it. Shanker had his people in Washington too. Piscitelli told me, on the other hand, that Robinson was a man of great honor: once he tells you he is with you, he is with you, and you can rely on it. So I never had a conversation with Robinson before the vote. Everyone assumed I had promised him something, but I never even had a conversation with him.

Next I called Amelia Ashe. "I don't like either Macchiarola or Weinberger," she said. "I like So-and-so from Virginia."

"But that person is not going to be the new Chancellor," I said. "And I need your vote. Don't waste it like that. I need you."

"Well," she said, "let me think about it."

So I called her up the following Monday and I said, "Amelia, you must do this for me. You're a Mayoral appointee and that is why you're there. I'm asking you to vote in a way that will be helpful to me."

"I'll do it," she said. She was really very nice. And then the vote was held and Macchiarola won 4-3. Everybody was shocked. As I told everyone, "That was the first time Al Shanker was ever beaten. And I did it." And I believe Macchiarola during his tenure made a significant difference.

7

Setting the Tone

ONE OF THE THINGS that Mayors do is to go out to the boardrooms of the major publications and sit down over lunch with the editors. The exchanges are generally lively. It is a way to get the editorial writers out of their ivory towers. And for Mayors it is a way to present their positions to the newspapermen. I like these lunches. And at night, when I get the papers, I turn first to the editorial page to see how I've done at lunch.

In April 1979 I was invited up to the *New York* magazine boardroom for lunch. With me I took Maureen Connelly and Dan Wolf.

The *New York* magazine editors wanted to talk about me and the way I handle things. And their thrust was "Gee, you are too responding. You ought to be more cautious. Don't get so far out front."

At one point Dan Wolf said, "I don't understand this. Here he is doing exactly what you would want a Mayor to do—he is not concealing anything; he is speaking out; he is taking an active role—and now you're saying that a good Mayor should be removed, a remote personality."

I followed that statement by saying, "Look, I am going to make mistakes. No doubt about it. But I will never be removed and I will never be remote. It is not my personality. You have had a chance to view it now. And it will not change. My own feeling is that I am an ordinary guy with special abilities. But I want the things that the average person wants. And so I do the things that the average New Yorker would do

63

if he or she were the Mayor. And it seems to be working pretty well, but the fact is I couldn't change myself if I tried."

Then they say, "Well, yeah, but you're not a Congressman anymore. Being Mayor is different."

"Oh, yes," I say. "I understand what it means to be Mayor. It is a very powerful position. And the power and the position have nothing to do with me."

"Well," they say, "but you have brought your own special personality to the job and you have made it more powerful."

I say, "Let me just tell you one story. I went to one of these David Rockefeller/Harry Van Arsdale* breakfasts for business and labor recently. It was held in the boardroom of the Chase Manhattan Bank—thirty leading bankers and labor leaders sitting around a table. When I walked into the room, every one of them stood up. They sat me between Rockefeller and Van Arsdale. Rockefeller said, 'Can I get you some coffee?' and he went up and got me a cup of coffee. Van Arsdale ran to get me a Danish. It was extraordinary treatment. And the reason it was so extraordinary is that neither one of these guys likes me and I suspect that none of the other twenty-eight people in that room ever voted for me, and they have each had several opportunities. So it is the office. Now, how do I know? Because half an hour later Senator Javits walked into that room. And over the course of one of the longest careers in the history of the U.S. Senate, Senator Javits has worked for these very people. He worked his ass off for them. And when *he* came in, only six people stood up and they sent a waiter to get him a roll. So you see I know a Senator is not a Mayor."

In addition to resisting too ceremonious a style, I was concerned from the outset not only to treat all interest groups alike but to be perceived to treat them alike. Early in the administration I had two memorable meetings—one with the gays and one with the blacks.

A group of homosexual activists had met with Ronay

---

*Rockefeller, until his recent retirement, was chairman of the board of the Chase Manhattan Bank. Van Arsdale is president of the New York City Central Labor Council, AFL-CIO.

Menschel and Herbert Rickman,* and they were not satisfied. They were demanding that I get Thomas Cuite, majority leader of the City Council, to agree to bring up the Gay Rights Bill in the City Council and pass it and to use whatever pressures were needed on him and everyone else, and they were not satisfied with the response that Ronay and Herb had given them. I had confirmed that response by letter. It was a very tough letter, saying that I am not going to tell anyone how to vote on something he or she perceives to be a matter of conscience. I continued by saying there were several other subjects—abortion was one, and the death penalty another—that were matters of conscience, and I wouldn't seek to influence people in their votes on those issues either. In cases in which people were not voting for the Gay Rights Bill because of possible political repercussions in their districts and they wanted help from me, I said that I would help them by campaigning for them when they were up for reelection, but that I would not break people's arms. This was the Gay Rights Bill that would do in the private sector what I had done by Executive Order in the public sector—end discrimination against homosexuals in the areas of housing and jobs.

So we held a meeting at City Hall. There were about twenty people in the room—men and women, all of them activists. Statements were made around the room that I was not doing enough for them. (I was thinking that if there was anybody who had taken flak on this and stood up on this issue, it was I. The public thinks that the very first thing I did on coming into office was issue that Executive Order. Actually, it was not the first. But the public sees it as the number one order of the administration.) And I'm taking all this flak. Then one of this delegation gets up and reads a denunciatory speech in which he demands that I inform the activists within seven days as to what I propose to do to implement this proposed legislation. Otherwise, they are going to take action at their meeting to decide what they will do vis-à-vis me.

In a very direct way I say, "Take it and shove it. You do

*Ronay Menschel was one of the original seven deputy mayors; Herbert Rickman was an Assistant to the Mayor.

what you want to do, but the one thing you should always know is, threaten me and you get nothing from it. Nothing. I will not be threatened or intimidated. I do something because I think it is the right thing to do, not because you can intimidate me, because you can't.''

Well, he became overwhelmed and shattered. (Later on, he said that he hadn't been threatening me and that I had picked on him.)

That kind of approach changes the whole mood of the meeting. I say, "There are certain things I won't do and certain things I will do. I will write the Council members and follow up with them. I will call the county leaders to urge them to call some Council members that they have some influence with. And I will testify personally in support of the legislation at the committee hearing instead of just sending a statement, which might ordinarily be done, and having some-one else read it.'' And that was the end of the meeting.

My impression is that out of these meetings there came a realization that my administration was not going to take crap from any group. I think somehow that realization percolated through.

The second opportunity to make this point clear arose when a group of blacks who said they were ministers arrived at City Hall. They wanted all the federal summer jobs to go to nonwhites. They wanted all of the money and who-knows-what-else-and-how-much to go only to nonwhites. Their de-mands were absolutely ridiculous. As it is, about 90 percent of the summer jobs go to nonwhites, in accordance with the federal guidelines. They go to the youngsters of families on welfare, and to youngsters from families whose income does not exceed the poverty level—then a maximum of $7,800 a year for a family of four or more. Those are the rules. They are not my rules. The Feds make the rules.

So these fifteen "clergymen" became very demanding and threatening. I said, "I am not going to do it. You do whatever you want to do. Goodbye." I got up and walked back to my office. And I notice that four of these guys are following me.

One of them says, "We are going to sit down and start singing and you won't be able to conduct business here until you give in to our demands."

And they sit down in the hallway outside my office.

I say, "Look, you can go outside the building and picket and sing to your hearts' content, but if you sit down as you are now and disrupt activities in City Hall, you will be arrested." I then went into my office.

Well, pretty soon a cop comes in and says, "They're sitting out there and singing. What do you want us to do?"

I say, "Remove them."

He replies, "What if they resist?"

I say, "Have you never heard the word 'arrest'?"

And that is what was done. They were carried away in the paddy wagon. And the word got out. No sitting in at City Hall. The fact is that I was denounced by Shirley Chisholm* on the floor of Congress for that action. But I happen to think it is to my credit—and people remember it. People know that I don't care if they are black ministers or white ministers, real or imagined; no unlawful disruptions will be permitted in City Hall.

And what applies to groups applies to individuals. Which reminds me of another story.

In addition to holding a town hall meeting and a constituent hour every month, I also go on the radio once or twice a month to answer questions on call-in shows.

I was on one of these shows when the call comes in: "Mr. Mayor, I live on West Twenty-third Street and I want to tell you about a problem. I was passing a theater on the block and I looked in the window and there was a two-hundred-and-fifty-pound naked lady cooking in the window. I find that objectionable."

I said, "Yes, sir, I understand. By the way, what is it that you find objectionable? Her nakedness, or the fact that she weighs two hundred and fifty pounds?"

"Both," he said.

I said, "Well, it's hard to believe. But give me your name and address and I'll look into it and then get back to you."

So when I got back to City Hall I called up Carl Weisbrod, who was at that time the director of the Midtown Enforcement Project, a group we set up for the purpose of cleaning

*A black Democratic Congresswoman from Brooklyn.

up the Times Square area. I said to him, "Find out what it's about and report back to me." Now, Carl is a young lawyer who I didn't think had a funny bone in his body. But what he sent me is this report:

to: Edward I. Koch, Mayor
from: Carl B. Weisbrod, Director
      Midtown Enforcement Project
re: Squat Theater, West 23rd Street

October 13, 1978

We have investigated the complaint regarding a production at the Squat Theater on 23rd Street during which a 250 pound woman was reported to have performed nude in a storefront window.

It is true that this performance did indeed occur as described. It was, however, part of a radical avant garde theater group's play entitled "Andy Warhol's Last Love." The play itself was not written by Andy Warhol. Nor did Warhol have any connection with this production which has been described as the reflection of recent immigrant experiences in America. The production was staged by an extended family group of Jewish Hungarian refugees who fled from Hungary because they were about to be arrested for not conforming to the standards of Socialist Realism of the East Bloc nations.

The play ended its run here in New York on September 15th. It is currently in production in Amsterdam, Holland where the group will be spending the Fall season. The scene involving the naked fat woman in the window was part of this group's theory about "inside" and "outside" theater. They created a concept of performing before two audiences—the audience in the theater and passersby on the street. The woman has been described as an authentic American witch who acts out a real witch's ceremony in the window. She was not cooking. It is doubtful that her act would be declared legally obscene.

This play, supported with a grant from the New York State Council on the Arts, was apparently very popular. It attracted an average of 90% capacity audience. It received good reviews except from John Simon. The theater group, consisting of 9 adults and 5 children, arrived in this country in June of 1977 under the aegis of the International Theater Institute. It received an Obie for the play, "Pigchild in Fire," in 1977 and has been invited to represent the United States at the Festival of Nations next Spring in Hamburg, Germany.

It is considered a serious group of artists who came to this country seeking freedom of expression through innovative methods.

CARL B. WEISBROD

Now, I have read the Squat Theater memorandum aloud on a number of occasions. In fact, I read it so often that my advance man used to carry it around in his pocket so that if I wanted to throw away my prepared text and speak in an extemporaneous way I could say what was on my mind at the moment and then end my remarks by saying, "I enjoy being the Mayor. Every day is an adventure. . . ." And then I might read the memorandum.

One of the times I read the Squat Theater memorandum was at a Congressional dinner in Washington given by the New York delegation. I had been asked to participate in the entertainment part of the evening, and what I thought I would do was read the Weisbrod memorandum.

Kitty Carlisle Hart, the chairperson of the New York State Council on the Arts, had been instrumental in putting the entertainment part of the evening together. So I am backstage getting ready to go on and she looks over my shoulder and says, "You're not going to read that Squat Theater paper, are you?"

I say, "Oh, yes, I am."

She says, "Well, you shouldn't do that."

I say, "Oh? Well, I am going to."

She doesn't like it because one of the key lines is that this theater was funded by the New York State Council on the Arts and she—Kitty Carlisle Hart—is the chairperson of the New York State Council on the Arts. And it always brings the house down when that line is read and then she is embarrassed.

Well, now it is November 3, 1979, a year after the original Squat Theater memo, and I am asked to go to the Museum of Natural History to give out the Mayor's Awards on Arts and Culture. I had made the presentations the year before and I'd agreed to do it again.

And it happens that the week before the event there was an

article in the *New York Post* to the effect that the Squat Theater group had been banned in Brussels. And the article went on to state that the ''authentic American witch'' who was reported by Weisbrod to weigh 250 pounds was now, a year later, reported in the AP dispatch and by the *Post* to weigh 350 pounds. The Brussels theater wants her to wear some clothes. Apparently she was prancing around its stage likewise absolutely naked.

That afternoon before the awards, I am in my office in City Hall and am thinking I might read the Squat Theater memo with the Brussels update, which my advance man is now also carrying around in his pocket, or I might read my prepared text, which is about how wonderful people like Kitty Carlisle Hart—who is one of the recipients—are, and all that they have done for the City. And I am thinking, Well, it depends on my mood. Then I get a message from Mary Tierney, a member of my staff who handles cultural matters, saying that Kitty Carlisle Hart has called and she is requesting that I not read the Squat Theater memo. Now, you have to understand, anytime someone asks me not to do something, I think, Well, I am going to do whatever I want to do. Nobody tells me what to read. And then it developed that what Kitty had told Mary Tierney was that if I insisted on reading the memo, then she would not come to the ceremony to accept her award. So I told Mary, ''Tell her not to come. Whatever she wants to do is okay with me.''

So we go to the museum—Mary hasn't been able to reach Kitty back, and I say, ''I don't care''—and the first person I see inside the museum is Kitty Hart. She says, ''You're not going to read it, are you?''

I say, ''Oh, yes, I am.'' Now I am sure in my own mind that I am going to throw away my prepared remarks and read the memo.

She says, ''Well, then I shall have to leave.''

I say, ''Suit yourself,'' and I walk off.

Then Barney McHenry* comes over and he says, ''Gee, I

*W. Barnabas McHenry, then vice chairman of the Mayor's Commission for Cultural Affairs.

understand you are going to read the memo and I am going to ask you not to."

I say, "Nobody censors what I read," and I walk away from him.

Then two or three other people come over, and I am getting angrier by the minute, and more convinced that what I have to do is to read this memo—although, I say to myself, If she actually leaves, then after she goes I will read the prepared text about how wonderful she is.

So I come on stage. Kitty Hart is on the stage too. First, sending word through Annette Kuhn, a member of my staff at City Hall, that she requests that if I read the Squat Theater memo she would like to be given an opportunity to say something. The others are not saying anything. Would I have any objection to her saying something?

I said, "Of course I don't have any objection." So I read the memo. And it gets a hilarious response. Now, it has to be understood that I am doing this the evening of the very day I have been physically assaulted by a doctor on the stage of the Hilton Hotel in front of 3,000 people* and everyone is aware of that attack and so they are all very sympathetic to me because all day long people were stopping me, asking me whether I was injured and telling me how much they appreciated what I had done in bringing a criminal complaint against the doctor. So there was a great deal of goodwill toward me.

Then Kitty Hart gets up and she makes a short statement, which goes something like this: "Ed Koch is one of the best stand-up comedians I know and he is a very good Mayor. But his statement as it relates to the New York State Arts Council is totally removed from what we do."

The key thing is, there you have the chairperson of the

*While I was addressing the annual convention of the American Public Health Association, Dr. Nayvin Gordon of San Diego, who was associated with the Progressive Labor Party, had gotten up onto the stage and socked me in the eye with a clenched fist holding an egg. He was immediately arrested on charges, with me as complainant, of third-degree assault, disorderly conduct and harassment. At his trial on March 21, 1980, at which I testified against him, he was found guilty of reckless assault and disorderly conduct. That summer, Gordon spent thirty days on Rikers Island and paid a $1,000 fine.

New York State Council on the Arts seeking to censor
something that is an art form. That memo is extraordinary,
and I deliver it pretty well. And the audience always loves it.
And she sought to censor it because it made her look bad. I
find that charming.

Not so charming was a little meeting I went to in February
of 1978 out in the Bayside section of Queens. During the
1977 runoff, I had attended a candidates' forum hosted by a
group called the Queens Civic Organization, a primarily
white and Christian group of middle-class homeowners. When I
had gone there, with Cuomo and the others, we had been
given a list of four demands to which we had to respond yes
or no before we were allowed to speak. We were required to
sign a statement.

One of the questions was "Will you fire any Commissioner
who lies to the public?"

I said, "Sure."

"Will you agree to meet with us within forty-five days
after you are elected?"

I said, "No. I will meet with you subsequent to my
election at some reasonable time when I find it convenient."

The other candidates, of course, said yes to everything and
signed.

Well, then I was elected, and the request from Father
Lynch,* who is appropriately named, comes in. (Actually, it
was more than a request. It was a demand.) I said, "Sure, I'll
go back out there. Set it up for a convenient time."

So, when we get to this school auditorium, we are told we
cannot bring in any security. Normally, several police officers
would go into the facility for the purpose of securing it, and
one would stay with me. Finally, we're told that one police
officer, Edward Martinez, may come in. So, I was there with
Eddie Martinez, Maureen Connelly and Bernie Rome.

When we went in, I had the feeling I was in some
Nuremberg stadium. There was a military band. There were
more than 1,000 people, chanting. They were thumping

---

*Father Eugene Lynch, pastor of Saint Mary Gate of Heaven Church in
Ozone Park, Queens.

standards on the floor. It was like mass hysteria and very militant.

I don't care, it doesn't bother me. In fact, I enjoy it.

The rhetoric coming from the stage from Father Lynch was to the effect that "We are going to demand that city officials come out here. We are going to put them on trial. They are going to have to answer questions. If we don't like their answers, we are going to ask them again and again until they respond to our satisfaction." It was the most hostile kind of atmosphere. So they marched me down front and seated me very close to the stage. Then they ordered me up and sat me at a small table by myself on one side of the stage. On the other side was a large table at which something like eight jurors were sitting, and then there was Father Lynch—the hanging judge—in the middle at his lectern. He said, "We are now going to place the Mayor on trial. He is going to have to answer these questions."

I said, "Fine. But before we proceed, I will make a two-minute opening statement."

He said, "You can have thirty seconds."

I said, "No, it will take two minutes."

They caucused for about five minutes, and they came back and said, "You can have one minute."

And I said, "No, I will take two minutes."

Father Lynch said, "Well, you can't have it."

I said, "Well, then, bye-bye, I am leaving." And I got up and left the stage.

I went down the stairs and Martinez said, "Let's go out the side entrance."

I said "No, I walk out the same entrance that I walk in. That is a rule, and don't ever forget it. We never leave by a side or rear entrance."

And we went out. And what is interesting is that while we are making our way through this mob, Bernie Rome says to Maureen, "Don't stand too close to Ed—he might get assaulted." And this throng is yelling and screaming pure hate. (My desire, to which I did not give in, was to turn around to these people and say, "How'm I doing?" But I didn't. I just smiled and waved.) When we get outside the school the press is all there, and they are saying, "How could you do this? How could you just leave? It has never been done before. You can't just walk out on a community group!"

I said, "Well, you know, they are holding a kangaroo court in there. But I am not a kangaroo.

"If they want me to speak, I am happy to speak; I will stay here for hours; but I will make an opening statement of two minutes. If they don't want to be that courteous to me, then I am not going to hang around here." And I left.

Then there was an enormous amount of flak in the press. "How could you do this?"

And I proceeded to say, escalating a little bit, "Well, you know, my feelings at the time were that this was sort of like the Jewish doctors' trial in Moscow under Stalin. I felt as if I were one of the doctors."

So everyone said, "Oh, he is accusing them of anti-Semitism." Well, maybe I was, because that is the way I felt.

Then Father Lynch and his crowd came down and held a press conference at City Hall: very denunciatory.

Then they said, "We want to have a second meeting."

And I said, "You put it all in an agenda, and I will go over it and decide whether the conditions are reasonable."

So the agenda was delivered. It was a very stilted agenda. They had the two minutes in there for me. They were going to ask the questions. And the agenda specifically said no closing statements. That was okay with me. They were going to have a report card on the wall, marking the five different items to show whether I passed or failed. I went back to the high school and answered their questions. To begin, Father Lynch asked me if ten minutes would be enough for my opening statement. I said, "Two minutes is what I asked for and all I need." Then at the end, Father Lynch said, "Well, I would like to make a closing statement."

I said, "Oh, no, you won't. There are no closing statements on this agenda. I am leaving." And that was the end of it. Except that on a Saturday morning about eleven months later, when I was holding one of my constituent hours in that same area, I had seen several people and then suddenly I looked up and there was this guy in a leather jacket and he said, "Do you know me?"

I looked at him and said, "Father Lynch." And then somewhat mischievously, "How'm I doing?"

And he said, "You are doing fine." And he said that to the press.

The following year, 1979, I was facing another of these what we might call constituent-community problems.

Shortly before my election, it had developed that a white police officer named Robert Torsney had shot and killed a black youngster in the Crown Heights section of Brooklyn. At the trial, Torsney used as his defense that he had blacked out as a result of a seizure of Jacksonian epilepsy and somehow or other had shot the youngster during the seizure. The jury found him not guilty on the basis that the shooting was unintentional. The leaders of the black community were quite understandably upset, and so I agreed to meet with them, as I always will in instances of this kind. Another one that comes to mind is the case of the death of Arthur Miller.* I attended a number of meetings as a result of that incident—always with the hope of delivering justice and calming nerves.

At the Torsney meeting, it was mentioned that these community people in Crown Heights were upset that they were getting inadequate police protection while the Lubavitcher Rebbe over on Eastern Parkway was in fact getting special police protection.

I said I didn't know anything about the special protection, but that I would have it checked out. I asked Bob McGuire if what they alleged was true, and he said it was. He said there was a patrol car stationed in front of the synagogue at 770 Eastern Parkway twenty-four hours a day. I asked him to find out whether that police car was required on the basis of a police decision or was it there as the result of a political decision. His feeling at that time and my feeling at that time was that probably it was placed there to protect the Lubavitcher community from attacks by the blacks. He said it was a very volatile neighborhood, that the Jews of this particular sect had

---

*Miller, 35, a black businessman from the Crown Heights section of Brooklyn, died tragically while being placed under arrest on June 15, 1978. He was innocent of any crime.

stayed while others had left and that there were lots of incidents of violence there. That was our suspicion—but nevertheless, he had a study made.

And sometime later, McGuire came in with a written report. It said that the first car had been put in front of the synagogue in 1966 by Mayor Lindsay. And it wasn't as a result of threats by blacks to Jews but rather because the Satmar Hasidic group had threatened to beat up the Lubavitcher. So the patrol car had been placed in front of the synagogue in order to prevent a fight between two Jewish groups. Additionally, the report showed that a second car had been placed in front of the Rebbe's home by Mayor Beame in 1977 during the primary. Obviously Beame had done it to curry favor with that particular group.

The police report also said that on the basis of manpower formulas, neither car should be there. The two cars cost the City half a million dollars a year, because you would have to figure that there are two police officers in each car on three tours, or a total of twelve cops for twenty-four hours a day. There was a third car which the police believed should be there that wasn't there on a regular basis. That one was in front of the mikvah, which is a ritual bath for women. That one, they thought, was needed on the day of the ritual baths for security reasons; but the others, they said, were a political matter. McGuire said, "If you want them there, they will stay there. But our study shows they should not be there but should be out traveling throughout the district."

I said to McGuire, "Get rid of them right away." And everyone was amazed at that. And everyone was sure that I would rescind my position after all hell broke loose.

First, by way of importuning me, Rabbi Groner called. He is the rabbi who functions as a sort of Papal Chamberlain of the Lubavitcher sect. He and two others came to see me, and they made their case. I said, "No, you have to understand—the cars will go." And they didn't believe it.

Then, in the summer of 1978, I went to Paris for a little vacation, and while I was there I got a telegram from the "French Jewish Community." It says, in French, basically: "Why are you torturing the Rebbe? Why do you refuse to provide him with adequate security? Why are you torturing the Lubavitcher?''

Well, I am visiting with Paris Mayor Jacques Chirac, and so I say to him, ''I have to tell you a little story about New York.'' And I explain to him all about the patrol car and the removal. And then I read him the telegram that was signed, ''The French Jewish Community.''

He says, ''They are a powerful community here—very powerful.'' And then, maybe a half-hour later, he says, ''Why don't you give them the car?''

I say, ''No, no, no, we can't. It isn't fair.''

Well, I come back from Paris and there is Rabbi Groner again for another meeting. On this occasion, I ask Bob McGuire to sit in with us. And Bob duly explains to Rabbi Groner that from the police perspective the car is not warranted.

And Rabbi Groner and the others begin, ''Well, you don't understand. The Rebbe is very special. It is as though he were the Cardinal. He has to be considered as though he were the representative of a foreign power, so to speak. Like an embassy person.''

I said, ''The first thing is that we don't provide around-the-clock police protection to the Cardinal. And secondly, you cannot be considered to be a foreign mission unless you want to give up your citizenship. And then if you are threatened, we will protect you in the same way that we provide protection to the other foreign missions.'' Here I was referring to Iraq, Israel, Egypt, the Soviet Union and others. And they do require special police protection because there are always terrorists after them. ''But,'' I said, ''you are not a foreign mission. You are American citizens. So that won't wash.''

Then they said, ''Well, the blacks will come and assault us. There are threats all the time on our people. The Black United Front led a group to within a hundred feet of the synagogue and they said, 'Let's get guns!' ''

I said, ''Yes. But that does not entitle you to twenty four-hour police protection. If the occasion arises that it is warranted, we will put a patrol car there on a temporary basis.''

Then they said, ''Well, we are telling you it will not go forward. We won't permit it.''

I said, "And I'm telling you that it will." Then they presented the same arguments and I gave them the same responses. And it went around for about four times in the space of this hourlong meeting. Finally, by now a little bit irate, I say to Rabbi Groner, "Look, Rabbi, you have given us the same arguments four times. And we have explained to you four times why they are not acceptable. Why are you repeating them?"

He says, "Because obviously you don't understand it. And we have to repeat it until you do." Now, he wasn't kidding, but I thought it was very funny.

So I said, "You are going to have to accept this. In order to make it easier, the cars will not both go right away. The one in front of the Rebbe's house is going right away. The one in front of the synagogue will go in thirty days."

They said, "We will go to the President and the Governor and we will get protection."

I said, "Go! But these cars are going."

Then, having accepted that they weren't going to change me on this, Rabbi Groner said, "Well, okay, but could we keep the car until the holidays are over?"

McGuire said, "That is okay with me."

I said, "Just a minute. You don't know what holidays they are talking about." Then I said to Groner, "Which holidays?"

And he takes out his calendar. He had a holiday every day up until October 31. Every day was a holiday. I laughed, and McGuire laughed. I said, "Okay, we will keep them until the end of October."

Some time after that I got a call from Bob Morgado.* His question was—and you have to remember that this was the year when Hugh Carey was running for reelection—"Mr. Mayor, would you object if the Governor put state troopers in front of the synagogue?"

I said, "You bet I would object!" They had obviously gone to Carey and he was willing to do it.

I don't know what the President would have done. They probably couldn't get him on the phone.

---

*Robert Morgado was Secretary to the Governor in the Carey administration. As such he was Carey's chief political operative.

8

Saving Money

IT IS TRUE that the popular perception of my first day in office is that I walked in the door of City Hall and issued an Executive Order barring discrimination based on sexual preference in city contracts, jobs and housing. This notion refers to Executive Order No. 4.

In fact, the first Executive Order, dated January 1, 1978, among other provisions, in its Section 3 brought the Community Development Agency, the Department of Employment and the Model Cities Program under direct Mayoral control. The effect of this action was a significant one. I had, during my campaign, lashed out at "poverty pimps," and this Executive Order sent a clear signal to all those who had vested interests in these programs that I meant to make good on my campaign promise to clean up the poverty programs.

For a decade, or since their inception, the poverty programs had been viewed by politicians, white and black alike, as the special province of the black political establishment. It was not uncommon to hear stories of newly elected district leaders in Harlem walking into the offices of these neighborhood facilities and asking point-blank: "How many jobs do I get?" The federal money that flowed into the poverty corporations was, in effect, being distributed as the largesse of the local political clubhouses. And the U.S. Attorneys, the DAs, the politicians and the press had all taken a largely hands-off attitude. The message sent by Section 3 of Executive Order No. 1 was clearly that I was not going to allow incompetence and corruption to continue in these poverty corporations. The fact was that the Federal Government had placed the corporations, collectively, in a kind of receivership. It had caused the umbrella organization, the Council Against Poverty, to be eliminated, and it had indicated that most of the individual programs were not code-compliant. Thus I was faced with the following choice: I could, through stalling tactics, preserve the programs as they were for perhaps a few more years, or I could clean them up and bring the whole program back within the federal guidelines.

I decided to bring them out into the sunshine, regardless of the political damage. I am white. I am Jewish. And this action, from the viewpoint of those who because of nepotism, incompetence or graft had something to lose, was heresy. A white man restructuring the poverty programs was a strike issue, and the strikers wasted no time going out.

The first skirmish occurred on January 15, 1978.

I was asked to go up to one of the major black churches— the Convent Avenue Baptist Church at 135th Street and Convent Avenue in Harlem—to read a proclamation on Martin Luther King, Jr.'s, birthday. I went up there with Basil Paterson,* and when we sat down near the altar I noticed that I was the only white person in the church. Well, I'm sitting there waiting to be called on and several things occur. Carl Flemister, a leading pastor in the City,† gets up to speak and he begins lecturing me. He is upset that I have issued an Executive Order barring discrimination on the basis of sexual orientation where city employment is involved. And he says that he hopes I will be equally conscious of the rights of the blacks and the poor—very caustic and, in my judgment, not nice from a minister. Okay. They call on me. I don't respond to his charges; I just start to read the proclamation. Suddenly I see this guy standing up and yelling in the balcony. And he's pointing down at me and yelling in this church, ''Don't let him speak. Send the Jew back to the synagogues!'' I mean you can't get any more vile than that. And I am just standing there and thinking, Well, somebody is going to get up and say

*My Deputy Mayor for Labor Relations, one of the original seven.
†The Reverend Carl Flemister and I subsequently became very good friends and we meet regularly.

something. Maybe Basil? Not a word in my defense from him. And this guy in the gallery is screaming away. Finally a couple of deacons, the church elders, get up and look at this guy in the balcony and one of them says, "Hush, brother." Then the minister quieted him.

I said to myself, "Hush, brother"?

I never got over that. I thought, What if Basil Paterson or Andrew Young got up and read a proclamation at Temple Emanuel on Warsaw Ghetto Uprising Day and someone in the congregation yelled, "Send him back to Harlem. Don't let him speak"? Why, there would be a storm of protest in the synagogue and in the community.

I did not, as they had hoped, roll over. Instead, as I had with the ministers and as I had with the gays, I continued on aggressively and up front, attempting to deliver services on the basis of need, and specifically not on the basis of who was threatening me or who had political clout.

In the person of Haskell Ward, one of Secretary of State Cyrus Vance's policy planners for African affairs and a product of the Ford Foundation, I found a brilliant young black man who was not a product of the black political machine to take on the poverty programs. I appointed Ward Commissioner of the Community Development Agency.

I had hoped that Ward would move to clean up clubhouse practices. And move Ward did. He found thievery, graft, extortion, nepotism, ballot tampering, payoffs and misappropriation of funds of all kinds. In the CDA's Annual Report for 1978 there appears a list of the corporations that were closed down in the first year of Ward's investigation. On just the first page of that list there is reference to wrongdoing in nearly every poor neighborhood in New York City—rip-offs by those who were supposed to help the poor.

But Ward made a mistake. He played by gentlemen's rules. He conducted his investigations not in the press by means of leaks, but behind the closed doors of his agency. One by one the directors of these programs were quietly called in and questioned outside the purview of the press. Thus, it was Ward's show and not the muckrakers'. In retrospect, it seems that the only way Haskell Ward could have saved himself from the torrent of attacks that rained down on him would have been to enter into a partnership with the muckrakers. As with Ward, so too with the rest of us: his strengths were his weaknesses. The Ford Foundation had prepared him for the investigation; the State Department had taught him discretion; but only the clubhouses could have taught him how to guard his flanks from the daily street fight on the front pages.

And what a news story it could have been: the City administration as muckraker. Every weekend Ward and I would take walks around the neighborhoods of New York. And every weekend we would review his past week's investigations. Often we were accompanied by Dan Wolf, who, as the editor of *The Village Voice* for nearly twenty years, knew as much about muckraking as anyone did. Ward would recite the facts he had uncovered and Wolf and I would speculate on how to get more, where to look and whom to turn. It was high drama, but it played to an empty house.

The restructuring of the poverty programs had several effects. These neighborhood corporations were brought back within the federal guidelines so that the maximum number of available federal dollars was made available to the poor. That was my goal, and it was achieved quickly and cleanly and without much notice. But at what cost? By midsummer 1978 the City's foremost black weekly, *The Amsterdam News*, was editorializing: "Mayor Koch is getting through this summer by the skin of his teeth. He is already on the ropes as far as black political leaders are concerned."* And by the following January, barely a year into my administration, when I appointed Ward my Deputy Mayor for Human Services, *The Amsterdam News* readers were being treated to steamed-up banner headlines like this:

January 27, 1979

NEW YORK AMSTERDAM NEWS

**Koch names Ward:
Blacks are enraged**

So I had done, as Mayor, what I had wanted to do, but hadn't done, as a Congressman. Those who told me in 1975

---

*The New York Amsterdam News, July 22, 1978, page 4.

that it couldn't be done were proved wrong. And those who said it couldn't be done except at great political cost were correct.

In the midst of the uproar Charlie Rangel, the redoubtable Congressman from Harlem, as a result of the restructuring, turned against me. He came into City Hall to ask me to take it easy on the black leadership—in effect, to leave them what was theirs. In the course of our conversation, Rangel said, "You know, Ed, you're running this administration as if you want to be a one-term Mayor."

And I replied, "You're exactly right, Charlie. And that's why I am going to be a three-term Mayor."

I at City Hall and Ward at CDA were the lightning rods for the attacks resulting from the program to bring all of the poverty programs back under the federal guidelines. But less conspicuously a little way up Church Street at the Department of Employment, where all the jobs programs are administered, Commissioner Stanley Brezenoff* was engaged in a similar— if not more radical—restructuring effort. Brezenoff took, for instance, the federal summer-jobs-for-youth program—which in New York amounted to 60,000 minimum-wage jobs—and he instituted at my request a lottery selection process for choosing the 60,000 recipients. Previously the jobs had been awarded from City Hall by Stanley Friedman, Mayor Beame's Deputy Mayor for Politics (a man I later described as "one of the smartest, ablest, most loyal people I know"). Friedman had chosen community leaders, district leaders, county leaders, members of the clergy, and he had given each of them a few dozen jobs to give away. During the days when Friedman had awarded the jobs, in 1977, for example, 76 percent of them had gone to nonwhites. Then I came in and said that the patronage process would be ended. And the clergy and the civic and political leaders said, "No, no, Mr. Mayor. We know who the good children are."

I responded to one priest, "Father, there are no bad children." And the names were put into the computer. In the summer of 1978, 92 percent of the jobs the Federal Govern-

*Another product of the Ford Foundation and later Human Resources Administrator and then president of the Health and Hospitals Corporation.

ment provided to the City of New York went to nonwhite youngsters. And that was just the start.

In DOE's Annual Report for 1978 there appears a list of employment programs that were defunded in that first year. The list runs seven full pages—single-spaced.

Meanwhile at the Model Cities Agency, Commissioner Richard Aniero was conducting a similar, across-the-board evaluation. One thing was becoming clear: the Koch administration was trying to cut the politics out of the poverty programs.

We found other abuses and took steps to correct them.

We found, for instance, that under the Model Cities scholarship program, the City had been allocating, year after year, $4.6 million for college-tuition grants. And when we examined the program, it was clear that of the $4.6 million, $2.1 million was being used as overhead expenses to pick students, largely black and Hispanic, and $2.5 million was being used for the grants. Now, that is ridiculous—the overhead exceeded 40 percent of the total budget. And we found that the people who were in the administrative part of this program were basically selected from one Harlem political clubhouse. I mean, how many people can it take to select 2,000 students? So we finally ended it. And there was a huge amount of screaming.

Specifically, we reduced the overhead from $2.1 million to $465,000, and got the Urban League and Aspira* to identify black and Hispanic students who would be considered for the grants. The balance of the money saved was used for maintenance grants for students. Then we found that the program directors were providing larger grants than were allowable under the federal rules and regulations. So we restructured that, and instead of sending 2,000 students to college with grants, which was what the money had paid for in the past, we took the total program less the $465,000 administrative-overhead costs and were able to send 5,000 students to college. Well, that is something.

Now, of course, the political people don't like this sort of

*From the Spanish verb "to aspire": an educational and leadership-development program targeted at Puerto Rican youth.

thing, and the parents who have their kids going to college who wouldn't have gone before—they don't know that their kids wouldn't have gone before. So they are not a lobby supporting us. But I don't mind. Let Charlie Rangel and the rest scream at me. Let them go outside and join the picket line.

I knew why they were screaming and yelling. They were screaming and yelling that I was ending their control of the poverty programs—I, a white Mayor, was actually removing the money from the black political-patronage system and making certain it was going to the black poor. I summed up my feelings on a number of occasions, saying, "If we had given to the poor all of the money that we have appropriated for the poor over the last twenty years, the poor would be rich."

A second way to save money shortly presented itself. When I took office I was told by my representative on the Board of Estimate that many water charges incurred by various institutions around town were being waived by the Board in an offhand way. I said, "We're going to stop that." I instructed my representative to begin opposing these exemptions. And as the City Charter was clear that such waivers had to be voted unanimously, I cast the first "nay" vote and, along with Carol Bellamy, effectively put a stop to the handout. She and I caused a joint resolution to be passed, and that resolution became effective on July 1, 1978.

But the problem remained: how to collect the estimated $4 million a year from the various hospitals, colleges, foreign missions, cemeteries and parochial schools that theretofore had been exempted.

All the missions together in New York City owed hundreds of thousands of dollars. They were billed for the first time beginning that July. This is not a tax; it is a user charge. If they had bought water from a private company, they would have had to pay, as they do for electricity. They are buying water from us and they have to pay.

Some of them said, "We won't pay."

We said to them, "We are cutting off the water." It was the same line that I used with the parochial schools, the universities and everybody else who came in.

"Well, we shouldn't be paying it," they said. "We're tax-exempt."

I said, "You don't have to pay. You only pay if you drink. Stop drinking, you don't pay."

With the Colombian U.N. Mission, which had declined to pay for thirty days, we had to go a little further. We told them we were sending up workmen to cut off their water if they didn't pay that afternoon. They delivered a check that day for $22,288.97.

The missions all asked for receipted bills in very contrite letters saying, "Could we have the bill so we could show it to our government? Because we didn't put it in the budget."

"Sure," we said, "we'll give you a receipted bill."

Well, then the big institutions came in. Columbia University, Fordham and a number of others. They wanted to see me. They came in and we met at City Hall.

I said, "Okay, who is going to speak?" So a couple of them start. And I listen. The same arguments I have heard a dozen times. "Okay," I said, "you are paying and that's it. If you don't want to pay, don't drink. But if you drink, you pay. Listen, you know what I said to Yeshiva University? 'You don't want to pay? Close your mikvahs!'* I assume that is where the water is going. I don't know. I mean how else do you buy two hundred and eighty thousand dollars' worth of water in a year? Whatever you did with it, you are going to pay! We have billed Woodlawn Cemetery in the Bronx for eighty thousand. And I didn't even know they could drink water."

*Jewish ritual baths.

9

Finding Money

SAVING THE CITY from eventual bankruptcy was not only a matter of finding better managers and using the dollars that we had more efficiently. The problem was political as well as financial and managerial—and the solution required federal and State help.

In the first week of April 1979, I focused my attention on Albany. The legislative budget was on the floor. The Governor's budget proposal included a $140-million cut over two years in revenue-sharing aid to the City. I needed eight Democratic votes to override. The Democrats were solidly behind the Governor. I went to work on them.

Our key person on the Democratic side was Abraham Bernstein. He was from the Bronx and had been very friendly toward the City, as opposed to Manfred Ohrenstein, the Senate Minority Leader from Manhattan, who hadn't been helpful at all on this issue. When we started calling people, we called the Senators who represented middle-class people, because they were the constituency that was to be most adversely affected by the cut. We needed that money for the schools, the police and other services. Those Senators were all in Queens, Brooklyn and the Bronx. We basically gave up on the Senators representing Manhattan because most of them were affiliated with Ohrenstein or the West Side radicals. My calls were always the same. I'd say: "Listen, this is important to me. And I want you to know that I will be supporting you and walking with you if you vote our way on this. But I will be opposing you and walking against you if you are on the other side.''

And some would say, ''Well, the Governor is very strong on this.''

I would say, ''Well, you may get the Governor to walk with you, but I will be walking against you. And you should know that.'' I was very direct. Now, I think normally this isn't done in as direct a manner as the way I do it. But that is my way. I just have no other way of negotiating. I can't be sophisticated about the political threat. Indeed, in an earlier situation, with the City Council, when members of my staff were bringing the Council members in on the Fuel Pass-Along Bill,* I did the same thing. The staff would say, ''Why are you threatening them?'' And I would reply, ''Well, why do you bring them in? If you don't want me to exercise that kind of political clout, then don't bring them in. I have no other way of doing it. I know these people and you cannot persuade them by logic. It can't be done.'' The same thing applied here. Only this time my staff members didn't even bother to try to caution me, because they knew it would have been a waste of time.

I called about ten of these legislators. My feeling was that most of them were not vulnerable, that they would win even if I opposed them. But my opposition would cost them money; and it would cost them time; and it would cost them worry.

I'd learned about this in 1973 in the Assembly race against Mark Siegel, who had caused his club, the Lexington Democratic Club, to oppose my bid for the mayoralty in 1973. In return, I supported a candidate against him in 1974 who was not terrific: George Spitz. Actually, if Spitz had won he wouldn't have been too awful, but he was no campaigner. I practically had to prop him up against the subway entrance and make his speech for him. I knew he couldn't win. But I can tell you that Siegel was absolutely crushed. After that election, which he won, he became one of my most ardent supporters.

---

*Legislation permitting landlords to pass along to their tenants the increased cost of heating fuel.

But to return to Albany, what was interesting in the course of all this negotiating was that we couldn't even use the Democratic phone in the Senate Chamber to hear the debate. Ohrenstein closed it down on us. I'd called up there during the debate and asked for him, and one of his staff people, a young woman, had come back to the phone and said, "The Minority Leader—and I'm so embarrassed, Mr. Mayor, to have to tell you this—said, 'You tell the Mayor I don't give a damn what he thinks!'" Then he stopped taking our calls altogether. So we had to arrange to get the debate via the Republicans' phone line, which was piped into our office. It was in that way that we were able to listen to the debate. Then, in order to get our instructions out to the floor, we had to use Warren Anderson's phone—the Majority Leader's phone, the Republicans' phone—and Anderson would call John Calandra, the Republican from the Bronx, who was being helpful to us, and Calandra would go and get Abe Bernstein, the Democrat. And that's how I got my messages through to the Senate floor.

It was essential to listen to the debate because, as the Senators attempted to get off the hook, they often misstated my positions. They said that they had promised they would be for revenue sharing, but only for revenue sharing and not for anything else, and that I had not asked them to vote in support of the whole override package. A lot of these things came in packages. So they would misstate my position in order to get themselves off the hook. Then I'd call Abe Bernstein* to get up and he'd restate my position. I drove them crazy.

At the end of all of this, we lost. We picked up only four of the eight Democratic Senators we needed. After the vote, Nat Leventhal† suggested that I call the Governor. Nat asked me with some trepidation, as if he thought I might not want to do it.

---

*As a result of his helpfulness to me in this instance, the Democratic leadership removed Bernstein as the ranking Democrat on the Senate Finance Committee, which resulted in his loss of some financial perquisites. I never forgot that.
†Nathan Leventhal, Deputy Mayor for Operations.

I said, "I have no problem with that." And I called Carey. I said, "Congratulations, Governor. You won."

He said, "Oh, there are no winners and there are no losers. Now I have to start the orderly flow of appropriate funds so as to get money to the City."

I said, "That's fine."

"That's fine" is not what I told the newspaper editorial boards, however. I started in on them the moment I knew the outcome. It was after 5 P.M., and all the editorial-board members at the *Times* had gone home. Next I called the *Post*, and was told that it would not be running an editorial on Carey's budget the next day.

The *Daily News* usually published an editorial the day after budget votes. And because we were sure it was going to do so, and that Carey's people—Robert Morgado in particular—would undoubtedly call around, I called the News editorial board looking for Mike O'Neill.*

I'd mentioned the matter first to Tom Goldstein.† He said, "Oh, no, you don't have to call. The editorials are already locked up. We can call tomorrow."

I said, "No, we are calling today." (I'm not putting Tom down; I just know how intense and persistent you have to be about this business if you want to accomplish anything. So I made the call.)

Mike O'Neill was not in at the *News*, but I spoke to Robert Laird. Laird had been Mayor John Lindsay's press secretary, and he is a very decent guy. I explained my problem to him.

He said, "You know, the editorial has already been made up, but let me go and tell them what you said."

What I'd said was "I worked very hard on this situation, getting Carey to provide the money administratively—and he hasn't and he can't, and it's smoke. That's why we need committed dollars. It would be ridiculous to think that these dollars would break the budget that he has up in Albany. That's silly."

"Well," Laird said, "I'll try to get your point across."

---

*Michael J. O'Neill, the editor.
†Thomas Goldstein, Maureen Connelly's successor as press secretary, 1980–82.

I said, "Please, be my lawyer and do your best."

Now, what's the result? That evening's edition of the *News* had an editorial that was totally Carey's editorial. But the morning edition of the same *Daily News* had a different editorial, two additional paragraphs. And the paper endorsed my position. And it shows how you can change things, because that editorial—the second one—was excellent. And if I hadn't called, it wouldn't have appeared. You have to keep after them, sometimes even torture them. In spite of himself, Carey generally gave us what we wanted.

I applied the same kind of pressure to President Carter, although he didn't fully appreciate it until 1980, and to be sure, I had to do it less directly.

"I think the Mayor's program is going to work."

From *The New Yorker,* June 30, 1980

My political relationship with Jimmy Carter had begun in an undiplomatic way. On October 1, 1977, the United States and the Soviet Union had issued a joint declaration on the peace efforts in the Middle East. It called for recognition of the legitimate rights of the Palestinian people and a withdrawal of the Israeli troops to the 1967 borders. Thus, the joint declaration was widely viewed as a retreat by the United States from its support of U.N. Resolutions 242 and 338.

The Jewish Press ran a page one editorial entitled "The Carter Sellout" in which it blasted the Carter Administration for endorsing a "Palestinian homeland on the very land Israel paid for with blood of Israeli soldiers in a war imposed on her by the Arab nations." After the jump the editorial continued: "By the United States' joining in the Russian resolution, the United States has effected a complete sellout of Israel! The shock was so great to Israel's Prime Minister Menachem Begin, especially after he was reassured of the United States' support, that Mr. Begin had to be hospitalized!"

Three days later, President Carter was scheduled to arrive at 9 A.M. at New York's LaGuardia Airport and to be flown by Marine helicopter to the heliport at the foot of Wall Street in Manhattan for his motorcade to the United Nations. The purpose of the U.N. stop was to deliver a message in support of the joint declaration. (Later that day Carter was to inspect the devastation in the South Bronx.) Mayor Beame, I, the Democratic contender, and others were lined up at 9 o'clock at the helipad to welcome the President to New York.

Late into the evening of October 3, Maureen Connelly, my campaign researcher, had worked with Ben Rosenthal* on a letter to President Carter for my signature. The letter began: "I fear that in this recent agreement the U.S. has abandoned its commitments to peace, to Jewish refugees, and to the protection of Israel," and it continued in that vein. There had been some discussion in my camp that afternoon about the content of the letter, but none about the manner in which the letter would be presented to the President. It showed. The October 4 letter incident is widely cited as an example of my uncontrollable side. The fact is, while I may at times be uncontrollable, that incident is an example, and a rare one at

---

*Benjamin S. Rosenthal, a Democrat from Queens and a longtime friend and Congressional colleague.

that, of poor staff work by the Carter advance people and my press office.

There were two things involved in the letter. The first was that I honestly believed it was necessary for the President to know he was wrong. Also, I felt it was necessary that I take a public position because I was running for the Mayoralty and people wanted to know where I stood. Garth was away that weekend, I believe. I can't remember all the people involved in discussing that letter, but they must have included Maureen, Eddie Costikyan, Dan Wolf and maybe Garth by telephone. This was after the runoff, at the time of the general election.

Well, we decided that I would give Carter such a letter, but that we would alert him to it in advance. Accordingly, our people called the White House advance people and told them that I planned to give the President a letter and asked, "Will it be okay?" We didn't want to take Carter by surprise or do something that would embarrass him. That was not my intention. Indeed, if the White House had said no, I would have found some other way to make my position public.

Since we never heard back from the White House, we assumed it was okay. Later it turned out that the President's advance people were told, but they never informed the President. So the President never had a chance to get back to us with a yes or a no.

There was another unfortunate aspect. We handed out copies of the letter at the heliport just as the helicopter was touching down. It might have been better not to do so, because then Carter's people would not have known of the letter in advance and would not have psyched him up so. As it was, one of his people, an advance woman in the crowd, saw the letter, read it and went out to the helicopter and alerted the President and Jody Powell to what was in store. So when the President got off the plane, he was stony. He greeted the others who were in the welcoming party and then he got to me. I said, "Mr. President, I have a letter for you," and he took the letter. In the meantime, Jody Powell, Carter's press secretary, had placed himself between the cameras and the President so as to make it difficult to photograph the incident, although there were photographs of it. And then the

President, instead of going to the microphone where he was going to make this wonderful statement about me and my election, went right to his car. He got into the car and rode off and didn't invite me to ride with him. He was absolutely outraged. So I went to the microphone and made my statement.

There was a big deal in the papers denouncing me and asking how I could have done such a thing. They said I had hurt the President, embarrassed him. The letter got me a lot of support from Jews and a lot of anger against me on the part of non-Jews and some Jews who thought I was putting Israel ahead of the City in some way. According to Israeli Foreign Minister Moshe Dayan, my letter caused Carter to reverse his Mideast policy on that issue, and he actually scheduled a meeting with Dayan that night to deal with the issue. It was worth doing.

Well, subsequently we had to get to the President to make him understand that he had to do something to make clear to the public that he was not angry. I went down to Washington several times, always working it out in advance with him. The first visit was with the New York Congressional delegation. They sat me next to Carter's chair so that when he entered the room I was right beside him. He sees me—it has all been choreographed—and he walks toward me with a big smile and says, "How is my good friend Ed?"

And I say, "Your good friend is terrific."

After that, I made an effort to be more supportive and conciliatory toward the Carter White House. Clearly, without the Carter Administration's help New York City's fiscal condition would be more difficult to improve. On several occasions during the winter and spring I was invited down to the White House for exercises in rapprochement. I always attended these sessions and never missed an opportunity to lobby the President for legislation that would be helpful to the City. Foremost among the needed legislation was the New York City loan-guarantee package.

In 1975, as I noted at the beginning of this story, New York City had found itself unable to sell its bonds. With weekly payrolls amounting to millions of dollars, the City had nearly gone under. Only the last-minute intervention of Governor Carey and the State Legislature had prevented a collapse. It was at that time that the Emergency Financial Control Board and the Municipal Assistance Corporation were created to lend credibility and dollars to a city that was desperately short of both.

The decision had been made to prop the City up. It wasn't an easy one, and there were those in the press and in Washington who advocated bankruptcy.

In my judgment, a default by the City of New York, or by any other municipality, would quickly lead to chaos. First, if the City went into bankruptcy, no one would sell to the City. No pencils, no trucks, no paint, no asphalt, nothing. We buy billions of dollars' worth of goods and services every year—and we do it on credit. We pay for these goods and services subsequently out of tax-levy dollars when the taxes come due. Now, what businessman is going to give us credit if we are in bankruptcy? Nobody sells to a bankrupt on credit.

Second, we would have no capital budget. Assuming for a moment that somehow or other, on a C.O.D. basis, we were able to stay in business with our operating budget, still we would surely not be able to persuade people to lend to us long-term. And that is how capital projects are financed: long-term—fifteen-, twenty-, thirty-year bonds. But nobody would buy these bonds if the City was in bankruptcy. And so the streets, bridges, water tunnels and sewers—the City's infrastructure—would fall apart. And those are the things that keep cities alive. Those are the things that a city has to offer people.

Then there is the law that applies in most states of the Union that fiduciary funds or various investing funds are not allowed to buy the securities of a bankrupt—even when the bankrupt becomes solvent—for a period of at least ten years. So for ten years we would be out of both the seasonal market and the long-term market. Well, now, without the ability to sell these notes and bonds, we could maintain neither services nor our infrastructure. They would have to deteriorate.

We would have fewer police officers, fewer firemen, fewer hospital workers and so on. Why should somebody stay here? The problem would be much worse than it now is. The businesses would leave. They would say: Well, you are not providing police protection and sanitation and the other essential services. As bad as city services are, they would have to deteriorate further if we couldn't sell our notes and bonds for ten years.

And there would be the stigma of a bankrupt city. There would be that hangdog psychological effect.

Now, what would be the pluses? The pluses would be that you could rewrite the municipal labor contracts, and also wipe out the debt that you owed to the banks and the other lending institutions. But you have to keep in mind that these banks and insurance companies may well not be the largest holders of the City's securities. Not at all. They sold their notes and bonds to other people. So what would you be doing if you went into bankruptcy? You would be ruining thousands of middle-class and elderly people who had put their life's savings into City paper. Do you really want to do that if it isn't necessary? I don't think so.

In 1975, during the first fiscal crisis, the City had gone to Washington seeking the Federal Government's help in guaranteeing seasonal loans to pay for operating expenses. That legislation was passed by a slim ten-vote margin in the House of Representatives, and with the caveat that New York was to get its house in order and not come back.

In 1978, once again on the brink of bankruptcy and still shut out of the public markets, we went back to the well. This time we had a two-fold plan: seasonal loans for operating expenses, long-term loan guarantees for capital projects. This plan, devised primarily by Felix Rohatyn, chairman of the board of the Municipal Assistance Corporation, was ready for review when the Koch administration took office in January 1978.* The Rohatyn plan was at that time viewed as ambitious, heady, something to bargain over. Most of the experts thought that the long-term loan guarantees would be stripped off the legislation and that the 1978 plan would ultimately look like the '75 plan. Nonetheless, with a new administration in both the White House and City Hall, our lobbyists took it to Washington.

---

*According to the Emergency Financial Control Board's agreement with the Treasury Department, the 1978 Four-Year Plan was due to be presented to the Federal Government on January 10—ten days after the Koch administra-

The Rohatyn-plan legislation had been drafted, in part, by Carter White House Treasury officials. W. Michael Blumenthal, then Carter's Treasury Secretary, was one of the bill's first advocates on Capitol Hill. But there were those in Washington—most notably Senate Banking Committee Chairman William Proxmire—who still recalled the 1975 caveat. The early indications were that the legislation—in any form—would never make it out of Proxmire's committee. Clearly a full-scale lobbying effort was required. And a full-scale lobbying effort is what the Senators on Proxmire's committee, and eventually in the entire Congress, received. The banks, the insurance companies, the corporations, the municipal unions, the City and State governments—everyone who stood to lose if New York went belly-up—pooled resources and stood together for the lobbying effort in Washington.

In our haste to get our hearings with Proxmire, we had to put our budget in order and have it adopted, because Proxmire had said that he would not actually hold the hearings he had scheduled unless we came to the hearings with an adopted budget. And I was scheduled to go to the Senate hearings a day after the budget was to be adopted, on June 6. That date had already been set. But Proxmire was saying if the budget wasn't adopted, no hearings. So this was a live-or-die issue for the City. The budget normally would be adopted before collective bargaining had ended; collective bargaining normally goes on well past the budget because the actual ongoing current contracts don't end until June 30.

Now, because we knew we had to do something of the kind, we speeded up the collective-bargaining operation with

---

tion took office. We asked the staff at Treasury to postpone it, so that we could redraft it. It was presented on January 20. Then there was a major push to lobby the long-term loan guarantees through the Congress, and to get the Financial Control Board enabling legislation through Albany, then to get the labor settlements. All that was done in just five months. It was like a three-ring circus. It is difficult to remember and to sort out who did what. I do know that it was primarily Felix Rohatyn who conceptualized not only the 1975 plan but also the 1978 plan. He is a financial genius and it was his plans that made it possible for the City of New York to twice avert bankruptcy.

the unions—and in fact, basically worked out the entire settlement, with very small issues left open. Our exposure on the open issues would be a maximum of $12 million. And what we did, therefore, was not complete the collective bargaining, because if we had we would have given the unions the open $12 million and that would have been it. We wanted to save some of that money. Well, everybody understood that.

In the meantime Jay Goldin was playing cute, as was Carol Bellamy,* but particularly Jay, who had not told us categorically that he was going to vote for the budget, although we were pretty sure that he would. Carol, meanwhile, wanted to stake out a position that would give her an independent role. And so she was saying that unless the budget, when adopted, included all labor-settlement costs, she was not going to vote for it. In view of Proxmire's ultimatum, that was a ridiculous position. So we called her in. And I remember that meeting. We said, "Carol, this is what we are settling for." We had been pretty clear about that. In fact, there had been an announcement that there was a $1.004-billion labor settlement.

She said, "But you have these items outstanding. I won't vote for it unless it is settled totally."

We explained that Proxmire had said I had to have a budget adopted before the hearings.

She said, "I don't care. I will not put my name to that. I will not vote for it. If you don't have the labor question totally settled I will tell the Proxmire Committee to vote against the loan-guarantee legislation."

I said, "You are endangering the legislation."

I can't remember her exact words, but they were to the effect that her honor as a public official was more important to her than whether we got this, and part of her credibility was not certifying a budget in advance of knowing to the last dollar what in fact that budget would ultimately include.

I said, "But Carol, ordinarily you adopt a budget without knowing down to the last item what will be included because

*Harrison J. Goldin, the City Comptroller, and Carol Bellamy, the President of the City Council, each with two votes on the eleven-vote Board of Estimate.

normally collective-bargaining settlements are not included in the budget. And after the budget is adopted, you go back and you amend the budget sometime in July. And we are not even doing that now. We really know what the last dollar is. It's between $3 million more and $12 million more. In a budget of $13 billion, that is nothing.''

''No, I will not do it,'' she insisted.

I am really at a loss here. I don't really know how to handle it, because we need her vote.

At that moment the phone rings. I am told it is Jay Goldin on the line. Jay says, ''I just want you to know that I will be voting for the budget.'' Now we have the votes.

I say, ''Thank you, Jay.'' Then I turn to Carol and I say, ''Carol, you are right. You shouldn't vote for the budget, on the basis of your feelings in this matter; I understand that. Jay just called me. He is voting for the budget. So everybody else will be, but you shouldn't do it. Tomorrow you vote against the budget. I am sure everyone will understand that. The meeting is adjourned.''

She broke into tears because her bluff had been called. I don't even know, frankly, what her game plan was; I don't know what she expected to get out of it. But somehow or other she was going to beat us up. And she was relying on the fact, I suppose, that she had heard that Jay had some doubts as to what he was going to do. I am sure he understood that he had to vote for the budget for the reasons I had given both of them. So it was embarrassing. She just broke into tears and left. Now, of course, she doesn't remember it—that it happened.

Meanwhile, back in Washington our lobbying of the Congress continued, with emphasis on the Senate and, more especially, its Banking Committee and, *most* especially, the committee chairman, William Proxmire. We kept the pressure on, but we also showed impeccable restraint.

I happen to like Bill Proxmire. I think he's an honest and fair man. He may be a little eccentric, but who isn't? It's the people who are a little eccentric who get things done. He kept our feet to the fire, and in that I think he did us a favor. I never agreed with those—Victor Gotbaum, in particular—who thought it would be helpful to dump on Senator Proxmire.

By June 6, when we went to Washington to make our case

before the Senate Banking Committee, we had cleared all the hurdles that Senator Proxmire had identified as the prerequisites. We had drafted a credible four-year plan. We had seen to it that the enabling legislation for a Financial Control Board that was acceptable to the lending institutions had been passed in Albany. We had achieved guidelines settlements with all the municipal labor unions. And, finally, we had seen our Fiscal '79 budget passed by the City Council and the Board of Estimate.

In Washington the question remained what the New York aid bill would look like. Senator Proxmire continued to take the position that New York could make it on its own. He recalled the caveat put on the '75 seasonal loans (that New York was not to come back) and cited the disappearing $600 million* in the labor talks as proof that the City hadn't mended its ways of financial gimmickry. Finally, he accused the banks of intimidating all the financial experts in the hope that the Senate Committee would be able to find only experts favorably disposed toward the New York legislation.

The middle position was presented in a letter written by Arthur Burns, the former chairman of the Federal Reserve Board. Burns, a man of unimpeachable integrity and independence, was presumably unintimidated by the banks' alleged conspiracy. In his letter he took a position in favor of an extended short-term loan program substantially the same as the one approved when he was at the Fed in 1975. The

---

*As Allen Schwartz recalls it: "[The Mayor] was saying...we have no money. His line was 'When the cupboard is bare you can't have a party.' And then the newspaper stories started coming out that there was money. And it got to a point where we were offering the unions a package that came to $600 million over what we had begun by setting as the ceiling. It was all in the papers. Ed went off the wall. He called in the numbers people and said, 'What the hell's going on here? You told me we were broke!' And they gave their usual 'It is a surplus; it is committed; it is underspending'—the usual litany of OMB jargon. Ed said, 'I just want all of you to know one thing. I am so mad I could fire every one of you! And if you ever lie to me again I *will* fire you! You have willfully misled me and I know it. And it won't happen again because I'm smarter than every one of you and you know it.' Well, they were dumbstruck. And guess what? It didn't happen again."

long-term loan guarantees for capital projects he described as an unnecessary "crutch."

Then I took the stand. I indicated that the City's most devastating problem had not been addressed by spokesmen for either of the other two views: namely, that the City's bridges and streets and tunnels and sewers were falling apart as a result of the City's not having had a capital budget for well over four years. My friend David Margolis had dismissed the long-term loan guarantees for capital projects as "pie in the sky," but down in Washington, on TV, I was going for them. I explained that the City might not go bankrupt next week or next year, but that eventually, if it didn't have a capital budget, its infrastructure would fall apart.

I explained that as a result of cutting more than 61,000 workers from its payroll, the City could probably continue to meet its payroll obligations out of local revenue dollars; but cut out of the public borrowing market, how would it find the moneys to repair its bridges, sewers, streets, water tunnels? I stopped short of predicting that if an extension of the seasonal-loans program was all that the Congress was willing to give us, the City would be forced to come back to the Congress for extension after extension, thereby becoming in effect a ward of the Federal Government. I did say that if the City went bankrupt it would almost certainly become a ward of both State and federal governments.

After four hours of my testimony, the day ended in a standoff. Proxmire declared he continued to have "an open mind," and the packed committee room erupted in cynical laughter.

But the field was open to a compromise. And a Senator emerged from an unlikely place to offer just such a proposal. Richard G. Lugar, a Republican, had served as Mayor of Indianapolis for two terms. Subsequently elected to the U.S. Senate, he had been a quiet presence on the Proxmire Committee; but as surprised New Yorkers were to learn, he had been doing his homework.

Our strategy had been not to overlook anybody on the Banking Committee, including the most conservative of the Republicans —people like Jake Garn of Utah and John Tower of Texas and Harrison Schmitt of New Mexico. None of these three, for example, was considered even mildly favorably disposed toward New York City. But we made out the City's case to each one of them; and in the end, we got all their votes except one. But the key was Senator Lugar. He had been openly critical of New York.

We knew that Lugar had recently given a speech in which he was critical of federal assistance to cities. Although he had been Mayor of Indianapolis, he was unsympathetic to the bind that cities like New York were in. He thought the Federal Government had gotten the cities into the bind and that that was a trend that ought to be reversed. When we first went to see Lugar he wouldn't even see us, and Philip Trimble,* who made the initial contact, got the impression from Lugar's administrative assistant that the Senator wasn't even close to the door on this one. But there was one sign. Lugar had a very sharp guy on his staff who had, I think, been the director of the budget in New Haven. And that guy knew municipal budgets. And he was following ours very closely. So they were at least interested. Well, then I came down to testify and the process began to come to a head; people started indicating what they would do. And it became clear that without some help from the Republicans on the Committee, the long-term-loan legislation was not going to fly.

Then Lugar appeared and, for whatever reason, he offered what in effect was the Republican alternative. And it wasn't bad. It set a specific deadline for balancing the budget (but I was committed to balancing the budget anyway, and as it turned out, I beat that deadline). It called for annual reviews by the Congress, with a one-house veto provision. But most important, it included the loan guarantees for capital projects. It trimmed off some of the dollars, but enough remained. It was acceptable. It was workable. So we went to work on it. And it sailed out of the Committee. There was an amendment that Senator Schmitt came up with that called for a productivity council, which was designed to force the City to take steps toward increasing productivity in the work force. But again,

---

*Then my counsel; later Deputy Mayor for Intergovernmental Relations.

we were already working on that. There were other amendments. It was perceived as a tougher bill on New York than the bill that had already passed the House. And the fact that it was Lugar's bill gave good protection against Republican attacks and the possibility of a filibuster.

The dickering took a month and a half. But at the end there was $1.65 billion in long-term bonds available because they had been guaranteed by the Feds for the purpose of capital projects—enough to keep the City's infrastructure together until it could once again sell its own paper in the public bond market. The whole process was anything but sexy. But that legislation was the bridge in the City's transition from the red to the black.

When the loan guarantees passed the House, I got a call from Speaker Thomas P. O'Neill. The margin in the House was ninety-two votes—and most people had said we couldn't get it at all. The Speaker said, "People voted for this bill that we never thought would. And they voted for it because they wanted to see you, personally, succeed." I thought that was nice.*

---

*In March 1983, I received the following letter from Senator Proxmire which, though its immediate occasion was a speech I had delivered urging universal military service, reflected in its last paragraph in the most heartening way the Senator's estimation of my job as Mayor.

William Proxmire
Wisconsin

United States Senate
Washington, D.C. 20510

The Honorable Edward I. Koch
The City of New York
Office of the Mayor
New York, N.Y. 10007

Dear Ed:

Thank you so much for sending me a copy of your fascinating speech proposing that we require all young people to serve our country in universal service for one year.

Frankly, I thought long and hard about this program and I flatly and completely and strongly oppose it.

In the first place, the cost would be colossal. I estimate not $20

The result was the Feds are stuck with us and we with them for thirty years! But there was no risk on their part, because they required us to mortgage general revenue-sharing and other moneys we get directly from them. There is no risk for them. If we fold up, they come ahead of everybody. And they are earning interest. On the '75 seasonal loans they made about $30 million. They charge us 7 percent. That's more than they charge foreign governments. Some foreign governments get forty-year loans at 1-percent interest. And we're a city—in the U.S.A. They should do this for us. They got us here. They said we had to pay welfare benefits, and then they didn't reimburse us for the costs. They mandated Medicaid. Those two items cost us $1 billion a year. Why, if we didn't have to pay just those two costs, *we* could lend money to Chrysler!

---

billion but closer to $60 billion. In the second place, it would wreck the Peace Corps, VISTA, and the other organizations that do a remarkably fine job based on the idealism of voluntary commitment and, in the third place, having served in the peacetime Army before World War II as a volunteer in 1941, I can tell you that a peacetime draft could come about as close to wrecking our military operation as anything I can dream of.

The military is just beginning to make some real progress based on paying volunteers enough to encourage people to come into the military and to make a career out of it. As a result, we have an Army, Navy and Air Force that has greatly improved in motivation and skill and retention rate over anything we've had before.

In view of the fact that the 1941 peacetime Army had such trouble with goldbricking over the hill in October and other protests against authority, I dread to think what this far less disciplined, less authority respectful generation would do if they were pulled into military or VISTA or Peace Corps or CCC or any other kind of government service on a compulsory basis.

As an overachiever yourself, Ed, you know that most of us only perform at about 10 percent of our potential. With a draft Army, I think it would be close to one percent of the potential of those who were drafted.

I say all of this to you because I have the greatest respect and admiration for you. You are doing a marvelous job as Mayor. You would have been a superb Governor and if you ever get nominated for President of the United States, I'd be for you all the way. You'd be a great President. But universal service—uh-uh, no way.

Sincerely,
William Proxmire, U.S.S.

So let's talk about Chrysler. It's a private company. It had done a bad job. Nineteen eighty was an election year. The Michigan legislators and lobbyists—the inner-city Democrats, unions, blacks—pressured Carter, saying they wouldn't be able to carry Michigan for him unless something was done for Chrysler. So the Carter people go out and try to save the company. They get the company a federal guarantee that will allow it to borrow $1.5 billion more. Under the Chrysler loan guarantee, the Federal Government comes after the banks: if Chrysler goes under, the banks get paid first.

The Michigan pressure groups got for Chrysler a better deal than we got for New York City. I opposed the Chrysler legislation. I spoke out against it. I was criticized by the Michigan Congressional delegation for doing that. So I wrote to them and explained why I couldn't be for it. I spoke with Coleman Young, the Mayor of Detroit, and explained to him my position. I said, "I'm not going to fight it, but in response to a question I told what I believe to be the truth. I will do anything to get aid for the City of Detroit. But not for a private company."

He said, "Well, at least you're consistent."

My thinking is very simple here. I am a capitalist in the sense that I believe in the capitalist economy. I believe it is in the interest of the United States that companies go in and out of business. If they are successful they stay. If they are not they fail. That is what has made our economy stronger than the socialist or communist economies. I said it with Lockheed and I lost and I said it with Chrysler and I lost. If you want to bloat the economy just take the element of competition out of it.*

In one way, the dark necessity of having to avert a bankruptcy and of seeking further aid from the Federal Government presented, to me at least, a silver lining. With nine years in the U.S. Congress behind me, I could present myself on Capitol Hill as a lobbyist of considerable force. I enjoyed not only the friendship and respect of my former colleagues in the

*In August of 1980, Chrysler Chairman Lee Iacocca and I made a bet: a box of Monte Cristo cigars against a bushel of apples as to who would pay off his federal guarantees first. Iacocca won. His loan was paid off in 1983.

95th Congress, but also the prerogatives open only to former Members. In the clubby atmosphere that exists on Capitol Hill, it soon became clear that the 95th Congress wished to see me succeed. In the same way that any one of them might have gone home to become a Mayor, I had. And now I needed their help in governing what was widely perceived to be the ungovernable.

To bolster the City's case, I appeared as a witness before the various committees, most notably Senator Proxmire's. I was friendly; I was easy; but I counterpunched; I bubbled with facts; I cajoled; I disarmed the Senators with my candor; and then I left them laughing. I knew what I was doing. And the editorial writers recognized what I was doing and let the word out. As early as February, editorials like this one from *Newsday* were beginning to appear.

A LOBBYIST WHO KNOWS THE TURF

New York City's own federal aid crusade has yet to attract throngs of converts in Washington. But Mayor Edward Koch's missionary work there—call it economic evangelism—may be starting to have some modest success.

This week the Mayor visited members of the Senate Banking Committee, which has rejected any further assistance to the city. Afterward there were supportive remarks from Senators Alan Cranston (D-Cal.) and Harrison Williams (D-N.J.), neither of whom was particularly happy with the committee's decision earlier this month.

Still, Koch and the city have a long way to go. In Albany, where an early bipartisan agreement on state aid to the city has materially strengthened the appeal for federal help, informed opinion suggests that the Senate committee's chairman, Senator William Proxmire (D-Wis.), has been so conspicuously negative that he can't back off now unless the city accepts very drastic terms.

Against that and some other harsh prospects, Koch's confidence that a practical aid agreement can be worked out may seem to border on carelessness. But the fact is that the Mayor's congressional experience is one of the city's prime assets right now. He knows how votes are counted—and how some could be changed in New York's favor. And just as the city's fiscal good faith is vital to any settlement so is good lobbying.

As Felix Rohatyn had pointed out in a January 11 memorandum to the Emergency Financial Control Board, the present crisis was every bit as "dangerous and unpredictable" as the fabled 1975 fiscal crisis. And it required every bit of my energy to negotiate. But the City of New York, like any major city, clearly couldn't operate without long-term borrowing. In the summer of 1978, my first year in office, it became clear we could get the guarantees.

In 1977 I had won without the support of the traditional power blocs. I was not supported by business interests. I was not supported by municipal unions. I was not supported by the realtors. I did not receive the public support of a single county leader. And I was not supported by the liberals and radicals of the New Democratic Coalition. Those are the power centers that in normal times elect Mayors in the City of New York. And in normal times, having come forth with their campaign contributions, organizations and expertise, these groups are accorded special entrée at City Hall. The Mayor always takes their calls; special waivers are available when possible; contracts are settled away from the bargaining table; provisional jobs are available to the friends and families of the chieftains; judgeships are dispensed according to clubhouse connections. By these techniques, and a hundred more, the powerful see a return on their investment.

Those rules did not apply after I took office. And although I didn't dwell on it, I made clear from the start that there were new rules in effect.

Some people—most notably a few officeholders and the editorial boards of the *New York Post* and the *Daily News*—had endorsed me. The same rules applied to them: no special favors, everything on the merits. The same was true in the case of Charlie Rangel. He supported me in the runoff after Percy Sutton had stepped aside. As a result of Rangel's decision I picked up a substantial number of votes, at least in Harlem and perhaps even City-wide. I took Rangel's calls—but as Rangel was the Congressman from Harlem, his calls would have been taken anyway. The question is: did Rangel get anything special from me when, in the course of restructuring the poverty programs, I found myself engaged in restructuring the black political-patronage system? And the answer is: nothing. That enraged Charlie Rangel. And he wasn't the only one who chafed at the new rules.

The 1975 fiscal crisis created, in the City of New York, a new power center. When Governor Carey caused the Municipal Assistance Corporation and the Emergency Financial Control Board to be created, he had, in effect, taken a great deal of the Mayor's and the Comptroller's and the Board of Estimate's ultimate control over the City's finances and entrusted that control to a small group of business people who were appointed by him. These business people—none of whom had ever held elective office—charted out the City's recovery plan. And to their credit, in the same way that a Lockheed or a Chrysler may be saved by the intervention of the Federal Government, they saved the City from bankruptcy. There was plenty of glory around for all, and all gloried in their achievement; the businessmen, led by Felix Rohatyn, who had set up the deal, and the bankers and municipal unions, led by Jack Bigel, who had financed it. They were, of course, the first to forget that it had been their system of special entrée that had helped set the course to the precipice. And when it came to the glory, it was their altruism that they stressed, not their self-interest. But had the City gone bankrupt, it would have been the municipal unions, businessmen and the banks—perhaps second only to the poor—who would have suffered the most.

So as a necessary step toward solvency, Governor Carey had trimmed the powers of the elected City government and added several more names to the list of those who might dictate policy to the locally elected officials. The result was that while the traditional centers of power had retained their previous positions on the flow chart, the members of the EFCB and MAC had been given full veto power over the elected officials' actions. Moreover, in the press and on the streets, Abe Beame, the Mayor, had been the one to take the heat for the City's fiscal collapse. In the minds of New Yorkers, City Hall had failed, and to the Governor and the special interests had been left the task of running the City.

But there was still a fiscal crisis in '78. And all of a sudden along comes this new Mayor who had been only on the periphery of that battle in '75. And it was fascinating to watch the special interests having to absorb that, and me seeking to establish my own reputation and authority with them.

After the primary, David Garth had started bringing in the labor leaders. They did not support me in the general election. But it wouldn't have made any difference, ultimately, if they had. Barry Feinstein, of the Teamsters, was the only one who was the slightest bit helpful to me. But I met them all: Al Shanker; Sam DeMilia; Victor Gotbaum; Jack Bigel, their consultant, and others. Then, after I was elected, there was a big meeting. I think the idea was to get everybody in line behind the Rohatyn plan that we were going to be taking to Washington. It must have been sometime in the middle of December 1977, because I remember Basil Paterson was there too. And Bigel is there, and as I have come to expect, he is doing the talking and taking command of the operation. And everything is wonderful and we are all on the same track behind the Rohatyn plan and Bigel happens to mention that we—the City and the unions—are partners.

I say, "Just a moment, fellas. Can I say something? There is no government by partnership or government by committee here. Let's make sure we all understand that. I was elected. Not you. We have a common goal here and that is terrific and we will be working together. You represent three hundred thousand people. I represent seven and a half million, of which your three hundred thousand are a part. And it is terrific when we are all on the same track. But sometimes we are not going to be. So we are not partners. And everybody should know that."

Then, after a hushed silence, they say, "Okay, we're not partners," and the meeting goes on. But that was the first time I can recall that it was laid out to them that this Mayor was not going to be their patsy.

This City had been brought to its knees by pressure groups. I am not suggesting that pressure groups are necessarily an evil—because in moderation, they are not. But these groups had been permitted, throughout a series of administrations, to invade City Hall and destroy the prerogatives of the Mayor. And Mayoral prerogatives had to reassert themselves if this City's management was ever going to make sense again.

Among the pressure groups, the banks are a major element. The banks are what they are: lenders of money. They are in business to make money, and they are an important pressure element when you are in a credit crunch.

The businesses in this town represent another element. To digress for a moment: The whole simplistic notion over the years was that we ought to put a businessman into City Hall—the "Mayor as businessman" approach. Ridiculous! As Mayor, you are dealing with the labyrinthine interrelationships between federal, State and City governments, and the solutions to problems lie somewhere in a balancing of interests between these governmental groups. The chances are you are not going to find a businessman who can do that. Nothing short of an able political craftsman will do. A businessman would be brought to his knees by the pressure groups alone.

Now, let me give you an example of something that we changed that has made a considerable difference in terms of keeping these pressure groups at arm's length. The municipal unions in this town are disproportionately strong. It is said that when Abe Beame was Mayor, City Hall couldn't go to bed without checking in with Jack Bigel. He was sort of the night watchman. And that has been ended. Now Bigel makes an appointment, he comes in, he goes out, just like everybody else.

On April 19, I went back to Albany. It wasn't the Board of Ed or the HHC or the enabling legislation for the Financial Control Board that took me there. It wasn't the dog law.* On April 19, my trip had one item on its agenda: Westway.

In the 1930s, an elevated highway had been built along the Hudson River stretching from Battery Park to 96th Street in Manhattan. By the mid-1970s, the highway was falling apart. In December 1973, a semitrailer truck fell through the roadbed.

---

*In August of 1978, the City of New York became subject to the new "Canine Waste Law." It was at that time that dog owners had to begin using pooper scoopers or be subject to a fine. I had gone to Albany during the 1978 legislative session to lobby for the bill.

Two months later all of the highway south of 45th Street was closed. Traffic, already snarled during the peak hours on the elevated West Side Highway, was rerouted to the city streets below the elevated structure—and it became more unbearable and dirtier and noisier. And, along with the decibel level, the public clamor grew for the politicians to do something to get traffic moving in an orderly fashion along the West Side. In 1974, the Beame administration proposed a 4.2-mile, six-lane highway called Westway to replace the old elevated highway. In 1975, the Westway project received the endorsement of Governor Carey.

Two years later, not a single sledgehammer had been swung toward building the new highway. The project was tied up in the courts, the community boards and the various agencies—federal, State and City—that must issue the appropriate permits. The plan called for 212 acres to be created with landfill, a tunnel to be constructed through the fill and parkland and housing to be created on the surface. I reviewed the project in late October of 1977, during the Mayoral campaign, and proclaimed it "an economic and environmental disaster." As the front-runner in the Mayoralty race at that time, I was quoted on page 1 of the October 28 *New York Times*:

KOCH CALLS WESTWAY A 'DISASTER' AND VOWS IT 'WILL NEVER BE BUILT'

During the postelection transition period, with the pressure on from the Governor and the banks, the unions and the business leaders, I called on David Margolis; Harold Fisher, chairman of the Metropolitan Transportation Authority board, and William Hennessey, commissioner of the New York State Department of Transportation, to make a study of the alternatives and furnish me with recommendations.

One of the alternatives advanced by the community groups who opposed the Westway project was the so-called "interstate transfer," or "trade-in," option. This option referred to the provision in the federal interstate highway regulations that allows municipalities to exchange federal highway funds for mass-transit dollars. In denouncing the Westway project, I had called for the trade-in option to be invoked. However, the Margolis study found that, in the circumstances surrounding Westway, there could be no assurance that the trade-in would automatically occur. The Margolis study drew as its conclusion that the Koch administration should withdraw its objections to Westway.

Throughout that first winter I hesitated. I had observed during the campaign that the final authority on Westway rested with the Governor, although I had pledged to try to change the Governor's mind. The Governor wasn't budging. During the campaign I had pledged to seek the trade-in. But in an interview with *New York* magazine I had said if the alternatives became Westway or nothing I would take Westway. Those, it now appeared, *were* the alternatives. Still I hesitated. The special interests stepped up their lobbying. Finally, on a ride up to Gracie Mansion one evening, I said to David Brown,* "Let's get it over with."

The Fiscal '79 budget was due to go to the printer. Should it or should it not contain the $80-million revenue the City would receive if the Westway right-of-way were sold to the State? In keeping with my campaign promise to keep everything in the City's budget aboveboard, I had to decide whether to include the $80 million. And so the trip to Albany was arranged.

There was no question that the Governor was not going to change his position on Westway. And if I could not change him, then with or without my consent, the highway was going forward. I was not going to reject the funding. So then the question became How do you negotiate with the Governor to get the best deal that you can?

David Brown, Phil Toia, Bobby Wagner† and Maureen Connelly went up to Albany the day before to talk with Robert Morgado. When I got to our motel that night they had been working on the problem all day, and they had gotten

---

*Deputy Mayor for Policy and one of the original seven.

†Robert F. Wagner, Jr., son of the former Mayor and my original chairman of the City Planning Commission. He later succeeded David Brown and Herman Badillo as Deputy Mayor for Policy.

some minor concessions. But the concession they had gone to get they had not gotten. The deal that I wanted was: I would withdraw my opposition to the project and make it graceful for the Governor to go ahead if he would agree that the State would be held responsible for all increases in the transit fare for the next four years.

I remember Maureen saying to me, "You've lost your mind," and I remember she looked at me as if I had.

I said, "I'll get it. You watch."

The next morning we all went to the Governor's office. After we got into the extended negotiating between the two of us and then with staff, I said, "Governor, I've got to have this. Otherwise I cannot do it." He knew I meant it.

He said, "Okay," and he turned to Morgado and said, "Do it."

Everyone was shocked except the Governor and me.

From the front page of *The New York Times*, April 20, 1978:

KOCH BACKS WESTWAY; CAREY PLEDGES TO SAVE 50¢ FARE AND RAISE AID

Governor Offers City $800 Million And Cost of New Riverside Park

10

Facing the Unions

MOVING INTO A MIDTOWN HOTEL at 8 P.M. on March 31 is a rite that occurs, for New York Mayors, every other year. It means that the Transport Workers' Union contract will expire in four hours.

On March 31, 1978, I joined my union negotiating team in a suite on the 39th floor of the New York Hilton. Two floors below, led by their chairman, Harold Fisher, the officials and staff of the Metropolitan Transportation Authority occupied a similar suite. The MTA is managed by a fourteen-member board. Four of the fourteen are appointed by the Mayor, six by the Governor and four by county executives. Notwithstanding the Governor's substantial clout, when settling the two-year contracts the MTA board had generally, though not always, allowed the contract to be formulated along lines dictated by the Mayor. The reasons for this tradition were, first, that the City bears a significant share of the cost and, second, that the transit settlement is generally cited by the municipal unions—fire, sanitation, police, hospital workers, librarians and so on—as the me-too model from which their contracts, to be negotiated two months later, will be fashioned. Also in the Hilton on the night of March 31 were Matthew Guinan, the president of the TWU, and his team, Victor Gotbaum of District Council 37 of the American Federation of State, County and Municipal Employees, Albert Shanker of the UFT, Barry Feinstein of the Teamsters and Jack Bigel, the union consultant. These men were installed in various suites and conference rooms throughout the hotel.

As I entered the Hilton, the question of the night, "Mr. Mayor, will the trains be running tomorrow?" was asked and reiterated by several dozen of the some hundred reporters, cameramen and photographers who met me at the front door. Patiently, and silently, I walked through them to an elevator.

I was walking a new road. Never before had the municipal unions— representing some 225,000 city workers—banded together at the bargaining table. Never before had there been a so-called "municipal coalition." The TWU, since it is not, strictly defined, a union of city workers—the MTA being a state agency—was not a partner in the coalition. But the TWU contract was viewed by the leaders of the municipal coalition to be the model in terms of raises, cost-of-living escalators, givebacks* and benefits for their contracts. Traditionally, the municipals have counted on the TWU to bring them top-dollar contracts. The traditional wisdom has been that the TWU, with 30,000-plus workers, can wreak more havoc on New York than all the municipals, with their 225,000. In a city of subway commuters, nothing can put the brakes on business faster than a subway strike.

The most novel aspect of the 1978 TWU negotiations was that when I entered the hotel, no one—anywhere— knew what the outcome of the bargaining would be. Other Mayors had walked into other hotels, but their activities upstairs had been a charade— a stunt for the cameras. City Hall staffers with long memories later said that they could not recall one time the fix had not been in prior to deadline night. Not since Lindsay in '65, they said, the year of the devastating Mike Quill transit strike, had the dimensions of the settlement not been known well in advance.

The 1978 negotiations had other very unusual aspects. Not only did we have a new Mayor and a new financial plan; we had the presence of the Federal Government in that labor negotiation. Indeed, the most important person at the bargaining table, and I am speaking figuratively, was the Federal Government, whether it was in the form of the Treasury Department or Proxmire. They were there and heavy-handedly so. And they had created a very difficult timetable.

*Benefits the union members would give up in exchange for other concessions.

Anyway, there we were on March 31 with a sense of an inevitable strike, because nobody was anywhere with the unions. They were all banded together in this coalition, and they had Victor Gotbaum doing the talking. And it occurred to me that there was one glaring weakness in all this: Basil Paterson, who was negotiating for the City, was relying on Victor Gotbaum for all of his judgments regarding the TWU, and the TWU had never given Victor Gotbaum any authority to speak for it. It had just sort of happened very conveniently for Victor that the TWU representatives weren't very vocal and they had just let all of Victor's rhetoric go by without ever disabusing anyone of the notion that Victor was speaking for them. So there we were in that hotel and relying on Basil to tell us what was going on. He would come in and tell us what Victor said and what Bigel said . . . and we were getting on toward midnight and there was going to be a strike, because there was no way we could pay what the municipal coalition wanted for the transit workers as well as their own people. No way.

This whole thing had been bothering me for several days. We had never heard from Guinan and the TWU directly. So what we did was get hold of Harold Fisher, the chairman of the MTA board, who was waiting around. No one had included him; no one had talked to him. And Matthew Guinan was just hanging around—the president of the TWU—while Basil talked to Victor. We were sliding into a transit strike without really knowing why. So we asked Fisher if he'd had any direct conversations with Guinan. He said, "Not really." He said he had never really been told what we needed, and so he had never really been able to make a real try with Guinan. So we told him: "We could possibly live and conclude a contract with the TWU if the contract came out in the second year with no more than a six-percent increase."

He said, "It's worth a try." So he got hold of John Zuccotti, a former Beame deputy mayor, who was in these talks playing an intermediary role, and the two of them went down to Guinan. They stopped the clock at midnight, and at 3 A.M. Harold Fisher came back with a 6-percent deal. It was close, but it involved some additional contributions from the

State and City. We decided that the City could come up with $17 million if the balance of an additional $17 million was picked up by the State.

David Margolis was present. When it comes to advice on business and labor matters, I have found he has very good judgment—the reason I had asked him to be at the Hilton for the TWU negotiations. And it was he who at 2 A.M., when we were on the verge of a strike, really prevailed upon me to back off. The question was whether to give the TWU a certain percentage increase, a percentage I thought was high in terms of the me-too effect that had previously existed with the other labor unions. I was for taking the strike. My feeling was that sooner or later we were going to have to take these unions on.

Margolis said, "This is not the place. Not this union. I believe you should settle right here. If you don't settle, there will be a strike and it will cost more. It always costs more. Once they go out, it always costs more to get them back to work. You can settle this thing for an additional seventeen million. If you have a strike, it will run into hundreds of millions. It just doesn't make sense. And what you pay them you don't have to pay the others."

I said, "Okay. Let's get the Governor on the phone."

Carey was at home. I put Harold Fisher on the line. And it was done.

At 3:30 A.M., I made my way down to the Trianon Ballroom—the same room in which little more than a year earlier I had announced my candidacy for Mayor—and stood before the TV lights with Matthew Guinan and Harold Fisher. We announced that the trains would continue running. And, as Lee Dembart of the *Times* noted on April 2, "[T]he transit settlement represented a successful surmounting of the first hurdle in the labor steeplechase that he [Koch] faced when he took office three months ago."

But there was hardly time to celebrate. There were several more hours of negotiations ahead, with the municipal coalition, whose leaders were anxious for a quick deal along the old me-too guidelines. And so it was back upstairs and shuttling from suite to suite until dawn. It was at that point, sunup, that the City's talks with the municipal coalition finally broke off, causing one of my weary staffers to quip: "The attempt at simultaneous orgasm failed."

Over the next several days there was yelling and screaming about linkage. And I remember a meeting we had one morning when it was decided—by Paterson and Margolis and Toia and Schwartz and all the other people who were there— that I should go out and say, "There never was any linkage." That was a mistake, not to take it on directly. Because there had been reports in the press about linkage—that was *their* word—and we had never challenged it. What I should have said was "Of course these municipal labor people wish to link their settlement to this State settlement. But we don't have any commitment to pay what we don't have. This settlement is being paid for in large part by State dollars. The State's got lots of money, but we're broke. We can't give our people the same."

When the municipal labor chiefs finally realized, a day or so after that, that I wasn't kidding about this "no linkage" statement, they were enraged. Victor Gotbaum, labeling me "a municipal disaster," declared to the reporters, "He is now lying. He's acting like a spoiled little child."

On April 18, a full two weeks after the transit settlement had been announced, I traveled to Kutsher's, a Catskills resort hotel, to address the fifth annual Association of Counties convention. While I was there I happened to mention that there were "too many loafers" on the City's payrolls. As a result of that observation, Al Viani, Gotbaum's lieutenant, characterized me as "either . . . stupid or a creep." And that is just a sample of the kind of invective New Yorkers found in their newspapers during the City's negotiations with the municipals.

After sixty days of on-again–off-again bargaining we finally reached a settlement. At 8:30 P.M. on June 5, I appeared with Gotbaum and the other labor leaders at the District Council 37 headquarters on Park Place and made the announcement to the press. At 9:30 P.M. I arrived at the Roseland dance emporium to attend the fund raiser that wiped out my 1977 campaign debt. The following morning I was on the Washington shuttle, and that afternoon I testified for four hours before the Proxmire Committee.

In the course of the negotiations, seven deadlines had been set and missed. The Proxmire Committee hearings were the final deadline. The Committee wouldn't take up the matter of the federal guarantees until all the labor contracts were in, and yet enough time had to be allowed to get the legislation out of committee and through both houses of Congress before the summer recess.

Michael Oreskes, the *Daily News* labor writer, had described the talks as "more than three months of tortuous and often bitter bargaining," and that was putting it mildly. Again, the unions were unaccustomed to bargaining with the City from across the table. And while not at the actual table, I was the City's chief negotiator, and I was determined to get for the City the leanest possible contract. I had promised the City's taxpayers an end to union excesses. I had promised givebacks. When it was all over, we had a lean settlement and no givebacks.

It was an 8-percent deal over two years, 4 percent in each year, and to this day I doubt that it had to be that large.* The reason that it was, in my judgment, was that our side was not handled well by Basil, and the largest culprit was the timetable set by the Federal Government.

Rupert Murdoch had been correct when he said to me, early on, "Basil Paterson is not a negotiator; he is a conciliator. And he will give away what he shouldn't give away." It's true, and there is no one nicer to sit down with to conciliate. He is a lovely, sweet man. But we paid more than we should have because the unions took advantage of Basil. Gotbaum admitted it—foolishly. He said to fifteen people at a Gracie Mansion breakfast that he had been shocked when Basil took the givebacks off the table. Of course, that is part bullshit. They would have given back fluff in exchange for dollars.

Anyway, what Basil loved to do was sort of get me alone in my office and then take advantage of me. He was my eyes and ears at the bargaining table—I had to listen to him. He would come in and pull his chair up very close to mine and

---

*The TWU's 6-percent deal was, in fact, a richer deal than the City's 8-percent settlement because of additional cash payments and the effect of adding 2 percent to the rate on the last day of the TWU contract.

put his hand on my shoulder and sort of lower his voice and say, "Ed, this is what we have to do." And then he would lay out some strategy.

One time he came in when the negotiations had broken down again. It was typical. He comes in and says, "We've got to get them off the dime. And the only way they'll come back is if we jump from six percent to eight percent. It will make the difference."

And I said, "Okay."

In hindsight, it was dumb; a mistake. David Margolis said to Basil, "Why did you do that? What did you get? I could understand going to eight percent if you were going to get a settlement. But what did you get for it?" And of course, Basil had no answer. That was the worst.

Ultimately we stuck with our 8 percent, and there was yelling and screaming, but we didn't budge, and that's what we took to Washington.

And there was, in fact, no linkage. As a result of the State participation in the TWU contract, according to figures published in the *Daily News*, a transit worker who made $17,000 in 1978 would receive an additional $2,485 by 1980. In contrast, a City worker earning $17,000 in 1978 would, under the terms of our contract, take in only an additional $1,640 by 1980. As Dennis Duggan of *Newsday* said, I'd weathered my bar mitzvah:

NEW YORK—The city's "Perils of Pauline" labor negotiations were building toward a successful end yesterday as the final pieces of a $13.5 billion city budget were being nudged into place, and Mayor Edward Koch was set to fly to Washington to try to convince Congress that the city is both a needy and a deserving case. It was then that a reporter asked him how he felt.

"I can hardly wait for the next snowstorm," he replied.

The response was typical of Koch. Part Woody Allen even to the delivery, and part New York wise guy, as in "ask a dumb question and you get a dumb answer." If you're a fan, you love it; if you're not, you think how long four years can be.

There are Koch critics who say that what you see is what you see. "He's all front, he's a municipal disaster," growls labor leader Victor Gotbaum.

"He's cool and articulate and one of the brightest men I

know," says close friend and confidant David Margolis, the president of Colt Industries.

"He's got guts, but sometimes guts can get you into trouble," says Anthony C. Russo, the city's top career labor negotiator.

The labor negotiations were the mayor's bar mitzvah. They were conducted in a fishbowl, and that didn't sit well with labor leaders, and at times, the mayor's inexperience showed. Yesterday, in talking about his total retreat on his long-standing demand for $100 million in union "givebacks," he admitted as much. "Sure that's a blow to my ego, but I still feel the principle was right—that people shouldn't get uniform allowances if they don't wear uniforms or holidays for giving blood. I gave in because I felt a settlement was more important than my ego."

Then the mayor revealed that at one point, the unions had offered to give him $10 million worth of givebacks, but only if the wage offer was hiked from eight to eight and one-half percent. "That would have cost the city at least $20 million just to salvage my ego," Koch said. "I could have done that and said, 'Look what we've got.' But, then, how could I live with myself?"

Some other scars are showing, too. There's one for Westway, the billion-dollar super highway that the mayor had promised would never be built; there's another for a labor contract that the mayor had said would not exceed $610 million.

"I'm making mistakes," Koch said. "But Rome wasn't built in a day, and New York City can't be changed in five months. This is a learning experience. Some of the experiences are painful and some are pleasant but they're all necessary. You may not come out smarter in the end, but you hope to come out wiser."

Is the mayor all style and no substance, or is his style beclouding the substance? "It's too early to say," labor consultant Jack Bigel said. "Five months isn't enough time to judge a man."

"I'd give him a B plus so far," says Queens Borough President Donald Manes, still plucking goodies from the city's budget late yesterday. "He's a hard worker and he's fair, and you can't argue with the results. He's got his budget in and he's got labor peace."

Koch's top political advisor bristled when he was asked whether the mayor had "paid off" the five borough presidents by giving them each $150,000 in appropriations for their own economic development offices in return for their agreement on keeping alive a similar $1.7 million mayoral operation at City

Hall. "That's B.S.," said John LoCicero. "This isn't duplication of effort. It's the mayor's own office and it's information he needs. I think the people in this city have a good feeling about the mayor despite Westway, the convention center and the job lottery, which made a lot of people upset. How do I know? Because politicians running for office are taking polls and they're finding that Koch is getting high marks."

The Koch style is unique: He is tireless, working long hours day after day. He can be biting. "This must have been the way it was when Stalin tried the Jewish doctors," he said in describing an unhappy confrontation with a Queens group—a comment that brought immediate protest and apology. And he's funny even in defeat. Last week, after the marathon labor-bargaining session in which he finally gave up on givebacks, a reporter happened to ask him what color his eyes were, and he replied: "Black and blue."

Today, he moves from a relatively new precinct—the office of City Hall—to one that, as an ex-representative, he is more familiar with: Congress. He brings that unique style with him. If it works, if Koch can bring home the money, he'll be laughing all the way to Gracie Mansion.

Late in the evening of March 30, 1979, the word came in that the operators of the tugboats in New York Harbor were going out on strike to secure a prevailing-wage agreement for members of their union who worked for the City. At the same time, word was relayed from the Department of Sanitation that the tugboat operators' strike would cause a major health emergency. The City held a contract with the Moran Towing Company. Moran tugs towed the City's garbage scows to the landfill at Fresh Kills on Staten Island and to the legal offshore dumping areas. If there were no tugboats, the garbage would pile up at a rate of 10,000 tons a day. Several alternatives presented themselves, and the City administration began its efforts to find a suitable one.

From the outset the gravity of the threat was clear. When you can't transfer the garbage from Manhattan, Queens and the Bronx by barge, then what you have to do is put it all in trucks and cart it, five and six hours per load, to the landfill in Brooklyn. When you do that, you use up all the manpower you have. Plus more manpower is needed, and that costs $500,000 a week in overtime alone. Meanwhile the streets can't be cleaned, because all the sanitation men are driving the trucks to Brooklyn.

That was the club they held over our heads. Now, what did they want? Not a better contract for themselves. They wanted prevailing wages for members of their union who worked, in other areas, for the City. City workers, unlike private-sector workers in the trades who work half a year, work fifty-two weeks a year and get better pensions; therefore the concept of prevailing wages for civil servants makes no sense. So we said no, and they struck us where they thought they could hurt us the most.

It never would have happened in previous administrations. A deal like that one would have been the subject of a sweetheart negotiation between this relatively small but powerful union and the Mayor. And the Mayor, whoever he was, would have paid what the union wanted, and the deal would have been blessed by the Comptroller—who in this case was Jay Goldin, and he certainly would have blessed the special deal because he was very close to and fearful of the unions—and the whole thing would be quietly done before anyone knew it.

Well, it didn't happen that way this time. I said, "No. We won't do it. We've already negotiated the municipal workers' contract and we will not give these people any more. If you want to strike, go ahead."

They did, and we went to court to get an injunction. But because these guys who run Moran's tugs weren't municipal-union members, we couldn't get the injunction. The best we could do was get the court to direct Moran to turn the tugboats over to us. Our strategy was: once we have the boats we will put our own municipal workers on them. They are in the same union as the strikers but are under the Taylor Law and cannot strike—like the guys who run the Staten Island ferry, for example.

The tugboat union agreed to our arrangement. But then some of the tugboat crews got wind of our plans, as they always will in matters of this kind, and they went down to the dock and put up a picket line. So when our eleven municipal ferryboat crewmen showed up they had to cross this wildcat picket line. And they wouldn't do it. I got a call from Bruce

McIver* in the City's Office of Labor Relations. He laid out the facts.

I said, "What can we do to them?"

He said, "We can direct them to cross the picket line."

I said, "Direct them to cross it! What else?"

He said, "We could suspend them."

I said, "Suspend them! Can we fire them?"

He said, "Well, we could fire them after thirty days if they stay out and don't do their work."

I said, "Terrific. Fire them as soon as you can."

He says, "Well, you know there can be escalating results."

I say, "That's okay with me."

He says, "Maybe we better have a meeting about this."

I say, "Fine. We'll have a meeting. You suspend those eleven guys and then come in to City Hall and we'll have a meeting this afternoon."

So we had the meeting. Allen Schwartz was there, along with McIver and Norman Steisel, the Commissioner of Sanitation. Steisel goes into what it's costing us and then he says, "And you know, my guys will wear out after not too long. They are working twelve- and fourteen-hour days."

Then McIver says, "And you know this ferryboat operators' group is not large. We could run through the whole group of them in less than a week. And then we wouldn't have anyone to run the Staten Island ferry."

I say, "No. We've made our point. We'll make an example of the eleven. You have eleven people who refused to carry out an order. Make examples of them."

Well, that kind of relieved them, and it was the end of the meeting. But Allen Schwartz stayed around. We decided that we had done everything that could be done locally and that the next step was to call on the Coast Guard.

I knew the Admiral—Vice Admiral Robert I. Price, a big, craggy-looking guy. I recalled welcoming him to New York when he received his appointment. As I am thinking about the way he looks, I am thinking, He's a real tough guy. This

---

*Bruce McIver—I dubbed him "Cool Hand Luke"—was my Director of Labor Relations and Basil Paterson's successor as the City's chief negotiator.

assignment won't be too big for him. He's probably over there on Governors Island just waiting for the phone to ring.

But nothing could have been further from the mark. My people called him and, as they told it to me, he became very vague and made statements to them about strikebreaking. And then he called the newspapers and made similar statements about how his men weren't scabs and so on. He actually said the Coast Guard wasn't going to help us. I was amazed by that. Really amazed.

I called Jack Watson, President Carter's adviser for domestic affairs, at the White House. I laid it out to him. He said he would need a little time: twenty-four hours. Then he took more than that. They were terrified of taking on the unions. Carter was running for reelection the next year and he didn't want to alienate the unions. The unions have more power physically and psychologically than I ever dreamed; physically because of what they can do and psychologically because of the fear they have implanted in so many minds.

Anyway, so I talk first to Watson and then to one of his people. And I tell them about the tugboat union's agreement not to cause further trouble and about the wildcat nature of the picket line. And ultimately, they did call Admiral Price to give him the order.

Meanwhile, I had gone up to Boston to speak at Harvard. When I come back I land at Newark Airport. And the car telephone rings. I am supposed to call Vice Admiral Price. So we pull the car over to a pay phone and I make the call. It's midnight. "Yes, sir," I say to the Admiral, "Koch here."

He says, "I am sitting here in this room with eight of my men. They are unshaved. And I understand that we are going to get a request from the White House. And I don't know what we can do." It is clear to me from his tone that he is still absolutely opposed to helping.

I say, "Admiral, that is not a request. It is an order. You are going to carry it out, aren't you? That is an order from the White House."

"Oh, yes," he says, "we will be carrying it out. But what I was really calling about is how we can work this out. We will need police protection."

I say, "What are you talking about? The union doesn't even object to what you will be doing. There's not going to be any trouble about this."

He says, "Oh, no. You don't know. I have six thousand people out on Governors Island who are hostages to this union. Their families . . . This union can do things."

I say, "Admiral, I don't believe you need police protection, but if you tell me you do we will provide you with it. But what we need is help pulling the garbage scows. And my hope is that you are going to be cooperative. And I want to tell you further, Admiral, I don't think you were very helpful in this situation when you said that you would not engage in scabbing or union-busting. What do you think your function is if not to serve the people of this City or country in time of emergency? You think it was scabbing when the State of New York called in the National Guard to run the prisons when the prison guards' union struck? And, as it happens, you are not even involved in a situation where the union objects to your presence. What is going on here? And even if it did object, wouldn't it be your function to carry out your orders?"

"We will be carrying out the orders," he said.

And they, in fact; did. In the end, the Coast Guard was helpful to us in bringing that strike to an end.

11

The Charlotte Street Project: The Politics of Urban Decay

ON OCTOBER 4, 1977, Jimmy Carter stood with Abe Beame on Charlotte Street in the Crotona Park East section of the South Bronx. Together they viewed the now-famous abandoned tenements and lonesome rubble that are prevalent in that area. The President pledged to make federal dollars available toward a large-scale rebuilding of the neighborhood. It was to be the cornerstone of his urban program.

Early on in my administration, I appointed Edward J. Logue, a master planner, to the directorship of the South Bronx Development Office. Logue's job was to develop a plan for the revitalization of the South Bronx. Having developed such plans in the past, Logue knew the values of symbolism and political craftsmanship.

His plan placed some of the first housing units on Charlotte Street. The project was, after all, to be built with federal dollars, and it had been on that very site that Beame and Carter had stood. But those people who had selected Charlotte Street for the President's visit had been press agents and advance men, not planners. And when the City Planning Commission saw the South Bronx plan, it raised serious questions about the choice of the Charlotte Street site. Textbook planning strategy runs counter to press-agent planning in these things. When press agents look for dramatic backgrounds, they seek the heart of the devastation. When planners seek to heal wounds on a city's face, they build from the existing strengths. They build from the periphery. Logue saw billions of dollars coming in. He thought he could build something out of nothing. The Planning Commission wanted to be sure that what dollars were actually delivered would be efficiently spent. They feared a funding interruption.

Herman Badillo took the lead on the South Bronx development plan. Bob Wagner became involved because the project would have to be reviewed by the City Planning Commission and he was at that time its chairman. He had a lot of doubts about the plan, as did the staff at City Planning. They delivered a statement to the Board of Estimate which supported the project but set forth some basic reservations. First of all, the statement noted, the level of federal commitment was diminishing. Did it still make sense to go at the area of greatest devastation? Second, the plan left unstated what would surround this housing project of 732 units that Logue and Badillo had proposed as stage one. From a planning point of view that didn't make much sense. The third issue was the notion of calling this project a co-op when in fact it wasn't. It was a Public Housing Authority project that might in the future become a co-op. And the final issue involved the actual funding. This project was supposed to be an additional federal commitment to the City. But in fact, as it was proposed, it did not involve new money for this first project: instead, it was taking 80 percent of the 1977 regular allocation City-wide for low-income housing and putting it into one location.

Before the Planning Commission issued its report there had been considerable debate within the administration, basically between Badillo and Wagner, about the good sense of it. The Housing Authority agreed that the plan wasn't really a co-op and that it didn't make sense from a planning point of view. The people from the Department of Housing Preservation and Development who were involved in the planning of the location agreed that it did not, from a housing strategy point of view, make total sense. And there was unanimity among the staff from City Planning that it should be opposed. It was an issue that ultimately came to me.

It was decided that Bob and Herman and I should go up there and look at the site. Herman drove. I sat beside him, and Bob was in the back seat. It was a terrifying trip, because Herman was so angry at Bob that he spent the whole time looking back at him while switching lanes and running stop signs. One was never quite certain where one would end up. There were a lot of sudden turns and dramatic stops. But we made it safely to the Charlotte Street area and drove around to a number of other sites, such as Plaza Boricua, which is a low-rise development that Herman said might be a model for Charlotte Street. Bob kept asking, "Why don't you put up additional units right next to this Plaza, instead of in a wasteland where no one is living and where clearly market forces have completely destroyed it?"

When we were through looking and talking, I decided that we should go along with Herman, in part for symbolic reasons. What difference does it make where you put the units? I felt that by that point the issue had become such a symbolic one that it was no longer a planning issue. The 732 units were no longer a housing project: they had become a test of whether there was a City interest in rebuilding the South Bronx. So Bob went along with it and got the Planning Commission to support it, even though the Commission members had a lot of reservations.

Then the proposal was readied to come before the Board of Estimate for its first vote. There was a very emotional meeting in my office at City Hall. Ed Logue was there. Herman was there. Bob Wagner was not at the meeting. Carol Bellamy at one point left the meeting and went outside to rethink her position. Bob helped persuade her, as she was walking around, to vote for it—basically as a leap of faith, because it was a symbol; therefore, even though she might have basic reservations about the soundness of the idea she should support it. She did, and it passed the first round.

Herman believed that it had to go back to the Board of Estimate for a second vote, because involved in the plan was a street-mapping change, and mapping changes have to go through the full ULURP* process. It was a mapping change that was probably never necessary; it is even now uncertain whether in a Housing Authority project a mapping change is really legally required. But the decision was made to take it back for a second time several months later.

*The Uniform Land Use Review Procedure, the process by which the City of New York clears proposed changes in land usage.

By that time a number of things had changed. Out in the neighborhoods there was an increasing feeling that the South Bronx was getting everything. So the Borough Presidents of Queens and Brooklyn were looking on the issue with greater hostility. Then you had the fears of many that the Federal Government's commitment was not a real commitment. Carol Bellamy had talked to Patricia Harris, the Secretary of Housing and Urban Development, who was very negative about Charlotte Street and about the South Bronx effort. Pat had talked to Jack Watson and did not feel that there was a real commitment that would justify putting 732 units of housing in the middle of nowhere.

Then we had to contend with the fact that the first time around Jay Goldin had been running for State Comptroller and Herman had been supporting him, Herman having designs on any City Comptroller vacancy. Jay was not going to upset anybody unnecessarily, and between that and his alliance with Herman, we were assured of his vote. He just went with it. But by the time the mapping-change vote came up, that race was over. Jay had lost, and he was embittered not only by losing but by the shabby way Herman had treated him. (In the final days, Herman had said things like "This creep—but I'm doing what I can to get him elected.") There were no truly warm feelings between them after that election.

The mood was very different, but the decision was made nonetheless that we should go ahead to the Board of Estimate despite the climate. Herman basically ran the strategy on going to the Board of Estimate. He decided we should go for a vote the first time the issue was considered by the Board, which meant it had to carry by a three-quarters vote, as opposed to laying it over to a second meeting, which would simply have required a majority vote. Bob Wagner again raised the question whether it was necessary to go to the Board of Estimate at all. The map change might well not have been necessary, according to the legal opinion of the City Planning Commission. Herman, however, thought it was important to have a vote.

In advance of the mapping-change vote at the Board of Estimate I sought to allay the fears of the Board's members. No one was sure of the level of the federal commitment. I called Jack Watson at the White House. The total project of more than 26,000 units had been costed out at over a billion dollars in a seven-year period. I wanted to know if the Feds were good for the billion. Watson, President Carter's special envoy for domestic affairs, wanted a meeting. City Hall was out: too much press exposure. Gracie Mansion was out: again too great a possibility of exposure. I suggested Herman Badillo's house in Riverdale. The meeting occurred there on January 16 at 7 P.M.

It was a sort of brief meeting—I had to leave at 8:30. Only Herman, Irma Badillo, Jack Watson and I were there. Watson began by saying that the President loved me and wanted me to know I was doing a very good job. He then said he was the President's man and that he too thought I was doing a very good job. "Now, let's talk about the South Bronx ...." Something like that. The thrust of what he said was "It's getting out of hand. We don't want to be up front with an enormous commitment of dollars that we don't know if we can deliver. We don't think we ever made that commitment."

I said, "Look, let's get something straight. The premise here is that the President said he wanted the South Bronx rebuilt. It's against the market forces. Nobody's being fooled on that. But I'm willing to do it ... with your money. Not with ours. We are going to maintain our present efforts. Anything above that has to come from moneys that the City of New York would not otherwise get. For us to proceed with this kind of design will require an up-front commitment from the federal administration that you will do whatever you can to get the massive moneys required to build. This plan calls for twenty-six thousand five hundred units of housing over the next seven years, with economic development going hand-in-hand. Now, let's get it straight. If you are not able to make that commitment, or if you have made it, as I believe you have, but now because of retrenchment in the Congress and other changes, you want to withdraw it, okay. I am not going to throw rocks at you. I just want it up front. I don't want a situation two years from now where we are up there doing our part and the Feds walk out. Because we can't go it alone. We will have to stop."

Then Herman said, "We don't need a deputy mayor

overseeing this project, and Ed Logue, and sixty staff people, if the Federal Government isn't going to come across with extra money. We can work on this area just like any other area. The Commissioners can take it over if the Feds want out. We can scale it down."

Then I said to Watson, "Jack, you have made a decision. I'll bet you have never read our proposal. Take it home. Give it to somebody. Read it. Get back to us. Maybe you don't like it. Maybe you want to get out from it. But tell us now. Don't leave us holding the bag two years from now."

Three weeks passed, and a letter was delivered to me from Watson certifying that the Carter Administration still intended to go ahead with the financing of the 26,500-unit project and that the Administration understood that the City's contribution would be nothing over and above that which the City would normally spend in any comparable neighborhood. The letter was delivered on Tuesday, February 6, at 5 P.M. It was simultaneously released to the press, and copies of it were made available to the members of the Board of Estimate. On Wednesday I went to Washington to appear before the Proxmire Committee for an interim hearing on the loan guarantees. I was in Washington all day. On Thursday I left for Albany in the morning and didn't return until the afternoon. When I returned I was told by Philip Trimble, my Deputy Mayor for Intergovernmental Relations, that the first phase of the South Bronx plan was going to go down before the Board of Estimate. The task of lining up the votes had been left to Herman Badillo. And Herman, a veteran of seven years in the U.S. Congress and himself a former member of the Board of Estimate, had neglected to line up the votes.

At 3 P.M. that Thursday, I went upstairs to the Board of Estimate chambers and made a speech that was somewhat impassioned. I said, "If you vote this down, it will be the end of the special South Bronx project." I said, "It will be the end of Herman Badillo and Ed Logue in the South Bronx. The Commissioners will be handling the South Bronx as they would any other part of town."

Well, with the exception of Bronx Borough President Stanley Simon and Staten Island Borough President Anthony Gaeta, they all voted agiainst it. So it went down 7–4. And that was really it. Kind of surprising. As it turned out, some of them didn't believe that somehow or other some of these moneys weren't going to be taken away from projects in their areas. Others were dismayed that the Watson letter didn't cite a specific dollar figure—a billion dollars or something. And some people just didn't like the looks of the plan. Now, some of these people, in my judgment, could have been brought around by Herman if he had tried to talk to them. There were no special meetings. He didn't bring anyone in to see me about this. He was flying blind.

After the vote he was furious. He attacked the Board of Estimate members who had voted against him. He called them clowns. He attacked their motives. He was very rough with them.

The vote was carried in the press as a terrible defeat for me. I took the position that no single vote on the Board of Estimate was a terrible defeat for me. I don't get these people to go along with me by offering them jobs and judgeships and special projects, as other Mayors did. There is no log-rolling with me. Maybe that is bad, but that is Mayor Ed Koch.

The following Monday, meetings were scheduled at Gracie Mansion on how to proceed. At noon the in-house people arrived. They were followed at 3 P.M. by the members of the Board of Estimate. Comptroller Goldin was at that time widely viewed as the leader of the drive to defeat the Charlotte Street proposal. After the 3-o'clock meeting, Goldin and I retired to a private room to discuss our differences.

I said, "Jay, I want to speak frankly and I want you to speak frankly. Our relationship is very bad and there is no question that I can hurt you and you can hurt me. I have no political aspirations other than to be the Mayor for the rest of my political life. You have other aspirations. Having me as your enemy is not helpful. Having you as my enemy is not helpful."

He said, "Yes. I agree with that."

Then he recited the litany of what was troubling him. He felt that I hadn't treated him with the proper respect. He said that I had taken him for granted. Hadn't invited him to Gracie Mansion enough. But you see, I knew what was really at the bottom of it. He was expecting a massive primary against him in his reelection race, probably by Herman Badillo. And by taking Herman on in the South Bronx and then sorting it out with me, he was in effect trying to get my support for him in the primary. Well, this primary that he was so concerned about was still two and a half years away. Nonetheless, Jay was absolutely correct in his assessment, because the next day Herman came in to see me and said that he was going to be running against either Jay or Carol; and subsequent to that he was on CBS-TV and giving it to both of them, saying that they had written off the blacks and the Puerto Ricans.

My meeting with Herman was an interesting one. He said, "We could put together a ticket. You, white; the Jews could be represented through you. Me with the Hispanics. And we could get David Dinkins to run for Borough President. At the State level we could get Basil Paterson to run for Governor." I just listened passively. Didn't say anything. I was thinking: What about Carol Bellamy, the Council President? Doesn't he want her?

I did say one thing. When Herman said "David Dinkins," I said, "Couldn't you find someone better than him?"

Later Jay comes in, and he and I have the following conversation: "Ed, Herman is attacking me viciously. Can't you restrain him?"

I say, "Jay, I cannot stop him. Herman has his own constituency. He doesn't speak for me in these political matters. In fact, since he became deputy mayor he has supported candidates I have not been supporting. And that is my arrangement with him. As long as he is not attacking *me*, I will not restrain him. Nor am I responsible for him. If he says something that is an attack on you, it is not an attack by me."

Jay says, "Well, what if my deputy comptroller, Marty Ives, were to attack *you*? Could I then say, Well, he doesn't speak for me?"

I say, "Jay, there is a big difference between Marty Ives, who has no political constituency, and Herman Badillo, who does."

Jay and Herman continued their fighting until they were finally separated by Herman's departure from City government. Nobody much noticed after a while, except perhaps the residents of Crotona Park East and the rest of the South Bronx. They wanted housing and economic-development projects and the government's help with establishing a new strong fiber in their neighborhoods.

Ultimately, the government did help. Ed Logue, to his credit, and Senator Alfonse M. D'Amato got together on a federally subsidized program that allowed the City's South Bronx Development Corporation to construct ranch-style houses in the neighborhood where Jimmy Carter had stood.

I went up there in 1983 to paint one of the picket fences in front of one of those new houses. Jay was there—he always comes to these media events—with his paintbrush.

They call it Charlotte Gardens. It will ultimately be quite nice. And it was nice to be with Jay Goldin at the ceremony, so that I could recall for everyone that he, along with Carol Bellamy, had been the one who had let the Feds walk away from their commitment to that area.

12

Minorities: Confronting the Issues

THE MONTHS OF DECEMBER 1978 and January 1979 marked the nadir in my relationship with the black leaders of New York. By then they knew I was serious about the cuts that had to be made. They knew the cuts would be made without regard to political fallout. And since the black community had been, up to that time, a protected area, they knew the cuts would have an impact on them as well as everyone else.

The black leaders lashed out. Charlie Rangel called my plan to close two of the City's seventeen municipal hospitals "planned genocide." A Harlem minister, the Reverend Vastor Johnson, pastor of the Empire Baptist Church, in revoking his invitation to me to attend a Martin Luther King, Jr., memorial service, called me "Dracula" and said he "could not guarantee the Mayor's personal safety in Harlem."

I answered the attacks and continued on the course I had set.

That December I addressed a problem that had been a contributing factor in the decline of housing in poor neighborhoods. It was well known that many tenants were using their welfare rent allowances not to pay their rent but to buy food, clothing and other items, even though welfare clients receive additional allowances for maintenance over and above the rent. Everybody understood this, but the net result was that when enough tenants in a building engaged in this practice, the landlord would find that he was losing too much money and he would walk away from the building. The building would go into arrears in its real estate taxes and the

City of New York would be forced to take it over. By December 1978, the City of New York owned more than ten thousand such buildings. In other cities the municipal governments allow these buildings to totally deteriorate. But in New York the City government was spending more than $75 million a year to act as landlord for these buildings that had become losing propositions and to provide services such as heat and hot water—and we were collecting only 30 percent of the rents due.

Our answer to this problem was to encourage the Federal Government to issue two-party checks, checks that had to be signed by both the recipient and the landlord before they could be cashed. A pilot project was planned for a section of the South Bronx where this housing problem was particularly prevalent.

On December 22, Charlie Rangel denounced the program. He said: "Mayor Koch's proposal to force two-party rent checks on welfare recipients as a means of guaranteeing a profit to landlords is cynical, irresponsible and another case of violating the rights of the poor and powerless."

The program was eventually killed by the Federal Government, which would not grant the needed waiver for the test program.

On New Year's Day, I announced my choice for president of the Health and Hospitals Corporation: Joseph Hoffman, a middle-aged white man with management experience, who had been the First Deputy Police Commissioner. The prospect of a cop running the hospitals further antagonized the black leaders.

And three weeks later, I appointed Rangel's nemesis, Haskell Ward, Deputy Mayor for Human Services. At a public meeting in Harlem, while he had been at CDA, Ward had foolishly refused to allow Rangel to be heard out of turn. The meeting had erupted in bedlam, and Rangel had never forgotten. Now Ward was to be the deputy mayor with oversight authority not only for the poverty programs but for HHC as well. Rangel was furious, and he stepped up his attacks.

Meanwhile, on January 20, partly because the Reverend Mr. Johnson had said he could not guarantee my personal safety in Harlem and partly because I enjoy walking around the City with Dan Wolf and Haskell Ward, the three of us had gone up to Harlem for lunch. Then we had walked across 125th Street and around in that area. People were very friendly. One guy said, "Mr. Koch, aren't you afraid to come up here?"

I said, "No, I enjoy it."

Shortly after that Charlie called me. I told him that I was going to appoint Haskell deputy mayor. He said he was not pleased. I asked him if he was going to attack Haskell. He said, "I am not going to dump on Haskell Ward. I don't like it but it is done."

Then I spoke to Basil Paterson. Paterson had recently resigned as deputy mayor to become Governor Carey's Secretary of State. He said, "Well, he's not my first choice, but you have done it and you should feel comfortable with whomever you have. I will support him and I will help him."

So *The Amsterdam News* has a party to celebrate going from a full-sized paper to tabloid size. The first issue in its new format displays the headline "KOCH APPOINTS WARD—BLACKS ENRAGED." And in the article both Charlie and Basil attack Haskell. I am reading the story and thinking, What's going on here? So I send Charlie a little note.

January 25, 1979

Dear Charlie:

I read in today's *Amsterdam News* your comments describing Haskell Ward's appointment as a "terrible affront to the Black Community." Didn't you tell me that you were not going to denigrate Haskell, that it wasn't helpful to do that from anybody's point of view—or did I misunderstand you?

Sincerely,
Ed

I wrote Paterson a similar letter: "You said you were going to support him. Do you call this support?" But I didn't send that letter because the same day the paper appeared, Basil called. He said he had just left Haskell and had read *The Amsterdam News* as he was being driven downtown, and that he had been surprised to see that statement in the paper. He said he had not said anything. He told me he had been asked by the editor, "Mr. Paterson, don't you think that Ward's being appointed is a denigration of the community?" And Basil said he had said, "I am not going to comment on that." But probably he had permitted that inference to be drawn. He certainly hadn't said anything positive. Then he said to me, "Oh, you tell Haskell that we have to have lunch as soon as possible. You, me and Haskell, up in Harlem."

I said, "Okay."

Subsequently Haskell said he had called Basil and Basil said, "Let's get together for lunch," to which Haskell replied, "Yes." Basil then said, "I'll call you back over the weekend" —and of course, he never called back.

Haskell Ward was not a team player. In many respects his independence was why he rose so far so fast. As Dan Wolf said to me, "Haskell's like you. Why should you punish him for doing the things that you would have done?"

On March 6, a Tuesday, I went up to Albany. Before I left, Ward came in and said, "I will be announcing the closing of PRCD"—the city-wide Puerto Rican Community Development Corporation. It was another one in the long line of closings that Ward had supervised under my restructuring of the poverty programs. A new corporation would be formed, and the federal moneys would continue to flow uninterrupted.

I said, "Fine. Show the memorandum to Herman. Tell him what you are going to do, so that he will be prepared for it. But you are in charge here." Then I left for Albany.

During the County Day ceremony I was attending in Albany, I spoke to José Serrano, an Assemblyman from the South Bronx. I asked Serrano about PRCD, and Serrano too told me that the program should be closed.

The following morning Maureen Connelly came into my City Hall office. She was carrying a translation of Herman Badillo's comments regarding the closing of PRCD that had appeared that morning in the City's major Spanish daily, *El Diario*. Badillo had attacked Ward viciously. He had called him negligent and incompetent.

Moreover, on the same page there was an open letter denouncing the closing. And the letter was signed by several legislators, including José Serrano.

Then the press came in. I said, "Well, when you have first-rate people in government you find that they have first-rate tempers." Then I called in Ward and Badillo.

Herman was at his smoothest. When the two of them were with me, he simply said, "I wasn't told. It took me by surprise." And the fact is that Haskell had shown him the memo. (Subsequently Herman said to me privately that he would not have attacked Haskell if Haskell hadn't insisted on handing out the press release.)

I said, "Well, why couldn't you have held back your attack until I came back from Albany?"

He said, "I asked Haskell Ward to hold the announcement up a day. He wouldn't do it. I had to defend my position."

Well, I could see I wasn't getting anywhere with Herman, but I was still troubled by Serrano's comments. I mean he is an intelligent, honest guy, and it was puzzling that he would do such a thing. So rather than get into a barnyard contest—such as I had with Charlie Rangel when the reporters came in to tell me that Charlie was calling me a liar and I said, "I will not wrangle with Rangel"—I thought, Who needs that? So I called up Serrano and said, "Yesterday we had a conversation. Let me repeat what I said, and if I am incorrect and didn't understand you, tell me. Didn't you say to me that you thought PRCD should be closed? And that you approved of what we were doing there?"

He said, "Yes."

I said, "Well, then, why did you add your name to the press statement in which you agreed with Herman Badillo's denunciation of Haskell Ward?"

He said, "When did I do that?"

I said, "Well, let me read it to you." And I read him the letter that he had signed that had appeared in *El Diario*.

He said, "Now I see. Mr. Mayor, you have to understand that Herman Badillo carries all our proxies in his pocket. *El Diario* knows that anytime Herman says something, they can automatically say, without checking with us, that everyone in the Puerto Rican delegation agrees with Herman Badillo. It is just a matter of fact. Surely that was something you knew when you took Herman into your administration. Let me put it this way: If *El Diario* called me up and said Herman

Badillo just said the sky is green, I would say, 'Of course the sky is green.'"*

I said, "Joe, you are an honest guy. I want you to know that I appreciate your candor. You have taught me something."

The effect of that newspaper blitz was that Ward came out looking bad. He had not effectively responded to the charges leveled against him. Badillo had gotten the better of him in a press battle. Herman was always good with the press, especially the Spanish press. There were those around City Hall who wished Herman Badillo had been as good with his staff, the Commissioners and the elected officials as he was with the reporters.

At the end of the month Ward was back on the hot seat.

And by then, so was Blanche Bernstein, my head of the Human Resources Administration. I had always defended Blanche. When the politicians were critical of what she was doing, I always said, "Don't attack her; attack me. She is carrying out my policies." She was brilliant at that, and fearless. The problem was that her own people couldn't work with her. She was hiring good people and they were quitting on her. My people were telling me that she was a terrible administrator. So it wasn't working out as I had hoped it would.

In the middle of March she was in a quiet period. That is to say, she wasn't being attacked and there were no picket lines out in front of her house and office and around the block. I called her in. I said, "Blanche, I want you to bring in Stanley Brezenoff as your first deputy for operations."

She said, "I don't need a first deputy."

I said, "No. We are going to have Brezenoff. That is the bottom line. He is a brilliant administrator and we need that at HRA. He will have the power of hiring and firing. And he will report to me. What I have in mind is like what we do at Health and Hospitals—a chairman who reports to me and a president who reports to me. One makes policy; the other carries it out. There is no conflict there. It will be like a bank or a big business."

*That has changed. Herman Badillo no longer exercises dominion over the Hispanic legislators. They are now independent of him.

She said, "Can I think about it?"

I said, "Sure." And that was it. Then I called Brezenoff to see if he would do it. He is a good soldier and he said that he would try to work with her.

A week or so later, on a Friday, we had the big meeting on this. Blanche said, "Yes, I will do it. But Stan will have to report to me."

I say, "No, Blanche. As we discussed earlier, Stan will report directly to me."

Blanche said, "Oh, that is very difficult. How can that be?" I explained the whole HHC setup again—I was looking for ways to make it easier for her. She said, "Well, when do you want to put this into effect?"

I said, "Wednesday."

She said, "I'll let you know on Monday."

Well, what then occurred was that somehow the story leaked out, and Lee Dembart of the *Times* came in to talk to Haskell. According to Haskell, Dembart already had all the facts, and he was going to write the story along the lines of "Bernstein is thrown to the blacks." Well, that wasn't the way it was. So Haskell gave Dembart a blow-by-blow account of the meeting. And when the story appeared on Sunday, it showed a lack of sensitivity on my part toward Blanche's feelings. Afterward, Haskell was very contrite about it. He said he had done what had to be done in order to defend the administration. The result was that Blanche abruptly resigned, Brezenoff became the HRA administrator and there were bad feelings all around. She came in that Monday and she was upset. We discussed the leak and what Haskell had done. (Subsequently I was interviewed by Jack Hamilton of WPIX. He said, "What are the best and worst things you have done as Mayor?" I said, "The best thing I have done is take politics out of the judicial selection process. And the worst thing I have done is the way Blanche Bernstein's resignation was handled.")

Meanwhile, my relationship with Charlie Rangel had collapsed again. Charlie and I had been friends, but the tie had been strained by months of charges and countercharges. For a year and four months we had planned to have lunch, but we had put off this lunch a number of times as a result of the aggressive statements Charlie kept making about me. On two separate occasions he called me a liar, and twice he said he was going to run against me. I get upset when people attack my integrity, especially people I have known a long time and who presumably know better. He wanted to have a very private lunch. I wanted to include Ronald Gault, who is black and who knew all that we were doing in minority hiring. I also wanted Dan Wolf to be there because of his exceptional ability to perceive sensitivities.

We went to Sweets Restaurant in the South Street Seaport on April 13, 1979. I must say we didn't have a good lunch. It cost $90. I paid. But it was well worth the price. Charlie began by citing a meeting we'd had prior to the runoff, when I had agreed to appoint as many blacks to top positions as Wagner, Lindsay and Beame combined. He said he had my commitment. Then he said I had agreed to give him "input" and that I hadn't. He said I had said that we would have a close relationship. He said, "I would like to go back to that."

I said, "No. We cannot go back. And I will tell you why. Everything we do is from this moment on. Charlie, you and the people around you have seared my soul with your rhetoric. We may have had some kind of commitment, but it is over. You have breached it with your attacks."

At that point he began to visibly sweat. And it was not hot.

I said, "And I want to tell you, Charlie, I do not expect you to support me next time around. There is no reason why you should. So let's take that off the table. Still, I want very much to work with you. But it will be on the basis of today."

He said, "That won't work. Ed, I'm sorry about the things I said. I don't know what I can do. But if it will make you feel good," he said, "I'll call a press conference and say I will not be running against you." He was very funny at times —he is a very good guy. And strange.

After lunch we went back to my office at City Hall. I said, "Sit down, Charlie. I am really distressed that we should be in this position."

He said, "Well, let me tell you what I need. I need someone in your administration who I can relate to. Someone I can call up and know I have input."

I said, "Let me think about it. But you know what the

problem is. I am looking for people all the time. Right now I am looking for judges. But the good, smart black lawyers won't apply. They are making so much money on the outside. We have asked seven outstanding black lawyers to apply— and they won't do it.'' I told him who they were. I said, ''You call them. Maybe one of them will listen to you.''

Charlie Rangel and I had come down a long road together. And where he was ending up was basically that it wasn't any good for him to be with me anymore. For a while he had thought he would have it both ways, but at Sweets I had made it clear he couldn't any longer. He couldn't attack me using words like ''planned genocide'' in reference to my policies and then turn around and expect me to love him. I don't care who you are, it won't go on long like that. What was also clear to him that day was that I was not going to change my policies to accommodate him. It was true I had said during the runoff that I would bring in more blacks at the top than Wagner, Lindsay and Beame combined. In fact, I would have done so anyway. I had said that, independently, and by 1979 I had almost fulfilled that pledge. But I no longer regarded it as owing to Charlie Rangel, because for his part he was supposed to be supporting me. And he wasn't. Nonetheless, my record on minority hiring was a very good one. It was affirmative action working without racial quotas, drawing into government the best that the various groups had to offer.

My employment practices were often misunderstood and often misrepresented in the first few years of my Mayoralty. But in retrospect one thing is clear: no one was hired or fired *because* of his or her color. In that there was a dignity for all.

In addition to restructuring and affirmative action, there was one other issue that became a major irritant in my relations with the City's blacks: my plan to save the money being wasted in the municipal hospitals and use it for *good* medical treatment.

One of the problems was that I had originally gotten off on the wrong foot. The first of my appointees to the chairmanship of the Health and Hospitals Corporation was Axel Schupf, an investment banker who had been credited with restructuring the financing at Brooklyn Jewish Hospital and saving that hospital from bankruptcy. As it turned out, Schupf hadn't done all that he was credited with having done at Brooklyn Jewish—and shortly after he took the chairmanship of HHC, Brooklyn Jewish was found to be in dire financial straits. Still, when Schupf arrived at HHC he was heralded as a hospital-financing expert. Nothing less would have done. HHC was at that time operating with staggering cost overruns, and by all indications things were getting worse.

The City of New York in 1978 was operating seventeen municipal hospitals. Of these, only two served primarily white patients. The Health and Hospitals Corporation, like the poverty programs, had long been viewed as the turf of the minority politicians. These were unspoken rules. And if more tax-levy money was needed to keep the hospitals functioning, then more money was appropriated under the general political heading of "keeping things cool." For me that wasn't good enough. I wanted to know where the money was going, how it was being spent and how it could be better spent. I appointed Axel Schupf to find out.

Schupf, the investment banker, was accustomed to the luxurious trappings of private industry. In his world, limousines and plush office furniture came with the territory. It was in this spirit that Schupf permitted an office party to be held during working hours at a country club in Nassau County. When all the City cars arrived in the country-club parking lot, they were greeted by a TV reporter with his camera crew. And when the reporter asked Schupf, on camera, how he could explain to taxpayers these City employees' partying it up on City time, Schupf, in a rage, shoved the reporter aside. It was priceless footage. And it signaled the beginning of the end for Schupf. At the end of the summer the end came.

In the meantime, he'd done almost nothing. On September 8 he asked for an appointment. I knew, having heard from Victor Botnick, a Mayoral assistant, that Axel was thinking of resigning. He was upset because he'd heard that I had met with Dr. Martin Cherkasky, former president of the highly regarded Montefiore Hospital, and Felix Rohatyn about stopping the hemorrhaging at the Health and Hospitals Corporation, which was costing us $500 million in subsidies a year. It was bleeding us bone-dry. So he came in. Robert Tierney, my counsel, was with me. Axel says to Bob, "I would like to speak to the Mayor alone."

I say, "No. I never speak to anyone alone. Bob will stay." The thrust of Axel's remarks was that he thought it was wrong for me to appoint a committee to oversee what he was doing. It was very hard to hear him because he was speaking so low.

I said, "Axel, why is that wrong? What is wrong with my getting the services of Dr. Cherkasky and Felix Rohatyn to examine what it is you are doing? In the first three months of this fiscal year you already have a twenty-million-dollar additional deficit. There is something wrong with that. All I am doing is getting *pro bono* the services of these people who know something. Dr. Cherkasky is an expert on medical care and Felix Rohatyn is an expert on money. What is wrong with that?"

He said, "You are undercutting my authority."

I said, "Axel, I am doing this not only with HHC. I am going to do it with other agencies. I have already done it with the Board of Higher Education, which Harold Howe* is examining."

Then he said, "But I was not a part of the decision."

I said, "Do you think Bob Kibbee"—he was then the Chancellor at the Board of Higher Education—"was in this room when I got Howe to examine his agency? This is not an attack on your integrity. We are not examining irregularities. As far as I know, there are none. We are talking about programs and getting the best out of the dollars we are spending. We are spending a billion dollars a year on medical care in its various forms, much of it out of tax levies. We are wasting a lot of money."

He says, "Well, I don't agree with the way you are handling it."

He then reaches into his pocket, as I had hoped he would, and takes out an envelope, as I had hoped he would, and he hands me a letter. The letter is very brief. It says, "I resign as Health Services Administrator August 8."

*Former U.S. Commissioner of Education under President Kennedy and executive vice-president of the Ford Foundation.

I said, "You mean *September* eighth, don't you?" He was flustered and said he would take it back and redo it. I said, "No, no, no, just write it in."

Once Schupf was out, the search was begun for a new chairman.

The search continued for over two months.

Meanwhile, Phil Toia and Dr. Cherkasky oversaw the budget of the municipal hospital system. Of these two, the up-front policy person was Cherkasky, my unpaid adviser. And Cherkasky seemed to enjoy the role. For years he had been the medical gray eminence around town. Now he was advising those who were running the largest chain of municipal hospitals in the Free World. I liked Cherkasky. The doctor was a man who could make the tough decision. He could take the flak. He was a stand-up guy. And Cherkasky liked me, for many of the same reasons.

Then, one Sunday in mid-December, I picked up the Sunday *Times*. There, on the front page, was his plan to close half the municipals. Clearly Cherkasky had gotten carried away. I called him up. "Martin," I said, "how could you be so goddamn dumb?"

The doctor replied, "No one has ever talked to me like that." That was the beginning of the end for Cherkasky at HHC. But it was just the beginning of the hospital-closings issue for me.

I was very much alone. The State and federal authorities basically wished to see the status quo preserved. The City people maintained that the status quo was too expensive; that it was wasteful; that a serious new look at medical-care delivery was essential not only from the point of view of the City's purse strings but from that of the people who needed health care. The core issue was empty beds. Nearly half the beds in the City's hospitals were empty every night. Yet the cost of a bed remained high—$250 to $300 per night—even when it was empty. Our questions were: Why should the City maintain some empty beds every night when what is needed is ambulatory clinic facilities located in the medically underserved neighborhoods? Why can't we close down some of these beds in order to have the money to open ambulatory-care facilities? Predictably, the local officials all agreed there were too many empty beds, but no one wanted a single bed closed in *his or her* community. And as it happened, the majority of empty beds were in two municipal hospitals in upper Manhattan.* It was only a matter of time before the Harlem leaders began invoking the old standby "racism" charges in their denunciations of the City administration's plan. And it was Haskell Ward, who held both the Deputy Mayor for Human Services and the chairman of the Health and Hospitals Corporation titles, who again became the lightning rod.

The pressures on Haskell Ward were enormous. First he had been entrusted with cleaning the fraud out of the poverty program; and then he had been placed by me in charge of making the municipal hospital system run efficiently. Both of these assignments required that he take on the black political establishment—he versus them directly. And they attacked him mercilessly. He was constantly referred to at public meetings as an "Uncle Tom," which he was not. It took a lot of courage to do what Haskell did. And it finally broke him.

Our final contretemps occurred in the following way. Our strategy for solving the hospital-beds problem was simple. The budget people and all the other experts who had been consulted agreed that both Metropolitan Hospital and Sydenham Hospital met the criteria for closing. Metropolitan was underutilized and had an enormous empty-beds problem, and Sydenham was delivering vastly inferior health care. So we announced that we would be closing both, and we went into battle.

Sometime after the announcements were made, it became clear that we would have difficulty closing either one; yet because of HHC's difficult financial situation, and because medically it made sense, we still pressed ahead beyond the hearings and in the midst of an enormous *Sturm und Drang*. It was clear to me after the hearings that if we closed both hospitals there would be an enormous loss of momentum for the administration, and it would be really impossible to facilitate anything else, anywhere else, toward the City's recovery. Nonetheless, it was crucial to achieve the closing of one that the two be bracketed together. We therefore made

*Sydenham Hospital in Harlem and Metropolitan Hospital in East Harlem.

efforts to get federal support to keep Metropolitan open, since clearly Metropolitan was a better hospital than Sydenham. The City introduced a special program it wanted to try out that would provide free medical care for the medically indigent not eligible for Medicaid to be paid for by the Feds, the State and the City. Washington was interested because it would be helpful to Carter.

We believed that if we went forward with the two closings and did not prematurely indicate a surrender at Metropolitan, we would ultimately prevail in getting the aid for Metropolitan that could help us keep it open. Haskell Ward understood this strategy. But because of the enormous pressures he was subject to, especially on the Sydenham closing, he wished to be perceived as the savior of Metropolitan. He kept wanting to make the public announcement on Metropolitan's continued functioning. And I kept telling him that if he announced we were keeping Metropolitan open, he would be giving up an opportunity to get the federal aid for that hospital that would ultimately make it possible to keep it open, and that then it would be the City that would be stuck with the mounting deficit.

It was never clear to me whether Haskell thought the Feds would come through even after a premature announcement; or whether he just couldn't think clearly anymore because of the torrent of attacks directed at him; or whether he just didn't care anymore.

Doubtless our plan could have been improved upon, but nevertheless to throw away that bargaining aspect on the merits would have been a great disservice. I kept saying that to Haskell.

Finally, there was a meeting at which we again reviewed HHC's overspending, and it was clear that it was going to come out somewhere around $150 million for the fiscal year. Joe Hoffman said that collections were improving, but that with all the people involved it was difficult for him to do all he felt he should toward addressing the overspending. In a voluntary hospital, when you don't pay your bills the hospital goes broke. In a municipal, the city comes in with a subsidy over and above the funds that were originally planned, and then it is the city that goes broke.

Anyway, we had a meeting in which it was decided that the management should be consolidated and that Hoffman should take control of our efforts to implement the closings plan. And that meant a diminution of Haskell's power. So I kept pressing him in the meeting: "Haskell, are you going to support this?" And he kept withdrawing.

After that meeting, Dan Wolf came in and said that Haskell was down in his office writing his resignation. So Dan brought Haskell back in and we talked about it. I said, "Please, don't resign now. We need you. It will be perceived as a weakening of the City's position."

He said, "But what is the purpose of staying on? Hoffman is going to do it all. There's really nothing for me to do." Plus, "You know I don't agree with your approach. I have told you to give up on Metropolitan."

I said, "Can't you wait a little? We need you to go down and make out our case in Washington."

He said, "Okay." That was on Thursday. All day Friday there were reports that he would be leaving. There was an AP report to that effect. So all the reporters came in at 5:30 in the afternoon. I told them the truth: "Haskell has not offered me his resignation, and I have not asked him for it."

Well, then there was a period of several days when there was a silence. Dan and Haskell went to lunch. They went to dinner. Dan reported that Haskell was in good spirits but that he, Dan, didn't really know what Haskell's plans were. He was thinking it over. Then the following Thursday, Haskell came in. With me were Allen Schwartz and Dan Wolf. Allen said, "Haskell, I would like to repeat to you a conversation we had last week when I came in to see you. At that time you said, 'Ed has a closed mind on the issue of Metropolitan Hospital. He won't make a statement on it.' And so we came in here and saw the Mayor, and at that time he said, 'The statement I would make vis-à-vis Metropolitan Hospital is: If HSA* and the State issue their reports and show that there is a way to provide better medical care and save money at the same time, then we will do what they recommend.' "

*The Health Services Agency, a federally funded State health-planning body.

Haskell said, "This conversation is serving no purpose. I don't wish to continue it."

I said, "Haskell, what would you like me to do?"

He pulled out a letter and handed it to me. It was his resignation, effective September 1, 1979. And I accepted it.

I said, "What shall we say to the press?"

He said, "I have no intention of talking to the press."

I said, "That's impossible. We have to make a statement. Why don't we make a joint statement in the Blue Room?"

And that's what we did, and it was very cordial. He got out like a gentleman. He had just run out of patience. It was sad, but understandable. He had been the object of a constant stream of abuse of the vilest sort for a year and a half, and it finally staggered him.

The press response to Haskell's resignation surprised me. Suddenly, after months of his being maligned, it was apparent that Ward had had friends out there, albeit silent ones. The editorial in the August 22 *Daily News* called Ward "A Dedicated Public Servant," which he was. The editorial continued, "Another black person in high office at City Hall will not reverse the polarization exposed anew by Ward's resignation. What is needed for starters is a heart-to-heart between the Mayor and the city's black political establishment."

And in Beth Fallon's *Daily News* column the next day, the City's black establishment spoke again:

> The real question is where does Koch go? To the black community it looks like he can't even keep a black Deputy Mayor *he* likes, never mind one that they like.
>
> "We're not recommending anybody to serve in this Administration," says one elected official. "Let him find his own—if he can. Anybody who served him would risk the same thing Haskell did, of having his credibility destroyed."

After Haskell Ward's resignation, it was abundantly clear to me that it was I the ideologues were after.

As though I hadn't already enough trouble with the black leaders, two weeks after Ward's resignation another issue was handed to me. Over the course of several weekends in late 1975 and early 1976, I had sat down with an interviewer from the Columbia University Oral History Project. Our discussions had ranged over many topics, including the Village Independent Democrats, the DeSapio races, the Lindsay endorsement, the Councilmanic race, and my first six years in the U.S. Congress. It had been an informal discussion. Our agreement had been that the originals of the transcripts would remain sealed at Columbia until 1996. The carbons were given to me. Once, I had tried without success to interest a publisher in them. After that effort the carbons had lain dormant in a box in Ronay Menschel's office.

In December 1978, after my administration had been in office nearly a year, a journalist named Kenneth Auletta expressed an interest in doing an all-inclusive *New Yorker* profile on me. Auletta was a man of boyish good looks and an engaging smile. He had learned his politics at the knee of Howard Samuels. In the 1970 Gubernatorial race, Auletta had managed Samuels' campaign. After his loss to Arthur Goldberg in the primary, Howard Samuels was appointed by John Lindsay to be the first chairman of the Off-Track Betting Corporation. Thereafter Auletta, along with Doug Ireland, one of Samuels' advisers and later a columnist for the *Soho Weekly News*; Michael Shagan, Samuels' advance man, and a whole host of his political faithfuls also went to OTB. There was no civil service at OTB, and by some estimates as many as forty of Samuels' campaign workers, past and future, feathered their nests at OTB and prepared for 1974. In '74 Auletta again managed the Samuels Gubernatorial campaign and they lost again, this time to a savvy Congressman from the Park Slope section of Brooklyn, Hugh L. Carey. And that was the end of the Samuels organization. From government service, Ken Auletta returned to journalism, finally becoming a columnist for the Sunday edition of the *Daily News*.

Thereafter Auletta applied to Maureen Connelly to do his *New Yorker* profile. And both Connelly and I were charmed by him. Days went by when Auletta would show up first thing in the morning and stay with us through meetings and public appearances and meals, with his tape recorder spinning away. We invited Auletta to read my mail. The doors to City Hall were opened to him. Finally the Columbia transcript copies were dusted off and provided to him. Such was my faith in Auletta's fairness that no one even read the transcripts before they were turned over.

Finally Auletta retired to his study to prepare the profile. Occasionally he would reappear to check a fact and ask an additional question or two over lunch. City Hall waited and waited. Then, on September 10, the first installment of the two-part series appeared.

The article provoked an enormous stir. It contained an excerpt from the Columbia tapes in which I had said that "the black community is very anti-Semitic" and, "to be fair about it . . . whites are basically anti-black." The offending section follows.

"I'm very conscious of being Jewish," says Koch. He is also conscious of and threatened by what he considers widespread black anti-Semitism. As a member of Congress, he seethed at black colleagues who voted against aid for Israel; he feared that their votes were an expression of their hostility to Jews. In his oral memoirs of 1975 and 1976, Koch reveals his innermost feelings and fears about race relations:

"I find the black community very anti-Semitic. I don't care what the American Jewish Congress or the B'nai B'rith will issue by way of polls showing that the black community is not. I think that's pure bull. . . . They'd like to believe that. My experience with blacks is that they're basically anti-Semitic. Now, I want to be fair about it. I think whites are basically anti-black. . . . But the difference is: it is recognized as morally reprehensible, something you have to control."

For Koch, as for all moralists, issues tend to be clear-cut; if it is wrong for whites to stereotype blacks, it is wrong for blacks to stereotype whites. Koch's views, unlike those of many liberals, are not clouded by compassion for the descendants of slaves, the victims of racism. He accepts no excuses, brooks no insults, applies but one standard. That one standard leads him to oppose preferential treatment programs as "reverse discrimination." The goal of the civil rights movement, he says, should be for blacks "to be treated like whites." He is disdainful of welfare cheats and probably wonders why more people do not struggle to escape poverty, as the Koch family did. To most liberals, all poor blacks are victims; to Koch, some are villains.

As a result of the article there were bitter denunciations, although my own feeling is that what I said was basically true. Nevertheless, when I was interviewed on the Columbia tapes it was not a question-and-answer or an in-depth interview. It wasn't an interview at all. I just simply spoke, and therefore those were my thoughts in 1975 and 1976 without any explanations. So in 1979, for example, when I spoke with Vincent Cosgrove from the *Daily News,* who asked me did I regret having said it, I said, "No. I do regret that the journalist didn't ask me if I wanted to update it, or had I any additional thoughts or amplifications." If he had, I would have said, "A substantial number of blacks are anti-Semitic and substantial numbers of whites are anti-black." Why should the question of racism be the one that can't be discussed? Is it really a shock when I say this? The Kerner Report from fifteen years ago said that our society is racist.

Now, as a result of the storm, I had a call from Charlie Rangel, who said that he would like to help. I said, "Why don't we get together at the mansion tomorrow and discuss it?"

He said, "Well, I thought maybe you should just simply call for the clergy to come in and talk the matter over. It is your show."

I said, "No, let's the two of us sit down and discuss this on Saturday and I will have some of my people there."

So that Friday night, I had dinner with Maureen Connelly, David Garth, Dan Wolf and several top members of my administration. And the purpose of the dinner was to work out where to go from there and, in particular, what to seek in the meeting with Charlie Rangel. Garth began by saying, "You have sixty days in which to ameliorate the matter. You have to use the right words." By that he probably meant either quotas or preferential treatment. You have to understand the storm that was going on in the press over this. And these people, Garth and Maureen in particular, thought that I had to give something. But it was clear that I would not.

Then Garth says, "Look, if Bill Green* loses in Philadel-

*William J. Green, a former Democratic Congressman who was running for Mayor.

phia it will be because the blacks voted for a third-party candidate instead of the Democrat. That could happen to you."

I say, "Let me just say that my reelection is not really a matter of concern. Because if I don't get reelected, it is okay. I am really not concerned about that anymore. If I do get reelected I will love it. And I expect to. But if I don't, it is not the end of the world." I think that kind of surprised him.

Then Maureen shifted over to "Well, for the good of the City, it is not good to have this polarization which is setting in. They will be seeking to make you out to be a Rizzo."* And they then pointed to a poll that showed that 70 percent of the whites thought I was doing a good job and 20 percent didn't; and of the blacks, 40 percent thought I was a racist and only 36 percent thought I was doing a good job. "That will enlarge," she said, and—using the language of Charlie Rangel—"you might rule but you couldn't govern." Whatever that means. The implication was that whether your constituents approve of what you are doing or whether they don't, you cannot survive politically if there is a perception of either confusion or, worse yet, racial conflict.

I said, "There is much to that."

Well, the next morning we had breakfast with Charlie Rangel, and the first thing he said was "I wish you had told me ten years ago that you believed that, genetically, blacks don't like Jews."

I said, "Charlie, why do you say that? I never said that. I have never talked about 'genetically.' I have said, and I would change the language from 'most blacks' to 'a substantial number of blacks,' that blacks are anti-Semitic, and for understandable reasons from their point of view. Jews are people who remain a presence in the ghetto even after they have moved out as residents. They still own the businesses there, and the blacks move in and the Jews still continue to do business, and they are the landlords to a great extent, and the blacks dislike them for that reason. The blacks dislike the

---

*Frank Rizzo, the outgoing Mayor of Philadelphia. Rizzo had a notoriously bad relationship with his black constituents.

Jews because everybody would like to have a scapegoat. The Jews have been the scapegoat not only for blacks but for the whites as well. Many whites don't like Jews, so why shouldn't blacks have that pleasure?''

He said, "Well, I am glad that you say that that is not what it is. It is not genetic."

I said, "It's got nothing to do with genetics, and you know it, Charlie."

Now, we had no intention of making a news conference out of this breakfast. When he walked in, I had said, "Charlie, there are reporters outside for a news conference apparently following this."

He said, "I didn't do it."

I said, "Well, I know *we* didn't do it, so it must have been you."

"Well," he said, "I did speak at a club last night, so maybe somebody called them."

Now, when we left the room and went out on the porch, the reporters asked Charlie to speak, and he recapitulated basically what had taken place. Then they go to the questions, and one reporter says, "Congressman, when you came in this morning, you said that the Mayor is suffering from a character defect. Do you still believe he is suffering from a character defect?''

At that point Charlie became very tough in his comments, saying, "Obviously the Mayor hasn't met many black folks and doesn't know us, and we are not going to be excluded, and if it was painful for him before it will be even more painful in the future."

Then they asked me, "Are you sorry that you said these things?''

I said, "I am sorry if I gave pain and anguish to people when these things were said. And I am sorry that they hadn't been expanded upon so people had my total meaning. But I am not sorry that I said what I said on the substance of it. I could have done it a little more intelligently or artfully.''

At that point Charlie said, "What the Mayor is trying to say is that it was *dumb*."

I laughed, and it was a genuine laugh. I said, "You say things so nicely, Charlie." Then we walked to the car and I put my arm on his shoulder. And that was really a first-class picture on the front page of *The New York Times*.

13

Reorganizing
the Administration

FOR SOME MONTHS PRIOR to taking action on August 4, 1979, I had been privately turning the matter of my top-heavy organization over in my mind. And contrary to the opinion of those who say the route from my mind to my mouth is a quick one, I had for those months kept my own counsel. It was not until a July 25 dinner at Gracie Mansion with David Margolis and Maureen Connelly that I actually spoke of my frustrations. But from there to the August 4 press announcement I moved swiftly.

On July 26 I asked Allen Schwartz to arrange a hideaway meeting over the weekend of the 28th with the two young men I intended to bring into the top echelon of the administration: Nathan Leventhal, the 36-year-old Commissioner of Housing Preservation and Development, and 35-year-old Robert F. Wagner, Jr., the chairman of the City Planning Commission. The calls went out that morning, and the meeting was arranged for Saturday, the 28th, at Allen's summer house in Rye, New York. It was there, at a backyard barbecue, that I offered Leventhal the Deputy Mayor for Operations post. Wagner's role was also discussed, but there was a problem with the Deputy Mayor for Policy position.

In the first year of my administration, that post had been held by David W. Brown. On January 1, 1979, the day after Brown's departure, Herman Badillo had assumed the Policy title—and at the time of the barbecue, no one knew what was going to happen with the erratic Badillo in the ensuing week.

So while Leventhal could begin immediately, Wagner had to wait and see a little. He and Badillo had fallen out over the Charlotte Street vote. Now the plan was to fire Badillo and replace him with Wagner. It was a touchy business and it required gloves-on handling. Throughout the following week we importuned the Carter Administration to hire Badillo—unsuccessfully as it turned out. They didn't want him either.

With Herman I knew I would be having trouble, so I left him aside for the moment and turned to the rest of the job.

I had won in 1977 with 48 percent of the vote; and that was not high considering that Cuomo, my major opponent, was running on the Liberal Party line. I decided to have Basil Paterson as a deputy mayor. And Herman Badillo came in at about that time. I definitely wanted Ronay Menschel—she had been with me in government longer than anyone else. I was going to have the whole rainbow. It turned out I ended up with seven deputy mayors. And to be fair, it was not such a bad idea, in the beginning, to show a wide basis of support for the administration. New Yorkers didn't really know me, and I had not won by a large margin.

After twenty months things were different. New Yorkers did know me, and with the seven deputies, things were falling through the cracks. People build up staffs. At his high, Herman Badillo had twenty-four people working for him, and many of them, it seemed to me, were incompetent. The payroll in his office amounted to nearly half a million dollars annually. For this what did I get? Joyce Purnick, then of *New York* magazine, came in one day and said, "Mr. Mayor, what does Herman do?"

I had to, in honesty, say, "I don't know; why don't you ask him?"

So I knew it had to end—counsels, administrative assistants, advisers to the deputy mayor—and I geared myself up. It was very difficult. And the first conversation was one of the toughest.

It was a Monday, the 30th. At about 9:30 in the morning I got a call from Phil Trimble. He was my next-door neighbor. I had known him since I had been in the City Council.

He says, "Ed, I just got a call from Howard Blum of *The*

New York Times, who said I am being replaced by Nat Leventhal. I told him I didn't know anything about it.''

I said, "Phil, why don't you come upstairs and we'll talk about it.'' Now, over the weekend I had had several conversations with various people about how to proceed on this, and now undoubtedly one of them had leaked the story to Howard Blum. And he is a very good reporter, who will take the bare notion of a story and by means of saying, "Well I know this, so you better tell me that if you want your side reported,'' elicit the whole story. He will obtain stories that it is not in the interest of any of the sources to divulge.

So Phil comes in, and he is a man who shows almost no visible emotion. In this case he seemed just totally drained. It was more distressing than if he had ranted and raved. I said, "You know, Phil, it just isn't working. I am going to make changes. And one of the changes includes yourself. I would like to help you get a job at the State Department. I have been working on that. So we will do this in a way that will be helpful to you.'' He sat there in absolute silence. He internalized it all.*

The next conversation I had occurred almost immediately. Diane Coffey came in and said, "What's going on?''

I said, "Okay. I'll tell you what's going on. There are going to be changes. Some people's titles will be reduced. Others will have to go altogether. Only Peter Solomon† and Haskell Ward will be unaffected. And Peter has said he will be leaving anyway. I'm going to tell everyone today. I have already told Phil. In your case, I am changing your title from chief of staff to administrative assistant.''

Well, she was absolutely crushed. She said, "It will diminish my authority with others.''

I said, "I don't think so. The truth is, chief of staff is not what you are. You are not running the Commissioners.''

She said, "I know that. I never wanted the title. David

---

*Phil Trimble was a brilliant lawyer; he ultimately served in a high position in the State Department, and he later became a professor at a California University. He is still a good friend.

†Robert J. Milano's successor as Deputy Mayor for Economic Development.

Brown gave it to me. But now I have it, and to take it away will diminish my authority."*

I said, "Well, I am resolved to do this. And the worst part is going to be telling Ronay. I am going to ask her to give up her deputy mayor title and to take the title of executive administrator." Now, Diane and Ronay are very good friends, and so that crushed her even more.

She said, "That will be terrible. Are you sure that is what you have to do?"

I said, "Yes. It has been the subject of discussion, and my mind is made up."

She said, "Okay."

Then I called in Ronay. And by that time it was clear to her what was going on. I gave her all the reasons. She said, "Well, there is really no reason. I have done a good job."

I said, "No question about it, Ronay. You are one of the best. But we don't need seven deputy mayors. And if I can't recognize that and change your title, then I can't do it with any of them. That is why I am doing it first with my friends and then with those with whom I don't have that personal relationship." Well, she is really a good trouper. I said, "I know you are going to have a problem with Richard." Richard is her husband, an early supporter of mine. I introduced them. "But if Richard were in a comparable position—if he saw that his office at Goldman, Sachs was not being well run—he would do whatever it was that had to be done and personal relationships wouldn't have anything to do with it."

She says, "Well, Richard always said that you don't care about personal relationships. He says it's one of your defects."

I said, "Well, I'm sorry if that's the way it comes over, but as I've said, government isn't for friends. It's not a sorority house here. I want my friends in government, but only if government needs them and they do the job. And you do it and you know it. But what you do isn't what a deputy mayor does. You don't need the staff."

---

*Diane Coffey is an extraordinarily able administrator. She runs my office. And I ultimately restored her title to her. And her authority was never diminished—with or without title.

She wept. She is a very strong woman. It was very difficult. The worst. The hardest. She said, "I will try it. I'll see if it works."*

The next person I spoke to was Phil Toia. He had been the Deputy Mayor for Finance. He came in. I had seen him the night before at Gracie Mansion at a labor meeting. I said, "Phil, this is very difficult, but I am going to end your position with the government. The reason is very simple: it hasn't worked. You are a guy with great ability. You are a guy who can take very complex concepts and explain them to someone like me in such a way that I can grasp those concepts. You are also a marvelous guy to have around. I like talking to you. But Phil, I asked you four months ago to take on the matter of our capital spending. You were to find a construction czar, and you haven't done it. You have procrastinated. I asked you to study the budgets of the deputy mayors to see where we could cut. And you procrastinated there. I asked you to form a revenue-enhancement committee. You got the committee, but they never met. You never called them together. What good are they if you don't use them? Phil, you didn't follow through."

He said, "Nobody has ever spoken to me that way before." He was very calm and well modulated. He said, "Well, I was going to leave after two years anyway."

I said, "Fine. It corresponds to both our wishes."

Then he said, "Oh, by the way, I have completed the analysis of the budgets of the deputy mayors and I will submit it to you along with my recommendations. I recommend that you should phase out my job. It is my opinion that the budget people can do all that we have been doing."†

I said, "Okay." And he left. He seemed relieved, in a way. I know I was. Having these conversations is like an ulcer:

---

*Ronay Menschel made the change work. She was one of my most trusted confidantes and advisers and ultimately became one of my representatives on the MTA Board. She is a brilliant, self-effacing and superbly talented person; and still a good friend.

†Phil Toia is a very able man. He is now a leading executive at a major bank and he is helping the city *pro bono* from time to time—and is still a good friend.

worry, worry, worry, painful, painful, painful, piercing. And then all the pus runs out and you feel better.

After that, Ronay came back in. She said, "Okay, but it should all be spelled out in the release, what everyone is doing and is to do. And Peter Solomon should be included in that."

I said, "You're right, and that's exactly what I have in mind. Peter said he was going to leave at the end of the year."

She said, "Make sure that gets in the release."

Then I called in Peter Solomon. And he fought tooth and nail. He said, "Well, you know, when I said I was going to leave I said that because it was my feeling that there were too many deputy mayors. But now that there are only three, I would like to stay."

I said, "Oh, I hadn't understood that that was your feeling."

He said, "Yes, that is what I had meant to convey." And the fact was that at that time Solomon seemed to be working out. So I said, "Okay. We can try it." And, of course, I had to tell that to Ronay.*

The next one was Herbert Sturz. He was on Martha's Vineyard on vacation. It was 10:30 P.M. I was at the mansion. He had just walked into his house for his vacation. He was very cheerful.

I said, "Hi, I just wanted to tell you what I'm doing." And I ran through all the changes. Then I said, "Now let me tell you what I'm doing with you. I'm changing your title from Deputy Mayor for Criminal Justice to Criminal Justice Coordinator. It will be no diminution of your authority. The fact is, the Charter title carries with it greater authority because you will now be in a position to hire and fire the Commissioner of Corrections." And I knew that he wanted to fire Ciuros.†

He said, "I can't do that." And he gave all the same arguments that Ronay had given and I gave the countervailing

---

*Peter Solomon left at a later time and returned to his investment-banking firm. He was subsequently helpful to me in my campaigns, and he is still a good friend.

†William J. Ciuros, Commissioner of Corrections.

arguments. Allen Schwartz was with me at the mansion, so I put him on the phone to explain the Charter designation and the effects of the change in terms of the powers given to the Criminal Justice Coordinator in the City Charter. And in the end they agreed that Sturz was not happy; that he might well have to leave; but that he and I would talk about it further the following morning.

I got into City Hall the following morning at 7:30 and there was this call from Sturz. He was protesting again. I said, "Look, let me tell you where I'm at. This is very painful for me and I wish you would help me. If you cannot, I will understand. But try. I am going to reduce titles. I have done it with Ronay and Diane and I am going to do it with you. But with you, on a substantive basis, you come out ahead. I'm not cutting your staff, as I am with the others, and I am giving you additional authority over the Corrections Commissioner. I would like you to say you agree with me, or at least that you are going to go along with it. If you can't do that, then you can let me say you are going along with it with reservations. And if you can't, then you can't. But I am not going to change on this."

Then his tone changed. He said, "Well, I'll try it."*

So that ended that one and I moved on to Herman Badillo.

I had left word the night before that when Herman came in the next morning I wanted to see him. It was August 4. I had dictated the press statement, and the reporters were gathering outside. A little after 9 A.M., there he was. I said, "Herman, it is bad. And I really think that the best way out of this is that I announce that you will be leaving at the end of the year along with the others. I have been trying to get you the HUD job. I have called Jack Watson and Rafshoon, Bob Strauss and Hamilton Jordan† on that."

He says, "Oh, you don't have to get me a job. I can get

---

*Herb Sturz ultimately became the City Planning Chairman. He is a specialist at bringing consensus to any problem. And I rely on him a great deal. And he also remains a good friend.

†Gerald Rafshoon, Carter's media adviser, and Robert Strauss, former chairman of the Democratic National Committee, the Carter campaign chairman. Hamilton Jordan was White House chief of staff.

one for myself. If it works out, okay. Or I'll go back to private practice. It's okay." He was really being very good about it. All he asked for was sixty days to relocate his staff.

I said, "Sure." And it became his doing, which was obviously in my interest.

He said, "I will say I am leaving at the end of the year, but I will probably leave before that."

I said, "I hope we are still friends."

He said, "Oh, sure." You worry about Herman because even when he is your friend he can do terrible things.

I said, "So we will make you a part of the announcement today."

And he said, "No. I will announce it myself."

I said, "Fine."

Nonetheless, with Herman, as I knew it would, the thing went badly almost immediately. Within a couple of days he was saying that he was leaving because it was impossible to work with such a "cowardly" Mayor. I thought: Hmm, after twenty months? What a coincidence. I knew the syndrome. It was the Bernie Rome syndrome. I knew our professional relationship was over, so I called him in again. I said, "Herman, it is distressing to me the way you are attacking me."

He says, "I have not been attacking you."

I say, "I view calling someone 'cowardly' as a personal attack."

He says, "Well . . ."

I say, "And, by the way, it is ridiculous. What are you doing? You are going to need me."

He says, "Well . . ."

I say, "Okay, so what are your plans? When are you leaving?"

He says, "Well, I am having difficulty reaching the partners of the law firms that I am negotiating with. They are all on vacation until after Labor Day."

I say, "Look, the reporters are constantly asking me, as a result of your attacks upon me, 'When is Herman leaving?' So can I tell them you will be gone at the end of September?"

He said, "Yes, you can tell them that." Very cryptic, yet stoical. You could see the nerve line move in his cheek. And that is unusual. Anyway, the next day he resigns again, this time effective the end of September.

Then, a week or so later I go down to a New York delegation dinner with the Members of Congress and I see Tip O'Neill. I go over to him and he is very hearty in his welcome, but then he says, "I want you to know that I had a terrible conversation recently with one of your former colleagues down here who was one of your vice-mayors."

I said, "Herman Badillo?"

He said, "Yes, he came down here and alleged that you were anti-black and anti-Hispanic. And he was going around saying the most terrible things about you. Ed, if you ever talk to him again I won't talk to you again."*

That is Herman's problem. He is very shrewd politically, but in the end he is always by himself. He could have led the Hispanic constituency in New York to terrific heights. They wanted him to. But no one could work with him. He is a one-man band, not an orchestra leader. And that is why they didn't want him in the Carter Administration. They didn't trust him. They knew that in the end he would be standing outside the White House calling them names. It was clear that that was the reason why.

Now, also, in one of my calls to Hamilton Jordan when I was attempting to get Herman into HUD, I said to Jordan, "Would you mind if I gave you some friendly advice regarding the firing of Califano, Adams† and the others?" It was the week following those announcements.

He said, "No, of course not. We were not pleased by the way it was handled."

I said, "What you should say is: 'We weren't pleased with the way we handled these firings. I would say they were B-firings. But we intend to do better next time.' And in that way you can defuse the thing."

*I, of course, thought: So I have to choose. How nice. And I didn't speak to Herman Badillo again until two years ago, when I saw him at the start of the New York Marathon. He was running, and he looked very perky. I said: "Herman, I hope you come in number one—but only in the marathon!"
†Joseph A. Califano had been Secretary of Health, Education and Welfare; Brock Adams had been Secretary of Transportation.

He said, "Oh, yes, that's pretty good. We'll try it out."
But of course, they never did.

Their problem with Joe and Brock wasn't the way they
handled it, although it wasn't handled well; it was the timing,
the rationale and the signal that was sent to the rest of the
government. Carter was responding to a situation in which he
was low in the polls. He wanted to gain popularity by making
the changes. That is what they were all about. But I was at a
high in popularity, 67-percent approval nineteen months out. I
made the changes not because I wished to enhance my
popularity but because I believed that the new structure would
make the government more efficient. Second distinction:
Carter changed the Commissioners, who are called Secretaries in the Cabinet in Washington, and he made them weaker
by those changes, while he strengthened the palace guard and
the White House staff, meaning Jody Powell and Ham Jordan.
Those guys correspond to the deputy mayors and the City
Hall staff. I did just the opposite. I didn't change a single
Commissioner. I strengthened my Commissioners by not
affecting them adversely. And I reduced the palace guard.
And thirdly, I did it in a way that was immediate and
all-encompassing, not day-by-day. The projection was therefore that this was not a Saturday Night Massacre but rather a
reassessment of the administration twenty months into the
term, knowing that changes should be made at the end of two
years, and announcing those changes with the consent of the
people involved.

III

Closing the
Budget Gap

14

The Transit Strike: A Victory for All New Yorkers

IN THE SPRING OF 1980, New Yorkers endured what is widely regarded in the City as the most crippling of strikes: a strike by the 33,000-member Transport Workers Union. For eleven days in April the buses and the subways stood still.

Fourteen years earlier, the year of the last transit strike, John Lindsay was Mayor. As an indication of how transit strikes are regarded, Lindsay's 1966 statement to the people of the City of New York, including the municipal work force, was "No one should travel into Manhattan . . . or into the business districts of Queens, the Bronx and Brooklyn unless he is engaged in the critical activities of providing food, fuel or medical services. . . ." By contrast, in 1980 I took the unions on directly. I forbade city employees to stay home from work. Clearly my view of the Mayor's role was different from Lindsay's.

My strategy toward the strike was twofold. One thrust was to keep the City going and in a spirit that would make it possible to survive a strike and not crumble. The other was to do what I could to influence the outcome of the contract negotiations, knowing that it was the State that had overall financial responsibility and therefore that my role as it related to the Metropolitan Transportation Authority board was that of a minority stockholder.

The role of the Mayor had never previously been tested. It is true that some of the fourteen MTA board members had been Mayoral appointees ever since that metropolitan-area transit-management board was created in 1966, but they had

171

been only a small minority. Still, even as late as the 1978 transit negotiations the transit settlement had been viewed in the City as the me-too model for the larger municipal-union settlements. Thus, as the City would likely be forced to pay its municipal workers raises roughly equivalent to those granted the transport workers, Governors had previously yielded to Mayors, because the Mayors had so much more at stake.

In the 1980 transit negotiations, every wage increase of 1 percent cost the State of New York $10 million, whereas in the City's negotiations with the municipal unions, whose collective memberships numbered over two hundred thousand, every point meant a liability of more than $53 million to the City. That certainly was reason for the other members of the board to consider the City's position. However, when I made my "no linkage" declaration following the TWU settlement in 1978,* I had in effect surrendered my me-too-based veto over the 1980 TWU settlement. Moreover, by linking my approval of the Westway project to transit subsidies by the State, I had ensured that any further increases in the MTA's budget would have to be funded by the State.

In 1980, the City therefore had only as much interest in the size of the settlement as there was life to the tradition of the old me-too days. But the me-too days were not so long gone, and the municipal labor leaders were sure to cite the transit settlement when their contracts came up two months later. In short, every point that the State gave the transit workers had the effect of making the City's negotiations with the municipals more difficult.

During the 1977 campaign, Congressman Stephen Solarz, a personal friend of both mine and Victor Gotbaum's, had had a conversation with Gotbaum that went something like this:

SOLARZ: "Victor, I don't understand the intensity of your opposition to Ed Koch."

---

*In 1978 I helped management reinterpret that me-too model by saying, after the TWU settlement, that the City was not bound by the transit settlement to give all its municipal workers the same increases. That was unheard of. I said there was to be "no linkage" between the settlements— and the union leaders went crazy. You see, it was to their advantage for their contracts always to be pegged to those of the region's most powerful union.

GOTBAUM: "Steve, there are people out there who resent the strength of the labor unions, and Koch is the candidate who will arouse them."

Given that response, it was no surprise that Gotbaum's 1977 pre-primary mailings urged his membership to vote for "anyone but Koch." In early April 1980, Gotbaum got a good look at his worst fears, as the following entries from my "Transit Strike Diary" will attest:

March 30. I met from 8 to 10 this morning with Dick Ravitch,* Bruce McIver and Bob Wagner. The core of our talk was that Ravitch had had a phone conversation with the Governor which made no sense to him. I said, "That happens all the time with the Governor. One simply doesn't understand what he says."

Ravitch said, "I have to make some decision. I will be guided by the City's needs. But as chairman of the MTA, my sole consideration really should be, What will be the impact on the MTA in terms of what we pay for a settlement?" In other words, he is setting policy, which is really not what he should be doing. He went on to say: "If both the Governor and you told me not to settle at a particular amount, I would abide by your decision. But if the TWU walks, the likelihood is that we will have to pay more to bring them back."

I said, "I really can't understand why everyone takes for granted that the City has to lose every strike. Why can't we prevail? In New Orleans there was a police strike and the City won. In Kansas City† and Chicago there were firemen's strikes and the City won. When you are dealing with police and firemen, you are dealing with lives, which is even greater than the inconvenience of a transit strike and the consequent loss of dollars. If you settle or make an offer of settlement that is responsible and they don't take it, you should not do something irrational and offer more than is reasonable and responsible simply to avoid a strike. I don't want a strike, but if we have to have one we should not run away from it."

March 31. Ravitch called me at City Hall at about 7:30 this morning and said that he had been negotiating all night and was

---

*Richard Ravitch had been appointed to the chairmanship of the Metropolitan Transportation Authority by Governor Carey.

†During the ensuing strike I was given to singing the chorus from "Everything's Up to Date in Kansas City."

very discouraged. He said that despite published reports, the fact is that the private discussions are not going well and they are very far apart. He said he would call Bob McGuire in the afternoon to alert him to the need to secure the MTA facilities and that he would like Tom Goldstein to leak that information so as to create an additional atmosphere of pressures on the unions.

At 7:30 in the evening I left Gracie Mansion to go to the St. Regis Hotel, where the Governor was with Morgado and Ravitch. Bruce McIver and Jim Brigham were with me. In the course of our discussions, Ravitch said that he thought he would go from his offer of 3 + 3 to 6 + 6 (that is, two one-year wage increases of 6 percent). He said he believed John Lawe* would bring back a proposal of 9 + 9 with givebacks of 1½ percent, which would put the settlement at 7½ percent. Ravitch knows that if he makes the offer and it is turned down, it will become a basis for demands after a strike is in progress. He said, "If Lawe cannot deliver a substantial executive-board vote, I will not accept it. We will stay at seven and a half and we will let them walk."

I said to the Governor, "You understand that before I accept any settlement that Ravitch brings to me, I will decide if it is helpful to the City. If it is not, my representatives on the MTA will vote it down. I know that you are against that; and you think I am going to nail you by blaming you for a higher settlement or an increased fare; but I have said to you that I won't do that even if I have to instruct my appointees to vote against the settlement in order to help the City in its negotiations with our municipal unions."

Morgado said, "No, he accepts that you won't attack him."

I said, "Governor, let's go over to the Sheraton Hotel so that we can be in touch with Ravitch regularly."

He said, "No, I want to stay where I am and be in touch with Ravitch by phone. I will only go to the hotel if Ravitch needs me."

I said, "Well, I am going to the hotel."

It was a rainy, snowy night. I walked into the hotel and there was one television reporter there. She televised me walking in, but she didn't ask any questions. The suite that I had was just a single room but near Ravitch's, which was a large suite taken by the MTA. In my room were Allen Schwartz, David Margolis, Bruce McIver and others.

---

*John Lawe was president of the Transport Workers Union. A congenial Irishman from County Roscommon, Lawe faced considerable opposition from within his union's more militant black and Hispanic ranks.

I explained what Ravitch was doing. David Margolis wanted to know whether I was committed to simply voting against a 9 + 9 or whether I would seek to get all the members to vote it down. Wagner said that he did not think the other members of the MTA would buy a 9 + 9. We then discussed whether Ravitch understood that I retained the right to do whatever was in the City's interest, including defeating any 9 + 9 he might bring back.

Then Jack Rudin called and he said he was with Harry Van Arsdale and Rex Tompkins* and they wanted to see me because they wanted to help.

I said, "There is nothing you can do. Ravitch is the negotiator, not me. I will tell him that you want to help, and if he wants to get in touch with you, he will."

What they would like me to do is share confidences with them, as if they were on our side. They are not on our side. They are on their own side. And if there is an additional side, it is the side of the labor unions. You have Harry Van Arsdale there. You have these people who will suffer losses in the event of any strike. Therefore, they don't care about the cost to the City; they only care about the cost to them. Understandable, but that is not what I have to worry about. I have to worry about the total cost.

So Jack Rudin was very upset. Then, later on, Harry Van Arsdale called and said he wanted me to come down. I said, "I am happy to come down, Harry, but you are not going to get me in that room alone with you. We will get Dick Ravitch and I will sit there and I will listen, but it is Ravitch who represents the MTA and who is doing the negotiations. You wouldn't want me to cut off his legs, would you? Would you do that to your negotiator?"

"Oh, no," he said. So that was the end of that conversation.

After our discussions about what Ravitch might perceive as my position, we agreed that I would tell Ravitch that I will oppose the 9 + 9. Brigham's staff had priced out the items that Ravitch had cited and found that the settlement could be viewed as giving as much as 11 percent. We were concerned that the unions would advertise the settlement as an 11-percent increase the first year and 13 percent the second. We feared that that would impact on our labor negotiations with the municipal workers, who would

---

*Jack Rudin is one of the City's real estate developers; Harry Van Arsdale is the founder of the electricians' union, Local 1199, and is president of the New York City Central Labor Council; Rex Tompkins is chairman of the board of the Dry Dock Savings Bank and a former chairman of the Real Estate Board.

want the same. Then Ravitch called and said, "The nine-plus-nine scenario won't carry. It will be rejected by the union. But we're still working on it."

I said, "I just want you to know that the figures don't check out. It is not a net seven and a half percent. It may be eleven percent or thirteen percent, and that would be a disaster for the City."

Ravitch seemed to bristle, and said that he was not interested in discussing the figures because he didn't think Lawe would be authorized to bring back a 9 + 9. I was then clearly on the record as reserving my right to actively oppose such a settlement with all the members of the MTA board, not just my appointees.

At about 2 A.M., Ravitch called again. He said, "The union's executive-board meeting is breaking up and they are going on strike." The chairman of the mediation panel, Walter Gellhorn, had proposed to Ravitch that the mediators submit a final proposal to the union of 8 + 8 and givebacks. Gellhorn had gone into the Labor Executive Committee and made the offer, but was shouted down without a vote and the strike was then called. This means that the union broke off the negotiations. So it is their strike.

The Governor arrived with Morgado just as the union was leaving to start the strike. The Governor thought the matter had been settled at 8 + 8, and he was stunned to find the Sheraton Centre in disarray, with the union leaving. McIver, Silver* and I went with the Governor upstairs. Morgado and several others of the Governor's group were there. I said, "We have to talk to the press." The Governor was reluctant to go downstairs. It was clear from the Governor's statement that he did not want to push on the Taylor Law† other than to say that the law would be enforced. I said, "Why don't you punish severely every member of the executive committee?"

He said, "I am not for that."

I said, "We should sue them civilly."

"No," he said.

I said, "Let's sock 'em."

Frucher‡ said, "You can only ask for a thousand-dollar fine maximum total from each individual."

---

*Edward Silver, an independent counsel retained by the City administration for the labor negotiations.
†The Taylor Law is the successor to the Condon-Wadlin Law: it is the State law that makes strikes by municipal or State employees illegal.
‡Meyer S. Frucher was Governor Carey's in-house labor negotiator.

I said, "I don't believe it."

Then we all went downstairs and appeared before the press. Nothing adverse was said. We all supported one another. I left the hotel at 3:45 A.M. and stayed the night at 14 Washington Place.

April 1. I left my apartment at 6:45 A.M., getting about 2½ hours' sleep. When I got to One Police Plaza, I met with Bob McGuire in his top-floor office. From his window I could see thousands of people streaming across the Brooklyn Bridge into Manhattan. I thought: There are the municipal workers coming to save the City. It was like the Russian Army coming over frozen Lake Ladoga to save Leningrad.

There was a briefing by Gene Connell* and then the first of the regular 8 A.M. press conferences at Police Headquarters.

Then I went to the Manhattan side of the Brooklyn Bridge and greeted the people who were walking across the bridge. They were all supportive of my position. They would say, "Keep it up," or "Don't give in." It was very encouraging. The press was really surprised. Then I went to the Staten Island ferry and received the same kind of supportive comments: "We love you." "We think you are doing fine." "Keep it up." "Stand tough."†

Carl Stokes from Channel 4 was there. He was amazed by the support I was getting. He said, "How come these people don't blame you? Any other mayor would be yelled at, and here they are supporting you. You must have been born under a lucky star."

I said, "No, I am a Sagittarian."

At about 2 P.M., I walked from Canal Street down Broadway to City Hall, and I received a good response from blacks, Hispanics, Asians and whites. All gave their support in roughly equal measure.

At about 11 that morning, I had a meeting in my office with our labor people. I said, "I believe that we should seek to intervene in the Taylor Law proceedings, because I don't trust the Governor to stand up."

Allen Schwartz said, "We should be supportive of Ravitch and

---

*Eugene Connell was an on-loan executive from the Telephone Company. Connell oversaw the City administration's comprehensive program relating to traffic and public safety during the strike. It was Connell's program that kept the City functioning.

†Some of the bridge walkers, particularly the Brooklyn Heights residents who were walking to Wall Street, recall most fondly my exhortation "Go out and make money!"

encourage the MTA and the Attorney General to pursue the contempt proceedings, the Taylor Law penalties and the filing of a petition with PERB.''*

I said, "Ravitch will do what the Governor wants, because he was appointed by the Governor. I want us to be able to sue the individuals."

Allen said, "Okay."

Then we called Ravitch and told him what we were doing. He had no problem with it.

Then the Governor called and said we should stay in touch. He said, "I believe we should oppose these penalties."

I said, "We should enforce the penalties."

He was very much upset, saying, "This is a matter that is controlled by the Governor and the Attorney General."

I said, "I represent the City and I'm one of the principals."

"I have a lot of experience with these matters," Carey said. "I know where the Taylor Law is good and where it is bad."

"I don't have the experience," I said, "but I have done a lot of reading." He was not happy.

Then I called Ravitch. He seemed to be supportive. I asked him to set up a time when we could meet that afternoon. At 2 P.M., when he hadn't called me back, I called him again. He said he was tired, but that if I insisted on a meeting, it was okay.

"You don't have to come down here," I said. "We will come to your place. Dick, we have to move. The Governor and Abrams† will seek to lessen what you do."

He said, "No, I called Allee.‡ Allee said Morgado called him and said, 'Do whatever Ravitch tells you to do.' So I told him to get the checkoff removed and to add the executive-board members as defendants."

I said, "I want to sue every picket!"

That afternoon, Allen Schwartz and I drove to Ravitch's apartment. McIver and Silver joined us shortly after we had arrived. Dick looked weary. As we sat sipping tea, Allen and I told Dick that amnesty from the Taylor Law fines and an attempt to get a waiver of the mandatory two days' pay for every day on strike would become a critical issue. I said, "We cannot grant amnesty or a waiver, and we must take the position that the

---

*Filing papers with the Public Employees Retirement Board that would automatically eliminate the TWU's right to a dues checkoff from its members' paychecks.

†Robert Abrams, the State's Attorney General.

‡Dennis Allee was the First Deputy State Attorney General.

matter cannot even be discussed. The penalties are mandatory, and if they try to get relief from the Legislature we will oppose them, even if it means running a candidate against every legislator who votes to waive or soften the penalties.''

April 2. This morning Allen Schwartz told me that Dick Ravitch called him last night and wanted him to talk to me. Allen said Ravitch felt he had been imposed on yesterday when we went to see him. He said he was very tired and had agreed to the meeting only because I insisted. We had come on very strong with Ravitch regarding the Taylor Law. Ravitch said he had been tired and had supported my statements yesterday, but on reflection he does not have the same strong feelings. He said that his job is getting these people back to work without regard to the Taylor Law.

Allen said he'd told Dick that I had a strong view that the Taylor Law must be enforced. Our feeling is that amnesty will become an issue in the bargaining and that we have to have a definite and consistent position. The MTA, the Governor and the Mayor should be taking a joint position against amnesty. Allen also told Dick that it was my position that there could be no waiver of any of the Taylor Law sanctions or of any fine imposed by the court on the union, its officers and its executive-board members.

What is clear here is that the Governor and the Attorney General are leaning on Ravitch and seeking to persuade him not to be supportive of the Taylor Law penalties. They are against our tough line. The fact is that Bob Abrams and the Governor are both in need of labor support and will do anything they can, if they will not be embarrassed, not to upset labor. And so they see me as an anathema on this subject. The one funny line that the Governor made when I spoke with him was that he can't find Bob Abrams. And it is true that Bob Abrams is not on the scene. And that is unusual, since he likes to be in the limelight with the public—but not on this matter.

Allen wants me to be very careful not to create a rift with Ravitch over this. He says Ravitch is more kindly disposed to me and to those around me—Bob Wagner and Allen himself—than he is to Carey, Morgado and Berger,* because he knows that we are fighting for the public interest, that we have no political agenda and that the City's future depends on the success of our efforts.

_____

*Steven R. Berger, a Carey appointee to the MTA board.

April 4. Today we had our labor meeting in the morning: Schwartz, McIver, Silver, Wagner, Leventhal. The feeling is that Ravitch is doing things on his own and is not as experienced as McIver and Silver would like him to be. He may be making offers that we will ultimately not be able to support. And because there is now a strike, we ought to see what we can get out of this strike, as we are already taking the inconvenience and the pain. I reported to the group that I had spoken to Ravitch last night after I finished the press conference. I called him from a street telephone. He was home eating, and he said, "Call me later." I called again about 10:30. At that time he said to me, "There isn't any movement. I think we are in for a long strike. Lawe is not in any control, and until he gets into some position of leadership he can't do anything. I don't expect anything to happen for a number of days."

I said, "I would hope that you will now seek to get back the right to have part-time employees."

His response was "We can't do that. That is a strike issue." And the thought flashed through my head, Doesn't he realize that we already have a strike? But I didn't say it. So that bothered me, because it is clear that we are now at the point where most people thought we never could be—namely, we are in a strike and we are taking it. We should be maximizing our position. Well, I reported this conversation to our group this morning. And they laughed, just as anyone would, about his characterization of a strike issue.

I then heard Silver say, "But now, look, the problem is that Ravitch is now almost at the breaking point. He may be so resentful of what you are doing to him—as he sees it, pushing him—that he may simply walk away from the negotiations and say, 'The Mayor will have to settle this his own way, since he is directing me and doing things that I am not supportive of.' He could blame it all on you. That is the danger. And therefore you should be very careful what you say to him, because he could go over the brink."

So I called Ravitch on the phone and I said, "Dick, I would like you to meet regularly with Silver and McIver, twice a day, because I am called on all the time and interrogated by reporters on what I am doing. I want to be in a position to say that I am working very closely with you, and the way to do that is for you to meet with my people."

He said, "I am willing to meet, but we can't set these meetings up, because I don't know where I am going to be. Everything is an emergency."

I said, "Dick, I would like to institutionalize those meetings. You tell me when—one P.M. or one A.M., at your convenience. And if you have to cancel them, fine. We will work around you, but they should be institutionalized."

He kept saying, "No, I don't think it is necessary. If you want to meet with me I am happy to meet with you, but I don't think it is necessary to do it that way."

I said, "Dick, I think it is." I could feel his pique at the other end of the line.

He said, "I have to get ready. I have to be in court this afternoon and I can't meet at one P.M."

I said, "We will meet whenever you want to as soon as the court proceeding is closed."

He said, "Okay. I will come down as soon as the proceeding is closed. I will come down to City Hall."

Then he said, "I don't want to meet with Carey's people." I had suggested that the meetings be with Sandy Frucher, and with McIver and Silver representing me, and Ravitch as the chairman of the MTA. Why he doesn't want to meet with Frucher I don't know. I suspect he doesn't like him.

Also, in the morning meeting Allen said that the Governor's people wanted to withhold the checks of the transit workers, checks that were payment for services performed before the strike. They had checked out the law and the law specified that if a private employer did that it would be a misdemeanor—a crime. But that the law had been amended several years back so as to exempt the State from that provision. It would simply be a breach of contract, in which case the transit workers would have the right to sue in a civil court, which would take weeks or months.

I said, "No, we are not going to do that. I don't think that is sensible either as a matter of equity or as a matter of public relations." So we dropped that.*

Well, Ravitch came in the afternoon. He was calm. His position was that the judge should not try to mediate but should simply impose penalties. It is our judgment that that is a mistake, that the judge can be helpful as a mediator. But we are not going to tell Ravitch how to run this thing. I did, however, say to Ravitch, "Look, what you have to do is make it clear that you are ready, willing and able to meet twenty-four hours a day."

---

*We learned later on that the transit workers and the Governor's office were spreading the rumor that it was I who had made that suggestion. In fact it was Sandy Frucher who had made the original suggestion, the night of the strike. I heard him say it. And we had turned it down at that point.

He said, "I am, and I have said that."

I said, "But you haven't said it in a way that is helpful. I have heard you, and I have seen you on television. What you have said is that you are ready and willing to meet as long as it is understood that the TWU is going to talk about givebacks, and until they are willing to talk about givebacks, you are not going to talk about cash [meaning increases]. Then you have John Lawe saying, 'We are not going to meet unless they drop givebacks from the table.' And it looks as if both of you are being intransigent. What you should say, Dick, is the following: 'I will meet every day. In fact, I am going to be at the Sheraton Centre at nine o'clock every morning. I will be there all day, and I want John Lawe to come. I don't care what he says about whether he wants to talk about givebacks or increases. I am there to talk about everything, and we are going to sit down and we are going to talk and we will lock the doors. I am there.' Then, Dick, have the television cameras there. They will be there showing that Lawe never comes—but that you are there. That means that they are intransigent and you are willing to sit down and talk."

The weekend of April 5–6 was a turning point. By then it was clear that although the dollar amount had not yet been fixed, the maximum penalties would be levied against the striking union and its membership. By then, labor's intransigence had been clearly demonstrated by Ravitch's declaration of his willingness to discuss all subjects at all times. And most important, during the first week of the strike New Yorkers had demonstrated that they were willing and able to take it. After four days of walking the surprises were over, and the momentum, albeit fickle, had alighted on management's side.

As Joyce Purnick of the *Times* reported on April 6 under the headline "KOCH IS AVOIDING THE NEGOTIATIONS, BUT HE REMAINS DEFINITE PRESENCE":

His city was struggling through the tangle of a mass-transit strike, the labor talks were at a standstill, relief was nowhere in sight and Mayor Koch was singing—walking tall, hands planted firmly in pockets, and singing "Everything's Up to Date in Kansas City" as he headed for one of his frequent news briefings at Police Headquarters.

"What's important to me is that the people feel psychologically up," the Mayor said. "They are reacting superbly. Superbly! They are the city's strength. And that makes my job easier."

Facing the most severe test of his 26 months in office, the Mayor is doing what comes naturally—personally rallying his constituency and happily walking the city's streets like a candidate in search of a campaign. Throughout the wearying week, Edward I. Koch has remained distinctly, ebulliently Edward I. Koch—playing the same flamboyant, aggressively public role that he has fashioned into his trademark.

"I am trying to shore up the morale," Mr. Koch said, explaining what he sees as his key responsibility during the strike. His role in the negotiations, he says, is to support Richard Ravitch, chairman of the Metropolitan Transportation Authority and its chief negotiator.

ROLE UNLIKE LINDSAY'S

Unlike former Mayor John V. Lindsay, who took a direct role in settling the transit strike of 1966—and ended up approving a 15 percent increase that most now consider excessive—Mayor Koch has not participated in the talks. He points out that the Transit Authority of 1966 was a quasi-independent city agency, while the Metropolitan Transportation Authority is under the aegis of the state, further removed from the Mayor's authority.

At the same time, the outspoken Mr. Koch has not been at all silent or passive about this strike. As the dispute enters its second week, some close to the negotiations are beginning to say that the role Mr. Koch is playing is every bit as central as John Lindsay's to the unfolding drama of the strike.

In the first few days of the strike, as he went around the city praising Mr. Ravitch and saying he would not insert himself into the negotiations, Mayor Koch repeatedly denounced the demands of the Transport Workers Union as "unreasonable," and injected the city directly into the tangle of legal proceedings surrounding the strike by threatening to sue the T.W.U. for more than $925,000 a day in damages.

Despite the support he expressed for Mr. Ravitch, he has refused to guarantee he would support whatever settlement Mr. Ravitch ultimately recommends, and confirmed that his four appointees to the 14-member M.T.A. board "might" have to vote against any recommended settlement he found too generous. "I am supportive of Richard Ravitch, but I am not going to give up my ultimate power of decision," Mr. Koch said.

THREAT TO RAVITCH SEEN

The Mayor does not control enough M.T.A. votes to scuttle a settlement. However, some persons close to the dispute say his threat to withhold support could do precisely what Mr. Koch says he does not want to do—undercut Richard Ravitch. And staying away from the table and preserving the right to denounce the settlement would also make it easier for Mr. Koch to blame others for an increase in the 50-cent fare.

The Mayor's top aides say he has been deliberately distant from the talks because he wants to avoid the appearance of a link between any transit pact and the city's talks with its municipal unions later this spring. "I am a participant—*not* a partner," Mr. Koch said before the strike began. But because he knows such a link is inevitable, the aides say, the Mayor is continuing to exert pressure from a distance.

"He says he's not involved directly in the strike, but he is," said Victor Gotbaum, who—as head of District Council 37, the municipal employees' union—has long been at odds with the Mayor.

"What he's doing is undercutting negotiations," Mr. Gotbaum said. "Every action he takes prolongs the strike. While he maintains he will not involve himself in the strike, he's using a magnificent manipulative technique.

"He's involved himself with the straphangers, and has made himself a victim, instead of looking for some kind of solution. I think going to all the bridges is fine. But he's avoiding his responsibilities."

DISPUTE WITH KHEEL

Mr. Gotbaum's words echoed those of Theodore W. Kheel, an observer for the Central Labor Council, who repeatedly attacked Mr. Koch last week for remaining aloof from the negotiations. (Mr. Koch, in turn, lashed out at "hired guns," which Mr. Kheel took to be an allusion to himself.) Others closer to the labor dispute argue that the Mayor is involved, but not overtly, and should acknowledge that.

"Ed Koch is the single most important party in those talks, whether he's at the table or not," says one labor expert who is neutral in the negotiations. "In a labor dispute of this magnitude, talks aren't conducted only at a table. They are conducted in an environment, and he is creating the environment. He is at the table in spirit."

Mayor Koch's answer to theories and allegations about his role in the talks is much the same every time he is asked. "I will participate when *I* think it appropriate," he says. "But I will never do an end run around the chief negotiator, the way other Mayors did. Under Beame and Lindsay the labor unions owned the city. No more!"

"They want me to do an end run around Ravitch," he said during a lunch in Chinatown with members of his staff.

"They're trying to play you off against each other," agreed Corporation Counsel Allen G. Schwartz, a good friend of the Mayor and a close adviser on the strike. Also advising Mr. Koch on the strike are the Deputy Mayors, and David Margolis, president of Colt Industries, an old friend who advised Mr. Koch during the 1978 union negotiations and, like Mr. Schwartz, closely mirrors Mr. Koch's view of labor relations.

Maureen Connelly, who provided key counsel as the Mayor's press secretary two years ago, has left City Hall for a position with David Garth, the campaign consultant, but is in touch with the administration and telephoned the Mayor once, he said, to advise him not to bother responding to Mr. Kheel.

REFUSES TO 'LAY DOWN'

"How can I not?" asked the Mayor. Asked to respond to the charge that some of his tactics might be inflammatory and could prolong the strike, Mr. Koch said: "We have two philosophies. One is to lay down and let them run over you. The other is to say we'll respond with all of our defenses. You just cannot lay down —the city is not going to take a dive."

"How many people believe we should give in? How many people believe we should give in only to a reasonable, responsible settlement?" he asked at a meeting of the Lexington Democratic Club, which is in his former Congressional District on the East Side, one night during the week. He asked for a show of approving hands, and got it, just as he had done, during his mayoral campaign, on the subject of the death penalty, which he supports.

"Do we want to do what's responsible?" he demanded of enthusiastic workers in the garment district who gathered about him and his retinue of television cameras the next day.

There and everywhere else he ventured last week, the Mayor implored New Yorkers to give him their support, and received expressions of it overwhelmingly. The Mayor's nervous energy, often betrayed in a tapping of the foot or the rapping of his knuckles on his knees, did not seem to flag till Friday, when he overslept ("It won't happen again," he said), and aides said he was holding up well.

"He is at his best in times of crisis," said Deputy Mayor Robert F. Wagner Jr.

Mr. Koch said, "the adrenalins are flowing," riding up York Avenue one evening after the rush hour traffic had thinned out. He leaned out of the window to ask a cab driver "How'm I doin'?" He was told "great," and he beamed.

"I think there's no life comparable to mine," said the Mayor of strike-bound New York City. "None. There is never a boring day. Never!"

There was something in the atmosphere of strikebound New York that made people, and not just me, ebullient. Women in their Madison Avenue business suits strode along wearing their Uptown nylons and their jogging sneakers. People pulled rusty bicycles out of basements. Everyone had an excuse for being a little late. On the rainy days, New Yorkers looked as if they'd just stood under a downspout. Somehow, all those things made people feel better about themselves and their city.

It was against this backdrop of rugged self-confidence that I reintroduced "wacko" into the Gotham lexicon. Every day, at every bridge, a faintheart would appear. Always there was one: abusive, crude and persistent. The fainthearts came in all sizes. Hundreds of supportive faces would stream by my traveling press conferences, but one faintheart would linger. I have always loved hecklers. And I have used them well. But when I discovered "wacko," I added a new dimension to my repertoire of anti-heckler devices. It caught on immediately. And it served to lift the public's spirit.

April 5. On each day of the strike, I have been out at the Brooklyn Bridge, at the Staten Island ferry terminal, on the Williamsburg Bridge, at the 59th Street Bridge. The purpose is to get around and show people where I am. To talk to them. The press has nothing to do but follow me around. So I am on the radio all day long with these running comments. It is really funny to hear the radio, as I occasionally do when I am in the car.

The most recent incident took place on Friday. On Thursday you had two people, a woman and a man, both part of the crazy movement, or wackos, as I prefer to call them. The woman was yelling obscenities. "You bastard." You know, like in a movie. I

"Guess who Mayor Koch called a wacko today."

From *The New Yorker*, November 10, 1980

ignored her. What can you do? She was a woman. You cannot respond with equal indignities. It wouldn't look nice.

Then you have the guy, and he was—well, he looked crazy. He had a helmet on and he just looked nutty. He was handing out literature for the United Labor Party or the Progressive Labor Party, the same group to which that doctor who assaulted me belonged. Really wild. And he looks as if *he* were going to assault me. And it may be a macho quality in me at this particular moment, after my success in wrestling one of these nuts to the ground, and my success in trying the case and getting him convicted, but I said to this guy, "Now, look, if you put a hand on me I am going to have you arrested."

Then yesterday another one of these wackos coming over the

bridge in the rain began to yell, "You union-buster, you! You strikebreaker!" And it was interesting because everyone else was cheering me. You have this one wacko. So I said to the press, "You know, the wackos apparently don't come out in the rain. Only one."

Then I went to give a pint of blood. There is a blood shortage. I announced it and said people should go give blood. If you tell people to give blood, you have to give blood yourself. So I went down to the blood bank in the World Trade Center. And it was street theater. The press and television were there. I played it very straight. They gave me the Lorna Doone cookie, and I said, "This is a first-rate Lorna Doone."

I include that because there is the question of How does the Mayor come over? Does he have to come over as a very serious person who is so concerned about the strike that you can see the tears or the rage in his eyes? No. Part of what I do is to be an optimist and tough, and I think also humorous at the same time. It is a delicate balance.

What I enjoy, of course, is having Victor Gotbaum express, as he has on several occasions, his frustration and distress that somehow or other the people are very supportive of what I am doing. He can't understand that. They are supposed to hate me because there is a strike. I haven't given the maximum statement yet. It is too provocative. You see, we are clearly able to cope with this crisis. Somewhere in the neighborhood of 88 percent of the people who work in the City are getting to their jobs. It is 81 percent in the apparel industry, and 90 percent in the printing industry. The City employees are 86 percent. It is way up there. At some point, I would like to say, "Mass transit. Do we really need it?" That would drive these union people crazy. Absolutely crazy. So I won't say it. Maybe at the end I will.

April 7. This morning the Governor called. He said he was going to ask Basil Paterson* to become involved in the strike. He said Basil could be used to deal with the dissenters in the TWU who are black and Hispanic. What he wants is to include Basil in a mediation panel. He said he wanted to pursue getting some of the work-rule changes and management prerogatives back. He referred to them as buybacks. His final statement was "Walter Gellhorn is more like Walter Cronkite." By that he meant that he didn't think Gellhorn was doing such a good job of negotiating but was more like an anchorman on television making announcements.

*At this time, New York's Secretary of State.

I reported to our labor people that Ravitch had told me that Sandy Frucher was creating problems for him by negotiating around him. In my telephone conversation with the Governor I mentioned that. He said, "No, Frucher would not be doing that."

I have the feeling that the Governor is seeking to bring the strike to a close by getting the work-rule changes off the table and signaling some kind of forgiveness on the penalties. I am against that, and I have said to the press on many occasions that there can be no amnesty from the Taylor Law penalties. I have said, "The Governor, Ravitch and I are against it, and only the Legislature can allow it. And I believe that since they are all running for office and know that the people of the City and State are against amnesty from the Taylor Law, they would not dare vote for it."

In the afternoon, there were reports from Albany quoting Warren Anderson* as saying that there would be no amnesty. Then John Marchi† called me to say that while he had once voted for amnesty, in 1966 (he referred to it as "one bite into the apple"), he would not permit it to happen this time.

Ravitch called in the afternoon and said that he had been very much distressed by the introduction of Basil Paterson's name. Then he said that John Zuccotti‡ was also going to be introduced by the Governor. Ravitch was opposed to that and said that he would make sure it did not happen.

April 8. I called Ravitch this morning at 7:30 from Police Headquarters in advance of the press briefing. Ravitch said he had killed the introduction of Zuccotti by the Governor and that it would not happen.

Then I called Ravitch again during our labor-panel meeting and asked him if we could meet today. We had decided that at that point what we should really want is the freedom to hire part-timers. Ravitch's position has been that part-timers are off the table and he will not pursue that avenue.

I said, "Dick, the judge at this very moment is making his decision, and Allen Schwartz will be calling us shortly to tell us what it is. We are at the highest point, with public sentiment in our favor. I think it is important that you come out of this with givebacks that are quantifiable."

---

*Leader of the Republican Majority in the State Senate.
†Chairman of the State Senate Finance Committee and the third-ranking Republican in Albany.
‡Governor Carey apparently considered that Zuccotti, a well-known lawyer and negotiator, might be able to settle the strike.

He said, "I am not interested in face-saving."

I said, "I am not interested in face-saving either. I am interested in saving dollars, and your single request is not adequate."

He said, "What would you ask for?"

I said, "The four items that are set forth in today's *New York Times* editorial."

The *Times*'s encouragement and advice were as follows:

New York, Working

It wasn't easy to get to Manhattan and back yesterday, the dreaded day after the holidays. For some, commuting meant long waits that wore their patience thinner than their useless subway tokens. But cheered on by Mayor Koch, a symbol of irrepressible resistance, New York worked yesterday. It worked because the people willed that it should. It worked because they understand what surrendering to the 12 percent-a-year wage increases demanded by the Transit Workers Union would mean: not only higher taxes and fares but also a punishing precedent for other municipal unions. And the defects of the transit system would remain untouched.

New Yorkers want a subway and bus system that can be operated for their convenience and comfort as well as for the benefit of those who work in it. Underground, they want reasonably clean trains with doors that work. In the streets, they want buses with signs they can read and engines that run quietly. The M.T.A. seeks contract changes to accomplish those aims:

☐ Foremost is a proposal to use part-time personnel at change booths that are busy only at rush hours. No one who has a job would lose it, but the M.T.A. calculates that eliminating paid useless time and evening overtime would save $21 million a year.

☐ The authority seeks to stop the 10 percent weekend differential given drivers for working Saturday or Sunday. That would save about $7 million, about the same as one percentage point in increased wages.

☐ The M.T.A. also wants to eliminate some unusual payments for report-writing time; bus drivers get 20 minutes a day to complete a form that takes about 10 minutes at most—and is often done within the paid working day. The saving might total $1.5 million a year for each minute eliminated.

FRED W. McDARRAH

On MacDougal Street in 1966. With the support of the Villagers who worked out of this storefront, I was able to carry all ten South Village (Italian) election districts when an Italian in the previous election had been unable to do so.

UPI

Examining the 1963 district leader election returns with Carmine DeSapio. If I had not defeated Carmine I doubt whether I would have had the credibility and support to go on to become Councilman, Congressman and, ultimately, Mayor. In a perverse way, all that I am today I owe to Carmine G. DeSapio.

FRED W. McDARRAH

Sixth Avenue and 8th Street in Greenwich Village: 1964. It was this picture—Robert F. Kennedy, Bill Passannante and me—that, when I produced it four years later in R.F.K.'s apartment, helped me gain his support in my 1968 race for Congress. Kennedy had thought I had opposed him in his campaign for the Senate. This photo proved I had supported him. His whole demeanor changed. I remembered what his brother Jack had said: "Forgive your enemies, but never forget their names," and I quoted it to him.

With Carol Greitzer, my running mate, and Marty Berger, president of the Village Independent Democrats, celebrating the returns in my first race for district leader.

FRED W. McDARRAH

Congratulating Nelson Rockefeller, on the Senate side of the Capitol, upon his swearing in as Gerald Ford's Vice President. Between us is New York City Mayor Abraham Beame; in the background is my Congressional colleague, and later New York State Governor for eight years, Hugh L. Carey.

With John LoCicero (left foreground) at an antiwar rally in Central Park, 1972. When I ran for the City Council in 1966, opposition to the Vietnam War was one of my issues. When I entered Congress in 1969, I was one of a small group of Representatives who had publicly declared their opposition to the war.

Thirteen debates in eleven days: Mario Cuomo and I were both tired and glad when those endless debates were almost over. In 1977 I began as sixth in a field of seven and finished on top. We made very few mistakes.

UPI

It got to the point where I could tell you how many people used which subway at any stop in my Congressional district.

GILLES PERESS/MAGNUM

Celebrating my victory in the 1977 Mayoral race with my old friends Charlie Rangel and Herman Badillo—and hanging on to Bess Myerson for dear life.

MARTY LEVICK/BLACK STAR

After the first cabinet changes, but before the midterm shakeout. Left to right: Bob Tierney, Herb Sturz, Ronay Menschel, Phil Trimble, Herman Badillo, Peter Solomon, Diane Coffey and Phil Toia.

Haskell Ward: on television
he was brilliant.

Basil Paterson:
a first-rate mediator.

Two success stories. Frank Macchiarola is universally perceived as a
great Schools Chancellor. He got the City's children reading and doing
math above the national average. Bob McGuire was the best Police
Commissioner the City of New York had ever had.

Dan Wolf: the person whose judgment has been for me, over time, the best. He has an extraordinary ability to sense what people are thinking even when they don't voice it. When people give me advice, I take his most often.

David Garth at his feisty best. He was a principal architect of my 1977 Mayoral election victory, and is a devoted friend. I couldn't have won in 1977 without these four factors: Garth, Bess Myerson, the New York Post endorsement and the endorsement of the Daily News.

Senator William Proxmire. Not withstanding his negativism, he ultimately helped the City of New York. He held our feet to the fire.

Carol Bellamy. At a *New York Post* editorial-board meeting in late 1981 the editors asked me, "Why is Carol Bellamy so popular?" I said, "It must be her high cheekbones. But," I said, "working with her is a horror show." Later I apologized to her for stating my feelings publicly, but I never retracted the substance of my comment. On this particular day the South Bronx/Charlotte Street plan's advocates symbolically interred both Carol Bellamy, the Council President, and Jay Goldin, the City Comptroller, for rejecting federal aid to rebuild the South Bronx. In the picture below I am standing with my deputy mayor—one of the seven— Herman Badillo, whose ineptitude at the Board of Estimate ultimately destroyed the plan.

The 1980 transit strike: When I saw the people streaming over the Brooklyn Bridge I thought of the Russian Army crossing frozen Lake Ladoga to save Leningrad. Every morning, on my walk back to City Hall from the 8 A.M. Police Headquarters press briefing, I would stop at the foot of the Brooklyn Bridge to encourage the walkers and confront the wackos. (Below) John Lawe and Dick Ravitch announcing the settlement of the transit strike. The City won the strike in the streets; the Metropolitan Transportation Authority lost it at the bargaining table.

Tony Gliedman, Commissioner of Housing Preservation and Development, a gifted administrator.

David Margolis, president of Colt Industries—a close friend, an adviser and one of the smartest people I know. In addition to everything else, he saved my life in 1981 in a Chinese restaurant when he applied the Heimlich maneuver as I was choking on my favorite cuisine.

Demonstrators (right) at Sydenham Hospital, peacefully protesting its closing. Cops under assault (below) defending the hospital from the mob that was bent on forcibly taking it over.

Campaigning with Walter F. Mondale (above) in 1980. I held my nose while voting for Jimmy Carter's reelection, but voted with pride for Mondale. With Governor Carey (below) I met Carter at the West 30th Street heliport during the 1980 Presidential campaign. I guess we knew more than he did about how he was doing.

Carter
Mondale
Koch

Addressing the 1980 Democratic National Convention in Madison Square Garden. It was here that the TV cameras caught Bella Abzug telling me to "Shut up!" as I said, "We cannot allow our nation to become hostage to the mad ambitions of the Ayatollah Khomeini." Later that year, at his request, I greeted Republican candidate Ronald Reagan (right) at Gracie Mansion to brief him on the City of New York's fiscal condition. The knowledge Reagan gained in this briefing resulted in his supporting, as President, New York City's receiving the $600-million drawdown of the federal loan guarantees, against the advice of his own Secretary of the Treasury, Donald T. Regan.

Robert F. Wagner, Jr., Deputy Mayor for Policy. Bobby is the repository of the City's history. He has unerring good judgment, a brilliant analytical mind and the skills of a diplomat.

Nathan Leventhal, Deputy Mayor for Operations. Nat is the best administrator I have ever met. He is totally dedicated to getting the job done, whatever the job is. And he is selfless and self-effacing: two very rare qualities in government.

The nuts-and-bolts crew: Bill Rauch (left), Maureen Connelly and Victor Botnick. Each of them is capable of doing whatever is required in a campaign. Rauch: the street campaign, any logistics and advance job. Connelly: all research and campaign managing. Botnick: the avenging angel.

Here I am towering above the City of New York like a colossus. This was taken from a boat in the East River with me teetering at the edge of the rail.

A sad moment: conceding defeat in the 1982 Democratic Gubernatorial primary election before the hundreds of friends who had gathered in the ballroom.

Conducting the All City High School Band on the steps of City Hall. No other job could ever provide the same excitement, challenge and satisfaction as being Mayor of the City of New York.

☐ Finally the M.T.A. wants a promotion process more like that of other municipal agencies. Now new employees move to the top of their grade within a year. Stretching this process out over three years could save more than $25 million.

If the M.T.A. can stand firm and win these changes, some of the spending increases proposed for improved maintenance would be covered. And the changes would increase the productivity of new employees. Standing firm will be difficult because other municipal unions are leaning over the balcony to watch, preparing to demand for themselves every half percentage point in wages that the transit workers win. Their expectations of parity are not necessarily reasonable. Some productivity issues of overriding importance to the M.T.A. may be wholly irrelevant in the case of other unions.

But one thing should make the job of the M.T.A. and the city negotiators easier: New Yorkers are walking and waiting to improve their transit system and to save their city.

Ravitch disagreed with the *Times*'s advice, and mine, as indicated in the rest of my log for April 8:

He [Ravitch] said, "Part time is not possible, and I know that we have a difference of opinion. I know that you would settle for a lower increase and no givebacks, and I want a higher increase and givebacks." [This, of course, is not accurate. I wanted the lowest increase *and* givebacks.]

I said, "Dick, let's meet tonight. How about ten o'clock at your apartment?"

He said, "I will have to call you."

I said, "It is very important that we meet, because it will be terrible if we go through all of this pain and inconvenience and end up with nothing." Then I put Allen Schwartz on the phone and he summarized the judge's ruling, which provided for a $1-million fine against the several unions involved, as well as a $250 fine against the officers, and a further court direction to John Lawe that the men go back to work. Then I got back on the phone and said, "Dick, again, we are at our maximum strength."

He said, "I agree with you, and we can get further things in the future contracts to come."

I said, "We will never be in the kind of position we are in today. We are surviving a strike. You can press for the maximum demands. Please, think about it."

At about 10:30, Dick Ravitch, Dan Scannell* and Lew Kaden†
came to Gracie Mansion, and they stayed until about 1 A.M. With
me were Allen Schwartz, Bruce McIver and Ed Silver. The
conversation was as follows:

First Ravitch went through the giveback question again.

I said, "I care about both getting a low increase and getting
givebacks. And if we go through this strike (and we are now
eight days into it) and you don't get anything back after putting
forty-one givebacks on the table, the people will say that we
suffered for nothing and that we should have settled the strike a
long time ago."

Ravitch said, "The Governor has turned into a hawk. He is
now more interested in givebacks than you are. I expect to see
him on the Brooklyn Bridge with you." What he was saying was
that the Governor, who shifts every day apparently, believes now
that a tough line is the best line and senses my success with it as
something to be envied. We ended the meeting with my trying to
get Ravitch to try to get the part-timers as the major giveback, to
which he replied, "How long a strike would you take for each
giveback? How many days for each giveback?"

I said, "Your mind-set is wrong. That is not the question. You
should say to yourself every day, 'I am going to win them,' and
then, day by day, you make a determination as to what you can
ultimately win. The labor people don't say, 'How many days
should I stay out?' They fight us tooth and nail. And that is what
we have to do."

April 9. This morning I went to Police Plaza, where I had my
daily press conference. In response to one of the questions from a
newsman, I said, "Our negotiator, Dick Ravitch, is willing to be
in a room twenty-four hours a day with John Lawe until the strike
is over. We never left the negotiations. It was the labor people
who left. We are always prepared to be at that table."

Then a reporter said, "Have you called John Lawe to tell him
this?"

I said, "No, but I am sure he is aware of it. But I will call him
as soon as I get back to the office."

I called Lawe when I got back to the office. I asked him if he
would come to the Sheraton Centre Hotel with Dick Ravitch and
stay there around the clock until an agreement was reached.

He, in his wonderful Irish accent, said, "The six-and-eight

*Daniel T. Scannell was vice-chairman of the MTA.
†Lewis B. Kaden was counsel to Ravitch.

offers were never cleared up. They are creating difficulties for me with my members. They are pushing me to the wall on that one. The Long Island Rail Road strike was settled at nine and a half percent. That is a problem for me." (I later called and checked with the MTA, and no such settlement had been entered into.) "Mr. Mayor," he said, "I would like to get movement as soon as we can. We will look at two or three of the givebacks."

I then called Ravitch and told him of my conversation with Lawe. Ravitch, in a very querulous voice, asked, "What did you mean when you said, 'We will always negotiate and be at the table'?"

I said, "By we, I meant you. You represent the Governor, me and the MTA."

He said, "I am willing to go there, but I cannot be there until three P.M., and I will stay only as long as it is worthwhile."

I said, "No, you have to say that you will go there at three P.M. and stay there twenty-four hours a day—that you will eat there, sleep there and so on."

He said, "I will not do that. I have to go home to sleep."

I said, "No, stay at the hotel. If you want, have Diane come to the hotel and spend the night with you there." He got angrier. I said, "I have every right to ask you to do that. I am making it possible to have the citizens do what they have to do so as to make it possible for you to do what you have to do."

He said, "I am not going to give up my family obligations, and you don't have the right to ask me to do that."

I said, "Yes, I do. That is the nature of government."

He said, "Are you suggesting that I am shirking my responsibilities?"

I said, "Not at all. I am simply saying that you have to be at the hotel."

He said, "I won't let you say that to me."

I said, "Okay, I will say that John Lawe is willing to work twenty-four hours a day at the hotel but that you are not."

He said, "You are threatening me."

I said, "No, I am not." And then he hung up.

At about two o'clock this afternoon Basil Paterson called me. His voice was very hostile. He said, "I heard that you told the *New York Times* editorial board that if I come into the negotiations as a mediator, I will give away the City."

I said, "That is not true. I praised you for your abilities as a mediator. I said to them, 'Basil was the chief labor negotiator and the Deputy Mayor for Labor Relations when he was in my administration. Now he is the Secretary of State and he provides good advice to the Governor. But whether he comes into this particular matter is dependent on whether Ravitch and Lawe want him to.'''

Basil said, "That is fine. That is my position also. I am glad I checked with you."

Then the Governor called at about 3:30. His opening words were "Ed, if you are going to make any announcements on the negotiations, I want you to first call me and let me know what you plan on saying."

I said, "What are you talking about?"

He said, "You announced that there would be around-the-clock negotiations starting today."

I said, "Okay, now I know what you are talking about. Let me tell you what I said. I have consistently said, and said it again this morning, that the City and the State and the MTA are prepared to have twenty-four-hour negotiations. I urged John Lawe to come back to the table and enter into these negotiations. The newsmen asked if I had told that to John Lawe. I said, 'No, but I have said it so many times publicly that I am sure he knows it. But just for the record, I will call him as soon as I get back to my office.' So I called him, and he said he would do that if I asked him to."

The Governor said, "Well, you know what Lawe is saying, don't you? He is saying that you are getting soft on the negotiations."

I said, "Me? You know better than that."

He laughed and said, "It is the two of us who are standing up. I want all the givebacks put back on the table, and I have told Ravitch that."

I said, "The problem is that Ravitch doesn't want to do that. He wants to go home to his wife and family at night. I told him to bring his wife to the hotel at night if he wanted to."

The Governor said, "I don't know if I want him in there alone. You know what happens when you bring people in and they make side deals."

I said, "Okay, bring the MTA executive board to the hotel."

He said, "You know there isn't one labor negotiator there?"

I said, "Yes, there is. Scannell is there."

He said, "Oh, yes, that's right. But we might want to have Basil Paterson in the room." I didn't say anything. He said, "But before I do that, I will talk to you." Then he laughed and said, "I like your city, Ed. I've just paid my taxes."

I said, "You, Ravitch and I have got to meet either today or tomorrow."

He said, "I am working on the budget tomorrow. I will call you so that we can get together."

Lawe called again and said, "I spoke to Ravitch at about one P.M. and he did not respond positively to the suggestion that we meet around the clock. Mr. Mayor, I have been avoiding the press, who have been trying to ask me about this. I would like to tell them that the Mayor asked that I meet around-the-clock with management and that I am prepared to do that. Is it okay if I say that?"

I said, "It certainly is, and thank you very much."

On the evening news it was announced that both Lawe and Ravitch had stated that they were now engaged in twenty-four-hour negotiations.

April 10. This morning I called Ravitch at 7:30 from Police Headquarters. I wanted to talk to him before I had my press conference at 8. He was very terse and tense on the phone. I very jovially said, "How are you doing? Are you getting enough sleep?"

He said, "Yes."

I said, "Well, what's up?"

He said, "I can't talk now. I'm leaving to meet with John Lawe."

I said, "Well, just give me a little briefing, so that I come prepared for my eight-o'clock press conference."

He said, "Well, there isn't much to say." And here he became very elusive. "I will be doing something over the next two hours but I don't want to say anything about it now. I know that you will be meeting with the Governor today at eleven."

"That meeting is with you, the Governor and me," I said. "Dick, you know that I am supporting you as the chief negotiator and not cutting off your legs or working around you. Even though we had our tiff yesterday."

He said, "I understand that."

I said, "Tell me what the Governor is going to do."

He said, "I would rather not tell you now."

I said, "You have to tell me now. I can't walk around all day long not knowing what is going on."

He said, "The Governor is meeting with Basil Paterson. Basil will probably be at the eleven-o'clock meeting."

I said, "Is the Governor introducing Basil into the negotiations?"

He said, "Yes." Then the tone of his voice changed and he indicated that, in effect, Basil would be superseding him. I could tell Ravitch was angry and was going to take some kind of action that would prevent that.

I said, "I want you to know that Basil is not going to come into these negotiations without your consent. And if the Governor tries to impose that, I will denounce him. I want you to be at that meeting today."

He said, "I will be at the hotel, which is only two minutes away."

I said, "I am calling the Governor."

He said, "No, don't do that. If I am not at the meeting when you get there, you can call me at the hotel. I have to leave now because John Lawe is waiting for me."

I said, "Okay. Goodbye."

When I got back to the office I called the Governor. He was out, but Morgado returned the call. I said, "It is my understanding that the Governor, Ravitch and I are meeting at eleven A.M. Is that correct? Ravitch knows about the meeting, right?"

Morgado said, "Yes. I personally called Ravitch last night and Ravitch told me that he had a meeting already scheduled and I told him he should adjourn that meeting and be with us." This statement was at odds with what Ravitch seemingly understood. And I believed Ravitch. Yesterday Bob Wagner was interviewed by a reporter. The reporter told him, partly in confidence, that when the reporter had interviewed Morgado, Morgado had referred to me as "arrogant and dumb." This will undoubtedly affect my relationship with him. I will never trust him again. He has always gone out of his way when he is with me to be supportive and say nice things about me. And this makes him very duplicitous.

At 11 A.M. I went to the Governor's office. With me were Bruce McIver, Ed Silver, Tom Goldstein and Allen Schwartz. As we were walking in we met David Margolis, and we all went upstairs to the Governor's office. With the Governor were Morgado, Rohatyn, Ravitch, Kaden and Frucher.

The Governor opened by saying, "I am distressed with the lack of movement. The mediators in these negotiations, especially the Gellhorn panel, are not very good. I want to bring in a new mediation panel. I want Basil Paterson and Joe Crowley* in there. The way it can be done would be that the chairman of PERB, Harold Newman, can make those appointments. The

---

*Joseph Crowley was a professor at Fordham Law School and counsel to the firm of Skadden, Arps, Slater, Meagher and Flom.

current panel is going to bring in a fact-finding report under the PERB regulations which is far too high in its recommendations. Basil can be a mediator as no one else can."

I said, "May I respond now?"

He said, "Yes."

I said, "My position on that matter is that there are people who want to indicate that there is disagreement among the Governor, me, Ravitch and Morgado. I continually say that we are united. Therefore I do not want any action to be taken that would subvert Ravitch and cut off his legs. The question is: Does the introduction of Basil Paterson help Ravitch or diminish his stature and ability to negotiate?" I did not want Ravitch to respond before me, because I could see by his face that he was weary of the subject, although very angry.

Margolis said, "Governor, if you introduce Basil as a mediator, or introduce him in any other fashion, you will be signaling to the people of this city that you are caving in. Basil is known in this town as a friend of labor. He was labor's candidate for the Senate before he withdrew from the race."

The Governor said, "That is unfair. Basil wouldn't do anything that is adverse to us. Are you saying that I can't control my own people?"

Margolis said, "It doesn't make any difference what reality is. And I am not commenting on Basil's performance during the 1978 labor negotiations. I am simply saying every labor person would see his introduction as a weakening of the State's position."

The Governor said, "I would not make the designation. It would be done by Newman of PERB."

Margolis said, "That would be transparent. Everyone would know it was you who did it, and you would be held responsible for a softening of our position. That is how it would be perceived."

Morgado said, "I believe it is important that Basil be appointed. It would be a strengthening of our position."

Margolis said, "You must be kidding!"

Morgado said, "I never kid." Then, turning to me, Morgado said, "When you called John Lawe yesterday you signaled that *you* were soft."

I said, "That is an outrage. Do you think there is anyone in this city who believes I am soft? Do you know anyone in the labor or business world who believes that?"

Morgado's face was livid with anger, and he said, "I don't care what you think."

I said, "I think you *will* care what I think."

At that point the Governor said, "Ed, I have never been disrespectful to a member of your staff, and I don't want you to be disrespectful to a member of mine."

Then Ed Silver asked, "What do you propose to do with the present three mediators?"

The Governor said, "They will be terminated by Newman."

Allen Schwartz then handed me a note, which I read out loud: "If you replace Gellhorn and his two associates, he may then file a report which would be adverse to us and set the dollars higher than he would otherwise."

Kaden said, "We have already en his report, and he is advocating givebacks that we want and he has left the number open."

At that point the Governor said to Ravitch, "What is it you in fact want to settle this for?"

Ravitch said, "It will not be settled for what the Mayor wants. Not at eight plus eight [he was referring to the mediator's last offer], because we are now in a strike and it will be settled for more."

I said, "You are wrong. You are stronger today than you were on the first day of the strike. The people are standing up. I was on the Brooklyn Bridge this morning speaking to people after the rainstorm last night. They are still strong. [In fact, they had appeared weary, though resolute.] Dick, you should give to the Governor and me a confidential memo as to what you are looking for."

At that point, Ravitch explained what he wanted to do. Over and above what he had already told us, he now said he planned to offer an additional cash payment and COLA.*

Both the Governor and I said, "That would not be acceptable to us."

I said to Ravitch, "Why don't you meet with Silver and McIver for me, and with Morgado and Frucher for the Governor, so as to keep things going?"

Ravitch said, "Are you saying that they should be with me in the room?"

I said, "No, but available to you so that you get our input."

Rohatyn said, "I understand your problem, Dick. I know you are not able to meet with everybody, but perhaps someone on your staff could meet with these people. Now," he added, addressing the rest of us, "we should come back this afternoon

---

*A cost-of-living allowance.

so that we can discuss what Ravitch would like to come out with."

Then, at Felix' request, the Governor stepped out of the room. While the Governor and Rohatyn were away, Margolis said to Ravitch, "If they appoint Paterson, you should resign. And you should speak up and say what you think about this."

Ravitch flushed and indicated his anger with Margolis by saying something like "Are you saying I am not doing a good job?"

When the Governor and Felix came back, the Governor said he was postponing his decision on appointing Basil for twenty-four hours.

After the meeting there was a press conference in the Governor's press room. There were television cameras and about fifty news people. The Governor spoke first, Ravitch second. Then the press asked questions, at which time I spoke, along with the others. The thrust of the press briefing had been "We are all working closely with Ravitch."

A reporter asked, "Why are we here?"

"Who called you?" I interjected, as though there were no formal press conference to the best of my knowledge, simply a meeting between me and the Governor, which was no secret. It was clear that the press had been called by the Governor's office to announce Basil's involvement, and that we had prevented it at our meeting. Indeed, my press secretary said that a member of the press said he had seen Basil in the suite, and McIver said he had seen Basil's advance man in the suite. So Basil was obviously there, but he didn't show. Later it was reported that he had left quietly through a side door.

After the press conference our group went to lunch. Margolis said that he thought the deal had already been worked out by Ravitch and Lawe. Allen suggested that the additional moneys— the cash payment and COLA—were probably to take care of the Taylor Law fines, which exceed $1,000 per person as of today.

At 5 P.M. we reconvened our meeting in the Governor's office. At that time the numbers people got to work on the value of the various givebacks. While that was going on, the Governor said, "Why don't the two of us go over to the party for Kevin Cahill? He just had his book published."* The party was being held at John Jay College. We went there along with Bob Wagner. On the

---

*Dr. Kevin M. Cahill was Governor Carey's chief health counselor. The John Jay Press had published his book of *Irish Essays*.

way back to the Governor's office, we heard several reporters express themselves on the radio in the following way: "The Mayor is missing. It may mean that something is happening." And here were Carey and I sitting in his car listening to this. It was interesting to see Carey's reaction. He said, in a stage whisper and with a noticeable bitterness: "The Governor kidnapped the Mayor."

When we got back to Carey's office, Allen Schwartz and David Margolis brought us up to date on the discussions with Morgado and Rohatyn. They said that Ravitch, who had not been at that 5 P.M. meeting, was at the Sheraton Centre Hotel and was prepared to make an offer with the Governor's blessing—two 8-percent increases over and above the roll-ups* and welfare benefits,† with some givebacks that would help pay the 8 percent plus a productivity-gain sharing of ¾ percent or 1 percent certifiable by auditors. Margolis said he thought that was acceptable, and so did Schwartz. Silver and McIver said they did not think Ravitch could sell it.

There were questions next about various aspects of the settlement. Allen said, "Shouldn't we have Ravitch here so that he can go over the proposal in front of us, and make sure that we are all in accord, since the Governor and the Mayor will be supporting it?"

Morgado said, "That won't be helpful. Ravitch is at the edge of his nerve bank. But you can rely on my assertion that Ravitch is taking his instructions from me and will carry out this proposal and not go beyond it without authorization."

Allen insisted that Ravitch should be there, and I said, "It is unreasonable that if the Mayor wants the chairman of the MTA to come here, Ravitch would refuse."

Morgado suggested that we call Ravitch and talk to him, so we got on the phone.

I said, "Dick, tell us what it is that you are going to be offering to the TWU."

Ravitch then outlined the offer, which was different from that described by Morgado. Morgado was in the room, but was not on the phone. I repeated what Ravitch was saying so that everyone could hear. Ravitch said, "In addition to the eight percent in the

*Roll-ups: A number of transit workers hired since the last collective bargaining were being paid, by argreement, at less than the "top" rate. Their salaries were to be rolled up to the "top" rate as part of this settlement.
†Welfare benefits: The New York City Transit Authority contributes a fixed amount to the TWU's health-and-welfare fund to provide health care and other benefits. This fixed payment was to be increased.

first year, we are going to offer a one-percent cash payment.* And weekend differentials† will not be given back to the MTA." The key for us was the additional 1 percent that Ravitch was including in his offer. According to Allen, this was Ravitch's way of giving money to the transit workers to pay their Taylor Law fines.

I said to Ravitch, "This is not what Morgado told us. I am putting Morgado on the phone." Ravitch again told Morgado the proposal in his form. Morgado did not flinch. He just sort of smiled, as though it were not different from his own. But in fact, there was a huge difference in dollars—and a huge difference in psychological impact.

My people then went back to the caucus without Morgado. The thrust of our conversation had been that we were off the hook. We would absolutely oppose any payments over and above the 8 percent that would in effect be giving the TWU back their Taylor Law penalties.

On the telephone, Ravitch had indicated that he was going to be making his proposals after he spoke to his board members. So after I finished my conversation with Ravitch, I had him put Wagner on the phone. I told Wagner that our four board members should oppose anything above 8 + 8. This was about 8 P.M. We then went out to dinner and didn't get back to the Governor's office until about ten o'clock.

At 11 P.M. I received a call informing me that a policeman had been shot in Far Rockaway. The Governor had not come back from his party. So I said, "Everyone should go home. I'm going to Far Rockaway."

At 6 the next morning, after three and a half hours of sleep, I got up and went over to Police Headquarters. McGuire said to me that the officer shot the night before had just come out of the operating room. He had lost his pancreas and other organs. He was in critical condition but stable.

After the morning press briefing, the newsmen reiterated that there were threats of a general strike and quoted Victor Gotbaum and others. I said, "It is understandable that labor groups are supporting the striking unions."

---

*This was to be a nonpensionable bonus of 1 percent tacked onto each paycheck.
†Weekend differentials are overtime payments awarded, usually on the basis of seniority, to maintenance workers. They are either time-and-a-half or double-time.

When I got back to City Hall, Wagner called me. He said he believed that Ravitch would come in with a 9-percent or 9½-percent settlement offer, and that the current proposal, which was close to the 9 percent that Ravitch was seeking to sell to the MTA board, would be turned down.

Then Allen Schwartz called. He reported that the Governor had been told that Ravitch was offering more than had been agreed to when Ravitch, Morgado, the Governor and I and the others had come up with the 8 + 8. Allen said Felix Rohatyn had tried to persuade the Governor not to accept the new proposal, which exceeded 9 + 9. Felix had said that he, Felix, would ultimately have to denounce it. Margolis had called both Felix and Morgado to make it clear that the City administration would not be supporting any such settlement.

At that point Nat Leventhal came in and said that I should call Jack Watson at the White House. In addition to our MTA subway problems, the PATH system* was threatening to go back on strike that evening. At midnight the injunction under the Taft-Hartley Law would expire; there was a no-contract/no-work clause in the contract; so unless the President declared a sixty-day cooling-off period, the PATH system would go back out at midnight. Nat said he had spoken to Peter Goldmark, Jr., chairman of the Port Authority, who controlled the management side in the negotiations, and that Goldmark had recommended that New Jersey's Governor Brendan T. Byrne and I call Washington. Their feeling was that Governor Carey shouldn't be involved here because the President would never do anything for Carey.

So I called Watson and said, "Look, Jack, we need this cooling-off period."

He said, "We're working on it. But don't tell anybody. We don't want the labor people to think the President is stepping in on the side of management. But if it is needed by midnight, it will be done."

I thought, Great.

At our 10:30 A.M. labor meeting, Allen Schwartz proposed, and it was agreed, that I should tell the Governor our position on the offer, so that there could be no dispute about it. When we got Carey on the phone I said, "We have computed the settlement, having gotten the details from Wagner, who got them from Ravitch, who was trying to sell it to the MTA board, and it

---

*Port Authority Trans-Hudson: a surface rapid-transit rail system in New Jersey with a Hudson River tunnel link to Manhattan, operated by the Port Authority of New York and New Jersey.

comes to a 21-percent increase, and in addition to that there are a whole host of extras which they are not even including as a part of the settlement cost.''

The Governor said, "That is not my understanding as to the figures. But in any event," he said, "look, good friend, I knew that you would have to get off of any settlement at some point because of the piranhas outside" (meaning the municipal labor unions).

After I hung up, it was agreed that I should call Wagner and have him make a statement on my behalf so that the MTA board would know my position: this settlement was too expensive for the MTA and should be voted down.

Wagner said, "It looks now like Dick Ravitch will have to break a tie, because the vote without Ravitch is seven to seven. The seven against are your four members and Bellamy, Berger and McAlevey.* Ravitch does not want to have to do that. But the Governor is at this moment talking to Bellamy and Berger to get them to vote for the settlement. It is my feeling that both Bellamy and Berger will ultimately succumb to the Governor's request."

Then Nat came in and said that Jack Watson had heard that the strike was being settled and that the White House now didn't want to issue the injunction on the PATH matter. So I called Watson again.

I said, "Jack, that would be terrible."

He said, "Well, there are these negotiations toward ending the MTA strike."

"Sure," I said, "we have been negotiating for eleven days. Nobody knows that it will be ended today. But even if it were ended you should issue the injunction. Why discommode one hundred fifty thousand people?"

He said, "One hundred sixty thousand."

I said, "Look, let me just say one thing to you. You will ultimately have to do it. You will do it next week maybe. And the President is going to look like an ass. It will be just like Iran. What you should have done early you did too late." I could hear him gritting his teeth. I guess they didn't like to hear Carter described as an ass.

He said, "Well, I understand. We will think about it."

Ultimately they issued an injunction and it was no problem for them.

*Carol Bellamy and John McAlevey, like Berger, were Carey appointees to the MTA board.

Then Bobby called again from the hotel to say, "The Governor called Ravitch and said, 'The Mayor wants to speak with you.' Ravitch does not want to call you because he believes you each already know your respective positions on the matter."

I said, "I did not ask that Ravitch call me. The Governor suggested that he call me. But I think that since the Governor suggested it, it is a good idea. That way there will be no misunderstanding at a future time."

Wagner said that Ravitch had asked him if I would release one City member to vote for the settlement.

I said, "Absolutely not; under no circumstances."

Wagner said that Simpson and Ravitch were up front in describing the settlement as a 22-percent increase, but as a result of alleged productivity savings they were saying it was a settlement of 7½ percent in each year.

Ravitch then called me, and I put McIver and Brigham on the phone. Ravitch said, "I don't have time to go over the figures with you now. Can I speak to you privately?"

I said, "Of course." And the others got off the phone.

Ravitch then said, "I told you from the very beginning that I respected your position, and I know that your position has not changed. The Governor said in his call to me that if I don't get a substantial vote the Governor will disavow the deal and it will become my settlement. What I would like you to do is release one vote."

I said, "No."

He said, "I don't mean one of your four. Have one of your four speak to the other three and ask one of them to vote for it."

I said, "No."

Then Wagner called again and said, "At the present time Steve Berger will abstain, instead of voting against the settlement. According to Berger, Berger and the Governor had a heated conversation on the phone and Berger offered to resign because he did not want to vote for it. Then he agreed to abstain. Ravitch now has the votes."

Ravitch then called to say that the vote was cast and it was now 9-4 with one abstention. And that was the end of it.

Bellamy said it was a "shitty settlement," but she voted for it.

Berger said it was "a bad settlement" and then he abstained. Both said they did not think the MTA could get a better deal if there was a continuation of the strike.

At about 4:45 that afternoon the Governor called again. He said, "Ed, I want to speak to you just as you speak to me and tell you my complaint. I understand that some of your people are going around saying that Morgado and I have undermined the City with the municipal coalition. I have always said that I will only enter into a responsible settlement and that it will always be a matter of the MTA board's judgment as to what is responsible. I have always said I want to know what the costs of the buybacks are. I will put those actual costs in the budget. They have to be costed out, and I told that to Ravitch and I am depending on his figure, which is different from yours. I want you to know that this settlement is computed at five and a half percent a year."

I said, "Governor, is that what they told you?"

He said, "Yes. That is what they say the settlement costs if you figure in the givebacks. And I want you to know that Bob Morgado is one of the finest men I know. And it is wrong of your staff people who are telling the press that he is duplicitous."

I said, "I have never said that to the press or to anyone else. But I do want you to know that when we were together at your office, I was very upset when Morgado said to me, 'I don't care what you think.' I then said to Morgado, 'You *will* care what I think.' "

The Governor said, "I don't believe that a member of my staff would ever say that he doesn't care what the Mayor of the City of New York thinks."

I said, "It was said in front of you."

He said, "I don't remember it."

I said, "There were ten people in that room. Go ask Morgado. He won't deny it. And then go ask Felix Rohatyn."

Our conversation ended in a friendly way, each of us saying that yes, we were friends, even when we could not be in accord. But even as I was speaking with the Governor, Morgado was calling the editorial boards and giving them the Carey-Ravitch line that this was the best that was attainable and that I had somehow been destructive to the atmosphere of the negotiations by being, in their words, "a cheerleader." What was the alternative? To roll over and slit our own throat?

For the first ten days of the strike Ravitch was not going to put forward anything that I didn't agree to, because he was scared to death that he would be labeled the guy who gave away the City. But then what occurred was that Morgado talked him into jettisoning his relationship with me. Morgado then tried to manipulate the editorial boards into giving the other parties kudos and portraying me as intransigent. He said that if they had done it my way there never would have been a settlement, just more pain. I know he did that, because a reporter related to me a conversation he had had with Morgado. But the thing was that it didn't work, because I had had an editorial lunch at the *Times* at which I had told them that the Governor and Ravitch would fold. And then it occurred, as predicted.

Now I wasted no time in expressing my disdain for the settlement. At 7 P.M. on the 11th, the television lights and photographers and reporters were all crammed into the basement conference room at Gracie Mansion. The strike had seemed to last longer than its eleven-day life. Nonetheless, the atmosphere was not one of relief when at 7:05 I stood before the cameras. My formal statement clearly articulated the City administration's mood:

> I have to state at the beginning—and I regret to have to say it—the people of New York deserved a better settlement. The people of this city faced the terrible disruption of the transit strike with courage and great spirit. By doing so, they gave the MTA an unparalleled opportunity to negotiate a reasonable contract. I am sorry to have to say that a majority of the MTA board proved to be of weaker resolve than the people.
>
> I spoke to Governor Hugh Carey and MTA Chairman Richard Ravitch this morning and expressed my strong opposition to their proposed settlement. The four MTA board members whom I appointed voted against the agreement. Regrettably, the other ten members of the board chose to give in.
>
> Over the next several days, different people will describe the settlement in different ways. But the basic fact is that it is too expensive—for the MTA and for the people of New York City. Next year it will add ninety-one million dollars to the MTA's present deficit of an estimated three hundred twelve million; in the two years of the contract it will add two hundred seventy-one point four million dollars.
>
> Although the City's government will not pay the cost, the City's people will, through higher State taxes and the very real possibility of a fare increase. This settlement will also raise the expectations of City workers way beyond what we can possibly afford to pay.
>
> The City won the battle in the streets; the MTA lost it at the bargaining table. For almost two weeks New Yorkers showed

they could withstand what many said was the worst that could happen to the City—and withstand it with grace, spirit, patience and courage. Their message will not be forgotten.

The editorials, as they appeared, were lukewarm. For us that was a victory. Up to that time, in every dispute between me and Carey, the editorial boards had taken the State's side. The Governor was, after all, the one who had rescued the City in 1975. The *News* objected to the size of the settlement and praised the City administration for coming up with a plan that permitted the City to function during the worst turmoil in fourteen years. The *Post* attacked the settlement and praised the givebacks. The *Times* of April 13 offered the most comprehensive picture:

The Unsettling End of It All

The confusion and tension in the streets of New York now move back to its politics. The people weathered a debilitating transit strike with remarkable composure, only to find at the end that there is no fair measure of the value of their sacrifice. How much money, if any, was saved by the agony? How much more might have been saved by struggling on?

Mayor Koch was a scrappy cheerleader. He kept up the people's spirits and, with sound emergency plans, kept the city's economy alive. Weather that was mostly good helped, of course. But the Mayor demonstrated a new public tolerance for horrendous disruption in the interests of saving public money and improving public service. Whether or not Mr. Koch is right to call the final settlement a sellout, he now personifies a new political reality that should make it possible, over time, to obtain more efficiency and value from all public employees.

But this was not the Mayor's strike and his outrage at the settlement, while understandable, is premature. He has not said how much longer he would have held out and what terms he would have accepted. His real concern throughout has been not the cost of the new transit contracts but the cost of their contagion in inflaming the demands of the other municipal unions that he must now confront.

The transit authority was already $200 million in deficit. To avoid irresponsible neglect of its equipment, it was bound to seek a fare increase and higher bridge and tunnel tolls—not to balance its books but to induce upstate legislators to support a further heavy subsidy. It could not "afford" any wage increase. Yet it finally settled for costs of $270 million more over two years—less the sizable fines it will collect from the strikers and the savings it can achieve with the new work rules obtained in the bargain. These may be worth $100 million, or less; only managerial skill, and time, will tell.

If these "givebacks" turn out to be trivial, then Governor Carey and his transit chief, Richard Ravitch, will have misspent a formidable public resolve. But they had to judge the costs of staying shut against the chances of saving $20 million, or even $40 million, but not more. They can't prove that they guessed right. Their stakes, in any case, were relatively modest.

To understand the Mayor's real anxiety it is necessary only to know that, whereas every 1 percent raise for the transit workers cost about $10 million a year, every 1 percent for those employed directly by the city will cost $50 million or more. And the city can afford such raises even less than the state. Mr. Koch wants to settle for less with his workers and he will want them to pay for their raises with still more valuable "givebacks" in work rules and practices. The reputation for toughness that he built up in the strike and emphasized at its end will be tested soon enough. His passion is purposeful, not narrowly self-serving.

In sum, New York's struggle for survival is far from over. The worst possible kind of strike has been survived, and that demonstration will not have been in vain. A new era of better transit management and value—for higher fares and taxes—may be ahead. And the settlement's precedent for other public employees may be marginally useful, or downright harmful. This is not a sport in which winners and losers are comfortably known as the clock runs out. It is the democratic politics of a proud but poor community whose crises will be recurrent and whose future remains uncertain.

Okay. But the real report card was out on the streets. All that weekend of the 12th and 13th I was on the sidewalks. What politician wouldn't have been? People jaywalked across avenues to shake my hand and thank me for standing up. New Yorkers were in a kind of euphoria that weekend. They had been called upon to run the gantlet, and they had done it with style.

15

Closing Sydenham Hospital

ON FRIDAY AFTERNOON, September 12, 1980, Secretary of Health and Human Services Patricia Harris called me. I was having a budget meeting in my office. Present were Jim Brigham, Nat Leventhal, Bob Wagner and Allen Schwartz. When I got on the phone, she said, "Mr. Mayor?" I responded by saying, "Madam Secretary."

She said, "I just wanted to inform you that a letter is being sent to you saying that the Office of Civil Rights has found that there is no Title Six violation as a result of the closing of Sydenham Hospital, and that OCR will continue to monitor the various HHC proposals and programs." The letter, thirty pages long, was a complete vindication of our plan and stated that it entailed no violation of federal law and no racism.

Then Pat said that she was a little distressed to learn that we were closing Sydenham on October 1. I told her that we weren't going to close it until October 15. "Oh," she said, "that makes me feel better." Then she told me that she had provided that report to everyone, including the local Congressman—meaning Charlie Rangel—and that she had personally called him.

I said, "I want you to know that things are going well, and you did it."

She said, "Well, the Metropolitan [Hospital] plan* is

*The Metropolitan Hospital plan was an innovative reimbursement system designed by Bob Wagner and Victor Botnick under which the Federal Government pays 50 percent of the costs of treating medically indigent New Yorkers who are not Medicaid-eligible. The program is still functioning.

going very well, but please don't refer to it as a 'bailout.' I've just read the *New York* magazine article in which it is called a 'bailout' and one of your successes. Other Mayors are coming to me now and asking that I do the same for their hospitals.''

I said, ''Pat, the Metropolitan plan, which is your plan, is remarkable, and it will be looked at by the rest of the country as something special.'' Here I was soft-soaping her, because she had given us heartache over this. When I hung up, the others in the room said they were surprised and impressed with how nice I had been to her.

''Well,'' I said to them, ''she is the sweetheart of Sigma Chi.''

Then, late Monday evening, the 15th, about sixty protesters, primarily black and drawn from throughout the City, began a sit-in in Sydenham Hospital's executive offices. Upstairs some seventy-five patients rested nervously.

Sydenham had been built in 1925 and was the smallest of the City's hospitals. Located in the heart of Harlem, it had been in the forefront of programs to allow black doctors to gain medical experience from which they had been barred elsewhere. It had been for many years an outstanding medical facility. But it was small, and modern medicine required larger and larger spaces for the newest equipment. In the 1950s Sydenham had fallen seriously behind the other municipal hospitals in terms of delivering first-rate medical care. Impartial studies during the Wagner administration indicated that the hospital should be closed and the patient load moved to the nearby and vastly more modern Harlem Hospital. John L. S. Holloman, who was president of HHC under Mayor Beame and who was black, also recommended the closing of Sydenham to the City Council. But always politics intervened. At the suggestion of closing Sydenham Hospital the Harlem leadership would howl, and City Hall would back down. The hospital, in effect, was being preserved as a cultural landmark, not as a hospital. But inadequate hospitals make expensive landmarks. Sydenham's projected deficit for Fiscal Year 1981 was $9.6 million—not staggering next to the Health and Hospitals Corporation's $338-million FY 1981 operating deficit, but nonetheless unnecessary. After all, nothing was being done at Sydenham that couldn't be done more efficiently, and with better equipment, at Harlem Hospital, or St. Luke's or Mt. Sinai, each of which was within a four-minute ambulance ride.

It was clear from the start that despite Sydenham's poor reputation as a medical facility, a reputation that most would not dispute, the hospital could not be closed without a fight. There had been numerous investigations and legal obstacles, but finally the date had been set. After all responsible efforts by the Harlem community had failed, the battle was turned over to the rabble-rousers.

The closing plan called for a one-month phaseout. From September 15 no new patients were to be admitted, and for the subsequent month the patients who were there were to be relocated to other facilities. On the evening of September 15 the rabble-rousers moved in.

At about 10 P.M., I received a call from Victor Botnick. I was having dinner in Chinatown. Victor said that about sixty demonstrators had taken over Sydenham. He said that the media were there and they wanted a response from me. I dictated a statement to Victor over the phone. Victor said that the situation seemed to be under control. There was an ambulance outside in the event anyone needed emergency assistance, and anyone coming to Sydenham would be taken directly to Harlem Hospital. I asked Victor to call Allen Schwartz to clear the contents of my statement. Allen edited the statement on Sydenham and it was released.

We discussed the sit-in the following morning at the cabinet meeting. It was the consensus that Allen should seek a court order with the hope that we could obtain some sort of sanction against the demonstrators. We agreed that there was a danger of crowds building up outside.

On September 16 at 11 P.M. Victor called. He said he had served a contempt order on Cenie Williams, who was there with the Reverend Herbert Daughtry, and that the order was returnable the following day in State Supreme Court. Bobby Wagner suggested we have a press conference to get our side of the story out. So we had a press conference. Present were

Bob Wagner, Allen Schwartz, Bill Devine and Madeline Bohman.*

Two of the reporters, who were black, were very antagonistic in their questioning, in effect saying, Wasn't I a racist for closing this hospital? That gave me the opportunity to point out that the Federal District Court, the Circuit Court of Appeals and Secretary Harris, in her thirty-page report, had all said the charges of racial discrimination levied against the City on the Sydenham closing were unfounded.

I then got a call from Bill Devine saying that the legislators, and in particular State Senator Leon Bogues, wanted to go into the hospital to see those who were sitting in. Devine said he didn't think we should make any exceptions, and I agreed with him.

Then Bogues called me. I told him that I understood the pressure he was under. I also told him that Anthony Watson, executive director of the State Health Services Agency, had called me today to say that it was outrageous I should be attacked as a racist when the Feds and the State were for closing Sydenham. Tony had said he was willing to say that publicly. Bogues said he knew all of that but that he had to appear at the hospital because Charlie Rangel had decided to stay in Washington.

I said, "You can go in, but tell them you called me and that I am willing to meet and talk with you, and that they have no commitment from me on what the police will do in removing people if they think it is necessary." I told him I would ask Bill Devine to let him in, even though Devine was opposed to it. I then called Devine while Bogues was holding on the other line. Devine said that he would be happy to let Bogues in, but he would appreciate it if he didn't stay for more than a half-hour.

Bogues then told me that he understood the demonstrators were trying to organize a citizens' committee to come down to see me and that they were going to seek the involvement of

*William Devine was the First Deputy Police Commissioner. Madeline Bohman was acting vice-president at the Health and Hospitals Corporation, since there was no president at the time. She is now executive director of Bellevue Hospital.

Vernon Jordan, executive director of the National Urban League.

I said, "It won't help. I won't change on this."

He said, laughingly, "I told them you wouldn't change your mind and if they wanted you to they should think about changing the name of the hospital to Mount Zion Hospital." That sounded anti-Semitic to me, but I wasn't inclined to pursue it.

Victor Botnick later reported the scene at Sydenham to me as follows:

At about 8:30 Monday evening, September 15, I received a phone call from a member of the Sydenham Hospital Community Advisory Board, saying that after a meeting held at the hospital earlier in the evening a group of fifty or sixty individuals had decided to sit-in at the facility to prevent the implementation of the closing plan that was to go into effect the next morning.

I called Bill Devine to learn whether the Police Department had been advised of the situation. He called back to say that the Operations Division had heard nothing but that he would have additional information in a few minutes because he was sending a lieutenant in a patrol car to ascertain what was in fact taking place. At about 9:20 he called back to advise me that a sit-in was taking place and that senior police officials were coming to the 28th Precinct to meet with me to discuss the situation and to determine what we should do. I called the Mayor, who was having dinner in Chinatown, and advised him that a sit-in was taking place at Sydenham and that I would have additional information once I was briefed by the police.

At about 10:30 I met with the police, and after a brief conversation it was decided that the implementation of the closing plan would in fact take effect on time the next morning, but that as long as patients' lives were not being placed in jeopardy and as long as the sit-in was confined to the executive suite of the hospital, no attempt would at that time be made to remove the demonstrators.

The next morning, September 16, at 8 o'clock the City officially closed the emergency room. That caused a certain amount of tension with the people who were sitting-in. Nonetheless, the official closing of the emergency room and the continued diversion of ambulances from Sydenham to other hospitals was implemented without incident. In addition, the process for discharging patients to their homes or transferring patients to other facilities was also implemented.

As a result of the discussion that had taken place earlier that morning at a cabinet meeting, a court order was obtained, and about 8 P.M. I returned to the Sydenham facility and we served the court order. When I had the opportunity to walk around the facility, I became concerned by the lack of security. Anyone who wanted to go into or out of the hospital was permitted to do so. However, at that point I decided that it would make no sense for me to intervene, since the situation seemed to be calm.

On Wednesday, against everybody's advice, I decided to go back to the hospital and was again alarmed by the lack of security and order. People were just milling about going into and out of the hospital as they pleased. Others were going in to visit the demonstrators; food was going through windows or through the door; and I was very much concerned and expressed my concern to the Police Department through Bill Devine. As a result, he decided to clamp down and made it very clear that no one was to go into or out of the hospital except those cleared by hospital security or visiting patients, that no additional people would be allowed into the room where the sit-in was taking place, and that anyone who wanted to leave would be permitted to do so but would not be allowed to return.

Next, at about 4 A.M. on Thursday, an additional line of barriers was placed on the sidewalk to prevent people from climbing in and out of the windows of the executive suite, where the sit-in was taking place. But the demonstrators were still able to communicate with their supporters by a voice amplifier. At my urging, the Police Department decided that it was in the best interest of trying to maintain order to cut the power to the amplifier and not let them broadcast over these speakers. The additional barriers and the restriction of access to the room and the restriction about no food going in through the window facing the street became a very heated issue.

On Thursday evening I returned once again to the hospital and was alarmed by the tension that existed in the vicinity surrounding the hospital and in particular the window facing the street where the demonstrators were located. The restriction limiting access to the facility caused additional concern, and State Senator Bogues called the Mayor requesting permission to go in. The Mayor, after careful consideration, decided to overrule the Police Department and permitted him to go in with an attorney with the proviso that they could not stay longer than thirty minutes and that they understood that anyone who decided to come out could not go back in.

On Friday, which was the eve of Yom Kippur, I went up early in the morning and noticed that additional barriers had been set up adjacent to the barriers already in place, and at my request a truck had been parked in front of the window to prevent visual contact between the demonstrators and the people on the street. I went back Friday afternoon and walked around and was concerned once again about the lack of decorum. I noticed that on one of the upper floors an effigy of the Mayor was hanging, and I insisted that the Police Department have it removed.

Chief Duffy* said, "But it is daylight."

I said, "This is the City of New York, Ed Koch is the Mayor, this is City property, I want the effigy down and I am telling you I want it down now."

Chief Duffy said, "Okay. You realize that it is still daylight and we take it down at your risk."

I said, "I will take the full responsibility. I don't believe that if the Police Commissioner, the Deputy Police Commissioner or the Chiefs of Operations or Patrol were here they would approve of the Mayor's being hanged in effigy in a building that we are supposed to be in control of."

So they cut the effigy down, and nothing resulted whatever. I just had the sense that this whole situation was a circus; it was absolutely nuts. As I continued to walk around, people would recognize me and start chanting my name, and the sit-ins, who were able to see me through the window, started to chant: "Botnick, the walls of Jericho will fall again."

By the walls they were referring to the barriers. I said to myself, Thank God I am here with a hundred cops. The number of pickets on the outside increased in the demonstration area, and the demonstrators inside kept yelling that they would accept food only through the window and from the "people," not the police. There were constant speeches to the crowd by the leaders that they could be nourished and receive their sustenance only from their followers, and now with the window restricted they could get no nourishment. They made the window a symbolic situation.

Assemblyman George Miller said to me, "Tomorrow is your holiday and we are going to destroy that holiday."

I said, "Sorry you feel that way."

It was clear to me that tension was rising, and I was extremely

---

*Martin Duffy, Borough Commander of Manhattan North.

concerned, and I expressed my concern to Bill Devine by telephone before going home to celebrate the holiday. As a result of my call, Devine ordered additional police personnel and additional barriers.

On Saturday at about 1:45 P.M., Congressman Charles Rangel, State Senator Leon Bogues, Assemblymen Edward C. Sullivan and George W. Miller and various other officials decided to go in and speak with the demonstrators. They were permitted to do so. The meeting, which lasted about an hour and a half, ended with Rangel and company coming out and attempting to make a speech. As they started to speak, the police noticed that the women at the front of the barriers were being moved to the rear and replaced with an organized group of males, who immediately began to taunt the police behind the barriers. The men standing closest to the barriers started yelling that the "walls of Jericho must come down" and picked up the barriers and started to throw them at the police.

As a result of that, the police reacted and dispersed the crowd. Fourteen police officers were injured and four patrol cars were damaged. In addition, I was told that only two demonstrators were taken to Harlem Hospital for treatment of minor injuries.

Saturday evening as I listened to the radio I heard a live interview with one of the sit-ins on one of the news stations. I couldn't believe that we still were giving them the right to make telephone calls. So I decided to call the number for the executive office of Sydenham.

The phone was answered, "Sydenham Free Hospital."

I responded by saying, "Not for long." I then called the Police Department.

I said, "Why don't you have the wires cut?"

He said, "How do we do that?—since we don't know where the wires are, and we don't want to cut off the entire switchboard system for the hospital."

I said, "Why don't you just have that particular number put out of service?"

He said, "That's going to take some time."

I decided to get the emergency New York Telephone number from the Police Department, and I then called the phone company and explained to the person who answered what the problem was.

He said to me, "Within one hour the phone will be cut off."

I received a phone call an hour later advising that the phone was no longer working. Contact from outside the hospital to the sit-ins was now completely restricted. As a result, a demonstration that was planned for Sunday where the police expected additional trouble took place but with no disruption whatsoever.

From Monday, September 22, through Thursday, September 25, conditions remained relatively calm. Those who sought to keep the hospital open by working through the system, namely Charlie Rangel, Leon Bogues and "the Citizen Committee," were experiencing difficulty with their plan. Sometimes Governor Carey was with them, sometimes he was not, but they had significant legal difficulties, in either case, and not much time to sort them out. Likewise, those inside the hospital—they had thinned to nine—who had taken the civil-disobedience route were becoming increasingly frustrated. For a week nothing had happened except that the City had continued pulling the plugs on them. First no lights; then no food, except what was supplied by the Police Department, no telephone and then no visual contact with the outside. At City Hall, Ed Koch was, of course, hardly relenting. He did not wish to seem intransigent, and yet all the reasonable boulevards had been explored prior to the closing date, and there was nothing left to be done. There was the feeling that all the efforts by Bogues and Rangel were just last-minute posturings; there must be a limit to the amount of time that they are allowed to occupy center stage and prevent the orderly phasing out of this hospital and the transfer of its employees and the dollars associated with this hospital to other facilities.

On Monday, September 22, at 3:45 P.M., Charlie Rangel came to City Hall with about thirty people for his citizens'-committee meeting. He was late arriving. The others were waiting for him out at the door.

We sat around the table. Roscoe Brown* was the chief spokesman. He said they wanted to keep Sydenham open as an acute-care facility with a functioning emergency room. A number of other people spoke, including Basil Paterson, Charlie Rangel and several black ministers. One point they made was that if the certificate on Sydenham was surrendered to the State, it would be harder for the group applying for a new certificate to get one, since the facility would not be regarded as a functioning hospital. They all spoke with restraint, and then I gave my side of the story.

I mentioned the OCR opinion that Pat Harris had issued

*President of Bronx Community College and an activist in the black community.

and said that copies had been made and were available in the back of the room. I said we were going to close Sydenham on October 15. Their spokesman said they had filed an Article 28 proceeding with the State, seeking a certificate to run the acute-care operation, and they needed six more months' time.

At that point I asked Tony Watson to speak. He stood up and said that he had stated publicly in the past that there was no need to have Sydenham as an acute-care facility. Then he said he didn't want to take a position on that now. I was shocked when he said that. I said, "Tony, I heard you on television and you said it would be foolish to think that there might be a need for an acute-care facility there." And I clearly indicated my displeasure with what he had just done.

Finally I said, "I am willing to do the following: We will close Sydenham on October fifteenth, but we will not surrender the certificate until sixty days from today, which will be November twenty-first. That will give you the opportunity to get a new certificate if you can." I said that the building would be sealed and that security people would be placed on the premises to keep the facility intact for the community group, and I also stressed that I would give the community group the key to the building if a certificate were issued or if they wanted to run the facility as an alcohol treatment or drug-detox facility. Then Carl Flemister* said that he thought he could sell the proposal if I extended the closing date two weeks. Horace Morris† nodded in agreement.

Ultimately we agreed to keep the hospital open to November 1, provided that no new picketing and other takeover measures occurred and that patients would be sent home when ready and long-term patients would also be removed from the hospital. Flemister said, "I think I can sell that and get the demonstrators out and end this."

Then we went back into the Blue Room and the press came over, and I repeated that I was going to extend the time to November 21 for surrender of the certificate. Flemister said he agreed with that, and Morris indicated that he agreed.

---

*The Reverend Carl Flemister is executive minister of the American Baptist Churches of Metropolitan New York.
†Executive director of the New York Urban League.

Roscoe Brown did not agree. He said they weren't getting anything.

On Wednesday afternoon, the 24th, during the public hearings conducted on bills to be signed, Bob Wagner came in and said it was urgent that I meet with our people who were meeting on Sydenham. I told him I would be there in five minutes. I joined that meeting at 4:30. The thrust of Allen Schwartz' remarks was that he had been in court with Judge Hilda Schwartz, who had said to both sides that she hoped the matter could be settled. If it could not be, she said, she would have to hold hearings on the City's motion for a preliminary injunction and all other requests, including the restraining order.* Allen said he thought she was afraid to make a decision that would place her in a position of having been responsible for removing the protesters from the hospital. He said she did not want to be blamed and was temporizing and urging a settlement. She had asked Allen if he would agree that if the sit-ins got out forthwith, we would waive any civil and criminal sanctions for their past violations of the law. Allen had agreed. She then asked him to dictate the stipulation on the record. Then she asked the lawyer for the nine sit-ins if they would agree. He said he could not agree but would take the proposal to his clients; he did not think they would agree to it.

During our meeting, Bob McGuire told us that the Intelligence Division of the NYPD had advised him there were members of the Communist Party, white agitators and others who might bring guns into the community. He said the agitators were looking for a confrontation with the police between then and Sunday. McGuire said he thought the sit-ins should be removed at 3 A.M. that night. He said they wouldn't be arrested but simply removed from the building.

Schwartz, Wagner and the others said that we should reach out for Rangel, Flemister, Morris and others to tell them how serious the matter was and ask them to help in getting those people out. I called Charlie Rangel in Washington. Bob McGuire got on the phone with me. We spoke for about twenty minutes. We told Charlie about the seriousness of the

*A court order to prohibit unlawful acts, including sit-ins, by the protesters.

situation. Charlie grasped the problem, and while we did not say that we contemplated moving the sit-ins out that night, it was clear that he thought that was the possibility. I asked him if he would go in and urge them to leave.

He said, ''That's a joke. Do you know how far up I am on their shit list?'' Charlie then asked what they were getting.

I said, ''We will waive criminal and civil sanctions.''

He said, ''These people have said they are willing to die. What you are offering them means nothing to them. They will enjoy it.'' Then he had to go vote. He called back about forty minutes later and we were still meeting on this issue. He said, ''It is clear to me that this is a very serious matter if you are still meeting.'' And he began to make calls, as did the rest of us. Rangel and Fred Samuel* really took the lead.

The net result was that, while earlier in the evening we had agreed that we would remove the sit-ins that night, we decided that it was far better to allow another effort to be made, particularly since Rangel said he believed the community saw my efforts to date as cooperation, and he feared that even if there was a real possibility of violence against the police, the community at that time was not aware of it. The community would view a removal of the sit-ins as undue violence by the police, he said, and therefore we decided that a special effort should be made the next day with the group that had been put together by Fred Samuel and Rangel. I said to McGuire during the course of our meeting, ''If you think the demonstrators should be removed, that is a police judgment and I will concur. This cannot be a political decision. It must be based on security grounds.''

He said that on the basis of his information, he believed the sit-ins should be removed soon. We all agreed that the matter could be tabled until we heard from the Rangel/Samuel group.

The following morning, Thursday the 25th, Fred Samuel called to say he was arranging to go in with a number of people to talk with the sit-ins. At about 5 P.M., I received a call from Charlie Rangel. He said, ''The sit-ins have indicated that if they have to leave, they will leave peacefully.''

*City Councilman from Harlem.

McGuire called about twenty minutes later. He said, "My people now know that there will be huge demonstrations on Saturday. The hospital workers' union has already distributed thousands of pamphlets urging people to come to the demonstration. We believe that the physical presence of a large number of police, which is now required because of the sit-ins, adds to the possibility of confrontation. And if the sit-ins were removed, the police could be returned to the streets."

I said, "That has to be a police decision."

McGuire said, "It is a police decision. We will remove them later tonight instead of tomorrow morning."

At 2 A.M. the cops moved in, and the removal was accomplished with a minimum of yelling and screaming.

The *Daily News* reported as follows:

Acting to prevent possible violent confrontations over the weekend, a hand-picked squad of police entered Sydenham Hospital early today and quietly carried out nine sit-in demonstrators. The action ended a 12-day siege at the Harlem hospital, which the city wants to close for economic reasons.

Chief of Patrol William Bracey, the Police Department's highest ranking black officer, led cops into the executive director's office, where eight of the nine demonstrators were asleep.

"We just walked in and said, 'You have to go,' and they said, 'We're not going,' and I said, 'Yes, you are—it's just a question of how you're going.'"

At a City Hall press conference, Bracey, flanked by Major Koch and Police Commissioner Robert McGuire recounted how uniformed cops took the nine men outside the hospital without arresting them and without a confrontation.

"No force was used," he said. "I must say there wasn't even any animosity. They even congratulated us on a job well done, and I said we'll do an even better job the next time."

But at a press conference outside the embattled 119-bed hospital at 123d St. and Manhattan Ave., which the city and state want to convert to a drug rehabilitation center, the ousted demonstrators—among them, Cenie Williams, the Rev. Herbert Daughtry and the Rev. Timothy Mitchell—said that the eviction was illegal.

"We were forcibly removed by at least 20 police officers who came in the wee hours of the morning," said Williams, director of the National Association of Black Social Workers. "We were denied our basic rights. We should have been arrested or allowed to stay in the hospital."

Clayton Jones, an attorney for the Coalition to Save Sydenham, added, "It was technically an assault on these people. The police had no legal basis for going in. That's what I call police vigilantism."

"The same unity we had inside, we're going to have outside," the Rev. Mitchell vowed.

The ousted leaders called for demonstrations by "a thousand people" today and tomorrow.

Koch said the decision to remove the demonstrators, who had occupied the hospital for 12 days, was aimed at restoring calm and avoiding a repeat of last Saturday's violence.

"On Wednesday," Koch said, "community officers informed me that continuation of the sit-in through the weekend could produce a potentially violent situation."

The mayor said he "reached out" for Rep. Charles Rangel (D-Harlem), Councilman Fred Samuel (D,L-Harlem) and State Sen. Leon Bogues (D-Harlem) and asked them to try to persuade the demonstrators to leave. "But they still refused to leave."

"It was only after this effort failed that Commissioner McGuire ordered his men to remove the demonstrators," Koch said. McGuire said police had received intelligence reports of the presence of the Communist Workers Party and of the "presence of guns."

"As far as I was concerned, it was too close for comfort," he said. He added that last Saturday the demonstrators "came as close as they possibly could" to exhorting the crowd to violence.

"My decision was made on Wednesday, and the order was given to Chief Bracey on Thursday," McGuire said.

Bracey said he entered the hospital with five community service officers—Lt. Kenneth Jones, Sgt. Howard Wallace, Sgt. Joseph Carter and Detectives Warren Blake and David Walker.

Bracey said eight of the demonstrators were sleeping and the ninth, Shakoor Aljwani, was at the window holding a walkie-talkie. "He said into the walkie-talkie, 'The police are here,'" Bracey said.

"We told them they were not going to be arrested and that we did not want a confrontation," he said. "They asked to caucus, and I said that given the fact that some of them are reverends and not likely to pull any funny business, they could caucus for five minutes."

"They caucused for three or four minutes and said they would not leave, but would prefer to be carried out.'' The demonstrators didn't want to be carried out by the community officers, though, because they said they are ''our friends.''

''They asked to be carried out by uniformed officers,'' Bracey said.

The nine men sat on the floor and each was carried out by a uniformed sergeant and three cops. They were carried beyond the barricades and put down. Bracey said the movement took 20 minutes and was accomplished without fuss.

On the afternoon of the 26th, Sydenham Hospital, for the first time in nearly sixty years, stood empty. It was ringed with police barriers, and a large contingent of police officers still remained on the scene. But the hospital was closed. Meanwhile the posturing by the elected officials continued.

That afternoon I got a call from Kevin Cahill. Cahill said he was calling at the Governor's request and that the Governor was meeting with the Harlem committee. We later found out that that included some of the sit-ins as well as Rangel and the others. Cahill asked me to keep the hospital open for more than sixty days.

I said, ''No, we are not going to do that.'' He indicated that he understood and agreed with us but he worried about what the Governor would say.

I said, ''Tell the Governor not to urge me to keep it open, because I won't. And if he criticizes me, I will dump it all on him, which I have not done thus far.''

Kevin laughed and said, ''I thought that is what you just did when you extended the surrender of the certificate.'' Then he laughed and said, ''I'm only kidding.'' But he wasn't really—that is what he believed.

Then I saw the Governor on television and he had really gone crazy. He talked about forming a committee to open the hospital. When he asked me, I told him that we would give him the hospital, and a long-term lease.

Predictably, the State's plan came to nothing and the hospital remained closed. To minority people across the country, the entire process was a kind of litmus test and a rallying point against the Koch administration. The old charges of ''insensitivity'' and ''arrogance'' were dragged back out and it was left to me to defend myself. As they had about the poverty programs, some black leaders later said privately the right thing had been done. But in public they were silent. The refrain was always the same. When asked about their silence, they would say, "Well, Mr. Mayor, you know if I spoke out I would lose my credibility." And so it was left to me and to the Commissioners to explain the closing of Sydenham Hospital. And we went through it time and time again.

A representative case arose on October 9, 1980, at one of my town hall meetings, this one at Tilden High School in the East Flatbush section of Brooklyn. It was late in the meeting. I had been taking questions from the floor for over an hour and three-quarters. I was looking to close the two-hour meeting on time at 9:30 P.M.. In the fifth row of the auditorium a teenaged black youngster in a red down jacket had his hand raised. I signaled him to the microphone. The exchange went like this:

Q. Mr. Koch, I have one question to ask you. If you're supposed to be doing something for the black community and the black neighborhoods, how come you're not doing anything? I see no progress being done.*

A. You see no progress. Well, let me—I think it's unfair, but let me tell you what we're doing, okay? We have a budget of thirteen billion six hundred million dollars. Regrettably, the poorest people in the City happen to be black and Hispanic. Put your hands down; I've got to talk a little bit here. Poverty is bad, no matter what your race is, and seventy-five percent of the poor people in the whole country happen to be white, but that isn't true in New York City. In New York City, poor people are overwhelmingly black and Hispanic. And what you should know is that fifty-six percent of our budget goes to twenty-six percent of the people who live in this City. They are the twenty-six percent who are below the poverty line, okay? They are overwhelmingly black and Hispanic. I'll tell you how we figured that: I'm going to tell you, because you opened up a door; I think it's important; I'll explain it to you.

*The entire exchange, and the entire town hall meeting, was taped by WNYC, the City's municipal radio station.

Q. I have one more thing to ask you, though.

A. I'll let you ask a question, but just let me answer this. We spend, in the City of New York, four billion four hundred million dollars on Medicaid and welfare. Can you imagine that? Four billion four hundred million dollars. And of that, one billion one hundred million comes right out of local tax-levy dollars, out of our budget, and that goes overwhelmingly to nonwhite people. That's a fact. We spend over a billion dollars for our Medicaid budget, and of the municipal hospitals, only two have a majority of white patients; all the others serve basically nonwhites.

Now, it makes no difference to us what the race or religion is; we serve people irrespective of their color. We have a Department of Employment that spends five hundred million dollars that the Federal Government gives us. Overwhelmingly that goes to nonwhite people, because they are overwhelmingly the people who fit the financial requirements that the Federal Government sets for getting those jobs. Let's take the Board of Education. That Board of Education spends three billion dollars. Of the children who go to school, seventy-one percent are nonwhites.

What I am trying to convey is that our budget, as big as it is, overwhelmingly, because humanity requires it, overwhelmingly our budget goes to black and Hispanic people. And it should. We've got to provide for the poorest of the poor, and we're going to, but I want to tell you what you have to know is: there are demagogues and ideologues who don't give a damn about the middle class. I speak out for the middle class. You know why? Because they pay the taxes; they provide the jobs for the poor people, and we're not able to do as much for them economically as I would like, but at the very least, I'm gonna recognize the sacrifices that they make. What's your next question?

Q. My next question is, You said you weren't going to close down the hospital, the hospital that you closed, right in the black community, but you closed it anyway, and I want to see why you didn't keep your promise about keeping it open.

A. I will explain that to you. Hold it, I'm going to explain it to you. Please, he's talking about Sydenham, and I want to give you, in two minutes, the facts. It's interesting that you raised it. We have seventeen municipal hospitals. In the whole country, the largest cities, they have a total of twenty-seven, of which we have seventeen in the City of New York. No other city in the country has more than one municipal hospital. We have seventeen. The fact is that we can't afford to have excess beds.

A hospital provides three services. One you would call the acute care—if someone needs to be in the hospital overnight, for two days, or weeks, or whatever. The fact is that Sydenham, which had one hundred nineteen beds, had only seventy patients in them, because the people in Harlem knew that the care they got there was not as good as the care they could get at Harlem Hospital, at Mount Sinai, at Saint Luke's—at any of the six hospitals in that area that are from four blocks to twelve blocks away. That's number one.

The second thing that the hospital provided was an emergency clinic. Do you know that Sydenham was so bad that if you were shot a half a block away, the Federal Government said to the City of New York: "You are not allowed to bring someone who's been shot in the gut or in the head to Sydenham even if they're half a block away because Sydenham cannot treat them at the emergency clinic"? Do you know what a cop said to me last month, so help me God? He said, "Mr. Mayor, if, God forbid, I'm shot and I'm in the foyer of Sydenham, please take me to another hospital."

Now, I want to tell you something else. There is a third facility that a hospital provides, and that is called an ambulatory facility. That is where you need day-to-day clinic care. The doctors have left the areas of Central Brooklyn and Central Harlem, to their eternal shame, but they have, and we need ambulatory facilities where people can come in and see a doctor and go home the same day. We're opening four clinics in the Sydenham area—four ambulatory clinics that weren't there before. And you know what else we're doing? We have created a nationwide demonstration project at Metropolitan Hospital in East Harlem where anybody who makes less than fourteen thousand five hundred in a family of four, who lives from river to river, from Harlem to East Harlem, is eligible to go without charge. Even though they're not eligible under Medicaid, they're medically indigent—but they're not poor enough; do you know what I mean? Those people get free medical service for members of their family. Middle-class people don't get that free service, but we're providing it for the people of Harlem. We think it will be a wonderful demonstration project. The rest of the country will look at it and say everybody should have that kind of care.

Let me close by saying this—it's nine thirty P.M., I want to close, hold it, we've been here two hours, please sit down. Now, you know, I told you that I've been Mayor for close to three years. And I've said that it will take twelve years to turn this town around. But I get involved in a lot of controversies and I make a lot of people mad at me, and so maybe at the end of these four years they'll say, "He's too controversial and we don't want him." And maybe they'll throw me out. That's okay with me. I'll get a better job, and you won't get a better Mayor.

16

New York and the Presidential Campaign

ON MARCH 6, 1980, eight months before the Presidential election and less than three weeks before the March 25 New York State Presidential primary, I and several government colleagues returned from a two-week vacation tour of China and Japan. When our plane was ten minutes out of Kennedy Airport the captain approached me. "Mr. Koch," he said, "we just got a call for you. The message is that the President wants you to call him before you talk to the press."

The previous Saturday, March 1, the Carter Administration's deputy to the U.N. Ambassador had cast a "yes" vote on a resolution rebuking Israel for continuing to place settlements on the West Bank of the Jordan River. Additionally, the resolution challenged Israeli sovereignty in Jerusalem. On March 3, at 10 P.M., after being criticized on the vote by Israeli spokesmen, including the Israeli Ambassador to the United States, Ephraim Evron, as well as American Jewish organizations and Senator Edward Kennedy, the Carter White House had issued a statement calling the vote an error.

Immediately after landing, I went to a phone and called the President. He was very jovial on the phone. He said, "Ed, I know you have had a wonderful time. I read all about it, and I would like to hear it from you."

I said, "Well, Mr. President, the Chinese are waiting for you in China. They said they are waiting for you to come over."

Then he said, "Have you been kept informed about the U.N. vote on Israel?"

"Yes, I have," I said.

He said, "You know, I would like to talk to you about it. When you hear what our side is, I think you will be pleased. I would appreciate your coming down and having lunch with me over the weekend. And could you not talk to the press until I have had a chance to talk to you?"

I said, "I'll be happy to come down and talk to you."

He said, "How about Saturday?"

I said, "Certainly, Mr. President. And I would like to bring along Jim Brigham, my Budget Director." If the President wanted to talk about Israel, I wanted to talk about Israel and the City's fiscal needs.

Carter said, "That's okay."

Then we had our airport press conference, and following my comments on China, one of the reporters added, "Have you heard about the U.N. vote on Israel?"

I said, "Yes. I am disturbed about that vote in the same way that Chairman Strauss is disturbed." Strauss had used that language. "But," I said, "I will hold comment on the details until I have all of the facts." Then I looked into the television camera and said, "I don't want to be a bull in a china shop."

Friday morning I called Eugene Eidenberg (an assistant to the President) at the White House and said, "I just want to find out, what is this lunch for? Are you bringing down eighteen Jews and are we all going to be lectured? Or is this a lunch for me?"

He said, "No, this is a private lunch for you and the President."

"Fine," I said.

That night Eidenberg called back saying, "The President would prefer that you not come down with Brigham and that it just be between the two of you."

"That's ridiculous," I said. "I have to have someone down there who has our budget numbers. I can't keep them in my head. And I want to talk to him about those numbers."

"Well, the President would prefer not to have him," Eidenberg insisted.

"I just want to make something very clear," I said. "I will do whatever the President wants me to do, but it is a waste of time. Nothing will come of it. It will not satisfy me and it won't be helpful to the President. I want Brigham there.''

Again he said, ''No.''

''Well,'' I said, ''I'm just telling you, you're wasting your time. You guys are calling me because the President is losing in New York and I know that and you know that. The fact is that if I had to call the primary now I would say that probably he would lose. But even if he wins, he will lose the general election because the Jews are not going to vote for him. In terms of what I can do for him, I am never going to leave him. I am not Jane Byrne.* But there is very little I can do to help him if the City's financial situation is such that I cannot balance the budget because the Federal Government hasn't provided the money it said it would. You should know that now. And you should also know that it is a little upsetting to me that when he is in trouble he calls me. He calls me on the plane. But over the last two months when I have called him on about six different occasions he never calls back. Watson or you will call back, but he never calls back. And that bothers me. If Carey, who has not been friendly to him, had called him, he would have called back.''

Well, Eidenberg is getting my message at that point, and he says, ''Okay, you can have Brigham come down, but just for the early part of the meeting. He can't stay for lunch. The President wants to talk to you on a macro basis, not on a micro basis.''

I say, ''Macro, micro, it doesn't make any difference. We have to cover these items. So we will talk on the micro with Brigham and at lunch he can talk on the macro with me.''

On the plane going down we met Jerry Rafshoon. Rafshoon was handling the President's media campaign. He knew I was going to meet with Carter. I said, ''You know you're losing New York. And what he did on the vote at the U.N. was terrible. For the first time the United States voted to support a resolution questioning Israeli sovereignty over Jerusalem and calling for the removal of the settlements while not imposing any requirements on the Arab states. Unless that is clarified and unless there is a television meeting where he explains

---

*The Mayor of Chicago and a Kennedy supporter.

what the situation is and responds to the fears that the Jews have that they are being sold out—and they can smell it; they have lived through two thousand years of this selling out, and they know when it is happening—Carter is going to lose." Rafshoon indicated that he thought that was true and that I should tell the President exactly what I thought and give him my best advice.

The first half-hour was in the Oval Office, and the people present were Watson, Eidenberg, Brigham, the President and me. The President asked about my trip. Then he said, "You know, I just want you to know that we are partners. I want to be helpful. I will never let New York City go into bankruptcy. I appreciate the support you have given."

I responded by saying, "Look, Mr. President, what you are saying isn't enough. You are saying that we will never go into bankruptcy and that we are partners. But what you have to say—and I am urging you to say in order to provide the credibility that is so necessary for me if I am to help you, and I will always be there, but I am talking about being able to substantially help you—is that you will do whatever you can to get the Congress to provide the money, a hundred million dollars this year and two hundred million next year. At the moment, through your Secretaries, after I called you and you have shaken them up, you have come up with ten million. Apparently you can't do more administratively; it has to be done legislatively. But the programs that the press is saying you are going to be cutting are the programs that would provide the hundred million to us. We have alternatives, because we understand that you have to make cuts. Brigham can talk to you about the cutting, and what he has said to me, and I am repeating now to you, Mr. President, is that you can save us dollars by deferring mandated programs."*

We talked about the Moynihan Medicaid proposal,† and what shocked me was that Carter didn't really know what it was. So Brigham explained it. The substance was that it would cost the Federal Government an additional $2.5 billion,

---

*Programs imposed upon localities by federal court decisions, administrative actions or legislation.

†For a federal takeover of 77 percent of Medicaid costs.

of which New York State would get about $600 million, and that would provide New York City with about $200 million— exactly what we needed for FY 1982.

He said, "Oh, that is ridiculous. I cannot add two and a half billion dollars to the budget and have other states complain that we have to raise taxes."

So Brigham said, "Well, if you tie that to hospital cost containment, you in fact save money. If you put the two together, you come out with a net saving of billions of dollars. It is the fair way to deal with this problem."

I said, "Please, consider the Moynihan bill."

Carter said, "I will get back to you on that." Then he said, "We will talk about Israel over lunch."

At that point Brigham left with Watson and Eidenberg, and Carter and I walked over to the family quarters for lunch. Rosalynn Carter was there, and so was Amy, lying on the floor watching television and reading a book.

Then we went in to lunch. Rosalynn, uncharacteristically, was very quiet, subdued, monosyllabic. Her complexion was bad, which was rare; normally it is very good. She looked distraught. The President looked okay, but he was very down. His whole manner was down. He opened up by saying, "If you don't mind, Ed, I would like to say a prayer over lunch."

I said, "Fine." So he said his prayer.

Then he said to me, "Now, you have some advice for me." He went right into it.

And this is what I said to him. I said: "Mr. President, you have to understand that the Jews for two thousand years have had people sell them out. There isn't a country on the world's face today except for the United States that hasn't at one point cast its Jews out. When Shakespeare wrote *The Merchant of Venice*, there wasn't a Jew in England. The Jews had been expelled three hundred years before."

He said, "I didn't know that."

I said, "The Spanish expelled the Jews in 1492. The Dutch expelled the Jews. . . . France today has announced that it is going to recognize the PLO. Giscard is inviting Arafat to Paris. So you have to understand that the Jews may sound paranoid on this matter of Israel, but they are not. They are being very realistic.

"And what they see, Mr. President, is that in the one country which has consistently given them support, that support has eroded. In the past we vetoed resolutions that were one-sided against Israel and that questioned Israeli sovereignty over Jerusalem. Then we got to the point where we simply abstained; and now we are supporting resolutions that have sanctions in them and are denunciatory. In the past it was always the President who saved Israel over the objections of the State Department. But today we have two people who are anti-Israel who are in the forefront of your administration: Andrew Young and Donald McHenry.* They are pro-Arab. They are not for Israel. They are for the Arabs. Andy Young has never asked for forgiveness for having referred to the Ayatollah as a saint. McHenry is even smarter than Young because he doesn't go as public as Young. He is just as vicious on the subject of Israel as Young was. And Cy Vance† is just part of the regular State Department operation and mentality: pro-Arab and anti-Israel. But in a nice way. I happen to know Cy Vance. He is an old friend of mine. It doesn't help. In the past, under Roosevelt, you had the same situation with the State Department. And the same situation under Truman. But it was the President who cut them off. The President makes the policy. Not the State Department. The Jews don't see that happening with you. And that has got to be addressed.

"There is also a religious aspect here. The Christian community has failed in every case involving the Jews. People said after World War Two that it could never happen again to the Jews. But it is happening again. Not in the same way, with concentration camps, but with the same disregard for the Jewish community's safety and security. You know, today in Argentina there are three hundred thousand Jews who are living on the edge of a sword. Today. They can be expelled at any time. They have already had their leader, Timerman,‡ tortured and expelled. You have the Jews in the Soviet Union. We would not take in all those Jews if the

*McHenry succeeded Young as U.S. Ambassador to the United Nations.
†Cyrus Vance, Secretary of State.
‡Jacobo Timerman, a prominent liberal newspaper publisher in Buenos Aires.

Soviets were to expel them all. And that is the way it is across the world. And it is Israel that has to be there constantly. And its security has to be safeguarded. And this isn't only the way religious Jews feel. This is all Jews. It is me.

"Finally, Mr. President, what upsets the Jews is that regardless of what you have done or not done, no matter what you say, they know you can't run again and you will never have to come back to them, and therefore once you are elected you may get worse on this issue. And they will have no control because you don't need them anymore—whereas if they support a Republican who is going to be elected for the first time, he has to come back to them. And I am telling you now that in my own judgment at this point, if Ford or Reagan were to be the Republican candidate, I believe the Jews would vote for the Republican in the general election.

"Now, the way you can address that, again in my judgment, and I urge you to do it, is to have a press conference. You should address each of these issues and convince the Jewish community that you are supportive of them. What you have going for you is your own religion."*

Carter said, "Well, I want you, first, to understand what happened. The resolution that we had was one which regrettably came up on a Saturday and I hadn't actually read that statement." (I am thinking: It is ridiculous that in a statement which relates to Israel he hasn't read every word. Ridiculous. He, Jimmy Carter, from Camp David.) Then he said, "I am against the settlements. When Sadat finds that he gets no satisfaction on that with us, he may go to the United Nations. He, after all, has to relate to his Arab brothers, and he is distressed that Hussein and Assad† are angry with him. So I believe we are helping Israel by seeking to reduce that antipathy and anger and the need to go to the United Nations. After all, it was I who was working on a treaty not only with Egypt, but ultimately with Jordan and Syria, and it upsets me that anyone could disparage my honor."

---

*Jimmy Carter's religious outlook was similar to that of Billy Graham. And Billy Graham was an energetic supporter of the State of Israel. Graham's ecclesiastical position required the resurrection of Israel.
†King Hussein of Jordan and president Hafez al-Assad of Syria.

I said, "Again, Mr. President, I believe that the Jews will probably vote for you in the primary. I am not sure that they will. But in the general election, I think they will go to Ford and Reagan unless you are able to reassure them."

He said, "Well, what can you do to help?"

I said, "Mr. President, no one can help you. Only you can help yourself. I read what Mario Cuomo said after he had lunch with you last week. And it didn't change one vote on this issue, the fact that he supports you. Every Jew is going to make up his own mind on this. And it will be because of what you say, not because of what *I* say."

Then Carter said, "Now, Ed, I just want to make one thing clear. I know you have supported me. You supported me early. But if you decide the day before the primary or the day before the general election that someone else would do better for this country or for the City of New York, I would understand—you are an honorable man and you would want to carry out any obligations that you had—I would understand if you decided that it was in the best interests of the country or the City, and you would be free to support anybody you wanted to."

That, of course, was purely self-serving. He felt it was necessary to say that—he having been filled in on my earlier comments to Gene Eidenberg. But it must have been very wounding to his pride: The President needs ol' boy Ed Koch.

Carter also said, "I want you to know that my being reelected is not the first priority for me."

I am thinking: I doubt that. But he felt compelled to say that too. There was a pause. I said, "Well, I can catch the two P.M. flight if I leave now." It was 1:40.

"Fine," he said. "I have kept you too long as it is."

"No," I said, "I have enjoyed it." And I went back to the City.

Back in New York, I wasted no time exercising my First Amendment rights. After my Saturday lunch with Carter, I was free to express myself on the recent U.N. vote, and on Monday I did so to two *New York Post* reporters.

In that interview at City Hall I described my feelings rather candidly. The most jarring note from Carter's point of view was my referring to five of his policy makers—Donald

McHenry, Andrew Young, Cyrus Vance, Zbigniew Brzezinski*
and Harold Saunders†—as "the Gang of Five." If I had not
just been to China (where the Gang of Four had recently been
tried), I might not have used that phrase. But I thought it was
a good phrase, and it certainly stunned them.

After the *Post* piece appeared, I got several calls. The first
was from McHenry. He was very quiet and moderate in tone,
but very intense. I picked up the phone and said, "Hi, Don,
how are you?"

He said, "Mr. Mayor, I am very upset. I don't know how
you could say that I am anti-Israel."

I said, "Well, I believe that."

He said, "Well, what is your proof?"

I said, "The resolution is my proof," adding, "You know,
Don, I like you personally, but I think you are an Arabist:
pro-Arab and anti-Israel. That is my feeling on the matter.
And you would not want me to say anything but the truth,
would you, as I see the truth?"

"Oh, no," he said.

The second call was from Cy Vance, at about 6:30 P.M. at
Gracie Mansion. He said, "Ed, I just got out of a press
conference and I denounced you, and I just want you to know
what I said."

I said, "How are you, Cy?"

He said, "It was terrible of you to call me anti-Israel and
part of the Gang of Five. And I have gone on television and I
have said that it is hogwash."

I said, "Cy, you know, I really like you. But I just believe
that you are an Arabist."

He says, "How can you say that?"

I say, "It is not that you are an evil man. It is just that you
were put in there [the State Department] to clean out the house
and you have become institutionalized"—a sort of *double
entendre* that I didn't intend at the moment. And I said, "I
mean in the best sense. They have taken you over. You didn't
get rid of the Arabists at the State Department."

---

*National Security Adviser.
†Assistant Secretary of State for Near Eastern Affairs.

"There are just as many pro-Israel people in the State Department as there are Arabists," he said.

"Well, that is the problem," I said—meaning Shouldn't the State Department reflect the Administration's position?

"It wasn't right, Ed, of you to do that," he complained.

"Cy, let me be truthful," I said. "All of the people you and I know think you are an Arabist." He laughed, and that was the end of the conversation.

Then Andy Young called and left his number, which I called maybe six or seven times. He wasn't home; someone took the message, but he never called back.

Then Governor Harriman called. He is very deaf. He kept saying, "You shouldn't have called for Cy's resignation."

I said, "Governor, I didn't call for Cy Vance's resignation."

But he couldn't hear me. He kept repeating himself, and then he said, "You should have called for Brzezinski's resignation."

Because we were still working on the budget, I was in continual contact with the Carter people—Gene Eidenberg in particular. They were very much upset by my statement, but they also yielded. I said to Eidenberg, "This will not alter my support of the President, particularly now that he has made a clean breast of it, so to speak, by admitting error." They knew they had a wild man on their hands, so they didn't seek a showdown. What was there to argue about? It was done. Next they were worried about what I was going to do to their budget. So they were trying to calm me down. The Presidential primary in New York was by then less than two weeks away, and Carter was clearly in trouble with Kennedy. He didn't need me too as his enemy.

On March 15, Carter went on the air with his budget message: $2 billion in cuts for Fiscal 1980, $14 billion in Fiscal '81. These reductions translated into $100 million in immediate revenue losses for New York City. I knew that if I was to get that $100 million back for New York, I would have to do it in the next ten days. I would have to have the deal in place by Primary Day.

Vice President Mondale called at 9 A.M. on the 19th. He said he would be able to deliver another $60 million toward our gap of $100 million. Some $13.8 million would be made up in two administrative programs—specifically, $8.8 million through a federal takeover of low-income housing projects and $5 million by recalculation of a general revenue-sharing grant. Legislatively, he said they were going to be able to provide an additional $10 million in revenue sharing, $1.5 million for foreign-dignitary protection and $35 million for targeted fiscal assistance. A total of $60.3 million. That left us with $40 million to go. Then the Vice President said that he was working on the hospital situation,* adding, "I will do anything to make life easier for you." Then he said, "The President and I will do everything I can [his language was odd here] to see that these proposals pass and get through the Congress."

I said, "You have got to do something about the hospitals, because Pat Harris won't do anything. She must be called because she is opposed to what we are doing. I think the President is afraid of her."

Mondale said, "Well, I ain't."

While these negotiations with the Vice President continued, I had twice postponed my press conference on the impact of the Carter budget proposals on the City. Finally, that afternoon at 1:15, we had the release prepared, and as I walked out of my office to go into the Blue Room for the press conference I said to Dan Wolf, "I don't know whether we will get any of these dollars, but now we have the paper trail that shows we tried."

Before the week was out, the $100 million was restored, albeit in promises, and with an extra $5 million as gravy, and I renewed my support for the Carter-Mondale ticket. But it didn't make any difference. While Jimmy Carter sat in the Rose Garden, Ted Kennedy had worked New York State, and it showed. But Carter was hampered by more than his refusal to campaign. There was the matter of his record. Continual announcements by the Cost of Living Council had indicated that there would be no respite from inflation. There were the flip-flop on the Israel vote and the continuing embarrassment

*The need to get federal support to save Metropolitan Hospital in East Harlem.

of Billygate,* not to mention the travesty of the hostages in Teheran. In the week prior to the primary, sound trucks crisscrossed the City's Jewish neighborhoods with messages like "A vote for Carter is a vote against Israel."

Primary Day found me sharing my favorite early-morning subway stop with the Vice President. As we stood at the northwest corner of 77th and Lexington, we fielded questions from the press. We sounded optimistic, but March 25 was a very grim day for the President. Kennedy beat him 59 percent–41 percent in New York and 53 percent–46 percent in Connecticut.† The Carter-Mondale ticket had been favored in both states.

In the evening I went up to Bob Strauss' suite at the Sheraton Centre, where the Carter people had their headquarters. From polling done during the day, it was clear that Carter was going to lose. The President's side conceded at about 9:30 P.M. Cuomo introduced Strauss, who conceded defeat, calling it "a bump in the road." Then Strauss asked me to close.

I said, "This was a Mailgram telling the President that he

---

*One day during the 1977 campaign, Garth had said to me, "I think we should get you and Billy Carter in a picture." Billy Carter was coming to New York to endorse "Billy Beer," and Garth knew about it. He is an old friend of Jack MacGregor, who had been Billy Carter's commanding officer in the Marines, and who had saved him from numerous courts-martial.

So, sure enough, one day into Garth's office walks Billy Carter. This was before it was well known what a wacko he was. He was absolutely drunk, and he was drunk all day long. That was his reputation, and it was based on fact. He is there with his manager, who is dressed all in white, Mr. Snake Oil, and with this Southern accent. They were a pair.

Billy Carter says to me, "You want me to endorse you?" And before I could say anything he says, "What are you, a Republican or a Democrat?"

Now, I don't want his endorsement. I don't want to embarrass his brother, anyway. So I say, "No, you don't have to endorse me." But we did take a picture and it appeared in the *Post*. And it was Garth who was able to arrange that. When you are running it is always helpful to stay in the papers. In the spring of 1980, Billy Carter was the subject of several investigations into his activities relating to the Libyan Government. It was those investigations which came to be called "Billygate."

†Coming from a slow start, however, Kennedy remained far behind nationwide.

has to be concerned about inflation, cuts to the cities and Israel.''

Then the TV reporters came over and I repeated the same message, saying that it was good the trouble had arisen so early because it would give Carter an opportunity to recoup. I repeated my statements concerning the Gang of Five and the need for the President to reestablish his primacy over the Secretary of State.

I was back at Gracie Mansion by 10:30 P.M. I called the White House and asked for the President. He took the phone quickly. His words to me were "Ed, you are a great man.''

I said, "You are very nice. I am just sorry that we did not carry the State for you, but we will try again in November.''

He said, "You are a good friend. You were there with me when no one else was.''

The following morning, Vice President Walter Mondale called to say that he appreciated everything I had done.

I said, "The President has got to get out and campaign and address the issues of inflation, cuts to the cities and Israel.'' He agreed. And I said, "I think he has to fire people in the State Department.''

He said, "Yes. And I will continue to work on the problems of New York City.''

I said, "In particular, do something about Pat Harris.''

The bargaining, of course, continued after the primary. It wasn't long before I started seizing opportunities to speak critically of the Carter Administration. I always prefaced my remarks with the little disclaimer: "I was with the President when he was in the desert and I will be with him when he crosses over into the Promised Land.'' Then I would add, "But the fact that you have my support doesn't mean you have bought my silence. I will always reserve my right to speak out.''

On June 6, I appeared before the Republican Party's platform committee. I was the first Democratic Mayor to do so in anyone's memory. And it caused a stir.

I had been told I could speak for fifteen minutes and that there would be no questions. I had prepared a sixteen-page statement outlining the City's needs. Then, in his opening statement, Senator Tower* said all the speakers would be limited to five minutes. So I just handed my statement in to the secretary to be read into the minutes and I spoke extemporaneously. As it turned out, the Republicans kept me before them for nearly three-quarters of an hour. We went over a lot of territory, including the federally mandated programs that we have to pay for out of our local tax-levy dollars, block grants and the need for a federal takeover of the Medicaid burden. They were with me on all of these items. It is common sense. It has nothing to do with anyone's party affiliation.

When the session was concluded, William Brock, the party chairman, said, "Mr. Mayor, you have made the most eloquent argument for a Republican Congress that I have ever heard. May I issue an invitation to you to join the Republican Party?"

I said, "Mr. Chairman, I respectfully decline."

Then we all went outside for the pictures. There I was asked by a reporter, "Mr. Mayor, isn't this political treason?"

I said, "If this be treason, make the most of it. But it ain't!"

A reporter said, "Who writes your lines?"

And I said, "Nathan Hale." Later I corrected myself. Actually it was Patrick Henry.

A week later, I went down to Washington to appear before the Democratic Party platform committee.

I hadn't been in the Sheraton Hotel there since its renovation. Now it is very much like a Hyatt hotel: atrium with huge interior towers and balconies, and so on. So as I am walking through this place, all I can think of is the Mel Brooks movie *High Anxiety.*

I get into the room where they are having the hearing and they put me on right away. So I say, "You know, it is particularly appropriate that we should be having this hearing here because this place is just like *High Anxiety.* And we all should be having high anxiety."

Then they started asking me about the City's fiscal condition and I said, "Look, let's get something up front here. The

---

*John Tower of Texas.

President has taken away two hundred million dollars from the CETA* program. Not next year. Not by Congressional resolution. This year. Because he's decided to. It's going to cost New York City twelve million dollars. When Nixon did that, they called it impoundment.''

Well, that certainly got their attention.

In the first three fiscal years of the Koch administration, the federal shortfall was $550 million. If anyone wonders, as some people have, why I faltered in my approach to the bridge over into the Promised Land, that is the reason. I got tired of hearing ''The check's in the mail.''

But there were other lessons as well. On April 24, President Carter had launched his military alternative to the failed diplomatic initiatives in Iran. The helicopter raid got about as far as the diplomatic initiatives had.

In Washington, the military attempt was viewed as a further indication of Zbigniew Brzezinski's dominance over the affairs of state. The raid had, after all, been opposed unreservedly by Secretary of State Vance. Vance had made his stand for uninterrupted diplomatic efforts. A product of his New England roots, he had characteristically placed his faith in patience and rationality. Meanwhile, the country wanted action. On April 24, Vance lost the fight, and within the week his resignation had been tendered and accepted. Always the gentleman, he stepped down with his virtue intact.

On July 17 I had lunch with Vance. With me were Dan Wolf, Allen Schwartz and David Margolis. It was very interesting.

I have known Cy Vance for about ten years. He is the best kind of WASP. As a result of being wealthy and going to good schools he wanted to give something back. *Noblesse oblige*, I guess. But more than that, he is fundamentally a decent man. He may not have been strong enough to get his arms around the Carter White House. He may not have had the energy. And certainly he wasn't the cunning and Machiavellian Secretary of State that Henry Kissinger was. But you

*The federally funded Comprehensive Employment and Training Act.

cannot know him without appreciating the fundamental honesty and decency of the man. And I respond to that.

I knew him when I was in the Congress. I knew him better when Matthew Nimitz* went to work at the State Department. We were always friendly. I had derogated him in the Gang of Five episode, and he took it quite well. Then, after he left the State Department, I saw him at a reception and I apologized for my remarks. Then I invited him to the aforementioned lunch.

In the course of the meal, I told him the story of Carter's calling me on the airplane when I was returning from China. Then I recounted my lunch at the White House, including Carter's claim that he hadn't read the resolution.

Vance said, "He read it and he knew what was in it. But he underestimated what the impact would be."

"The Jews know that," I said, "and they are not going to vote for him in the general election. They believe that if he is reelected he will sell them out."

Vance nodded and said, "He will."

And indeed Carter would have. How do I know? He said so. He supported the sale of AWACS planes to Saudi Arabia, and when he and Nixon and Ford were returning from Anwar Sadat's funeral on October 10, 1981, Carter, interviewed on the plane, said that he thought the United States should recognize the PLO. That is what I call selling out Israel.

Meanwhile, I hadn't made much progress in collecting on Carter's promises to the City. In March, just prior to the primary, I had done my best toward eliciting discretionary moneys from the Carter Administration, but I hadn't been too successful. In August I saw that as Mayor of the host city for the Democratic Convention, I had another bargaining chip. I attempted to use *that* chip to promote my laundry list in an attempt to buy federal largesse, and the White House didn't like it.

On August 4, my people told me that the Carter people were absolutely livid with me and that they would seek to get me sometime after the election.

---

*A Manhattan-based lawyer and personal friend.

Clyde Haberman, a *Times* reporter, asked me if I thought the role I was taking was a dangerous one. I said, "I don't think so. We got nothing from them before."

He said, "People at the White House say you can't play hardball with the President or you will suffer."

I said to Haberman, "Did we get anything from them when we played softball? We have received no budget-balancing support moneys to date. We have gotten only earmarked programmatic aid, and even that is far reduced overall."

The following day, Bob Strauss called. He said, "Let me talk very quietly with some understanding of your concerns. You look bad and we look bad. And what you are saying is not helpful to the campaign. No player in this looks good, and what you hope to accomplish simply won't happen. Let me tell you what the President is doing to help you. One: Eizenstadt* is working on the countercyclical aid with Congress. The President will be announcing his new recovery plan, which will help you. Two: Eizenstadt is working to make progress in the other areas that you are concerned about.

"Ed," he continued, "your statements are very important. And when I talk to the Governors, they all ask, 'Doesn't he get any advice from you?' And I say, 'That S.O.B. doesn't take advice from anybody.' But they are all asking, 'Can't you turn him off during the convention?' "

I said, "Bob, I need your help. And there are two things of the four things I need that the President could do with a stroke of his pen. One is getting the federal standby guarantees made available immediately. The other is getting the Census Bureau to include the stock-transfer tax† as part of our formula for general revenue sharing, which would give us thirty-five million dollars annually and two hundred million by way of back claims. Then the President could help us with the Congress in getting Medicaid legislation, which he has not supported."

---

*Stuart Eizenstadt was one of the President's domestic advisers.
†Only City tax levies were included in the federal formula. The stock-transfer tax was a State tax. The Koch administration sought to have it viewed as a City tax because virtually all of the stock-transfer transactions in the State of New York occurred in the City of New York, and all the revenues raised by the stock-transfer tax came to the City.

At that point Strauss said, "Stop! Don't give the fourth item to me. Let me go to work on these three items first. You are meeting with the President tomorrow," he said, referring to a planned motorcade uptown from the 30th Street heliport. "Would you like to be alone with him, or is it okay if Cuomo and Rangel ride in the car?"

I said, "I can't talk to him in the car with anyone else there, but I leave that to you."

"I will tell them," he said, "that the four of you will ride in the car but that you and the President should have fifteen minutes alone later on in the morning. I hope out of that meeting will come a positive statement by you for the press."

Midsummer was a difficult time for Carter. The President's attempts to rescue the fifty-two American hostages were stalled. The Russians had invaded Afghanistan, and all Carter did by way of response was ask American athletes not to compete in the Moscow Olympics. The Kennedy threat wouldn't go away. Ronald Reagan was gaining in the polls. And Billygate was playing on the evening news.

I wasn't helping much either. During a construction tour of Madison Square Garden, the site of the forthcoming Democratic Convention, I called Billy Carter a "wacko." Worse, I said that if Billy hadn't been the President's brother he would probably have been indicted. Meanwhile, Governor Carey, who had never been friendly with the Carter Administration, continued to wander between flirting with Kennedy and seeking a favorite-son designation for himself.

All the campaign fact sheets indicated Carter had to win New York in November. And New York was drifting away.

On August 7, the President came to town to address the annual convention of the Urban League and to do what shoring up he could with the State's political leaders. I was at the West 30th Street heliport to welcome him with the Governor and Congressmen Robert Garcia, Mario Biaggi and Charles Rangel. The President's advance woman informed me that I was scheduled to ride alone with the President in his limousine to the hotel where he was to give his speech. Later, when the helicopter landed, she started to have me take the lead in greeting the President, but I told her, "No, protocol requires that the Governor go first."

When the President emerged, he shook hands with the Governor and me, and not very heartily. Then he went over to the Congressmen, all of whom were doing what they could for him, and greeted them with enthusiasm. Then the President and I got into the limousine with Robert Dunn, one of his staff people. The first thing I said was, "Mr. President, may I raise some issues with you? I am told we won't have an opportunity to talk later on."

He said, "Okay."

Then, before I could start talking, he said, "I want you to know that every time I pick up *The New York Times* you are there beating the hell out of me. You have done me more damage than any other man in America. When I have problems politically or with my family, you are attacking me and not supporting me." It was clear to me that he was really angry.

I said, "Mr. President, I was with you when you were all alone and few were with you." (I was referring to the previous August, when his popularity rating stood at 23 percent in the polls.)

He said, "I know that. And I also want you to know that I have a commitment to New York, no matter what happens."

I said, "Mr. President, I am for you. I was for you and still am. But I also have an obligation to New York City, and I need help."

At that point he looked away and stared out the window and waved to the crowds. They were not waving back. In fact, they stood mute, with some of them giving him the thumbs-down signal. He obviously was not listening to me. Then he said, "I am listening to you, but I am waving to the crowd."

So then I read to him my list of items: (1) changing the revenue-sharing formula to take account of the stock-transfer tax; (2) the $900-million standby loan guarantees; (3) Medicaid relief; (4) budgetary support of $100 million.

As I started to explain the problem of the Census Bureau and the stock-transfer-tax definition, he said, "If it is so easy and general revenue has been around for so long, why didn't you get it from Nixon and Ford? Give me a memo on this, because you can't expect me to have the details. I will give it to Watson.''

It was clear to me that he was absolutely angry and threatening. We really had no further conversation. When we got to the Hilton Hotel, he jumped out of the car and got ahead of me.

When I returned to City Hall, I told my people in our budget meeting what had happened. In the middle of all this, I returned a call from Don Manes, the Queens Borough President. He went on for five minutes about his diet, telling me that he had lost thirty-four pounds and wanted to arrange to call me every Friday, so that we could check on each other's weight. I said, ''You mean Fatsos Anonymous?'' Then he kept going on about going out to eat at a Chinese restaurant. It was just bizarre in the context of what I was going through with the President and the budget.

Then, at 6:30 P.M., the Governor called. The thrust of his remarks was that it was clear the President was playing hardball and indicating that if people didn't go along with him, he would take revenge.

I said, ''Listen, you and I are not going to be frightened.''

He said, ''That is true. Even if he wants to take revenge on me and you, he is never going to do it to the people in the City and State because he needs them. Unless he turns around, he's going to lose.''

I said, ''I don't believe we are going to get a nickel in help from him, judging from my conversation with him in the car.''

The next day, the 8th, the fallout from the limousine meeting began to be interpreted by both sides. First there was a conversation with the Vice President.

I said, ''Fritz, I don't know whether you got a report from the President on my conversation with him in his car, but I thought he was rather snappish.''

He said, ''Yes, he was irritated, but it is a passing matter. It was the wrong day to be with him, and on the wrong day with him it is better to be elsewhere. When you spoke to him, was he going to or coming from his Urban League speech?''

I said, ''He was on his way to make the speech.''

''Well,'' he said, ''that is part of it. Things like that make him very uptight. He was worried about the reception his speech would get. I understand at one point he wasn't even listening to you."

"Well, he was looking out the window waving to the crowds," I said, "but the crowds weren't waving back. Then he got mad at me."

"That is executive privilege," he said.

"I want you to know, Fritz," I replied, "that I really want you as the President. And since I can't have you this year, I am for him. And when I talked with him it was because I was told that I would have fifteen minutes either after his Urban League speech or before it in his car to talk to him and that I should take the matters up with him directly. So I did. I told him that I have a responsibility to this city and that is why I was pressing the items on him." Mondale said that he understood. "He asked me to send him a memo on the items, which I am doing. Could I also send you a copy of the memo?"

Mondale agreed. "Have your memo delivered to me at the Sheraton Centre on Monday, and have your representative call my representative and arrange to meet me at the hotel to explain it all to me. Ed, what is most important is that we come out of this convention upbeat and in good shape. And you can depend on my working on what you need, as I know Bob Strauss is doing."

I said, "The Governor suggests that the President meet sometime during the convention with him, Pat Moynihan and me to talk about what we can do together."

Mondale said, "I'll pass that on to the President."

Bob Strauss called me an hour later. "Would it be presumptuous of me," he said, "to ask what this Carey meeting is that you have asked for?"

"The Governor thought it would be helpful to have a meeting with the President to straighten things out," I said. "I suggested that Moynihan be part of it."

"You know," he said, "the President is goddamned angry at Carey. But he says, 'About Ed, I am hurt. He came out for me when few people did, and I appreciate that. But his quips and his cute remarks tear me apart. He hurts me. I am not angry, but my feelings are hurt.' I told the President," Strauss continued, "that 'Ed is almost obsessed with his problems in New York City. Every time I speak to him, almost every word he says is a replay. He says you can do these things with a stroke of a pen.' And the President said to me, 'He used that phrase with me too—"with a stroke of a pen."' "

Predictably, we went into the Democratic Convention with no more largesse than a fistful of Carter Administration promises. But having done what I could, I reveled in my host role.

Sunday, August 10, was the beginning of all the cocktail parties relating to the convention. I went to about sixteen of them. The highlight of that day was a reception at the Lone Star Café. It was for the Texas delegation. They had a singer and a country-style band there and were really whooping it up when I came in. They asked me to come up on stage, so I did. I said, "I understand that you come from a teeny-weeny state and that you folks are afraid to go out at night. But don't worry, I'll protect you."

That evening I went to the Radio City Music Hall. There were about four thousand people there, at a welcoming event for the delegates. The master of ceremonies introduced Jay Goldin, then Carol Bellamy and then me. We all made some very upbeat remarks. Then the Governor was introduced and they cheered him. Then he did something that was really dumb. He said, "As you know, I am for an open convention."* And he had to know that he was speaking to a mixture of delegates. At that point, a majority started to boo him and a minority started to cheer him. Well, you know, it is never a good idea to divide an audience. But instead of getting out from under, he tried to continue by saying, "Let me tell you about 1924 and the convention we had at that time. They stayed here for a hundred and twenty-five ballots, and if you do that we will be able to keep you in our city for a longer period of time. We would love that." It was a very dumb, unentertaining remark. I was standing off to the side of the stage and I said to Michael Patterson, his press secretary,

*That is, a convention in which delegates, although pledged to specific candidates, would be free to vote as they wished.

"Did you tell him to do that?" Patterson looked up to heaven, closed his eyes, crossed himself and said, "No."

I said, "How is he going to get out of this?"

Patterson said, "He will sing his way out."

And sure enough, as the crowd was booing him, Carey said, "Now, I want to sing a little song for you, but I want our Mayor to come out here with me." So I go out onto the stage and he begins to sing this song which nobody ever heard of, it has no melody, he can't sing it, I can't sing it, the crowd can't sing it. It was so silly and funny that they began to cheer us, and then we left the stage.

The following day was the first day of the convention. It was the day I gave my welcoming address. I got to Madison Square Garden at about 6:30 P.M. and went over to my seat in the New York delegation. For about an hour I was interviewed by just about every news publication and TV station imaginable. About halfway through, I noticed that three burly security guards had appeared in front of me and that they were making it difficult for the press to interview me. They were standing right in front of me and wouldn't move. They said they had been sent over by the Democratic National Committee, and it was pretty obvious that they had been sent to prevent me from talking to the press. So I decided to take a walk around the hall and see if they would go away. When I came back they were still there, and they closed in on me again. So I said, "I don't know who you guys are, but you had better stay at least six feet away from me or there will be a nasty little news story about you."

Then I went up onto the speakers' platform. I knew that the delegates weren't listening to the speeches, so I just ignored the hall and spoke to the TV cameras:

As Mayor and as a Democrat, I am delighted to welcome the 1980 Democratic Convention to New York.

In many ways, this convention will be a repeat of what happened here four years ago. Then we met and chose the next President. And now we'll be doing that again. But in other ways, things are different from what they were four years ago. Here in New York they are very different. Four years ago we were on the edge of bankruptcy. But the nation came forward, and with its help, and that of the State, New York has come through. Our budget is balanced for the first time in more than a decade, and our spirit has never been better.

I know you'll enjoy our restaurants, our theaters, our stores and our museums. I hope also that you will find a chance to enjoy the richness of our neighborhoods, for while New York is Wall Street, the Metropolitan Museum and Lincoln Center, it is also a city of small towns—a city where a hundred and fifty ethnic groups live in relative harmony, where, as Cardinal Cooke told me, Mass is celebrated every Sunday in twenty-three languages.

New York is unique, but New York is also America. This is your hometown. Many of your ancestors came through this port. We welcome you, their children, back tonight.

But the New York a visitor sees is not all there is to this city. We have our mean streets. We have the South Bronx, Harlem and Central Brooklyn, where hope is a scarce commodity and unemployment is almost twice what the nation experienced at the height of the Great Depression. These too are New York—another New York. They are also America—a forgotten part of America.

Their poverty, their unemployment and their despair—and the poverty, unemployment and despair of similar areas in every city in this country—should be a national responsibility, but they are not. Here in New York we pay a total of one billion one hundred million dollars for our local share of Medicaid and welfare. The people who receive this aid come not just from New York, but from the rest of the United States, and indeed, the world. This should be a national responsibility. If we did not have to bear this burden, we would have no trouble balancing our budget. We could lend money to Chrysler.

What is true of New York is also true of the rest of urban America. Close to four out of five American cities face severe fiscal problems, and the cause is not mismanagement, but their obligation to pay for what should be national responsibilities.

When Mount Saint Helens exploded, Congress appropriated eight hundred fifty million dollars for relief. But while New York's South Bronx, or Los Angeles' Watts, or Boston's Roxbury crumbles and decays, there is no similar response.

And while urban America declines, while cities pay for the needs of the nation's poor and unemployed, other areas of the country are growing rich from their natural resources.

Just as certainly as this nation could not endure half slave and half free more than a century ago, it cannot exist half rich and half poor today.

When it has come to cities, Congress has added to our burdens, rather than reducing them. It has mandated programs for cities and states without providing the federal dollars to carry them out. When I was a member of Congress, I was as guilty of this as anyone else. I want to atone publicly for my mistake. I urge you to take the stand that either federal mandates should be removed, or the dollars provided to carry them out. And I'd like to say to the present members of Congress: if you don't, then may God punish you by making you a mayor for a year.

It should also be kept in mind that foreign policy has further added to the problems of urban America. Since 1973, the year of the Arab oil embargo, energy costs have gone up dramatically. Today we still depend on foreign oil. We should be ashamed of ourselves. And we should also recognize just how costly our failure has been. Here in New York, our government energy costs have nearly doubled in the past two years, to four hundred million dollars.

Dealing with the problems of New York and other cities will not be easy in a time of inflation and retrenchment. No one could know better than the Mayor of the City of New York the distance between good intentions and the solution to basic problems. But dealing with problems is what this party has been about ever since it was founded here in 1792. What it will take is a return to the basic ideals of this party. It will also take toughness, and a willingness to put aside past attitudes.

I think the Democratic Party and the country can learn a lesson from New Yorkers. Let me tell you a story that happened when I was running for Mayor. The story has to do with crime. And by the way, I want to point out that although New York is number one in many ways, we rank twelfth among cities in the number of reported crimes. The story expresses the sort of attitude I think we need to overcome our problems.

I went up to a Bronx senior center and told two hundred senior citizens: "A judge I helped elect was mugged recently. And do you know what he did? He called a press conference and said, 'This mugging of me will in no way affect my decisions in matters of this kind.' And an elderly lady got up in the back of the room and said, 'Then mug him again.'"

We've got to be tough. We've got to face realities. We've got to set our priorities and stand up to those who are mugging our cities.

And we've got to show the same attitude abroad. We cannot allow our nation to become hostage to the mad ambitions of the Ayatollah Khomeini, any more than we can allow our cities to be held hostage to neglect. We cannot allow Iranians who call themselves students to trample on our hospitality and violate our laws. Enough is enough. I say: Ship them back to Iran, and do it now.

In closing, let me say: Do your best for the party, enjoy New York and have a great convention. And remember, we are you, and you are us. Like New York, the Democratic Party has a long and glorious history. Like New York, we are composed of many different, and not always harmonious, elements. And like New York, the party not only has endured, it has prevailed.

After I spoke, I hung around the Garden for a little while. But I was home for the 11 P.M. news, and it was really funny. I was watching my speech, and when I got to the part about the Iranians, the camera cut to Bella Abzug, who was a delegate, and you didn't have to be a lip-reader to make out her comment, which was "Shut up," and you could see the anger on her face. Then the following day Charlie Rangel was quoted as being opposed to my speaking out on foreign affairs. I replied that "Charlie Rangel should speak out more on foreign affairs. Oh, yes, he speaks out on South Africa. But he has not spoken out on, for example, Israel. He could have denounced Jesse Jackson when Jackson was photographed kissing Yasir Arafat on the cheek. But he was silent."

On Wednesday, the 13th, I went to meet the President at the heliport with Cuomo (then Lieutenant Governor), Carey and Moynihan. It had been agreed—at least, so I was told—that the four of us would be riding in the car with the President, who was coming in to the convention from Newark Airport. When the helicopter arrived, the President came over to greet us. When he got to me, he whispered in my ear, because of the noise, that he wanted to thank me for "the hospitality that New York City has provided the delegates. They are having a wonderful time."

We got into the car and the President asked, "Where is Hughie?"

Cuomo said, "He's supposed to be with us."

I said, "I'll go look for him." But the car door was locked from the outside, and we had to knock on the window between us and the front seat.

When the door was opened, Cuomo ran out past the reporters to the outside of the heliport. When he came back, he said, "He's gone," adding, "If I'm asked, I'll say to the press that I made a mistake and took Carey's seat and that's why he didn't get into the car."

I knew that wouldn't fly, but fortunately the question wasn't asked.

The basement ballroom in the Sheraton Centre was packed with about five hundred people when we arrived. There was a lot of television coverage also. When Carter got to the podium, the first thing he said was that he wanted to thank Ed Koch and the City of New York for the hospitality and the reception we had provided for the Democratic delegates. The place was filled with Carter-Mondale signs, and the President came over to me and pointed to one woman in the crowd who was holding a sign that said "WE LOVE KOCH" and he laughed.

That afternoon I went to a birthday party for Miss Lillian at 860 United Nations Plaza. I went over to her as soon as I saw her. She looked better than when we had gone to the Vatican together.* We took a very nice picture together touching cheeks. Then she called out to the onlookers, "He is a very nice man, but he lies about me. He says that I always win at poker."

In the afternoon, I went to a party at O'Neal's Balloon at Lincoln Center that was given by Speaker Tip O'Neill. We appeared on Channel 4 together, and he was asked if Kennedy would support Carter at the convention. He said he hoped so but did not know. He sounded, as did all the others, very careful, even ponderous. A reporter then asked me the same question. I said, "Yes, indeed he will. He will be on the dais with Carter. And if he isn't, I will have lost a quarter."

*Mrs. Lillian Carter, the President's mother, had headed the Presidential delegation to the funeral of Pope John Paul I. I had been one of the President's representatives, and we had all traveled together to Rome and back. When I returned to City Hall I was asked about the flight, and I said—perhaps indiscreetly: "Well, you know, Miss Lillian is very smart, and she's wonderful to be with. On the way back she played poker nonstop for twelve hours, and she really cleaned up." Well, that little statement played around the world.

So, a week later I saw her on television. She says, "Why, that Mayor Koch is such a liar! How could I play poker for twelve hours when we were only on the airplane for six? And I only won a quarter."

It was marvelous.

That evening I went to Madison Square Garden early to a dinner hosted by Bobbie Margolis for the foreign ambassadors who had come from Washington for Carter's acceptance speech. As I was entering the room I saw Treasury Secretary William G. Miller. He had a big smile on his face, and I said to the crowd, "This Secretary is the most important Secretary in my life."

And he, with equal verve, said, "And the most generous."

Later on, after the speeches, the U.S. Chief of Protocol came over to me and said that Secretary Miller wanted to speak to me for a few minutes. I asked David Margolis to come along.

We went into a separate room and chatted for about fifteen minutes. David raised the subject of the standby guarantees* and asked what Miller's view was.

"Well," Miller said, "I am not sufficiently familiar with the situation yet, as I was with the Chrysler guarantees. But I understand we have lawyer problems."

I said, "Those problems are far less than existed in the Chrysler situation."

He said, "That's true, but there I knew everything from the beginning and here I have to familiarize myself."

I said, "The guarantees are very important to me and to the City."

He said, "I understand that, and I am certainly sympathetic. Now help us get the President reelected."

I said, "I will certainly try."

After we left the room, David said that he perceived Miller as being both totally political and a lightweight and that if we pushed hard enough, and now, we would get the standby guarantees.

On Thursday, the last day of the convention, I was scheduled to attend a luncheon at the Plaza Hotel. The program for that luncheon, at least the part that I had to attend, was so confused as to be almost unbelievable. First the chairman of the luncheon got up and introduced Bob Strauss, who, he

---

*The federal loan guarantees for capital projects were not all granted at once. They became available at the discretion of the Secretary of the Treasury in increments of $300 million.

said, would be introducing me. It was the first Strauss had heard of it. He got up and said he was pleased to do it—a little statement about me and the City; and then I went on.

I welcomed everybody and said the City was on a high without drugs, and then I read my Squat Theater memo. Then I said, "Hearty appetite!" and started to leave the stage. At that point the chairman came up from behind me and whispered into my ear, "You should acknowledge the Governor, but don't ask him up on the stage." So I go back to the mike and say, "It is now my privilege to acknowledge the presence of the great Governor of the State of New York, Hugh Carey. Governor, stand up and take a bow." Well, nobody gets up. Then I said, "Hugh, where are you?" And then it was clear that the Governor was not in the room and that the chairman had blundered by making it obvious that the Governor hadn't made it. So then I said, "He must be out looking for his car."

Well, now, that comment had a little life of its own. The story is that after Carey took his walk at the heliport his aides attempted to cover for him, or themselves, by saying there had been a mix-up and that the Governor didn't know he was invited. Okay. But then they added a little something on: "Of course, Mayor Koch asked a security guard three times how to get into the President's car." Of course I had not. When I was told of their little ploy by my press secretary, I told him to relay the word to Carey's press people that if they continued to do things like that I would respond. And they knew I knew how to do it. They probably thought that that was what I was doing at the Plaza. It was not. I had no wish to embarrass the Governor, but they would never believe that. After all, the delegates leave town. And then it is still me and the Governor.

Toward the end of August, Joel McCleary came in to see me. McCleary was Carter's statewide campaign manager in New York. The word always was that McCleary was very close to Hamilton Jordan, that they had worked together closely in 1976. McCleary was a Harvard-educated WASP turned Buddhist. He was thirty-three years old, smiley and pudgy. He said he was putting together the campaign for the fall and how much did I wish to be involved? I said, "I have an informal press conference every day, and I will speak out there when it is appropriate."

He said, "Mayor Beame took a very active role four years ago. He provided us with substantial numbers of City workers."

I said, "We can't do that. We do not have a patronage operation; therefore there is nobody in the government we can call to come help. Anyway, even if I could, I wouldn't. That's one difference between me and Abe Beame."

Then he said, "Well, Mr. Mayor, how committed are you actually to the President?"

I said, "I am supportive, but without much energy on my part. Because of the last U.N. resolution on Jerusalem,* I don't think the Democratic Party will carry 50 percent of the Jewish vote."

McCleary said, "Well, Israel has been acting rather badly. It may be that some people perceive people around the President as being anti-Semitic, but the people around Reagan are really scary."

I said, "You won't be able to sell that in New York. Reagan was California's Governor for eight years—two terms. Can you point to a single fascistic action on his part?"

"No," says McCleary.

"Right or wrong," I said, "more people are frightened of Jerry Brown on that point than they are of Reagan."

He says, "Mr. Mayor, what will it take to get you more involved? I think, for instance, that you should be telling people about how Kemp-Roth† will destroy the City and State."

I shook my head. "It won't sell. The sophisticated people who are rich are for Kemp-Roth. It is money in their pockets. And nobody else understands it. If you want me to get

---

*On June 30, 1980, the Israeli Parliament approved a bill reaffirming Jerusalem as Israel's capital. As a result, the Security Council, under Arab pressure, passed a resolution calling upon all nations that had embassies in Jerusalem to remove them. Those that did not would have been subject to a cut-off of Arab aid and contracts. The United States did not veto, but rather abstained, and as a result twelve countries removed their embassies from Jerusalem.
†The three-year federal tax-cut bill.

involved, one thing would be the Moynihan Medicaid legislation.''

"You mean if the President comes out for the Moynihan Medicaid bill you will get actively involved?'' he said.

"No,'' I replied. "The President came out for a federal welfare takeover when he was running in 1976. Nobody would believe him today if he said he was 'for' the Moynihan Medicaid bill. Certainly not I. But he's got a Democratic Congress down there. If he got it through, or at least really tried to get it through, I could get interested. But if he can't get it passed now, he never will. Especially if he isn't there next year.'' Well, that sort of ended the meeting.

A few days later I got a call from McCleary: "Mr. Mayor, Hamilton Jordan is coming to New York and would like to meet with you.''

I say, "Fine.''

So on September 3 we have our meeting on the porch at Gracie Mansion—Hamilton Jordan, Joel McCleary, Pat Caddell* and me. They were a half-hour late arriving because they had been around the corner with Steve Ross.† They first got their drinks—Scotch, bourbon and wine—and then we began to talk.

Caddell took out his poll for New York, and the reading showed that the President was ahead of Reagan in a two-man race, and that he was also ahead in a three-man race including John Anderson. They all said they were very confident that they were going up. Caddell said, "And you, Mr. Mayor, are the most popular political figure in New York State, according to our polls. The poll results show you at fifty-four to twenty-two percent favorable in the State of New York— higher than Moynihan, who is the next-highest, and considerably higher than Javits.''

Then they asked me what I thought about the President's chances. I said, "My discussions with the people of New York City do not correspond with your poll. I know the Jews are unhappy with Reagan and will probably not vote for him

*Patrick Caddell was president Carter's in-house pollster.
†Steven J. Ross is chairman of the board, president and chief executive officer of Warner Communications. He has been a generous financial backer of Governor Carey and of other Democrats.

because they think he is dumb, and they won't vote for a dummy. But they are not happy with Carter either. They will probably ultimately vote for Carter, but I don't think you can count on it at this moment. Also, you are getting the benefit of Reagan's dumb mistakes. They should have sent him to China, as I suggested."

Page 1, August 29, 1980

The *NEW YORK POST*

'SEND HIM
TO CHINA!'

Mayor Koch has a hot tip to Republicans on how to win the election: send Ronald Reagan to China.

"Ronald Reagan will commit hara-kiri"—Japanese ritual suicide—in the presidential campaign, because he "has hoof-in-mouth disease," the irrepressible Mayor predicted today.

McCleary said, "That was a terrific headline, especially when you said that he is going to commit hara-kiri." McCleary asked Jordan if he had seen the headline. Jordan said no, but then McCleary pulled out another *Post*, which said something like "Jordan says we don't need to carry New York," and McCleary said, "I can't wait till the President sees this."

Jordan is a very smooth, very engaging person, and he doesn't talk too much. Though he was obviously the head of this contingent, he allowed McCleary to do most of the talking. At that point McCleary said to me, "Tell Hamilton what is on your mind."

I told Jordan about the failure to get budgetary support over the last three years. I said, "I am for the President and I will vote for him. But the major contribution I bring to the President is my credibility. And I will never say anything I don't believe, and the people of this city know that."

Hamilton said, "I know that too. But you tell us that the Feds have failed you by about five hundred million dollars over the last three years. Eizenstadt says we have gotten the City a lot of money. And the President doesn't understand why we have this dispute."

I said, "You are talking about apples and oranges. They did give us the programmatic moneys.* But we have had to lay off or attrit eight thousand cops."

Hamilton looked astonished and said, "Eight thousand? It is hard for me to grasp that number. That is more than any city I know of has."

Then I continued and told them, "For this semester we have laid off twenty-two hundred teachers." He looked astonished again. I said, "What you are comparing is not comparable."

He said, "Well, the President doesn't understand it."

I said, "I visited the President in March and I told him that we needed the Moynihan Medicaid bill. He said he couldn't do it because you were going to have a balanced budget and that it would cost two and a half billion, of which New York City would get two hundred million. Now you don't have a balanced budget, and the President is spending billions of dollars of extra money, so there is no longer any reason for him not to be for that bill."

McCleary said, "You told me the President had to get it passed by November."

I said, "What I conveyed to you was that he had to be for it and had to take every measure on his part to pass it before November. But if it is not passed because of Congressional opposition, then I would not find fault with the President so long as he did everything within his power to try and get it."

Jordan said, "We will look at that."

McCleary said, "Let's talk about Israel. Tell Hamilton what your feelings are."

So for the next forty minutes we talked about Israel. The first thing I said was "Let me make it clear that the overriding priority for me is to get budgetary support for this city. But if you are asking me do I have other concerns which will not affect my support for the President but which I am concerned about, the answer is yes. I believe, as the Jewish community believes, that the things he said in the past on Jerusalem's always being Israel's capital, the Golan Heights'

---

*Moneys earmarked for special projects—thus not providing direct budgetary relief.

never being returned to Syria and the West Bank will no longer mean anything. I don't agree with what you have done on voting for the resolution to censure on Jerusalem and abstaining on the latest U.N. vote. You are responsible for the embassies' leaving Jerusalem, and there is no reason for the position that you are taking."

Referring to Carter, Jordan said, "What can he do to convince the Jews that he is for them and that if he is gone the Egyptian–Israeli peace pact won't be finished?"

I said, "I don't know, but it has to be more than a promise. It has to be something tangible. How about putting a U.S. military base in Israel so they know you will be there?"

Jordan said, "They don't want it."

I said, "I'm surprised at that."

And so it went. They asked if I had any other ideas. I said I didn't but that I would think about it.

Two days later I got a call from Gene Eidenberg and we went through it again.

He says, "Ed, we would like you to speak out for us on Israel."

I said, "No. The reason you are calling me is because I have credibility with the people of this city. They know I will never say anything that I don't believe. And until you people change your position I will not defend it. I will not be a Judas goat. You will have to find someone else."

For the rest of that week I questioned my advisers about what moves the Carter Administration might make toward salvaging its chances with the Jewish community. In the end it was decided that Carter would need to provide three things: an assurance that vetos would be used on Security Council resolutions that were anti-Israel, a pledge to withdraw from the General Assembly if the United Nations should expel Israel and a pledge that the United States would not furnish the Saudis offensive weaponry, including bomb racks for the F-15.

Although New York's budgetary needs remained top priority, the Carter Administration's position on Israel was becoming a matter of some urgency. In the latter half of September, the talk at the United Nations was to the effect that the Arabs were going to attempt to have Israel expelled from the

General Assembly. I, for my part, denounced the United Nations as a "cesspool of anti-Semitism."

On the 29th of September I met the President at the West 30th Street heliport. When Carter shook my hand, he also whispered into my ear, "I am going to be saying something on Israel and the General Assembly."

I said, "What I hope you can say is 'If the General Assembly expels Israel the United States will withdraw from the General Assembly.'" Then we got into the President's limousine and rode across town. In the car were Governor Carey, Mario Cuomo and Liz Holtzman.* The President was in town to address an ILGWU† convention at the Sheraton Centre. He had recently acquitted himself superbly in the Billygate scandal. The crowds were cheering him again. He said, "This is a good response."

I said, "Mr. President, I have taken you from the heliport about fifteen times and only once has the crowd not cheered you. That was when I took you to the Urban League. And that crowd wasn't hostile, just motionless."

Carter said, "Yes. I remember that very well. That was the day you gave me hell, and I was thinking, Well, Ed Koch has his people out there standing with their arms against their sides."

When he got to the hotel and made his speech, Carter did in fact come very close to saying what I had suggested. The speech was cleverly written. On first hearing, it sounded as if Carter had pledged to withdraw the United States if the General Assembly expelled Israel. The wording was just deceptive enough to fool the *Post* headline writers, who ran an evening headline: "PREZ TO U.N.: 'LAY OFF ISRAEL OR WE PULL OUT!'" But Carter had left himself room to maneuver. He had merely suggested, not promised. All in all, it was a good day for the President in New York.

The following day was a good day for me. After months of haggling and hours on the phone to Washington, an additional $300 million in standby loan guarantees was made available

---

*Brooklyn Congresswoman Elizabeth Holtzman, the Democratic nominee for Jacob Javits' Senate Seat.
†International Ladies Garment Workers Union.

to the City by Secretary Miller. Characteristically, the Carter Administration had waited to move until the last day of the federal fiscal year. Nonetheless, the $300 million was finally in place. My convention meeting with Miller had paid off.

And it wasn't a bad day in New York for Ronald Reagan either. Very cleverly he had said, when asked about his position on the loan guarantees: "Oh, I changed my position on that a long time ago. I changed it when Mayor Koch was elected and began doing the things that needed doing here to straighten it out. That was always my position: that until they started straightening things out, you couldn't ask the rest of the taxpayers to bail out the City if the City was going to go on with its extravagant ways." I may have said that I thought Governor Reagan was "dumb." But I was changing my mind on that.

As the Presidential election swung into its final month, one thing was clear: both major candidates viewed New York's forty-one electoral votes as crucial to their chances of success. And all of a sudden the Southern peanut farmer and the Western movie actor were New York's best friends.

'I love N.Y. better than you!' 'Oh, yeah, well I love . . .'

From the New York *Daily News*, Friday, October 3, 1980

I appreciated the irony here. I also recognized opportunity. So I set about seeing what I could get.

While Reagan was in town his people called City Hall. "Would the Mayor brief the Governor on the problems of the City?" they asked.

"Of course," I said.

And we set a date.

On October 5, Gene Eidenberg called. "We understand that you are going to meet with Governor Reagan," he said. "We're really concerned about it and what he will make of it."

"Gene," I said, "there is no way in the world of my turning down the request of a Presidential candidate who asks that I brief him on the problems of the City of New York. If I were to turn him down I should not be Mayor. I have said to everybody, 'I'm for Jimmy Carter, but I will brief any State-wide candidate.'"

He said, "Well, when you leave the room it is a question of what you will say. Are you going to say 'Reagan impressed me,' and so on?"

I said, "Gene, I'm a big boy and I know what is appropriate to say."

He said, "I'm sure you do, but you know everyone says you are the key to New York City."

I said, "I'm glad they say that; and I have said, as you know, 'The key to New York City is the Feds' taking over Medicaid.' You have heard me say that, haven't you?"

He said, "I certainly have." Then he said, "Well, okay," and his voice trailed off.

It was during this period that I was going around saying, "Thank God for the two-party system."

After the Eidenberg call, the White House apparently decided that bigger guns would be needed to keep me in line. On the 9th, Bob Strauss, the President's campaign chairman, called. On the 10th he and I sat down in the lobby of the Barbizon Hotel to discuss what I was up to and what the Carter Administration could do about it.

I asked Strauss if he would prefer talking privately. He said, "Anything we say is going to be straight talk. Mr. Mayor, we need you. And everywhere I go I am told that you are hurting us and hurting the President. You should be for us. And when you meet with Reagan, we worry about it. I am told that you think Carter is anti-Semitic. I want you to know that there is a big difference between the Carter Administration and the Reagan people. They have a number of people who would be very bad for Israel.''

"Look, Bob,'' I said, "nobody can tell you that I have attacked the President, because I haven't. Whatever I have said has been positive. I am not now energized as I would be if the President came out for the Moynihan Medicaid bill. The President sent two letters to Abe Beame supporting a Medicaid takeover in 1976, and he still has not done it. If you want to get me energized to the fullest, he will have to do that. As I told Jordan, that means he has to send a message to Congress or introduce his own bill. And with respect to meeting with Reagan, I should be impeached if I refused to meet with a Presidential candidate. Regarding the Jews, I want you to know that I will never say anything I don't believe. As I told Jordan, I will not be a Judas goat, and I don't believe in the President's policies. In fact, I blame him for the fact that twelve countries have removed their embassies from Jerusalem, including the Dutch. They did it because we abstained on the U.N. resolution and it carried. Our abstention was just like a 'yes' vote. If the President wants me to do anything for him regarding the Jews and Israel, it will happen only if he does two things. The first is that he admit it was an error to abstain on the vote on Jerusalem and declare that in the future whenever there are resolutions that are flawed or unfair and adverse to Israel we would veto and not simply abstain. The second thing is to state that we recognized Israeli sovereignty over Jerusalem, and that could be couched in terms of West Jerusalem. Why shouldn't we place our embassy in West Jerusalem? It is terrible that we don't recognize Israel's sovereignty over Jerusalem or over West Jerusalem.''

Strauss said, "You don't understand that we could blow the peace treaty if the President said anything about Jerusalem. He has it all scripted out. Begin and Sadat have agreed to everything, with Begin having a right to sign off. You have to trust Carter on this.''

I said, "I am never going to do anything I don't believe in. If he wants me, that is what he is going to have to do. If he doesn't I am still for him, but I won't say anything on this issue."

He said, "Well, the fact is that I don't believe you could bring us anybody anyway."

I said, "You're absolutely right. I never claimed I could bring anybody to vote for the President. Others think I can. I know I can't. But it is nice that they think I can."

Strauss said, "If you say nothing, you lose votes for us. But if you speak for us, you don't lose votes and you don't gain votes." Then we got up to leave.

At that point I said to him, "I want you to know that I have said publicly that if for any reason I can't get through to the President if he is reelected, I would call on you because I like you, trust you, and I think you are one of the best."

He said, "I am vain enough to like your saying that, and I am smart enough to know that it's bullshit." Then we both laughed.

Then he said, "After you meet with Reagan, I hope you will say that you are supporting the President and that you prefer him to Reagan. You should say that you should be impeached if you refused to meet with a Presidential candidate but that you don't believe Reagan will be in the White House."

I said, "Be assured that I will say something appropriate and supportive of the President."

When I was a first-term Congressman, I was invited to speak to a Congressional prayer breakfast. The subject on which I was to speak was "Judaism." Feeling myself unprepared, I went to the Congressional Library and read up on "Judaism." After my speech I took questions, and the questions were on Judaism. As the session drew to a close, I knew there was one question that had gone unasked. And so I said, "There is one question you are not asking me, fellows. And that is 'Do Jews have dual loyalty?' No one ever asks that about the English, or the Irish, or the Italians. But they do ask it about the Jews." Then I raised my right hand and said,

"I pledge to you that if Israel ever invades the United States, I shall stand with the United States."

As I became aware that I was getting nowhere with President Carter on the Moynihan Medicaid bill and on the rewriting of the revenue-sharing formulas, I turned, because Carter was turning me there, to the question of the Administration's support of Israel. And I did so knowing that the dual-loyalty question was always in the air.

A few days after my meeting with Strauss, the Vice President called. "Ed," he said, "there's a very bad relationship developing between you and the President. Can I correct it?"

"Look," I said, "do you want me to tell you what the problems are? I have repeatedly told them to Gene Eidenberg, Hamilton Jordan and Bob Strauss, and they don't do anything about it."

"Never mind them," he said. "Talk to me."

I said, "Look, there are two areas in which I have problems with the President. The first is Medicaid and the other is Israel. Let me first talk about Medicaid." Then I gave him all of the budgetary background as it related to my conversation with the President in March, when he had shown a total lack of knowledge of the Moynihan Medicaid bill. "You will not get me energized," I continued, "unless I get a message to Congress from the President, or legislation with his name on it."

Then I said, "On Israel, there are two things the President did that I oppose and don't accept and won't defend: one is the original resolution denouncing Israel on the West Bank, which we voted for. I believe, no matter what the President says, that he knew what was in the resolution. The second is the more recent resolution on Jerusalem, which in my judgment caused twelve friendly countries to withdraw their embassies. I hold him personally responsible. Poor Holland. It withdrew because of the resolution. Now, insofar as my relationship with the President is concerned, that will never be restored. I want to tell you in confidence that I think he's a mean and vindictive man. After the incident with his brother and my calling Billy a wacko the President said to me, 'You have done me more damage than any man in America.' I knew at that point that our relationship was over, and the fact I'd come out for him in August of '79 when few others did meant nothing. Fritz, I've been in politics since 1960, and I know the question is not 'What have you done?' but 'What are you doing for me?' You should understand that I'm never going to need anybody's endorsement because I'm never running for anything—not Senator, not Governor, Vice President or President.* I'm not like my crazy Governor, who's running for President. I will only be running for reelection as Mayor, and if I'm popular it's because I'm honest. I say exactly what's on my mind. So if you think I'm important, which I don't . . . I don't bring a single vote.''

"Yes, you do," he said, "or at least you can take them away."

I said, "If that is so, he's going to have to change his position on Israel and say that in the future we will not just abstain but veto, and we will place our embassy in West Jerusalem." And then I concluded, "Well, I've probably told you more about penguins than you want to know."

He said, "No, I'm interested. But Ed, you're wrong about the President knowing what was in the [Jerusalem] resolution. I went to see the President the Monday after the resolution was passed and I showed him the language, and the President turned white. He said, 'I didn't know the language on Jerusalem was there and they didn't take it out, as I told them.' I told him to tell the American people we were wrong.''

"You should know," I said, "that I know the decision on abstaining was made by Carter. I have spoken to Muskie,† and he told me that he, yourself and Carter were together and the decision was made at the highest level.''

Mondale said his recollection was that the Administration had voted for similar resolutions in the past. He said, "Our record on military and economic assistance, preventing the

*This was a speech that I gave publicly and privately countless times. And it was one that later haunted me.
†Former Maine Senator Edmund Muskie, Vance's replacement as Secretary of State.

PLO from becoming a member of the World Bank, denouncing terrorism, opposing a PLO state, never forcing Israel to accept anything by threatening, our fifteen-year oil contract with Israel, our preventing an Arab boycott of Israel, our not continuing the Nixon and Ford games of eight years, the President personally monitoring and negotiating the Egyptian–Israeli treaty, denouncing the Soviet Union on emigration—Carter and Mondale provide a record the Republicans cannot match.''

''Look, Fritz,'' I said, ''I'm voting for Carter, and I expect you will recall I told you in the Rose Garden I was sorry that *you* were not running for President. And the major reason I am supporting Carter is because he said that you would be his candidate to succeed him and that he would support you. But it was Carter's decision on the U.N., not yours. If they want me to campaign strongly for Carter henceforth there will have to be vetoes, and our embassy will have to be in West Jerusalem.''

In October I got a call from William Safire, the columnist. He said, ''Ed, can you remember back several months ago to a lunch you had with Cyrus Vance, whom you wanted to make up with after he had left Washington?''

I said, ''Yes, Bill, I had such a lunch.''

He said, ''When you got the soup dish, someone asked, 'Do you think Carter will sell out Israel after his reelection?' And Cyrus Vance said, 'Yes.' Ed, I want you to confirm or deny that story.''

I said, ''I am not going to confirm or deny any private conversation I had with someone at lunch. Otherwise people will stop eating with me.''

Safire then said, ''Do you know the Washington game Wave Off?''

I said, ''No.''

He said, ''That's strange. You were in Washington.''

I said, ''Yes, but I didn't go to any parties.''

He said, ''Well, the game is played in the following way. If a reporter whom you trust tells you he has a story, but he doesn't want to go with it unless there is some confirmation, he will repeat that story to you, and if it has no basis you will say, 'Wave off.' "

I said, "I will not wave you off that story."

He said, "You are a straight shooter."

That same afternoon George Arzt of the *Post* came in and said, "You were not at President Carter's meeting with Jewish voters in Forest Hills. Was that deliberate?"

I said, "Yes."

He said, "What was the reason?"

I said, "I don't believe in his policy on Israel and I am not going to defend it. I am for Carter because he is best for the City as it relates to City issues, but I will not be his emissary to the Jews."

"Does that mean you won't go to any Jewish meetings?"

I said, "I won't go to meetings that are called for the purpose of discussing his Israel policy. But I will go to meetings of concern to the general public. You know Carter has hurt Israel enormously. There was the censure vote. There was the abstention on Jerusalem. I would say Carter is responsible for those twelve countries' removing their embassies from Jerusalem."

When he left my office, Arzt told my press secretary he had a bombshell. I lay awake half the night thinking about the Arzt story and the Safire story to follow.

On October 15, the *New York Post* ran this page 1 headline:

KOCH SHOCK
FOR CARTER
He refuses to be go-between
for Jewish vote in New York

Meanwhile, I had urgently called Cy Vance's office to alert him to the Safire story. His secretary said he was at that moment on an airplane returning to New York from the Far East. I thought of doing what Carter had done—namely, calling the plane and asking the captain to tell Vance not to talk to the press until he calls the Mayor. But obviously I wouldn't do that.

The next morning I had reached him on the phone. He said, "I never said that. You have to call Safire and tell him I never said it." Well, now, the lunch had been three months before. And Cy Vance is an honest man. Furthermore, it isn't my policy to comment on conversations I have at lunch with friends.

I said, "Okay, Cy. I'll call him and tell him." At that moment I regretted having played Wave Off.

I then called Safire, and he was quite upset; he said he had already written the story, but that he would try to rewrite it within the deadline. It was in fact rewritten and the Vance episode omitted. Even without Vance's comment, Safire's column which appeared October 15, entitled "The Fate of Israel," was a powerful condemnation of Carter and his position on Israel and its effect on the Jews.

From there I let the story go. It was not my intention to grievously hurt Carter by further introducing an emotional issue in the final stages of the campaign.

On October 16 the President was back in New York. This time he was scheduled to hold a political rally for the TV cameras and then attend the Alfred E. Smith dinner, a political classic that is hosted annually by the Cardinal of the Roman Catholic Archdiocese of New York. The 1980 Al Smith dinner was the only time during the campaign, with the exception of the debates, that Carter and Reagan sat together in the same room.

The evening began with the obligatory ride from the heliport.

When I picked up the President there, he was coming in from Hofstra University, where he had held a town hall session. I was the only one meeting him, since the others in his entourage were arriving with him. When he alighted from the helicopter, he greeted me with "Mr. Mayor, you have a wonderful city." That was his only direct remark to me.

When I got into his car, Moynihan, Carey and Cuomo got in too. Cuomo and I sat in the jump seats. There were none of the customary crowds as we rode to the Sheraton Centre Hotel. Carey began again with the bike lanes. He said to me,

"You gotta get rid of the bike lanes.* They are terrible."

I said to him, "Look, they probably are terrible. We're gonna give them a chance and keep them till spring. If the ridership doesn't increase, we'll pull them up."

Carey said, "If you don't pull them up now, I won't give you the money to pull them up."

I thought, What arrogance. And Cuomo says to me, "Isn't this ridiculous that he should talk about bike lanes here, with the President in the car?"

When we got to the Sheraton Centre, the President went to a holding room and we walked into a small ballroom packed with about five hundred people. When Cuomo, Carter's New York State campaign cochairman, walked in there was applause, and when I walked in there was half applause and half booing. I just simply raised my thumbs high in the air as though they were all cheering. I saw signs saying "SAVE SYDENHAM HOSPITAL." It was clear to me that it was an organized demonstration to support the President and to attack me. It didn't bother me at all, especially since four or five people whispered to me, "You're doing terrific."

Then we get on the platform and they bring out Anthony Scotto of the longshoremen's union. I'm thinking: Aren't they crazy to so compromise the President with a convicted felon and labor racketeer?

The President delayed coming in, and so, first, Carey went to the microphone to amuse the crowd, and he began to sing. It was just silly. Then Moynihan took the mike and he hadn't yet even taken off his hat, which made his performance all the more bizarre.

Moynihan said, "We're for the President. We need Jimmy Carter. He's come out for a federal takeover of Medicaid."

Cuomo was sitting with me, and he whispered, "These two guys are outrageous. The President never said anything like that. Moynihan will get us into trouble."

I laughed. Then the President came in and received a huge cheer, and then one of the union leaders introduced him. That

---

*The bike lanes were lanes set aside on City streets for the exclusive use of bicycle traffic. They were instituted at my insistence and lasted about two months.

same chairman introduced Carey and Moynihan, and they both got tremendous cheers. Then he introduced me. At that moment the President was one foot away from me and to my left. When my name was mentioned about half the audience cheered and half booed. Maybe there were more boos than cheers. As that occurred, the President visibly flinched and moved two feet away from me, clearly wanting to disassociate himself from me. I put my thumbs in the air like a prizefighter or as though I were in Yankee Stadium, where they boo politicians and where I make believe that the booing is applause. And I do it to drive them crazy. Here too I wanted to drive them crazy by responding in such a way that anyone seeing me would think they were cheering me. At that point I leaned toward the President and said, "See, Mr. President, you don't really need me."

I was thinking, If you had any real brains you would come to my defense—not that I need you to, but you would hold up my hand, associating yourself with me. Instead, you walk away.

From the rally I went directly over to the Waldorf for the picture-taking session at the Al Smith dinner. It was to begin at 6:15 P.M. I had sent my advance man out to get me some studs for my full-dress shirt. I told him to bring them in for under $5. He did. I changed into white tie and tails in a room right off the room where the pictures were to be taken. At 6:15 I was ready. The advance man came in and said nobody had appeared for the photo session except Ronald Reagan. He said, "The Democrats are all still over at the Sheraton Centre, and the Cardinal is in Rome. It's just you and Governor Reagan."

I said, "Okay." And that's where I first met the Governor.

Afterward we all went into the ballroom for dinner. I was seated on the dais next to Nancy Reagan. Rupert Murdoch, the owner of the *Post*, was opposite me. I kept having trouble with one of my shirt studs, and Nancy kept helping me with it. At one point she said, "If you ever need your shirts repaired, I will be happy to sew them for you. I do it for Ronnie."

I asked her if she had had any time to relax, and she said no. We agreed that we loved the movies. I recommended

Ordinary People to her. Then she asked me, "What day is this?" I knew exactly what she meant. She was in a constant, twenty-four-hour daze going from place to place. We talked about how the last three weeks are the most difficult. She said she couldn't wait for it all to be over.

Then Rupert came over and I introduced him to Nancy. He said the *Post* was going to endorse the Governor on its front page the next day. I told Nancy that that was very important and that without the *Post* I couldn't have been elected Mayor. Rupert said, "No. You would have won anyway."

The speeches were very interesting. Carter came in at 9:15 P.M., and I thought he was very heavy-handed. He said, "I gave my good friend Mayor Koch some advice earlier. I told him not to get too close to Governor Reagan. On the Governor's 'I Love New York' button, the paint is still wet." The crowd booed and did not laugh. Carter's hostility to Reagan and me was obvious. Reagan spoke before the President, and he was excellent—very light, witty and charming. I watched the news when I got home. The difference between the two was startling. When Carter spoke, his meanness came through, and Reagan, looking at the audience, seemed very distressed and nonplused by Carter's attacks on him. On the other hand, Reagan's comments about the President were never vicious and were well received. Reagan won that one overwhelmingly.

The morning after the Al Smith dinner I was to meet with Governor Reagan. The Democrats were worried by the meeting. Mario Cuomo and Donald Manes, Carter's State-wide campaign chairmen, had each denounced the meeting as abetting the enemy. But I had persisted in my statement: "I should be impeached if I didn't meet with him. Don't you know that if he wins he will be the President, and if he loses he will still be the leader of the Republican Party for the next four years and, as such, one of the four or five most influential opinion makers in this country? How could it be good for the City for me not to brief Governor Reagan on the problems we face here?"

On the 17th at about 10:45 A.M. Ronald Reagan came to Gracie Mansion. We had set up a press conference on the lawn, and there were about fifty local reporters who had arrived at 10. I was told by the Reagan staff that when he arrived I should wait on the porch until the national press got out of their cars, and then come down as Reagan opened his door, and then lead him onto the porch. When he arrived we did exactly that. I had arranged with the local press that he would stand with me at the top of the porch steps, before going inside, and we would wave, which we did. When setting up the meeting, his staff had requested the following: that he and I sit next to each other on the same side of the table (they specified this so that we would not appear to be in an adversary relationship); that the briefing would be twenty-five minutes, to be followed by a press conference, and that the Governor wanted Sanka and jelly beans, which we provided.

As we walked onto the porch he said to me, "Nancy said to tell you that anytime you need help with your shirt studs, just call on her." We both laughed.

The day before the briefing I had discussed the strategy with Nat Leventhal, Bob Wagner and Allen Schwartz, and we had agreed that I would make the presentation and that we would focus on only three issues: (1) Medicaid takeover by the Federal Government, (2) the $600 million remaining on the federal guarantees and (3) removing federal mandates requiring us to do things with our money and not with theirs.

In my statement to Reagan, after I laid out the history of why the City was in the straits it was in and how we were getting out of them, I stressed the three issues on which I needed help. I briefed the Governor in eight minutes. Then I turned to Brigham and asked him if he had anything to add.

He said, "Governor, let me show you two of our charts." The charts had been prepared and were sitting on an easel. He explained them. The first described our operating budget in the five-year period from FY '76 to a GAAP*-balanced budget in FY '81.

After that I said to the Governor, "The three things that we need help on are, first, Medicaid and welfare. Medicaid costs us seven hundred forty-one million annually and welfare three hundred fifty million. Governor, if we didn't have to pay this, New York City could lend money to Chrysler."

I said, "The second thing is we need your commitment

*Acronym for "generally accepted accounting principles."

that the Feds will provide the remaining six hundred million in federal loan guarantees; and the third is that the Feds will end their mandates unless they are willing to pay for them.'' When I had stated the three requests, I said to him at that point, "Governor, do you think God hears my prayers?'' which was a reference to the right-wing Moral Majority minister's comment to the effect that God does not hear the prayers of a Jew.

And then, with a certain amount of restrained anger at Carter for having referred to that matter the night before, he said with a laugh, "I know God hears your prayers.'' Then he said that he was amazed at what the City had done and that he would like to congratulate me. On the question of welfare, he said that he would like to remove the Federal Government altogether; by reducing federal taxes, he would enable the states to raise whatever money they needed for that purpose. He said he was not willing to agree to have the Feds take over Medicaid costs because medical care provided by government, he said, had proved in some cases to be five times as costly as that by the private sector. He said he was open-minded about what could be done.

He expounded on what he'd done as Governor of California on welfare reform and was pleased when I told him we had reduced the number of ineligible welfare recipients from 18 percent in 1973 to 6 percent in 1980, and that we were no longer number one in welfare grants; that the grants themselves had not been increased since 1976, and that now we were number eleven in the country in the level of grants.*

At the end of our dialogue, Reagan volunteered, "Mr. Mayor, I just want you to know that I agree with you on the Mideast and I think it is terrific that you are standing up and saying the things you have been saying.''

Then I said, "Governor, we're going outside to a press conference, and it would be nice to be able to say something positive if we can. Could you say you agree that the City should get the balance of its federal guarantees—the six-hundred-million-dollar question—for next year? Could you

---

*In July 1981, the State Legislature passed a 15-percent grant increase. That brought the City of New York to seventh in the United States.

also make a statement about relieving us of the burden of the federal mandates even though you can't agree on the Medicaid question?''

Reagan had brought three people with him: Lyn Notziger, his press secretary; Stuart Spencer, a campaign consultant, and Martin Anderson, domestic-affairs adviser. At that point Nofziger interjected, "Mayor, if you promise to keep the press conference brief, we'll do it."

I said, "It will be brief."

Then we went outside, and there were now about 150 reporters—TV, radio and newspapers. I simply introduced the Governor, without a statement of my own.

He then, both on his own and in response to questions, said that he was for providing the $600-million drawdown on the loan guarantees, and he said that the Federal Government should not impose mandates unless it paid for them. In response to a question as to whether he would support me on the Republican ticket, he smiled and indicated my record, mentioning how we had kept the budget down compared with the State and federal governments. Then he said that he would support me on any ticket.

I then walked him over to his car and said goodbye.

When I returned to the porch to face the press I was asked, "Do you think his position on Israel is better than Carter's?"

I said, "Yes."

Before he left, Reagan had said to the press that he wanted to applaud me for speaking out on the Mideast, that it had had to be done. He'd indicated his support for my position, which was no surprise, since I had attacked the Carter position on the United Nations versus Israel and the Carter Administration's refusal to veto sanctions against Israel. One other question that was asked of me in the press conference was "Were you angered by the statement of Jody Powell which, in effect, dismissed you when you said you wouldn't go to a Jewish function to speak for him on Israel?"

I said, "Regrettably, campaign aides do their candidates great damage, but I will not let Jody Powell's comments affect my relationship with the President."

As a result of that October meeting I changed my assessment of the Governor. At that meeting he had displayed common sense, decency and a familiarity with the issues. He was not dumb.

Three days later, on October 20, Jimmy Carter was again in town. This time he was scheduled to attend a fund raiser for himself in Chinatown and then to speak to a $17-million Democratic Party fund raiser at the Sheraton Centre. The Carter forces had read all about my meeting with Reagan. And they were not pleased. (It was not long after this that my advance man had a discussion with one of Mondale's speechwriters at a Carter-Mondale campaign stop. The advance man said, "So, Marty, what are they saying about Ed Koch in Washington these days?" And Marty Kaplan, the speechwriter, replied: "I think there is probably more speculation about the motives of Ed Koch than there is about any other person's in the world, including the Ayatollah.")

At 5 P.M. I went to the Silver Palace Restaurant in Chinatown to attend the Carter fund raiser. I stayed there about a half-hour. When the President came in, he was cool but correct toward me. He had a smile on his face but did not display the normal warmth that he had shown from time to time in the past.

After that, I went to Gracie Mansion to attend a farewell party for Harry Tishelman,* who was going to the Small Business Administration. When I arrived at the mansion, about 6 P.M., I went in to see Harry and say hello. There were about a hundred people in the reception room.

Then I was told that the President was calling. I went into the library to take the call. A Presidential aide said that the President wanted to see me in his suite at the Sheraton Centre as soon as possible. I told him that I had to put on my dinner jacket and asked him if I had time to change. He said, "He would like you to be here at ten after seven, because he has another meeting at seven twenty-five."

I said, "Okay, I'll be there."

As I was leaving the mansion I told Allen Schwartz about my call from the President. I asked him if he wanted to go to

*My original Commissioner of the Department of Finance.

the meeting. In the car with me were Allen; my press secretary, Tom Goldstein, and John LoCicero.

When I went up to the twenty-first floor to see the President, there were about ten security people outside his door. I waited for a few minutes and then one of the guards said, "Okay, you can come in now." Allen and I walked toward the door and then another security person said, "The President wants to see you alone."

I said, "Fine." I walked into a big sitting room. There was a basket of fruit on one table and a bar. Then another Presidential aide offered me a drink. I said I would have club soda. He said they had only Coke and Tab, so I told him I would like a Tab. The President came into the room about five minutes later.

He said, "Sit down, Ed. Where is your tux?"

I said, "I didn't have time to change, so I brought it with me and I will change later."

Then we went over to the couch next to the window. "This election is very close, and I need your help," he said. "I know you are always saying that 'Jimmy Carter is better, *but*.' I just want you to stop saying 'but.' What I would like to do after the election is have you, Carey, Moynihan, Holtzman and me go to Camp David and go over what is helpful to New York, including changes in Medicaid. But I need your help because whenever you say something up here it affects me all over the country, like in Florida. I need help with the Jewish community. The polls are very good and I am going to win, but I want your help." He was very intense about it.

I said, "I have been telling your people about two things, and let me respond to what you are saying. I won't even go into the Medicaid matter, since you are familiar with that. On Israel, I will never say anything I don't believe."

He said, "You could mention all of the good things that I have done for Israel. You don't have to keep knocking me on it."

I said, "Muskie told me that it was your decision to abstain on the last U.N. resolution regarding Israel. And on the last two resolutions, you have been extremely harmful to Israel. I really believe that, and I won't say anything different."

At that point his face turned gray, and if he could have thrown me out the window and gotten away with it, I believe he would have. For a moment I thought he was contemplating it. Then he said, "You could at least do what Ezer Weizman* and Begin do, which is mention all the good things I have done."

"I have no hesitation in doing that," I said, "but I want you to know that as a result of our abstaining on the last vote, twelve nations removed their embassies from Jerusalem. Even poor Holland—the Dutch, who are so good on Israel—had to leave because they did not want to be in violation of a U.N. resolution. You should have vetoed that resolution. Muskie said it was flawed [that is, one-sided in its requirements of Israel vis-à-vis the Arab states], and if a resolution is flawed you should veto it and not simply abstain."

Then the President said, "You are not going to help me."

I said, "Mr. President, I hope you won't forget that when very few people were with you in the summer of 1979, I was with you. But you should know that I don't have any political aspirations for higher office and I don't need anyone's help. The reason I am the Mayor is that everyone knows I am honest. And by that I mean intellectually honest. And I will never say anything I don't believe and I am never going to shut up. I will get reelected as Mayor. And even if I don't, that is okay with me." The color did not come back to his face. I continued, "If you want me to say the things that have to be said, then you will henceforth have to say that you will veto U.N. resolutions on Israel if they are flawed."

He said, "I can't do that. You don't understand. The whole thing would fall apart if I did that."

I said, "Well, I can't say anything more than that."

At that point he stood up, and of course, I got up. His teeth were clenched as we shook hands and he in effect motioned me toward the door. Then one of his aides came in and whispered something in his ear and asked me if I could wait for a few minutes. I didn't know what was going on. The

---

*Israeli Defense Minister.

President then walked into the bedroom, and at that moment Joel McCleary came in. He asked me how it had gone, and I said, "Terrible."

He said, "What happened?"

I said, "I'm sure the President will tell you." Then the President came back into the room, but he said nothing further to me. I said, "Am I excused?"

He said, "Of course."

The next day Robert Tierney, my counsel, got a call from Joel McCleary. McCleary said that somehow or other things had gone awry and that the President hadn't done what he was supposed to do. According to McCleary, the President was not to have broached the Israel question. Instead, he had been supposed to tell me that he would be coming out for the Moynihan Medicaid bill. McCleary said that the campaign people were very much upset with the way things had worked out.

Perhaps Carter had allowed his passions to rule his head and had decided to attempt Presidential intimidation as a way to bring me into line. Or maybe McCleary was not telling the truth, and the campaign people had scored a late-night victory for Moynihan Medicaid. What was the difference? I'd gotten for the City something that we needed. But I was not told about it before my regular 11 A.M. press conference that day.

At that press conference, I was asked by a reporter what the President had said the night before. I said, "With respect to Medicaid, he said after the election was over he would like to sit down with Moynihan, Holtzman, Carey and me at Camp David to discuss the matter. That does not particularly excite me, since it is just putting off a determination by the people in power. It should be the Reagan people who would talk about sitting down after the election, not the Carter people. And the President should be saying that the Feds will be taking over Medicaid in some form and supporting the Moynihan bill."

At 5 P.M., while I was working on my announcement to be made at the National Conference on Mass Transit Crime, John LoCicero came in and said that the White House was upset that I had dumped on the President. He said the President was now for taking over Medicaid to some extent by supporting the Moynihan bill.

I said, "No one told me that. I dumped on the President because all he said was that he was putting off a decision till after November."

Then I called Watson at the White House. I said, "Jack, I am now being told that the President has come out for the Moynihan Medicaid bill. Is that true?"

Watson said, "Yes, it's true, and we were surprised that you dumped on it."

I said, "What I dumped on was his statement of last night, which was not adequate. Is this a conspiracy on your part? [Meaning not to tell me and to do it this sloppy way.] If he had told me, I would have praised him, and we certainly would have had a better time in his hotel suite."

Watson laughed and said, "If it is a conspiracy, it must be a conspiracy to defeat ourselves, because it certainly does not help us."

I said, "Well, I'll get the word out to the press."

I called Hamilton Jordan the following morning. His office said that he was on vacation. When I got back from lunch there was a message that he had returned my call, so I called him back immediately.

I said, "Hamilton, I see that you do return your calls. If anyone tells me that you don't, I will give him good evidence that you do. Now, how is it possible that I wasn't informed that the President was supporting the Moynihan Medicaid bill? I attacked what the President said as inadequate. It is terrific what he has done, and I know that you had a lot to do with it and I am very appreciative."

He said, "Well, we fouled up. I don't want to take credit for getting him to do it. And we didn't do it the way we should have. But I am glad that you are pleased." Then Hamilton said, "We are only one point apart in the country, and obviously we are concerned."

I said, "Let me tell you what the President can do as it relates to the Jewish community. It would get the support of the Jewish community and would certainly get him my support. He should henceforth say that whenever there is a flawed resolution in the United Nations we will veto it, and not simply abstain. And there are other things that he could do.''

Jordan said, ''Well, I would like to meet with you to talk about it. But would that satisfy you? You have indicated that no matter what he does, you won't be satisfied.''

I said, ''If the President does that regarding the resolutions, along with some other things, I can be supportive of him on Israel.''

He said, ''Let's meet and talk about it.''

I said, ''How about this Saturday?''

He said, ''No, I would like to do it before then.''

The next night, the 23rd, at 7 P.M., Hamilton Jordan came to Gracie Mansion with Joel McCleary. We sat in the living room. He seemed very cheerful and he was quite expansive. First he reported that Carter was doing well in a whole host of states. He wanted to know my opinion on New York.

I said, ''If the election were held today, he would win a plurality. Maybe by Election Day he can win a majority. But anything could change that between now and the election—such as if a significant issue were to catch on, as it did in the primary, when Carter lost.''

Jordan said, ''Joel is very concerned, even though the polls are good, because he feels an undercurrent, particularly in the Jewish community, against Carter.''

McCleary said, ''I have never seen such venom directed at Carter as I have seen in the Jewish community in Brooklyn, and it is getting worse. How can we change that?''

I said, ''I believe you can change that by taking the following measures which the Jews are very much interested in as they relate to Israel. First, say that henceforth you will veto flawed resolutions at the United Nations and not simply abstain. Second, say that you recognize Israeli sovereignty over Jerusalem and that you will place the U.S. Embassy in West Jerusalem. Third, say flatly that if Israel is expelled from the U.N. General Assembly we will withdraw from the Assembly, instead of saying that we will 'reconsider our position in the Assembly,' which is Carter's current position. And fourth, say that you will not sell bomb racks to the Saudis.''

Jordan said, "The President is very upset. He doesn't understand why the Jews don't trust him."

I said, "If you had been deceived and persecuted for two thousand years, you would develop a certain paranoia, and that paranoia may in this case rest on fact." And then I recited my little history lesson on how the Jews had suffered over the years. We talked about the French and their anti-Semitism and the fact that Prime Minister Raymond Barre had issued a statement indicating his distress at the bombing of a synagogue but spoiled it by saying in effect how awful it was that in seeking to kill Jews the bombers had killed three French Christians.

McCleary said, "The only time I ever disagreed with my wife was when we were both going through France and I said that the French were collaborationists with the Nazis and that I understood how the Jews feel about them."

Then Jordan said, "It is not possible for me to understand how Jews feel because I am not Jewish, although my grandmother was Jewish." Then he said that his grandfather had been Lieutenant Governor of one of the Carolina states.

I said, "I'll bet he did not mention the fact that his wife was Jewish; otherwise he would never have gotten elected."

Jordan laughed and said, "You couldn't get elected today if your wife was Jewish." Then he said, "I don't know if I can do any of those things, but I will get back to you. What do you think would happen if the President couldn't do those things because he felt it would undermine Sadat? What would happen if he gave assurances, but not in writing?"

I said, "You don't understand the Jewish mentality on this. They don't trust Carter. They know that no matter who the next President is, Israel is going to suffer. But if it is in writing, the candidate will find it more difficult to retreat from what he says, even though retreat he will."

Jordan said, "Now I understand what you mean. But what happens if the President can't do those things? What will they do?"

"They will say, 'You don't want to do this? Fuck you!'"

He laughed and said, "I understand that. And I am really sorry that you and I didn't get to know each other a long time ago." I believe he was entranced by my obscenity, because I don't think officials in high office generally talked to him that way. At that point in the conversation, he called me Ed instead of Mayor.

The next morning Jordan called at 9:15. He said, "I really enjoyed last night. I have a better sense of things, and we are working on those items, but you have to give us time."

I said, "There isn't much time left."

He said, "I know, and we will try to work faster than we did on the Medicaid issue."

Then he said, "I read today that Billy Carter met with Arafat. We don't know what that buffoon has done now, but we don't think he did that."

I said, "Wacko, not buffoon."

Then he said that he would get back to me within twenty-four hours with something more definitive, adding, "I want to repeat what I said last night. I only regret that we did not start earlier; but we have four more years to work on it."

I said, "I always enjoy our conversations."

Jordan called me back at 3:30. He said the President had been interviewed and he wanted to read me some of the President's statements. The thrust of the statements was as follows:

1. We will withdraw from the Assembly if Israel is expelled.
2. We oppose the creation of an independent Palestinian state.
3. Henceforth, flawed resolutions on Israel at the United Nations will be vetoed, not simply abstained on.
4. We will pledge not to sell Saudi Arabia bomb racks for its F-15 planes.

I told Jordan that the language wasn't as strong as it should be for the purposes of an ad, but it was terrific and he had done a lot in twenty-four hours.

I called Jordan back at 5 o'clock and told him that I had issued a statement which was congratulatory toward the President. I then read the statement to him. Then I said, "I know it was you who did it, and I want you to know that I want to be helpful. If there is something you want me to do in the campaign, even though I get the bends when I have to leave the City, I will be happy to do it."

He said, "That's good. Would you go to Philadelphia or New Jersey?"

I said, "Yes."

He asked, "How about Miami?"

I said, "Yes."

In the final week of the Presidential campaign I did what I could for Carter. Immediately after the President's Israel statements in the Oval Office, the Carter-Mondale Committee took out a full-page ad in both the *Times* and the *Post* which outlined the President's new position.

I said privately, regarding Carter's change: "It's amazing what fear will do."

On the 28th, a friend called to express the Reagan camp's distress with what I had done. My source said they were "hurt."

I said, "They don't have to worry that I will hurt Reagan. I will be supportive of Carter because he has come a long way, but I won't attack Reagan on this issue. Anyway, everyone knows I'm not going to change anyone's vote."

My source said, "I told them that."

"Have you told them," I said, "that they should take out an ad setting forth the five points that are in the Safire piece? And that they should correct their statement in support of the Vaticanization of Jerusalem?"

My source said, "They are doing that."

On the 29th I left for Miami, with an intermediate stopover in West Palm Beach. Carter's emissary to the Jews was on the move.

My schedule had been written by the Carter campaign people. Apparently they had never worked with someone who campaigns as hard as I do. At the Palm Beach Mall shopping center in West Palm Beach we found few voters. There were several TV cameras and a dozen or so reporters. What voters there were in the mall ran for cover when they saw my herd thundering down on them. A forty-five-minute stop was cut to fifteen, with the emissary reduced to asking shopkeepers, "How'm I doing?"

At the Century Village condominium in West Palm Beach I found some voters by the swimming pool. Saying, "Your children sent me here to bring you back to New York," I moved in on the Jewish vote. For twenty minutes I took all the questions the crowd of a hundred or more could think up. Clearly the middle-class Jews of West Palm Beach were distrustful of Carter. I outlined the President's recent statements, the bomb racks and so on, but it was too little too late.

In the afternoon our group flew to Miami Beach, where a series of non-events had been scheduled. Finally, at 5:30 P.M., the event of the day occurred. Wolfie's Restaurant on Collins Avenue is the premier Jewish delicatessen in Miami Beach. I had arranged to meet my then eighty-five-year-old father there. The press had taken over the rear half of the restaurant and made it over into a TV studio. A long table was set with generous helpings of pickles, cole slaw and corned beef. At 6 o'clock my father entered the restaurant.

I said: "Papa."

He said: "Eddie."

"Papa."

"Eddie."

It was as if we hadn't seen each other since the last war. Papa was brought over to the table and the interviews commenced. He played with his food and expounded on the demographics of south Florida. He fudged brilliantly on Carter. When the first round of live-to-New York interviews was over, Papa left me at the table and got up to work the front half of the restaurant. He had not actually put a bite of food in his mouth. At 6:15 he was called back to the table; more interviews, more fudging. He pushed some cole slaw around his plate. At 6:25 he got up to make a phone call. On his way back from the phones he worked the front room again. At 6:40 the TV crews were tearing down their lights. The pencil press were asking their last questions. Papa said, "Rose has made dinner. I have to go home." And he left. His had been the tightest bit of political legwork my group had seen all day.

On the 30th I drove to Philadelphia to be with the President at a rally for Jewish leaders that was held in the downtown YMHA.

Before I went on stage, I saw Steven R. Weisman of the *Times,* who was with the President's entourage. He told me that the night before in Washington they had all been very much interested and amused by my comment about Carter. My comment was that if he didn't keep his commitments about Israel, "He should rot in hell." Weisman said, "They don't understand you in Washington as we do, because you are different from what they are used to."

I was the third speaker preceding the President. When I began my speech, I got a warm welcome. I began by saying, "If I didn't live in New York City, I would love to live in Philadelphia." (This was said to undo any ill will that might have arisen as a result of my speech a few days earlier before some New York bankers who had compared Philadelphia's municipal labor contract with New York City's contract. They had said, "Mayor Green's contract was for a one-percent wage increase and your contract was for eight percent." And I had responded by saying, "Would you want to live in Philadelphia?")

Then I said to this group that I was an emissary for President Carter and that I was proud of it. People laughed at that, because I had theretofore said that I wouldn't be an emissary to the Jews because I had disagreed with positions that Carter had taken. I said there was nothing wrong with Jews' being concerned, especially about Israel, and that there were lots of non-Jews who were concerned as well; otherwise, Israel could not exist.

Then Carter spoke and he outlined the four positions.

When we left the hall, I drove with the President to *Air Force One*, on which we both flew to New York. I told him that his speech had been superb. He responded by saying, "Why shouldn't it be? It was written by Ed Koch."

When we got on the plane, the President walked into the press section in his sweater. I had already taken off my jacket and just had my vest on. A number of pictures were taken of the two of us together. Then the President went forward to bid farewell to some visitors. I decided to walk back to see the press, and I ran into Stu Eizenstadt. Then the President appeared again. I was standing between the President and Eizenstadt, and more pictures were taken. It was obvious Carter wanted this done.

Then the President came back into the press section with

me, Tom Goldstein and my advance man, Bill Rauch. He sat down and asked me to sit next to him. More pictures were taken.

While we were on *Air Force One*, we talked about Jody Powell. The President said that Jody was his closest friend. Jody had been with him early on when he ran for Governor of Georgia. He said that in the beginning, when they'd had very little money, they used to stay in the same hotels, sometimes in the same room, sometimes even in the same bed. Jody had been his driver, and then he became his press secretary during the Gubernatorial campaign. Carter said that when he'd gotten tired and had to sleep for a while, Jody, who had heard his speeches so many times, would be able to give Carter's answers for him.

I asked the President about Hamilton Jordan. He spoke very highly of him. I mentioned that Hamilton had told me that his grandfather had been Lieutenant Governor of one of the Southern states. The President looked bewildered when I said that. He said Hamilton's uncles were farmers and had been involved in civil rights causes. It occurred to me that Jordan's story to me about his grandmother's being Jewish wasn't true.

When the plane landed at Kennedy Airport, Carter said to me, "You will go with me in the helicopter to the City."

I said, "Okay."

As we were about to leave the plane, we hesitated in the front by the door. He said, "Do you want to go out first?" I couldn't tell whether he was joking or jabbing. Of course, I followed him out.

When we got into the helicopter, we met Jody Powell. Powell and the President started reminiscing about something that had happened at Carter's first Gubernatorial conference. On that occasion Powell and Jordan apparently had gone into a bar and, as Powell put it, had picked up the girlfriends of some guys who had gone to the men's room. When they were leaving the bar at midnight, they were beaten up by the guys whose girls they had danced with. Carter said that Powell had the biggest black eye he had ever seen.

I told Carter the story about the Goldwater Republican

whose life I had saved in 1964. He was having an epileptic fit, and I shoved *The New Republic* into his mouth to save him from choking on his tongue. I said, "He rewarded me by voting for Goldwater anyway."

Five days later, President Carter was defeated by Ronald Reagan by a margin greater than that by which Franklin D. Roosevelt beat President Hoover in 1932.

17

The Transit Fare: The Politics of Labor Organization

THE FISCAL YEAR 1981 budget made provision for maintaining the 50-cent City subway and bus fares only with the State assistance Governor Carey had promised over a four-year period in return for my support in 1978 on Westway. But notwithstanding his promise, I was concerned.

I had reasons for my concern. The Governor's budget indicated, on analysis by the City's experts, that the State would make up the City's transit shortfall with State discretionary moneys. But I knew that discretionary moneys come earmarked for specific programs. I didn't need new programs I need gap-closing money. And Carey was very elusive on that subject. He was so elusive, in fact, that I began publicly referring to his pledges to help as "smoke." And that, no doubt, antagonized the Governor. We arranged a meeting for February 7, 1980, in Albany.

At our meeting the Governor was very talkative and said that the condition of the State was not good.

I said, "I understand your budget, but the bottom line is that I am relying on your commitment to provide all the moneys agreed to in the City's financial plan."

His response was "I know you always say that you have personal and public commitments from me, and I have taken that position as a member of the Financial Control Board. But why is it that you always, when referring to Carter, say that those commitments made by the President are subject to Congressional approval? I too have to get legislative approval, and why don't you say that?"

I said, "Governor, the State is different from the Feds. You will remember that Proxmire said that the Federal Government should not be there at all and that it is the State's obligation to help the City. And I agree that whatever we get from the Federal Government is extra. We don't have the same demand on them that we do on you, and I am relying on you to keep your commitment."

He said, "You have my ironclad assurance on the fifty-cent fare. And I am using the word 'iron' instead of 'steel' because iron breaks." At that point I thought, Well, that is something. He has gone absolutely bananas. Then he said, "Anyway, my promise was conditioned upon Westway, and Westway is not going forward."

I said, "Westway is not going forward because your Commissioner has not given the two licenses required."

He said, "That is not it."

I said, "Yes, it is. Nothing can happen until your people give us those licenses."

Then he said, "Well, what are you going to say this afternoon at the legislative budget hearing?"

I said, "I am not going to attack you. I will just simply say that in the budget the funds are not there, but that I am convinced, on the basis of your statements to me, that the necessary funds will be forthcoming." Then I handed him a list of the State's failures in Fiscal '79 and the State's failures in Fiscal '80. To that he said nothing. He just looked at them.

Then he said, "You know, Ed, you are a national figure, and I am only a local figure." I don't know why he said that or, if, necessarily, it was true. But it was obviously on his mind. And somewhere, he always has a reason for his off-the-wall statements.

The fare rose to 75 cents.

18

Taking the Heat

IN THE STATE OF NEW YORK there is a residential real
estate development-incentive program known as the Section
421-A tax exemption. Under this program a real estate
developer may be entitled to a ten-year real estate tax exemption that starts at 100 percent and drops by 20 percent every
two years. Enacted in 1971, the 421-A program was designed
to bolster flagging real estate development in marginal neighborhoods. The program requires that, to qualify for the exemption,
the new development must replace a "functionally obsolete"
building. The 421-A program has been used countless times
by various developers in various parts of New York State.

On the corner of Fifth Avenue and 56th Street in Manhattan
had stood for many years the Bonwit Teller Building. In 1981
that corner would have to have been considered one of the
choicest pieces of real estate in the entire State of New York.
The Bonwit Teller Building had by that time been acquired by
a highly successful real estate developer.

Donald Trump was a man in his mid-thirties. He was the
son of a Brooklyn real estate developer who had very close
ties not only to the Beame administration but to other political
figures at the very heights of government. The elder Trump
had early recognized the stuff of entrepreneurial success in his
son, and he had given him free rein in his by then considerable real estate empire. The son had quite naturally focused
his attention on Midtown Manhattan—Midtown Manhattan
being, after all, the commercial center of New York State
and, by some estimates, the world.

On acquiring the 56th Street property, the younger Trump announced a project commensurate even with his own ambition. The Trump Organization, he said, would raze the nine-story Bonwit Teller Building, a great favorite of Art Deco aficionados, and construct in its place a sixty-eight-story steel-and-glass tower containing 320 condominium units and vast areas for commercial use on the lower floors. To be called "The Trump Tower," it would cost, he said, $155 million to build. The $407,000 one-bedroom condos and the Trump Tower's jewel, its $3.15-million triplex, would both be ready for occupancy in late 1982. For this Donald Trump wanted an estimated $30-40-million tax exemption under the Section 421-A program.

Anthony Gliedman was my Commissioner for Housing Preservation and Development. Gliedman, like Trump, had his roots in Brooklyn. He knew the Trump Organization from its gigantic Trump-Warbasse and Trump Village subsidized housing complexes in the Coney Island section of Brooklyn. And Gliedman was no newcomer to politics. He knew, as well, the considerable generosity of the Trumps when campaign-contribution time came around.

When Trump's 421-A application was filed, there was soon a call from the Manhattan Borough President, Andrew Stein. Stein had, earlier, been the subject of damaging news stories as a result of his accepting the use of a sumptuous summer house in the Hamptons free of charge from another Manhattan real estate baron, Sylvan Lawrence. In that call Stein arranged a meeting with Trump to which he invited Tony Gliedman to discuss the 421-A exemption on the Bonwit Teller site.

Gliedman attended the meeting. Trump and Stein were what I would describe as utilizers of the "Old School Tie network." They were accustomed to deals cut with public officials over drinks. But if they had not misjudged Gliedman's discretion, they had clearly misjudged his mettle. On March 20, Gliedman denied the Section 421-A exemption.

Trump was furious. That evening he called Gliedman. "Tony," he said, "I don't know whether it's still possible for you to change your decision or not, but I want you to know that I am a very rich and powerful person in this town and there is a reason I got that way. I will never forget what you did."

As it happened, I was in Washington that day. When I got back there was a call from Donald Trump. He said, "Mr. Mayor, you know how much I like you and how I think you are doing a superb job. I have never asked you for a favor and I never will. But I want to call your attention to a miscarriage of justice being done by one of your Commissioners."

I said, "Oh, which one?"

He said, "Tony Gliedman. He has turned down my application for a Section 421-A tax exemption. And I am entitled to the exemption."

I said, "There is nothing I can do for you in a matter of this kind. Indeed, if I ever told a Commissioner to give or not give an exemption on the strength of my position, as opposed to the Commissioner's doing what he felt was right, they should throw me out of office. I never have and I never will make such a request. If you think you have been treated unfairly and that you are entitled to the exemption, you should take an Article 78 proceeding and have the court make the final determination."

The following morning I called Gliedman and requested a memo on all aspects of the matter, including the phone conversation. On April 3, the Gliedman memo having been received, I sent Tony Gliedman the following response:

> I have your memo of March 27 regarding the statements of Donald Trump. I am shocked that Trump would threaten you as is implicit in his comment which you stated. I want you to know that I am delighted that you exercised your independent authority in this matter in the way that you did. And, in the words of Donald Trump, "I will never forget what you did." Hopefully, my comment carries more weight than his in this town. You are a good man. Keep up the good work.

> *Ed*

Subsequently Trump went to the courts and, after a series of appeals, he was finally awarded the tax break by the state's highest court, the Court of Appeals. In a statement issued by me on July 5, 1984 I called the ruling "outrageous" and "unfair." During the course of the litigation the city won some rounds and Trump won some rounds. The city's lawyers didn't have to continue the appeals process through all its phases. In fact, Trump won the first round and we could have left it at that. I directed our lawyers to continue the suit because I thought it was wrong to give tax breaks for luxury apartment houses, but I was overruled by the state's highest court.

In the mid-1970s, the City of New York's building industry had been in the doldrums. But by 1982, thanks to an atmosphere of economic recovery in the City, there were more than three hundred building projects under way. In the 1970s the City had taken to granting tax exemptions and abatements as a way of spurring development. By the 1980s these incentives were no longer, in many cases, necessary, particularly on the East Side of Manhattan's Midtown area.

As early as my first year in office I had asked my City Planning Commissioner, Bob Wagner, to study the tax incentives and zoning formula with an eye toward limiting both the tax breaks and ultimately the skyscrapers themselves. Finally, in mid-May of 1982, Wagner having since become a deputy mayor and Herbert Sturz having replaced him as City Planning Commissioner, my administration took its proposal to the Board of Estimate.

When it became clear that we were serious about limiting the building of skyscrapers and the use of the tax-abatement program, the real estate mavens began to call me up.

I got a call from developer Jack Rudin saying, "Why did you do this?"

I said, "To protect the City's revenues."

He said, "How can you accuse us of greed? All I want to do is be a good builder and help the City."

I said, "Oh, come on, Jack. Of course there is greed on the part of the builders. There is nothing wrong with that. It is not evil. And in my statements I don't mention you by name. You have your point of view. It is your money and your property and you want to maximize it. I understand that. But what you should try to understand is that I have my view. We have tax revenues to protect so as to be in a position to deliver essential services, and we have the quality of life in an area of Manhattan to protect. I am not a city planner. I have to rely on people like Sturz and Wagner to tell me that an area is being exploited. They say we have encouraged enough building of skyscrapers on the East Side. And I believe them. Therefore I am not going to change my position."

Well, he wasn't satisfied. They were all calling up, all the builders who had plans to build in the affected area. They wanted to come in to see me, to seek to change my position. Wagner and Sturz said I shouldn't see them, but I said, "Sure, bring them in."

It was the morning of the Board of Estimate vote. The first one in was Jack Rudin. He was very much excited and said that in effect, we were taking his property.

I said, "Oh, come on. I don't believe that. But if you do, what you should do is go to court. You just go right ahead and sue us. I won't consider it an attack on our friendship." Well, he looked as if he could kill me. I said, "You are very angry, Jack, and you shouldn't be."

He said, "I am more than angry."

I said, "Well, there is nothing I can do about it, because we are not going to change on this."

He said, "Why did you have me come in?"

I said, "You asked to come in. You called. You wanted to come in. Therefore I am seeing you." He left in a terrible fit.

The next one in was George Klein, another developer. He was a little calmer. "This zoning change," he said, "is going to cost me millions of dollars. We acquired property. I have forty-eight million dollars in this property. And now you are going to make it impossible to build on it. We are going to sue!"

I said, "Of course you should sue, George. I am not suggesting that you not protect yourself. I do what I have to do and you do what you have to do. We can still be friends. Don't be angry."

He said, "I am angry."

I said, "Well, I understand. But we are not going to change on this." So he left.

And in the afternoon we prevailed at the Board of Estimate.

Now, why do I tell these stories? It happens that Jack Rudin, George Klein and Donald Trump were at the very top of my list of campaign contributors when I ran for reelection in 1981—and they were at the top of my list of contributors in 1982 when I was running for Governor. It is not as if I hadn't known that when they were in my office. And while I care, that fact did not in any way prevent me from ordering that the Trump decision be appealed and standing fast for the City's position on Midtown zoning, notwithstanding the objections of Jack Rudin, George Klein and others.

19

New York
and the New President

IF IT HAD BEEN LEFT to Jimmy Carter, the fifty-two Americans who were taken captive by the "students" in Teheran would probably never have been freed. And if it had been left to Alexander Haig and others, the City of New York would never have been able to show those fifty-two Americans how we had suffered with them. When it finally appeared that the hostages would be released, I sent to President Reagan, on January 7, 1981, a letter requesting that New York City be designated the official host city for the returning Americans.

"Reminiscent of our traditional postwar tributes to returning war heroes," the letter promised, "we plan one of our greatest ticker-tape parades down Broadway to salute these men and women who have undergone so much." In response to that invitation the City administration heard nothing for two weeks. Yet the planning for the parade continued. Finally, on Friday, January 23, with the returning Americans actually on a plane and headed for West Point, I received a strange call from Secretary of State Alexander Haig. In a very friendly voice, he said to me, "Mayor, the President gave me your letter and asked me to respond to it. We are suggesting that you not have the parade. A lot of these people will not be up to it for medical and psychological reasons. We don't think you should have it."

I said, "Well, it is too far along, so we are going to have it. I can certainly understand that some may not come. And they should all certainly check with their doctors. But we know that some of them wish to come. And we also have our own hostage from New York City and we believe that he is going to come." Then, knowing that Haig might try to persuade me to the contrary, I changed the subject. I said, "I want first to congratulate you. I think it is wonderful that you are now the Secretary of State. And I want you to know that when I was in the Congress, all of us knew that you were the one who was saving us from a junta in the event Nixon sought to do something because of the difficult matters he was involved in."

He sort of laughed and said, "Thank you. I appreciate that."

Then I said, "I want you to know that whatever you can do to make sure this doesn't happen again with hostages and whatever you can do to punish the lawless, I am with you."

He said, "We know how much you have done so far. We are very appreciative. We want you to know that at the top of our list is stopping terrorism. It is no longer human rights. Human rights is second and stopping terrorism is first." Then, out of the blue he said, "We don't know where the hostages are going to land."

I said, "Well, they are going to West Point."

He said, "That has not yet been decided."

However, by that time I knew the hostages were already in the air, so I was certain a decision had been made as to where they were going to land. So, in a sense, he wasn't telling the truth. That was the end of our conversation.

After Haig's call, it was clear we were going to get no help from the Federal Government's agencies in coordinating the tickertape parade. That made for difficulty in terms of communicating with the returning Americans and arranging for their transportation and accommodations should they wish to come to New York for the parade. But there were several alternative lines of communication, and my staffers got together with Council Majority Leader Thomas Cuite to determine how best to proceed.

There was one clear path. One of the returning Americans had lived in the Gravesend section of Brooklyn. And his wife and their two children had continued to reside there during his captivity. Barbara Rosen had become, in the 444 days of the hostages' ordeal, a minor media figure. She had led various causes that had required communication between the hostages' Stateside families. Her husband, Barry, had been press attaché at the embassy in Teheran. Barbara Rosen knew about reporters; she knew what constituted a news story, and she had been the subject of more than a few. At public functions she attended during the time of the captivity, Barbara had made the acquaintance of Tom Cuite. Tom was, after all, a prominent Brooklyn politician who got around his borough with the best of them. At our Friday-afternoon meeting, it was decided that my advance man and Cuite would go to Mrs. Rosen's house the following morning, as she was preparing to leave for West Point, and deliver to her fifty-two letters of invitation to the parade, one for each of the returning Americans. When they did, she told them she had tentative commitments from two other hostage wives to whom she had spoken in the previous twenty-four hours.

Meanwhile, on that Saturday morning, an editorial had appeared in *The New York Times*, which in effect denounced the notion of a parade on the Haig ground that all these people would want was peace and quiet. The *Times* editors were the first of a fainthearted group who spent most of the following week discouraging people from feeling good about the hostages' return. All that week I was ever their opponent. Every time I saw a reporter I was asked if the parade was still on, and every time I said, "We will have a parade if only a single hostage wants it."

On Saturday night there was, quite understandably, no word from West Point. Sunday passed, likewise with no word from West Point. Monday morning arrived. The parade was tentatively scheduled to take place three days later, and as yet we had not a single confirmed guest of honor. The fainthearts' ranks grew. City Council President Bellamy told me she had been mistaken when she had cosigned the letter of invitation to the fifty-two. Governor Carey indicated he would be too busy preparing for his trip to Japan to attend.

At 11 o'clock Monday night, Barbara Rosen called to report she had acceptances from twenty-two former hostages and their families for the parade. But the schedule of events in Washington, she said, would make it difficult for all twenty-two to be in New York by Thursday morning. "How about Friday?" The parade was pushed back a day, and the City Hall planners bent themselves toward staging the extravaganza on that day.

On Thursday morning I went to a thanksgiving service at St. Patrick's Cathedral. I was the only government official there. The service marked the return to freedom of the hostages. Barbara and Barry Rosen had just gotten into New York. And they were at St. Patrick's.

After the service, a priest came over and motioned to me and the Rosens to come with him. The priest said, "I don't know what protocol calls for: who should go first?"

I said, "They go first."

We went to the side of the altar, where Cardinal Cooke greeted me and the Rosens, and then he took them by the hand and walked out into the sanctuary before the congregation, where everyone cheered them. It was very moving. Then the priest motioned for me to join the Cardinal, but I didn't want to push myself forward. Another repeated the invitation: "Remember," he said, "you own this church"—meaning that I go there so often. So I took a few steps out and just stood innocently off to the side watching the Rosens. Cardinal Cooke motioned for me to come forward. I pointed to myself as if to say, You mean me? He nodded Yes. And then the church erupted in cheers that were for me. We all then knew that the parade would be a success.

The Cardinal said, "Tomorrow will be an even bigger and better day."

As we were walking out together, Barry Rosen said to me, "I'm sorry about the editorial."

I said, "Oh, *The New York Times* has its head screwed on backward. They don't know what they're doing. The entire city is in love with you and wants to do this."

As we were leaving the church, one bystander yelled, "You gave it to the *Times,* Mr. Mayor. You told them where to get off—bravo!" Others said, "We agree with you, Mayor," "Right on, Mayor," "Let's have the parade, Mayor," so I'm sure Barry Rosen got the idea.

At 3 P.M. I went to the airport to greet the rest of those who were coming to New York for the parade. I stood at the red carpet with Tom Cuite and Jay Goldin. Carol Bellamy stood at the end of the line; she was sulking. In my car back to the city was Moorhead Kennedy, the highest-ranking member of the delegation, with his wife, Louisa, and their two sons. I told them that we had blocked off traffic on the expressways before only for the President and the Pope. They really enjoyed the ride, and so did I. I asked Moorhead how Carter's reception had been in Germany. He said, "Mixed. There was a good deal of strain. A lot of people were not pleased with him. But then, we really don't, and didn't, know what he had been doing while we were being held by the Iranians."

I asked him, "What about the guards?"

He said, "They did their job. There were some good ones. Some of them would find books for us to read. The Iranians are a very emotional people. It was a mistake to let the Shah into this country."

I said, "It was a mistake to let him in before we got all our personnel out of Iran."

He said, "No, I think the personnel would have been very much upset if they had been told they were leaving so that the Shah could get into the United States."

The crowds were huge everywhere, especially in the Waldorf lobby, where people were just jammed to the rafters and screaming with emotion.

The next day, the fainthearts ate crow. It was 26 degrees and windy. Yet despite the cold, some 2 million New Yorkers crunched together on lower Broadway to catch a glimpse of the parade. They had waited and hated too long. Now they could cheer.

I didn't hear much else from the Reagan Administration that first January. It was not that there was hostility there— just the opposite. As he had indicated in his campaign, and as he had reaffirmed later, Reagan was happy I ran New York. I had been doing the kinds of things in New York that Reagan believed needed doing. The new President even said he only wished he could do as well with the federal budget. For my part, I didn't really know what to think about President Reagan.

The first move toward friendship and cooperation was the

President's. And it was made on February 3. I was invited along with nine other Mayors to attend a morning briefing at the White House. As usual, I was early—the first of the ten to enter the conference room, which is adjacent to the Rose Garden. As I looked around, I noticed that two of the pictures had been changed. Presidents Coolidge and Eisenhower had been moved in. One of the President's staff people was present. I said, "Why Coolidge?"

He said, "The choice was deliberate. Coolidge was thrifty and he balanced the budget."

I said, "I think he'd do better with Teddy Roosevelt. People liked him better, and the President obviously agrees with them or he wouldn't have appropriated Teddy's term 'bully pulpit.'"

At 11 the other Mayors arrived, and then Vice President Bush came in. He said, "I can only be with you a half-hour, but the meeting will be chaired by Sam Pierce, our new HUD Secretary." Samuel Pierce's contribution was to announce his new first deputy at least twice. It was clear he didn't know too much yet. Edwin L. Harper, deputy director of the Office of Management and Budget, did most of the early talking at the session. He set the tone. Basically, what he said was "We're going to have spending controls. This country is now experiencing inflation at sustained historic highs. It is so bad that there are now inflation expectations. People have come to expect that inflation will continue. President Carter said last year he had a balanced budget. Then he said he had a twenty-nine-billion-dollar deficit. In December he said it was sixty-two billion. Now we know that the total deficit last year was eighty-two billion. The Federal Government does not have its house in order, and it is that which is our top priority. Everyone from every sector of the society will participate in the cutbacks we will have to make. Only the truly needy will be unaffected."

Mayor Tom Bradley of Los Angeles said, "What about the UDAG* grants?"

*Urban Development Action Grants. These are federal moneys granted to municipalities by the Department of Housing and Urban Development in the form of loans to businesses which, when repaid, are repaid to the municipalities.

Pierce said, "I am thinking at this moment of eliminating them. That function, under my proposal, will be taken over through block grants under community-development funding." All the Mayors were upset with that. They said that UDAG was important and that the money would have no significance if it was distributed per capita through community-development funding.

After about a half-hour the President came in. He was wearing a garish California-style blue plaid suit. He went down the line and shook hands with everyone. My seat at the table was to his immediate left. Pete Wilson from San Diego was to his right. The President said, "Gee, I didn't want to interrupt what was going on. Maybe there should be a red light outside the door, like a stage light, warning me not to come in." Then he said, "I'm just here for the pictures." At that point, the door opened and television and still photographers came in, in three shifts.

After they had left, the President talked about his subminimum-wage proposal for unemployed youngsters below the age of 18. He said, "When I was a young man I used to work for a construction company as a summer job. And the boss would reach into his pocket and pay me in cash. There was no auditing and no forms to be filled out. Filing withholding forms is a huge expense. My three-year-old daughter appeared on *General Electric Theater* and I had to get her a Social Security card. Shouldn't Social Security be given only when you are a permanent member of the labor force?" From this I drew the conclusion that the President didn't want people to pay taxes on subminimum-wage jobs.

Richard G. Hatcher from Gary, Indiana, said he had some objections and he hoped that the President would let him furnish a memo before they went forward with it.

The President said, "Of course."

I said, "Mr. President, I don't know if it works or not. It has been the subject of discussion for a long time. You should have ten test cities for the program, and I am offering New York City for that purpose." The President laughed, as did the others, but I thought he put it in his head. Tom Bradley said he too would sponsor such a program.

Then the President said, "I don't think we will be competing for jobs. This morning I looked through *The Washington Post* and there were thirty-five half-pages of want ads, so there are lots of jobs out there.''

Also at the meeting was Murray L. Weidenbaum, chairman of the Council of Economic Advisers. I found him to be less than articulate and convincing. Weidenbaum said, ''The economy is in much worse shape than anticipated. Every indicator indicates more inflation and unemployment. There will be no quick fix. It's going to take years. Nineteen eighty-one will be a period of economic medicine which hopefully the Congress and the people will take. The centerpiece is large across-the-board family income-tax reductions, which will reduce inflationary pressures instead of worsening them. We are now taking a hard-nosed look at the spending side of the budget.''

At noon we went to lunch in one of the dining rooms. I sat to the President's right and Wilson sat to his left. The President mentioned a little story in response to Wilson's having asked him about his name and his Irish ancestry. The President said, ''During the time of Queen Victoria, there were nine Irishmen who had sought to kill in support of Irish freedom. They were sentenced to death. Public pressure brought on Queen Victoria caused her to commute the sentences and instead to send them all to Australia. Later on, someone checked to find out what had happened to those nine. Eight of them had become public officials throughout the British Commonwealth, and the ninth one had become Mayor of New York City after World War One.'' It was a very lovely story. Then the President said, ''I think that should be made into a television series.'' It occurred to me that that is what he constantly thinks of. He thinks like a studio executive. He had mentioned television several other times, including the reference to his daughter.

My early impression of the President was that he was a very decent and honorable man but rather simplistic. As I flew home, my thought was: I hope for the best, because it is clear he is not a hard worker and he will delegate responsibility. The question is To whom?

About six weeks later, in mid-March, President Reagan came to New York to confer with Senator Alfonse D'Amato.

They had an espresso in a restaurant on Mulberry Street in Little Italy. After that the President went to the Waldorf Hotel to meet me.

When I got to the Waldorf I waited in the lobby at the side entrance on 50th Street. A member of the President's staff asked me to follow him into an elevator. With him were two people. What is strange about it is that no other President I have worked with would ever have done that. He would have entered the elevator alone and insisted that everyone else get out. I told a Presidential staff aide, Richard Williamson, that this was a mark of a very special person and that the President should continue the practice.

When we got upstairs, I noticed that the President had with him a box from Ferrara's Bakery. When we walked into the Presidential suite, Nancy Reagan got up to greet us. First the President kissed her and then he handed her the box. She opened it and it was filled with cannoli. She took one of them out of the box and asked, "What is this?"

I said, "They're cannoli. They're filled with ricotta cheese, and not whipped cream as it looks. They are wonderful. But you must put them in the refrigerator if you are not going to eat them right away."

Then we went into the sitting room, where it had been arranged for the President and me to sit on two hard-backed chairs for the photographers.

When the pictures had been taken, we went over to the room's two sofas and sat facing each other. Coffee was brought in. The President had with him Rich Williamson and David Gergen. He mentioned my earlier suggestion of a subminimum-wage experiment in New York City. He said that Congress had legislation to enact it for the country. I repeated, "Why not try it out in New York City and Los Angeles? Tom Bradley has offered to have an experimental program there as well."

The President said, "Did he say that?"

I said, "Yes, he did. And it would be better to try it out first before you change the laws."

The President said, "That is a good idea. We will look at it."

I then told him that the City administration wasn't trying to get him to change his plans on cutting the budget. I said, "Wherever I go, I always say, 'The President came into office by the largest sweep in the country since F.D.R. beat Hoover in 1932, and he is entitled to put his plans into effect.' But," I said to the President, "we do have alternatives, and I have two memos here for you. One of them is a detailed memo and the other is a summary which shows how you can cut twenty-two billion dollars elsewhere and enhance your revenue by fifteen billion so that you won't have to reduce mass-transit operating subsidies, Title Twenty funds* and food stamps. I don't expect to discuss all this in detail at this time, but perhaps we could arrange for David Stockman to meet with my budget people sometime next week."

He said, "Of course."

Then he said, "I have good news for you: not all of the things you want, but two out of three. We will give you the Brooklyn Army Terminal and the Elgin Theater, but not the Astoria Studios."

I laughed and sang a little song that goes: "Two out of three ain't bad."

And he laughed. Then I said, "The other issue I wanted to discuss was the mandates."†

He said, "Oh, I have good news for you there too. We are going to administratively, if possible, and legislatively, if required, end your need to retrofit the subways. And we will allow you to continue to dump the sludge into the ocean."

I said, "Mr. President, that is wonderful. Our figures indicate that ending the 504 mandate will save us thirty million dollars annually and ending the sludge limitation will save us seventeen million annually."

---

*Funds that may be used at the discretion of the localities for such projects as day care, senior-citizen social needs and home attendants.

†The 504 mandate requires localities to make mass-transit facilities equally accessible to the handicapped.

As it turned out we were later able to acquire the Astoria Studios and to perform a 6.75 million dollar renovation there—all with federal funds. I was also later told that the President's initial reluctance to help was the result of his fearing that New York would take too much of the film studio business from Hollywood. In 1983 nearly as many feature-length films and full-length television specials were made in New York City as in Hollywood, so his fears were not based in paranoia.

Then I said, "Now, I have one more matter, and that relates to Westway."

Williamson said, "We have a statement on that."

I read the statement; it said that the Reagan Administration favored Westway and it had made the environmental permits available. There was also some language in the statement about the President's not getting involved in local controversies. I said, "It is important in my bargaining with the Governor that he know that you are not imposing Westway on us. You have honored your commitment to provide the federal permanent subsidies. Whether or not it goes through is for the locality to decide. If the Governor knows that he needs my agreement, he will provide the operating subsidies that I am seeking from the State."

The President said, "That sounds okay to me. When I was in California and we wanted some roadways in some cities, the localities stopped us. That is appropriate when they don't want them."

At that point Williamson said, "But we have this statement that we have issued."

I said, "If the occasion arises where you can repeat your understanding that it is the locality which ultimately must approve, that will help me."

President Reagan didn't like Carey; it was clear that he enjoyed my sally. He said, "I think I can do that."

At the end of the meeting I went downstairs with the President's press secretary, James S. Brady,* Williamson and Gergen. They stood in the back of the room as I answered questions from the press. I went over all of the areas. When I left, Brady said to me, "You make my job easier. I didn't have to make any corrections or additions."

That is not all Brady said that day.

I had been effusive in my praise of Ronald Reagan's personal qualities. At the Waldorf press conference I had said, "I am not here to defend Ronald Reagan. But I'll tell you, I like him. He's a man of character."

The attacks on the Reagan cuts had already begun in

---

*This was before Brady was shot and severely incapacitated in an assassination attempt on the President.

earnest. Reporters in the rear of the press conference were particularly concerned that day with comments Detroit Mayor Coleman Young had made that were antagonistic toward the President. As Brady watched me and discussed Young, he delivered one of his well-known throwaway lines: "Now, which one of them do you think we'll try to help more?"

IV

Staying On

20

The 1981 Election

PRIOR TO 1981 there had been five "fusion" Mayors in New York's history. Seth Low was the first, in 1901, followed by John Mitchel in 1913, Fiorello LaGuardia in 1933 and 1937, Robert F. Wagner in 1957 and 1961 and John V. Lindsay in 1965. A "fusion" candidacy means, of course, a candidate's running with the endorsement of two or more parties. In the case of the original five fusion Mayors, that second-party support had come in every case from a minor party. For example, when LaGuardia won in '33 it had been as a Republican running with the support of the City Fusion Party. In '37 when LaGuardia won his second term, his backing had been from the Republicans and from the American Labor Party. Likewise, in 1965 Lindsay had won as a Republican with the backing of the Liberal Party.

What I proposed in 1981 was a significant variation on the fusion theme. I wanted the center. I wanted the backing of the two major parties. My design was to run as a Democrat with the backing of the Republicans.

My contention was a simple one. As stated by me innumerable times during debates and on street corners: "I will accept bipartisan support in order to strengthen my hand in dealing with Washington and Albany, each of whose help New York needs. In Albany one-third of the government, the State Senate, is Republican. In Washington it is two-thirds, the Senate and the White House. If I can go to Albany and Washington with a Republican as well as a Democratic endorsement, I believe I'll have a greater call on those capitals.''

I also had in mind a kind of insurance policy. I had always believed that I would be the subject of an attack by the radicals in the Democratic Party and that they would try to deny me reelection. I had known that for several years. It was always that way with me. The radicals don't like me. And they have good reason, because I despise them. By the radicals, I am talking about the Bella Abzugs and the Herman Badillos. I am talking about the elitists and many of those who are in the reform clubs. They are living in a fantasy world. Most of them are not Communists, although some of them may be. Most of them are just uninformed, totally naive, unthinking or just dumb. These are the people who have always been my opponents. They want to remake the world.

It is not possible to remake the world. You can fix parts, but you can't remake the world. I have also come to the conclusion that everything moves like a pendulum. At first they say, ''Oh, let's end all the discipline in the schools. Let's have a school without walls.'' So all the kids are in this building and they are running around and they are not learning anything, but everybody is having a good time, they think. Then they go to take a test, and they find out they can't get into college. They can't read and they can't write. But they have had a good time! People realize it can't go on this way. So they put the walls back into the schools—a little discipline and a little testing. Now, that will last for maybe ten or twenty years and then we will go back to the old way. That is the way life is. You can't get too excited. You can just try to lessen the swings.

Now, I realized that I was never going to get their help. And their pressure was very much like the pressure that many blacks wanted to put on me—that somehow or other, unless I did what they wanted me to, even if I didn't agree with what they wanted, I couldn't get reelected. There is nothing immoral about it. It is very political. Very understandable. But I would not give in. I want to be very careful that I am not describing them as Communists—no. But nuts nonetheless. They are the fringes—there are nuts on the right and on the left. So how do you prevent yourself from being pushed in that direction, if you want to be reelected? Without giving in? You build a constituency. I built that constituency.

Then, I knew that I could lose in the Democratic primary. The primary is a very special election. If 50 percent of the people who are qualified to vote come out in a general election, in a primary it is likely to be about 25 percent. And they tend to be the most militant. It would be mostly the fringe groups that come out, on the left and on the right. The center doesn't come out to the same extent. So I decided: wouldn't it be nice to have the Republican endorsement, so that people would have a way to vote the center even though the fringe might win the Democratic primary by bringing out every nut in the City, in the same way that Lindsay lost the Republican primary in 1969? That was one time when those from the conservative fringe came out, and they were able to beat him. I want you, said I in my head to these people, to know it won't help you. Because I will get the Republicans' endorsement and I will run on their line, so it won't be worth anything to you to beat me in the Democratic primary.

And I had good reason to believe I could have the Republican endorsement. The Fiscal '82 budget was a peculiarly simple one. It fell between hard times and hard times. That is, it was relatively simple because there was money around. The Fiscal 1981 cuts had been heavy enough that new ones were not needed in Fiscal '82. The City was actually able, in FY '82, to hire additional street sweepers and cops. There was money because the effects of the Reagan budget cuts were still a year away. There was money because the '81–'82 recession hadn't hit yet. Luckily for me, the FY '82 budget was an election-year budget. Unluckily, I had let my guard down a bit.

The tension was missing, and it was nice that it was missing. Many of the budget meetings were canceled because there wasn't anything to talk about. I had given Wagner the job of putting together my covering letter that goes into the brochure submitted to the Financial Control Board and which is given to the press and published in the papers. He took a long time putting it together—working from my draft ideas— and when it came back it wasn't his usual extraordinary work, but it was adequate. When I read his concluding paragraph, which was a restatement of what *Standard and Poor's* had said about bringing order out of chaos, I knew there would have to be an additional line to the effect that we were not yet out of the woods—something like "We have taken great strides," but not so as to paint either an entirely gloomy or an entirely rosy picture, because things were not at that time either all gloomy or all rosy.

Now, Wagner was not at that meeting, so I gave the redrafting job to Brigham and I explained what I wanted. Brigham wrote the conclusion, and he sent it to the printer without showing me what he had written. When he came in with the book on the day of the presentation, I read what he had written and it was exactly what I *didn't* want. He said, "I hope you like it."

I was fit to be tied. The sentence he had inserted was as rosy as you could make it. It read: "New York City's a better place now than it was a few years ago—a better place in which to work, to raise a family, to visit and to spend leisure time." Immediately I knew that that sentence would be used against me in the campaign. But it was printed, copied and practically handed out. It was too late to change it. And I couldn't say anything to Brigham then because I didn't want him down during his public presentations.

I waited until after we had done the presentations. Then I told him how hopping mad I was. He was contrite. What good could it do? He was leaving; he had done an incredibly good job, except as it related to this one little sentence. Nonetheless, I could see my opponents with numbers from God-knows-where waving this letter and saying, "The streets are dirtier. You call that better? Unemployment is up. What do you mean, better, Koch? Show me better!"

And they would be right. I never claimed that from 1978 to 1981 I had made things better. It was a period of drastic reductions. We were lucky when we stayed even. All I ever said was "I got the biggest bang for the bucks we had available."

According to a poll conducted the previous December by my pollsters, Penn and Schoen Associates, as I went into the primary two-thirds of the City's blacks regarded my perfor-

mance in my first three years in office unfavorably. Herman
Badillo's Hispanic constituency was somewhat warmer: according to the poll, 55 percent of the City's Hispanic population regarded my performance favorably. The City's Irish
regarded me favorably, by a margin of 71 percent. And the
December poll revealed that 78 percent of the City's Italian
community regarded me favorably. Moreover, the same poll
indicated that I would have held, at the time, a "comfortable
36-point lead over Mario Cuomo in a general election and a
38-point lead in a four-way primary." Cuomo, of course, not
only had been the runner-up to me in the '77 election but was
the highest-ranking Italian-American politician in the State of
New York.

All this did not, however, discourage Herman Badillo from
attempting to find a candidate to run against me. That
candidate, according to Herman's theory, should be Italian
and palatable to the unions and the minorities. As Herman
saw it, it would be his business to deliver the minority vote to
my opponent. There were various rumors as to whom Herman
wanted. The one I heard that made the most sense was
Congressman Mario Biaggi.

A long career as a political maverick had taught Biaggi
many things. He had learned the wisdom of hearing everyone,
but making his own judgments. He had learned to trust his
instincts. As a veteran of a half-dozen sessions in the U.S.
Congress, Biaggi had learned about getting off the railroad
track when the train was approaching. Years in his chosen
profession had taught him the necessity of being, above all, a
practical man. Years as a maverick had made him respectful
of leaders but not beholden to them. Lastly, Mario Biaggi had
observed when people talked. He knew when it was good for
him and he knew when it was overstated. Since the beginning
of 1981, Biaggi had allowed his name to be floated as a
possible candidate for Mayor. On February 20, Biaggi called
me.

I said, "What's up, Mario?"

He said, "I'll tell you when I get there. But I will tell you
that I am not coming in to ask you for anything."

When he came in, ten minutes later, I saw him alone. He
said, "You know, Herman Badillo and the others are using

my name. I just want to tell you that while they have asked me to run against you, I am not going to do it. Badillo told me that Frank Barbaro* is going to run against you. I told Herman, 'Good. Now you have an Italian candidate, so you don't need me.' I just wanted to tell you, Ed, that I am not going to run against you, and I wanted you to hear it from me.''

I said, ''I really appreciate it, and I hope you will be supporting me. I think I have been a good Mayor.''

He said, ''Yes, you have. Cuomo said you have made a better Mayor than he would have.''

Mario Biaggi was by no means the only potential candidate my opponents had interviewed. In mid-January a group calling themselves ''The Committee for a Mayoral Choice'' had come into being. This group ostensibly sought to ''debate the issues'' and promote a Mayoralty election that would be ''a contest, not a coronation.'' They were troubled by what they saw coming. Ironically, one of the things that most troubled them was the June primary. They saw, as I had seen, that no major threat could be mounted between January and June. Therefore, having realized that a longer campaign could only abet their ultimate purpose, they sought a September date. Their purpose was, of course, to unseat me. They were successful only in the first respect.

The Committee for a Mayoral Choice faced serious yet humorous difficulties from its inception. Immediately it encountered organizational problems, like the one concerning the use of James R. Dumpson's† name. In the group's position paper of February 4, his name appeared on the list of signers. However, Dumpson had never agreed to sign the paper, and on the 4th he issued a letter to that effect, thus forcing the committee, on the 11th, to admit ''a foul-up of communications at our end.''

It is not surprising that there were foul-ups in communication. This group, comprising people of all ideological persuasions,

---

*Assemblyman Frank Barbaro from the Bensonhurst section of Brooklyn.
†Welfare Commissioner under Mayor Wagner, Human Resources Administrator under Mayor Beame and dean of the Fordham University School of Social Work.

was united by only a single thread: their wish to see me beaten. Besides that, they had little in common. What, for example, would Bernard Rome, my former campaign treasurer and OTB chairman and a moderate Republican, be doing in the same room with Gloria Steinem? Similarly, how could Bob Milano, my former Deputy Mayor for Economic Development and a conservative Republican, ever get together on a set of issues with Ray Harding, the State's Liberal Party chief? John Lindsay came to one meeting, but he couldn't countenance the presence of Bella Abzug. And on it went. The group might have been a microcosm of my political opponents, but as such, it suffered the same ills from which the larger group suffered. No one could keep that group together for more than ten minutes.

For me, the committee was what kept life interesting. No one likes a fight or a joke better than I do, and from the coalition I got both. No sooner had they announced their existence than I was on the attack. For starters I labeled them "elitists." Then I went on to describe what I meant. " 'Elitist' means a very inbred group of very rich people who go around telling everybody what to do and how to suffer. They have an ideological leaning—it's radical left for everyone except themselves. *They* live high on the hog. But maybe one of them will come down here with the rest of us and gather up the courage to run against me. It's a God-given right to run, if you've got the guts. Come on in; the water's fine."

But running was not what the coalition's members had in mind. Their wish was to tell someone else how to run.

Ultimately the committee did what Richard Nixon had done in Vietnam: they declared victory and folded their tent.

Beginning the last weekend in July and continuing right up until Primary Day, with the exception of one August weekend off to tape commercials, I was on the streets of New York all day every weekend. The campaign days would begin about 10 A.M. and they would last until about 4 P.M. There would be an hour out for lunch. Similarly, I went street-campaigning many weekday evenings after I left City Hall.

The customary drill was three advance men, each building crowds on street corners and leapfrogging stops, with me rolling out of my car for fifteen or twenty minutes at a time.

In this way I was able to make as many as twelve appearances in a campaign day. I would stand on a plastic milk carton, make an introductory statement through a bullhorn that was equipped with a microphone, take fifteen or so questions and then move on.

I like campaigning, and I've always liked it. That, for one thing, makes me different from most campaigners. And it shows. I am generally ahead of schedule. There is another reason for that: I do not believe the individual handshake, which politicians traditionally believe is magic, has any applicability to votes or non-votes.

What is important is that you are there and that people know you are there seeking their support. The touching of the flesh is overrated, and it slows you down. That doesn't mean I don't shake hands; I do. But it is far more important to establish voice contact by just yelling "Hi!" and getting people to respond.

Over the first weekend in August, first Garth and then Maureen went campaigning with me to see how the response was. I was in the Rockaways at the swimming pools, on the Coney Island boardwalk, at the Bronx beach clubs and on street corners in between. And they saw the tremendous response that was there. They liked to frighten me by saying that this poll was lower than that one. They always liked to say that I would turn people off with my directness and that I should soften up and serve up some pap once in a while. Well, now, on that weekend I probably saw five thousand people: Jews, Italians, blacks, Irish, Hispanics, you name it. And they all responded with interest and with candor, almost to the last soul.

On Sunday evening the same weekend, after the last stop, Maureen and Allen and Joan Schwartz and I went to see *Victory*, an awful film. During the movie Maureen's beeper went off and she went out to use the phone. When the movie was over and we rejoined her, she said that she had the latest polling result. In the Democratic primary it was 62 percent for me, 11 percent for Barbaro and 3 percent for Smith.* In

*Jim Smith of Brooklyn, who dropped out of the primary.

the Republican primary it was 68 percent for me and 15 percent for John Esposito.*

I turned to Maureen and very slyly said, "Well, I guess I better change my personality and do things differently."

In the meantime we had tirelessly pursued endorsements, and not without success. In 1981 it wasn't, in most districts, a difficult thing to endorse my reelection. My principal opponent in the Democratic primary had turned out to be Frank Barbaro, a former longshoreman. Barbaro's record in the State Assembly was extremely liberal and pro-union. But he was not a particularly likable or persuasive candidate.† In the debates he was notable mostly for the grating style of his personal attacks. His natural strength lay in the 20-percent anti-Koch left fringe. That would be some of the unions, the minority leadership and the extreme liberal groups like Americans for Democratic Action. Sadly for Frank Barbaro, he was never able to cut any inroads into the beefy center of the vote.

The center was my country, and I guarded it jealously. But that is not to say I sought nothing else. Having come out of the reform movement, and having generally in the past enjoyed the support of the reformers, and having run my administration by the traditional reform code of no jobs or judgeships for political favors, I felt I was entitled to the support of the more moderate reform groups.

I gave to John LoCicero the job of lining up the reform support. LoCicero was the logical choice. A former district

*Assemblyman John Esposito, Republican from Queens.
†On July 23, for example, Barbaro stood on the Brooklyn Bridge to announce that he had the backing of twenty-nine union leaders whose union memberships totaled four hundred thousand. Barbaro's choice of locations was calculated to remind working people of my supposed treacheries during the 1980 transit strike. Barbaro accused me of "union-busting" during that strike. To this charge, I answered, "We didn't bring in other people to run the trains and buses." In City Hall we did not regard Barbaro's reminding people of my performance during the transit strike as wise, as most people regarded my performance during the strike as one of my best.

On September 1, I trotted out my own union supporters: the firemen, the corrections officers, the cops and the sanmen. They were joined by the restaurant workers, the ILGWU, the longshoremen and the International Union of Operating Engineers. In the end, the union endorsements were a standoff.

leader from the Village Independent Democrats, and my campaign manager in 1977 and 1981, LoCicero was a man who knew the rocky Manhattan liberal terrain as well as anyone. Moreover, LoCicero and I went back quite a way together, and our relationship has been an interesting one. As I moved perceptibly to the center, LoCicero has remained an only slightly reconstructed liberal. Therefore, John has often found himself in the position, in his own mind, of guarding me from myself—which, of course, occasionally enrages me. Still, he is a clever and likable man, and a man so ingenuous in some political situations that it has always been impossible for me to disapprove of him for long. In my heart I love having a reformer's reformer as my "patronage dispenser." I enjoy that irony.

But what LoCicero did on the liberal fringe in 1981 did not entertain me.

In May, G. Oliver Koppell had come to see me. He is a Bronx reformer, an Assemblyman, and he wanted to talk about endorsing me. After a little sparring around, he said, "What I want to know is, Is there still a problem between you and myself? I want to clear it up."

I said, "No. We start at zero. You crossed me up when you came out for Cuomo, and I always get even. So I opposed you in the Borough President's race. Now we're even. That is my rule, and it is an inflexible rule. It is the only thing I have going for me. You take me on, the next time I take you on. And then it depends on what you and I do vis-à-vis each other whether we go forward from there."

He said, "Good. I am glad that's straightened out. Now, if I come out for you this time, will you understand if my club opposes you? They are trying to take on the regulars in some judicial races."

I say, "No. That isn't the way it works. If you support me I am a loyal person and I will not oppose you. I believe in supporting people who are supportive of me—that's the rule. But if your club doesn't support me, I will do what I can to defeat them. I don't know if I will be successful, but I will give them a run for their money."

He looked at me shocked and said, "Well, isn't it important that I support you?"

I said, "Ollie, let me ask you a question. Is it very difficult to support me? Do you think I'll lose without your support?"

He looked up and said, "I wouldn't say my supporting you is exactly a profile in courage. No."

I said, "No, nor would I. I appreciate your support. It is important to me, but it doesn't make up for your club."

He said, "Okay, I understand that. I am with you." And he left. Later on, he insisted on representing me at the Bronx CDV,* which is comparable to the New Democratic Coalition in Manhattan and the rest of the City—a coalition of liberal groups,† not important in terms of the broad spectrum in the City but worthy of a news story as it relates to whom they endorse. John says they are less radical than the NDC; I can't tell the difference.

So at the CDV meeting each candidate is allowed four minutes. Koppell takes three of mine and uses them to apologize for supporting me. He says something like "Notwithstanding how bad Koch has been to us, I will still be supporting him. I hope you will all forgive me." And he leaves Nat Leventhal one minute to discuss my record. Rotten. So we lose the CDV. It didn't bother me, except that our people hadn't done their job. LoCicero hadn't made the calls that were necessary to keep them at "no endorsement."

Then Denise Scheinberg comes in. She is from the Bronx; she knows these people; she works for me and she has been excellent in the area of helping people with their neighborhood complaints. I guess she had been called on by John to help with the CDV. So she comes in and she is very much upset. She says, "I hope this won't color your point of view toward these clubs, because they are very good."

I say, "It doesn't color my point of view. I will do what I can to destroy them. I don't know that I can."

She says, "I am very upset because we didn't do any calling."

I said, "Don't feel bad. It is really unimportant." I was

*Committee of Democratic Voters, a Bronx-based Democratic Party reform group.
†The New Democratic Coalition is the City-wide organization of reform clubs, both regular and insurgent.

thinking, Why *didn't* these people make calls? But they hadn't made them.

I also did not enjoy the way John handled the NDC. I still can't believe the way he did that. I said to John subsequently, when I really chewed him out, "Look, my own feeling was: Don't go in. Denounce them! Say you don't want their endorsement and that is the end of it. But if you go in, which is what you have done, then try to have an objective. The objective cannot be to get the endorsement for me. That is impossible. The objective is to have less than sixty percent willing to support Barbaro, and then you get a position of 'no endorsement,' and that is the objective. If you are going to reach that objective, call the people who have to be called to be there to vote for me or no endorsement."

Well, he hadn't done it. Instead, at one point on the second ballot, John's strategy had been to walk out with my supporters so as to remove a quorum. Not possible. Not only not possible but not even done correctly, because on the second ballot I got 27 percent of the vote, which means that not all the people who were for me were asked to walk out.

Well, then we had a set of additional losses—the VID candidate for district leader and the Gay Democratic Club. And then the ADA. There Bob Wagner spoke, and ADA came out for Barbaro. There was no pulling operation to stop it.

I said to John, "You have to understand. ADA was formed in the late forties, as I recall by Mrs. Roosevelt and Hubert Humphrey, in order to prevent the radical left from taking over the Democratic Party. In fact, they had a rule in their constitution to prohibit Communists from joining ADA, because they were so fearful of the radical left's coming in and taking over the Democratic Party. Now, what is interesting and almost ludicrous is that ADA has *become* the radical left in the Democratic Party. They are a fringe element. Who cares about ADA? I don't." And I don't. They are not a factor. But the losses we sustained in all these groups showed a lack of organization.

We were more successful in our search for press support. On August 25 I met with the *New York Times* editorial board, and on August 26 I met with the *Daily News* editorial board. In both cases, I received a very warm response.

At the *Daily News*, I told Mike O'Neill that I wanted him to know how much I wanted the paper's endorsement again and that I knew I couldn't have won in 1977 without its endorsement. Sam Roberts* said, "That's true. We gave you access to a group of people who otherwise wouldn't have been supporting you." Here he was referring to the *News* readership among blue-collar workers.

I said, "That's true. I knew that if they heard me they'd agree with me, and you made that possible."

Then O'Neill said, "We don't want to say what we are going to do now, but I do want to say that we are not sorry we supported you in 1977." I thought that was really a lovely way of saying it. It was the comment of a friend and someone who truly thought I had done a good job.

The *Times* interview was extremely friendly. Punch Sulzberger† was present. Max Frankel‡ was on vacation. I told them in a confidential way of my intention to appoint someone to open up the unions to minorities and to end extortion by some minority groups against legitimate contractors.

At the *Times* we also spent a lot of time talking about *Times* columnist Sydney Schanberg's article on homeless men and women. I described my recent visit to Penn Station and the Moravian church, and they seemed quite affected by it. I told them that we were going to pick up shopping-bag ladies in a van each morning, on a voluntary basis, and take them to facilities for help. I told them that I expected only three shopping-bag ladies initially to accept our aid, but that we would try it.

In the end, all three major dailies endorsed me.

On the whole, things were going very well.

As if I hadn't been lucky enough to have the Israeli Prime Minister in town the weekend prior to the election,§ on

---

*The *News* city editor, now a reporter for the *Times*.

†Arthur Ochs Sulzberger, the publisher.

†The editorial-page editor.

§Menachem Begin stopped over in New York for a meeting and the night on Sunday, September 6, on his way to Washington.

Monday, the 7th, the last day of the long Labor Day weekend and three days before the scheduled September 10 primary, I had President Reagan in town for a check-presentation ceremony at Gracie Mansion.

Monday, September 7, was a day that was highly charged with politics. After thirteen years, the New York City Central Labor Council, under Harry Van Arsdale, had decided to revive the once-prestigious Labor Day parade. The parade was scheduled primarily as an attack on President Reagan's opposition to the air-traffic controllers' strike. This function of the parade was obvious in two ways: the striking controllers and their families, some seven thousand strong, marched at the head of the parade, and President Reagan was pointedly not invited to attend.

Having taken note of the Labor Council's nonhospitality, and recognizing the need for some kind of pro-organized-labor message on Labor Day, the Reagan forces hit upon a clever countermove. President Reagan would take that day to come to New York and present me with an $85-million check for the Westway project. In that way the President could at once signal his support for a project that would generate a lot of jobs and was strongly supported by most of the City unions and simultaneously knock the anti-Reagan Labor Day parade off the front pages.

For my part, I got it both ways. It was a dream day. First I got a parade; then I got a check.

Now, in fact, the Labor Council people really didn't want me marching either; but you can't have a parade in New York and not invite the Mayor. So they invited me to sit in the grandstand. But I never sit in the grandstand. I love to march—have always loved it. So I said, "Thank you very much; yes, I'll be there." Then I was contacted by Vincent Bollon, president of the Uniformed Fire Officers Association, who had endorsed me, and asked if I would like to march with them. They had been told that I always march. So I said to Vinnie, "Sure, I'll march with you."

Now, what you have to remember is that Van Arsdale had cooked up a whole routine whereby Barbaro marched at the head of the parade with all these Central Labor Council guys, and the electricians, and God-knows-who. Barbaro was their man, and they wanted to show him off in the best light. But no one recognized him, I was told, because he was surrounded by all those union officials.

Meanwhile, a little way back, there I was with Vinnie Bollon and the firemen. Everybody knows me, and everybody loves the firemen. So I thought I was in a pretty good spot. Now, I didn't want to get to the parade lineup too early, because it was clear that there were a lot of Barbaro people there and a lot of TV cameras and I didn't want a confrontation, so I stood around the corner with Bob Tierney and Joe Hynes* until I was told it was time to start marching. From the very beginning there was a lot of jeering and some cheering. The jeering came partly from random people in the crowd, but it was mostly initiated by about fifty Barbaro supporters who walked along the sidewalk with signs and hooted and heckled me all the way from 26th Street to the reviewing stand at 42nd Street. I smiled through it all. The press was there and kept asking me how I felt. And what I said was: "You know, in New York parades are for support and opposition. There is a lot of street theater involved. Half of these people who are booing are going to vote for me anyway. I am not upset by it—I close my eyes and I pretend that I am in Yankee Stadium, where everyone boos but they are cheering in their hearts. That's the way this crowd is." In my own head, I was thinking: Some will vote for me and some won't. Who cares? I am the Mayor of all of the people, and that includes organized labor.

So I would smile when they hooted at me and raise my arms with thumbs up, which is what I like to do in parades. And if some of them were being particularly vile, I would give them the thumbs-up, but what I was thinking was that it was my middle finger. And they could tell from my intensity what I was doing. I always kept my reaction under control because I didn't want to be either quoted or photographed using obscenities. But I can tell you that every one of those fifty Barbaro screamers who trailed me up Fifth Avenue knew he was the object of obscenities in my mind.

Then after the parade I went out to the airport to pick up

*Joseph Hynes, then Fire Commissioner of the City of New York.

the President for the check ceremony at Gracie Mansion.

The next day, the roof fell in. Over the course of the summer, three lawsuits had been brought that challenged the City Council's new districting plan under the Voting Rights Act of 1965. The lawsuits charged, in effect, that the new Councilmanic lines discriminated against minorities. The Districting Commission's gerrymandering would, they claimed, decrease minority representation on the City Council at a time when the minority population in the City had actually increased. I was prepared for that. I had known when I signed the districting bill on June 5 that there would be lawsuits. There had often been such lawsuits in the past.

But this time things were different. This time one of the plaintiffs further charged that polling sites had been moved without proper notification to voters. Subsequent checking would show that they had also been moved without what was called "pre-clearance" by the Justice Department. Under a provision of the Voting Rights Act of 1965, three of New York City's five counties—New York, Bronx, and Brooklyn—had large enough minority populations to require a pre-clearance by the U.S. Justice Department of all polling-site changes. This provision was designed to prevent the kind of Election Day hanky-panky that used to occur in the South, like putting the polling places far out in the country where only white folks with horses could go. However, in New York City an example of the polling-site changes that had occurred was one in the Bronx where a school had burned down and so the polling site had been moved around the corner to a barbershop. Unfortunately, owing to incompetence at the Board of Elections, these changes had not been reported to the Justice Department. It was for this reason that the primaries were halted.

At once it was clear what Albert Vann's motive had been in initiating the case. Vann, a State Assemblyman from the Bedford-Stuyvesant section of Brooklyn, had never been friendly toward me. As the leader of the Black and Puerto Rican Caucus in Albany, Vann had done what he could there to thwart our legislative initiatives. He had opposed the candidates, whether black, white or Hispanic, whom we supported. With the help of Cesar Perales and the Puerto

Rican Legal Defense Fund, the other two plaintiffs in the suit brought before the three-judge panel, he had effectively postponed the 1981 primaries and, in the process, was seeking to use the postponement as a way to paint me as an enemy of the minorities.

We moved immediately to correct the irregularities, and the postponed primary was held on September 22. Despite polls that showed my strength overall had ebbed 10 percent in the interval, it turned out that I won 60 percent in the Democratic primary and 66 percent in the Republican primary. I won very strongly in every area except the black districts, where I got about 30 percent of the vote. In the Democratic primary, Barbaro received 36 percent overall and Melvin Klenetsky* 4 percent. The landslide figure is generally agreed to be about 55 percent, so it was clear that this win was a landslide, and it was described that way in the papers. Of course, everyone noted my weakness in the black areas, and what I said about that was "Blacks are angry against government. They believe that government is the oppressor, and even if this government over the last four years has been decent and fair—as I believe it has been—they don't believe it." And then, of course, I was aware that there was the matter of my personality. I will not pander and I won't say the words that they are accustomed to hearing, because I believe in equal treatment, not preferential treatment. I believe in putting money where the need is, not in allocating it on the basis of race. That is not going to change. Now, the Hispanics understand me better. And so they voted for me in larger numbers: about even, at 47 percent of the vote—a split with Barbaro, with about 8 percent going to Klenetsky. I was not elated by the margin, although it was overwhelming in size—second only, I was told, to Mayor Robert F. Wagner's 63 percent in 1961.

The morning after the election, as I always do, I went to the subway stop at 77th Street and Lexington Avenue to thank the voters. And they were very friendly. Between 7 and 8 A.M. I guess I saw five hundred people walk by. Of those, three said they hadn't voted for me. Everyone was really

*An adherent of Lyndon LaRouche and the U.S. Labor Party and a perennial candidate in New York State and elsewhere.

nice, shaking my hand and congratulating me, and I would say to the cameramen and the reporters who were there, ''Just wait, there will be someone along here who doesn't like me. He will be coming along in a minute.''

And then, sure enough, one man came by. He said, ''Well, don't thank *me*. *I* didn't vote for you.''

And I turned to the press and said, ''See, I told you there would be one.''

Midway between the primary and the general, I had some explaining to do. Not only were the Republicans wondering what they'd got in me;* Democrats everywhere wanted reassurance about my loyalty to the party. The opportunity arrived in mid-October in Baltimore. What I said there I'd said many times privately, but on the record it was played as major news. I presented the following open letter to the members of the Democratic Advisory Group:

To my fellow Democrats:

Like others at this conference, I am deeply concerned about what has happened to the Democratic Party. I am concerned as a Democrat. I am concerned as a Mayor who has to deal with large federal cuts—cuts that are to no small extent the product of our failures. And I am concerned as someone who, when in Congress, shared in many of the mistakes that have brought us to where we are.

The record of the last three Presidential elections is a striking demonstration of just how badly we have failed. For a majority party to have lost two elections by landslides and to have narrowly won the third with a candidate who seemed to be running against his own party's record is extraordinary. Certainly it is possible to put down the candidates, to argue that if only our message had been clearer, our media advisers better, the outcome would have been different. But to take that approach misses the larger point. In 1980, the American people rejected not just our candidates but our party as well.

I believe that over the past decade the national Democratic Party lost the sense of where it came from, what its purpose should be and what the reality facing America was all about. My

---

*In answer to a reporter's question about an upcoming trip to a Democratic Party conference in Baltimore, I'd said, ''We are going to Baltimore to find ways to topple the Reagan Administration.''

fear is that we will not rethink our role, but will accept the present assault on government—either out of desperation or out of hope that Republican cuts and Republican economics will drive the public back to the Democratic Party. Such an approach, while it may bring back some short-term benefits, will not serve the long-term needs of the people or the party.

The problem is not that we became narrow and ideological like Britain's Labour Party, but too often in recent years we have allowed ideologues to determine our direction to a degree that never happened under Wilson, Roosevelt, or Truman. The problem is not that we became an elitist party, though there were times our candidates seemed more focused on the concerns of the editorial boardrooms than on those of the public, and times our new procedures for making the party more democratic made it less representative.

What happened over the last decade is that we became the party of the status quo, the party of government for government's sake, the party of abstraction. Rather than seeing ourselves as the inheritors of a dynamic, pragmatic, humane tradition, we sought to embalm our past successes—the New Deal, the Fair Deal, the New Frontier, the Great Society—in regulations and programs. We lost touch with reality.

We became unable and unwilling to recast programs that, however well-intentioned, had faults. When some pointed to abuse of welfare, Medicaid and food stamps, we avoided the issue. When job-training programs did not work, we put more money in. Poverty programs provided jobs for the people running the programs but often did not help the poor. We looked the other way. When it came to crime, though we talked tough, we consistently sided with the need to protect the civil liberties of the criminal, not the victim. Just look at the way we structured the LEAA.* Is it any wonder the program is being disbanded?

We conferred on special interests—particularly friendly special interests like labor, environmental groups, organizations for the handicapped—the right to set our legislative agenda. We believed that a mandate from Washington—to make transportation "accessible to the handicapped," to make waters "swimmable and fishable," to provide special education to the emotionally and physically handicapped—could solve problems without money or, in some cases, even without the necessary technology. We remained locked into busing as the way to correct the inadequacies of ghetto schools, even after blacks, whites and virtually every

*The Law Enforcement Assistance Administration.

scholar who looked at the issue agreed busing was not the answer. We supported racial quotas to end discrimination, even after it became clear that quotas were pitting race against race, ethnic group against ethnic group, rather than helping to bring about racial harmony. In foreign affairs, as Russia dramatically increased its conventional arms buildup, we continued to follow the defense policies that had served us adequately before the Vietnam War.

Understandably, America—beset by inflation, high interest rates, an uncertain position in the world and a declining quality of life—rejected what we were offering.

Since the 1980 election, our response too often has been an echo of the President's program, not an alternative. Probably the single greatest mistake the President has made so far was not to accept the Democratic tax program, which was as ill-conceived as his own, and which, when it failed (as it surely would have), he could have attacked. Just consider that it was the Democrats—not the Republicans—who gave the oil barons a break on the windfall-profits tax that will cost $16 billion over the next five years.

The answer to the present state of the Democratic Party should not be the abandonment of what we have stood for, but rather its refinement and reform. Certainly government needed to be cut. But there is a broad middle ground between where we used to be and what the Republicans are advocating. It is on that middle ground that we should be standing. We need to return to the basics of what the Democratic Party has stood for.

We also need to return to the constituencies that have provided the party's basic strength in the past—to New York and other cities, to regions like the Northeast and Midwest, which bear a disproportionate share of the country's problems.

As we reshape and refocus our program, I think there are certain fundamental Democratic initiatives which need to be kept in mind:

—Poverty must be treated as a national problem. This means that over time, the cost of welfare and medical assistance should be assumed by the national government. This does not mean that welfare and medical assistance should simply continue in their present forms. Indeed, all too often present welfare programs have discouraged work and encouraged dependency, while Medicaid has pushed up the cost of medical care without improving its quality.

—The Federal Government has an obligation to provide shelter.

Without federal subsidies, the poor and even the middle class will not have adequate housing. Again, this does not mean that we have to simply continue existing programs. The Section 8 program—with its deep subsidies, its tax shelters and its lack of accountability—is both lavish and flawed.

—Washington has an obligation to help local governments rebuild their deteriorating physical plants—not only through direct local grants, but through the creation of a new Reconstruction Finance Corporation.

—Certainly the Federal Government has an obligation to ensure employment, though here the emphasis should not be on the kinds of job-training programs tried in the past—programs that far too often trained people for jobs that did not exist. Instead, the emphasis should be on an overall economic strategy, which does not simply rely on tight money and on targeted assistance to education.

—There needs to be greater flexibility in programs to assist local governments through the elimination of mandates and the creation of block grants. But block grants should not simply become the equivalent of a return to States' Rights, as seems to be the thrust of the Reagan program. There have to be minimum standards.

—The Federal Government must have a role in curbing the current epidemic of crime. Right now the Federal Government spends only $4 billion a year for criminal justice to provide domestic security, while it spends $220 billion a year on defense. The Federal Government should assist in the construction of state and local prisons. It should take over responsibility for the prosecution and incarceration of heroin offenders. It should ban the manufacture and sale of Saturday Night Specials.

—Washington cannot abandon assistance to mass transit, as it currently plans. It makes absolutely no sense to remove subsidies for the most energy-efficient form of transportation, a form of transportation that serves the least affluent Americans, while we continue to subsidize the growing of tobacco.

—While I believe in a strong defense I think it would be a terrible mistake for the Democratic Party to exempt it from the search for waste and inefficiency.

What I am advocating does not represent a return to big spending and even bigger government. It does represent a return to the basics of what the Democratic Party at its best has been all about. I believe we can afford the kind of initiatives I have outlined, particularly if we eliminate the $16-billion windfall-profits-tax giveaway I mentioned before and restore the 70-percent tax rate on unearned income. That would provide an additional $40 billion over the next five years.

In short, I believe we can recapture the American public by recapturing the center of American politics. I believe our strength today lies, as it did in the past, in our ability to be the party of balance, of tolerance, of competence and of common sense.

On the evening of the general election, we gathered at the Sheraton Centre to await the returns. Before we went to the hotel, however, we held a reception at Gracie Mansion—maybe 150 people. Those things are never really much fun for me. Too many people. You can never have a real conversation. And then you have the problem of the people who were left out who should have been invited, and the ones who are there . . . Eeaaauugh! And at this party, that was compounded because we invited the Governor and he put it on his public schedule, so undoubtedly people read about it in the press.

Now, the Governor came, to my surprise, and he brought Engie.* And right after they showed up, David Garth arrived. Garth comes over to me and says, "Why is the Governor here? He doesn't belong here. He's not your friend."

I say, "David, how can you not invite the Governor? Who knew he would actually come? But you have to invite him." And the fact is I'm glad we did invite him because it gave me an opportunity to watch the way people—and these were sophisticated political people—related to the Governor and Engie. And what was happening was immediately clear. When the Careys entered the room, the room moved away from them. In a room of 150 people they stood by themselves. It was Engie. She seemed to put people off.

One incident occurred when they were leaving. Engie took me aside and said, "Did you know that I got an award from Hadassah last week?"

I said, "Isn't that nice."

She said, "And the week before, I got an award from B'nai B'rith."

---

*His new wife, Evangeline. My own impression of Engie is that she is sensitive, shy, a superb businesswoman and a great comfort to Hugh Carey. I like her.

I said, "Isn't that nice."

Then she said, "And I have planted a whole forest in Israel. Someday you and I will have to walk in that forest."

I said, "Isn't that nice." I was thinking, Every time she sees me she has this button in her brain that goes off and she spews out what she thinks a Jew would want to hear.

Thereafter, we gathered at the Sheraton Centre to await the returns. Garth didn't want me to go downstairs until 11. It was very smart of him. The election wasn't being covered by television all evening long, as it usually is; there would just be interruptions in the regular programs to give spot bulletins. But David knew that it would be the lead story on all the 11 P.M. newscasts. And the stations were all equipped to go live. So we waited . . . and waited.

Maureen kept calling up and saying, "Send him down—the press is dying."

And Garth kept saying, "I won't, goddammit." He kept waiting "for the numbers to drop," whatever that meant.

With 40 percent of the vote counted, I was holding at 77 percent. At 60 percent of the vote, it was 76 percent. Maureen called upstairs again with the new numbers. David said, "What did you say?"

She said, "Seventy-six percent."

"You see?" he said. "I told you it would drop."

The final result was a 75-percent majority, carrying every Assembly district in the City of New York. It was the biggest majority a New York City Mayor has ever received in modern times.

21

The Race for the Governorship

IF I HAD BEEN THE ONE in my previous races to make the rounds of the power brokers, in 1982 I was *the* power broker to be courted by those who were contemplating a run for the Statehouse in Albany. There were plenty of possible contenders and they weren't shy about coming in to make their respective cases.

Of course, in its early stages the 1982 New York Gubernatorial campaign was played out against a backdrop of uncertainty. Hugh L. Carey, the Democratic Party's two-term incumbent, had not, in the early weeks of the new year, declared his intentions.

It was rumored that Edward V. Regan, the State Comptroller and a Republican, and Jack Kemp, a Congressman from Buffalo and President Reagan's pet supply-sider, would decide between them who would ultimately represent their side.

On the Democrats' side it was, early on, really a waiting game to see where Carey would go. The word was that Mario Cuomo, Carey's Lieutenant Governor, would follow Mary Anne Krupsak's 1978 lead and run against his boss in the primary. Additionally, there were Stanley Fink, the Speaker of the Assembly, and Carol Bellamy, the President of the City Council, each doing a little traveling and extra phone-calling to New Yorkers. Among the Democrats, nearly everybody said that I was the strongest candidate, particularly in the areas of the recognition factor and demonstrated ability to raise the kind of dollars required for a serious State-wide attempt. On the negative side were numerous pledges I'd made—particularly a much-heralded one before Israel's Western Wall in Jerusalem—that I would never seek higher office. Additionally, I was inexorably identified with New York City; thus a city-slicker rap might be used effectively against me with Upstate voters. There was also the matter of the betrayal factor in the City. New Yorkers had, after all, just given me the biggest majority in the City's history. How, they would reason, could I possibly have the chutzpah to leave town?

The other contenders reasoned the same way: it was difficult for many of them to imagine me, sitting where I was in late 1981, deciding to move to Albany. Among these was one Lewis Lehrman—a man of independent means, a dynamic-looking man and a conservative Republican with ties to the White House. Lehrman was a newcomer to New York State politics. Only shortly before, in fact, he had been a bona fide resident of Pennsylvania. Nonetheless—in the face of Ned Regan and Jack Kemp, not to mention Warren Anderson and James Emery, two old hands in the Legislature—Lehrman was determined to seek the State's highest office.

Two things separated Lehrman from the others: unrestrained ambition and a personal fortune to match.

When Lehrman arrived on the State-wide scene, he seemed to most observers to have come from nowhere. Not to me. Six months before, I had considered him for my then-vacant Deputy Mayor for Economic Development post. Considered him, that is, until the interview.

It was David Margolis who had suggested that we talk to Lehrman about the position of deputy mayor. First, David and Allen Schwartz interviewed him, and Allen, at least, came away with the impression that Lehrman had lots of ideas but that those ideas were not necessarily sound. Nonetheless, he was a presentable guy, and we had been looking quite hard, and Lehrman obviously wanted the job. So David and Allen suggested to me that I talk to him, and I agreed.

Prior to the meeting, Allen said, "I would suggest two things before he comes in. One, that under no circumstances should you offer him the job during this meeting. Let's talk about it a little more. And two, that you will let him do some of the talking. Listen to what he has to say."

I said, "Okay. Bring him in."

When Lehrman was admitted, I said, "Okay, if you were the Deputy Mayor for Economic Development, what would be the first thing that you would do?"

He said, "The first thing would be to abolish the personal income tax. It discourages companies from coming here and people from working here."

I said, "Well, how much revenue do you think the City raises a year from that source?"

Lehrman says, "Oh, about fifty million."

I looked at Allen and said, "Allen, how much do we get from the personal income tax?"

Allen said, "About eight hundred fifty million; eight hundred million from residents and fifty million from nonresidents."

Lehrman, shocked, says, "Really?"

I said, "Okay? Well, what's the next thing you would do?"

Lehrman, forging ahead, says, "Well, I believe that the City government should just be delivering the *essential* services and nothing else."

I said, "Oh? Tell us. What are those essential services?"

Lehrman responds, "Police, fire, sanitation—and that's it!"

I said, "No education, Lew?"

After a moment of silence, Lehrman responded: "All right—yes—education too."

I concluded the meeting by saying, "Look, I've got a number of people to interview, and I'll be back to you one way or the other."

After Lehrman left, I made it clear to Allen it was going to be "the other."

When Lehrman came back six months later, he was seeking support for his Gubernatorial bid. He began by saying that he was going to raise about $6 million. Then he said, "Mr. Mayor, I want your advice. Upstate Republicans tell me that I don't have a chance because I'm Jewish. But what I have to say to them is 'Look at Ed Koch. He got seventy percent of the vote in Bay Ridge against two Italians, Esposito and Barbaro.'"

I said, "Look, what you have to do is *flaunt* being Jewish

if you are told that it is a weakness. Tell people that you don't have to be Jewish to be against crime. Take very tough positions and use that for a slogan if you like."

He said, "Thank you. It's going to be very important to me to know that I can call you from time to time."

I said, "Of course you can call me. I'll be happy to talk to you. But I am also going to tell Warren Anderson and Jim Emery, who may run, that I am talking to you and that I will be happy to talk to them as well. I can't afford to have any enemies. I need them in the State Legislature."

He said, "Oh, I understand that. That's okay with me."

After he left, I thought, He's a strange duck, but probably very able.

Two weeks later, another Republican came calling. This time it was Ned Regan, the State Comptroller—and the result of his visit was an interesting one.

Ned said, "I expect to be running, but I would think twice about it if Warren Anderson were to enter the race."

I said, "Well, what do you think the Governor will do?"

He said, "The Governor is an extraordinary person. When he is good he is very, very good, and when he is bad he is absolutely terrible." I thought, That's *my* line.

I said, "Well, if you decide to run, I hope you won't run on the City's back."

He said, "Well, I would never do that. I would criticize the MTA, though."

I said, "That's okay. You certainly should be criticizing them. I do it all the time."

At the end of the meeting, I said, "Look, I am not committed to supporting Carey, although I would hope to be able to, and I would certainly hope to be able to support a Democrat. But it will not necessarily happen that way unless they—the Democrats—pledge to do what has to be done to help this city. Now, let me just go a little further. I would not be upset if you were to win, because I believe that you are motivated toward helping the City, and I know that you and I have had and could continue to have a good working relationship. I think as a result of this meeting you and I will have a positive relationship throughout this upcoming campaign.

And if I ultimately support Carey or another Democrat, you may be sure that my support of him will never be in the form of negative comments about you."

On December 21, Mario Cuomo came to City Hall. The Lieutenant Governor had, by that time, pretty much decided that whatever the Governor did, he, Cuomo, would be running for the top spot. He had looked at the field, as it stood at that time, had decided he was the best-qualified and was presenting himself at City Hall to see where I stood.

Now, Cuomo had been my chief opponent in the Mayoralty race of 1977. In 1978, following the defection of Mary Anne Krupsak, Governor Carey had tapped Mario to be his running mate. Together they had beaten back a not-so-powerful challenge by Perry Duryea and Bruce Caputo.

Cuomo had languished as Lieutenant Governor. If Carey was morose and enigmatic with the electorate, he was just as difficult with his Lieutenant Governors. Like Vice Presidents, Lieutenant Governors have pretty much outlived their usefulness by the time Inauguration Day rolls around. Yes, they are "a heartbeat away." But as long as that heart is beating, they are without official duties and dependent on their chief executives to give them projects. Most running mates are chosen to "balance" the ticket. Therefore they are as unlike their chief executives as possible. That is good on Election Day, and bad for the rest of the term. All this was the case with Carey and Cuomo. Not only did Cuomo have to bear being publicly ignored by Carey; he even had to stomach his insults. Carey had publicly said things, when asked about Cuomo, like "He doesn't do anything." But Cuomo had, for the most part, borne that cross gracefully. He had, instead, amused himself by being active in the Carter campaign and by ruminating about his political future.

Mario Cuomo had been critical of me when I extended the invitation to Governor Reagan to be briefed on the problems of New York City. He had thought that might hurt Carter. Then, once that election was over and Carter had lost, Cuomo called up about coming in to see me. I said, "Sure," but it ended up just being a telephone conversation. Now he was concerned that the reporters were going to try to stir up a fight between us, and he wanted to make sure that we understood each other. He said, "I have said publicly that my critical comments about you relating to the Presidential campaign were based on the fact that you are the most powerful Democratic spokesman in the country and that whatever you say has an extraordinary impact. And I have also said that you turned out to be right by seeing Reagan. It was right for the City in that now you have access to him. If you had refused to see him you wouldn't have that access. Now, that is not to say that I hadn't wished that you'd be more critical of Reagan, but the fact is that even if Carter had won in New York it would not have changed the outcome of the election. So it is clear you did the right thing there."

I said, "Well, isn't that nice."

Then he said, "People have asked me if I will run against you again. And I have said no. First, I couldn't win. And second, I wouldn't know how to do a better job than you are doing." Then he laughed and said, "And I'm not going to run against Carey either. Even though Carey will probably lose— and he is very vulnerable—I owe him too much and it wouldn't be right to oppose him."

I said, "Somebody will."

Six months later, in June 1981, Cuomo came in for breakfast. He wanted to update me on his plans. He said he was considering running for Attorney General, but if Carey were to drop out he said he would consider running for Governor. It was clear at that time that he was upset by the shabby way Carey had been treating him.

I said, "Why don't you do what I do with some of my opponents' criticisms? When a verbal attack is unwarranted on the face of it, the public doesn't accept it, and you only give it greater credibility by responding in kind. I hit him where I know it hurts him the most. I deride him. I don't mention him by name, because I know what he wants most is to have his name in the papers. Don't deal with the charges directly: when you disparage them you disparage him."

He said, "Well, if I run . . . well, what are your plans regarding endorsing someone for Governor?"

I said, "The Governor fouled up the State takeover of

Medicaid. Now the likelihood is that will cost the City of New York almost a billion dollars a year. I am not committed to the Governor. I will be keeping my options open."

He said, "You know, your credibility Upstate is amazing. Normally a Jewish Mayor from New York would be just what they hate. But they like you."

I said, "Oh? Isn't that nice."

Then, back at City Hall the following December, Mario said he didn't think that Carey would run, but that in any case he, Mario, would not be running with Carey, as his running mate. And of course, implicit in that was that he would be running against him in the primary. I knew that that couldn't be good, ultimately, for either me or the City of New York—because I knew Mario and I suspected that he would seek to torture me* and therefore the City for beating him in 1977.

On January 16, 1982, I left for an eight-day vacation in Spain. In my absence, the *New York Post* sponsored a coupon campaign to draft me for Governor. While I and my traveling companions, David Garth, Dan Wolf and the Margolises, ate tapas, drank sherry, toured castles and museums and went to a practice bullfight, first the *Post* and then other papers in the City and in other parts of the State began weighing the ramifications of my possible entry into the race.

In short, while we were away the Governor possibility spread like wildfire. Everybody wanted to know: "Why is David Garth in Spain with Ed Koch two days after Governor Carey announces he won't run for reelection?"

Maureen Connelly was in New York saying, "Now, now. Let's not jump to conclusions. The trip was planned in

---

*A year into Governor Cuomo's administration, I tempered my view. In the beginning I really thought we would suffer in appointments and philosophy. To Mario's credit, so far his appointments have been quite good, in some cases excellent and in very few cases substandard. Also, in the early part of his administration he took on the unions, which I regarded as a real shock, by proposing layoffs in his State of the State Message. Most important to date, in my view, he has not designated political crazies like Herman Badillo and Bella Abzug to high positions in his administration. That the City and I, as Mayor, still have to worry about how he will respond to union demands over the next four years is clear. But my first fears, thank God, have not yet been realized and hopefully will not be.

November. The one doesn't have anything to do with the other." But not everyone was believing her.

By the time I returned, the "Koch for Governor" proposal had caught on, a fact made abundantly clear when, in the early evening of January 25, my traveling companions and I walked down a gangway at Kennedy Airport and into the lounge area, which had been set aside for a full-blown press conference. For a half-hour I was asked in every conceivable way whether there was any chance of my running. Of course, I kept my options open.

After I'd talked to the press, David Garth said to me, "You're not serious about this, are you?"

I said, "No. Not really . . . ."

He said to Maureen, "Okay, let's see how he looks."

So they took a poll. And it showed I was very high in job rating; doing very well Upstate, in the suburbs, in the City. I was beating everyone by 37 or more points.

At my regular morning press conference on Tuesday, the 26th, I announced that I would be taking thirty days to decide whether I would run. "I don't think I can string this out any longer than that," I explained, adding, "It enhances my ability to find out what these people [the other possible contenders] are going to do."

In fact, it was my original intention to take the thirty-day hiatus to see who would be most helpful to me in Albany. But as the days passed, two things happened. First, the 1982 Gubernatorial campaign came to a halt. Everyone's money dried up. None of the other contenders could move until I moved. And second, the discussions within my circle of advisers began to indicate to me that I should not be too hasty in dismissing the possibility of running.

During the thirty-day hiatus, those discussions became a full-fledged debate, with nearly everyone I saw, including passers-by in the street, becoming involved. Most of those who spoke up urged me to run. Among those who knew me best, however, there was a common concern and one that I myself shared: Could I be happy in Albany?

On February 9 I had a conversation with Nat Leventhal, in which he said that he might be leaving. I told him I hoped he would stay on, at least until the budget was passed.

He said, "Well, then I would have to stay through the labor negotiations, and they will be tough. That takes us to the end of the year. You go to Albany and I'm out of a job."

I said, "I hope you will come to Albany too, if I go."

He said, "I couldn't afford to go to Albany and pay two rents."

I said, "You could stay in the Executive Mansion—Louis Lefkowitz* stayed there while Rockefeller was Governor."

He said, "I don't think so. Anyway, what you should do is what you think is right for you, irrespective of what I say *I* will do."

I said, "I haven't told anybody whether or not I think I will run, but I believe I will. You are the only person I have told that to."

He said, "You could have a tremendous impact upon the State, but you would probably not like living in Albany."

I said, "That is a major concern, but I am sure I could get accustomed to it. Warren Anderson tells me that basically, what is required is to stay in Albany three nights a week."

On the down side was a lot more than lifestyle. And here Garth and Connelly dominated the debate. Early on, as far back as a November 22 meeting at Gracie Mansion, Garth had suggested that I position myself so as to be available for a Vice Presidential designation. At the same meeting, Allen Schwartz had first broached the Gubernatorial plan. Garth's view was that I should not run for Governor, not because I could not win but rather because it wasn't worth winning and giving up the Mayoralty. He believed the Mayoralty to be a more prestigious job from a national point of view—meaning if I was ever to run for a higher office. Allen argued that the Governorship was not only winnable but preferable to the Mayoralty in that the State would have greater financial resources than the City. And at that meeting I had said no to both of them.

On February 16 Bishop Sullivan† came in, and this is what

---

*Attorney General of the State of New York, 1957–78.

†A former professional baseball player who became a bishop of the Roman Catholic Church, Joseph Sullivan was also a Koch appointee to the board of the Health and Hospitals Corporation.

he said: "I would like to tell you why I think you shouldn't run for Governor. You have done a marvelous job here in the City, and you have been able to speak out for New Yorkers. I don't know if you could do the same in Albany, where you would have to work with the State Legislature. It is not the same as working with the City Council. They are much more difficult. One thing that you have given the City that is well known is an intangible thing, and that is the spirit and excitement and the sense that we can overcome and the pride that New Yorkers now feel. As I have said on many occasions, 'If someday Ed Koch got up in the morning and said he no longer wanted to do the job, it would be all over for New York City. The spirit would end, and we could not recover from that.'"

I said, "You have been very kind to me."

He said, "I don't know if I am imposing or out of line."

I said, "Not at all. Your advice is very important to me. Now let me tell you why I might run. The power has shifted to Albany, as a result of the New Federalism and the block grants, which go directly to Albany from Washington. And when I look at the other candidates, I don't think they are terribly good."

Then he said, "You know, Mr. Mayor, two of our bishops went Upstate recently and both are complaining and want to come home. They are New Yorkers from the City, and they don't like it up there. I worry that you will not like it either. What will you do with yourself up there?"

I said, "Well, I think about the personal separation from my friends here in the City for long periods of time and missing the modest lifestyle that I have in New York City."

He said, "Yes. But I want you to know that whatever you decide to do, I wish you well."

On Saturday, February 20, I met with the Speaker, Stanley Fink. And he urged me to run.

I said to him, "Do you think I could get along with you and Warren Anderson?"

He said, "Absolutely. You know, when you come to Albany and talk about criminal justice and legislation we are very courteous to you, but that is not your jurisdiction and it does not impress us. But if you were the Governor it *would* impress us."

Then I went to a police officer's funeral and then to a meeting with the Hispanic Advisory Council. After that I went to David Margolis' house for lunch, and Allen Schwartz and Dan Wolf and David went over all the arguments for and against. I made up my mind there, privately, and told no one at the table of my decision.

On Sunday morning I met with Bob Tierney and Judah Gribetz* at my apartment in the Village. We talked about issues and appointments. Judah pointed out that the next Governor would have five appointments to the Court of Appeals.† He also said that, according to the Governor's personality, he could be bored or busy every minute of the day. I was concerned that I wouldn't have as much to do as Governor as I had as Mayor. Then he said he thought a New York City residence could be arranged for me so that the Governor's life wouldn't have to be conducted entirely in Albany.

From there I went to Ross Sandler's‡ apartment for a small lunch and then to David Garth's. When I walked in, I clapped my hands and said, "David, I'm running."

The next day, Monday, February 22, we made the announcement at Gracie Mansion. And the reporters felt that they had been taken. They had never believed a politician before, but they had believed me when I'd said I was never going to run for any office other than Mayor.

The room was packed with television and print reporters and photographers. I read the announcement, and then the press really came at me. It was not a great success. What about my vow to serve twelve years? Didn't I have a responsibility to those who just elected me? What about my pledge at the Western Wall? I was in agony—not at all my jocular, light, happy self. And it showed.

On Monday evening, I was given an advance copy of the April issue of *Playboy* magazine, the issue in which an

---

*Judah Gribetz had been counsel to Governor Carey 1975–78.
†New York State's highest court.
‡Then my administration's in-house expert on public transportation.

interview with me appeared. Right away it was clear to me that there was going to be a backlash because of my comments about the "sterility" of the suburbs, the futility of rural life and the foolishness of Carol Bellamy, whom I referred to as "a pain in the ass."

Garth was very much worried and distressed.

That night there was a story in the *Times* about a statement by Donald Harrington, in which he implied that I did not deserve the Liberal Party's support, and my response, which was to the effect that Donald Harrington was personally motivated and that it had been he who had lent support to the homosexual slur campaign against me in 1977.

That was not the last of the homosexual issue in 1982. A flyer that surfaced in New York City in July used the old "VOTE FOR CUOMO, NOT THE HOMO" taunt. And when Mario Cuomo was asked for his comment, he did not disown the piece; his only comment was "That issue is irrelevant."

And that was not all. At the end of July it was reported that Bernard Ryan, Mario Cuomo's northeastern campaign coordinator, had recently appeared before a political-science class at Albany State College and during his remarks had once again repeated the false 1977 homosexual–brawl–in–Koch's–Greenwich Village apartment slur. There were various explanations as to how the old lie had found its way into the classroom, but no one denied that he had rekindled the slander.* And Mario Cuomo, true to form, did not either admonish or fire him.

My most immediate problem was still, of course, the Upstate New York newspapers, such as the Fredonia-Dunkirk *Evening Observer,* that had picked up the *Playboy* story:

Candidate Koch Says
Rural Life Is A 'Joke'

NEW YORK (UPI)—Mayor Edward Koch, who recently announced his intention to run for governor, says living in the suburbs is "sterile," and rural life is a "joke."

Koch, who will need upstate support to win the governor's mansion later this year, told Playboy Magazine that he did not want to be governor because it was a "terrible position."

*See Albany *Times Union*, July 29, 1982, page 1.

He also described City Council woman Carol Bellamy, who would become mayor if Koch becomes governor, as a "pain in the—."

The mayor's remarks, which were made in December, were published in the magazine's current issue.

Koch has since changed his mind about the governor's job. On Monday, he announced he would seek the Democratic nomination for governor in the fall election.

The Greenwich Village resident told Playboy that living in rural areas was a "joke," and he ridiculed suburbia.

He was quoted as saying, "Have you ever lived in the suburbs? It's sterile. It's nothing. It's wasting your life."

When questioned about time wasted in city subways, Koch said, "As opposed to wasting time in a car? Or out in the country, wasting time in a pickup truck when you have to drive 20 miles to buy a gingham dress or a Sears Roebuck suit?"

Koch, who has previously told reporters that living in Albany would be a "fate worse than death," told the interviewer it was "small town life at its worst."

On Tuesday the mayor told city hall reporters he was only being "honest" in the interview and had made the comments about rural life to counter what he perceived was an inference by the interviewer that people were leaving the cities for rural America.

The magazine also quoted Koch as describing Ms. Bellamy as a "pain in the—." He also accused her of not doing a good job on the board of the Metropolitan Transportation Authority.

Koch told the magazine he was not a homosexual, would not wear a toupee even though he was balding and would not walk in Central Park at night because "that's just tempting fate."

When I went to bed that night, I didn't sleep well. I woke up at 3 A.M. and again at 4 A.M. I decided that I had probably blown the election. Then, as I thought about it, I thought maybe I could make it acceptable. I decided to call Allen Schwartz. It was about 4:45 A.M. He was very sleepy. But I read him both articles.

He said he thought *Playboy* would be harmful, but that the Liberal Party story was basically harmless. Then he said the only way to deflect the *Playboy* problems would be to keep all my comments about them very light.

On Tuesday morning, I went over to see Carol Bellamy to apologize. I said I had made the comment four months before, and in fact it had been played in the press previously, because I had said the same thing about her at a *Post* editorial-board meeting that I had attended the week the *Playboy* interview was being conducted.* She seemed to understand. It occurred to me that she thought I had blown the election, but that nevertheless, because she was waiting to succeed me if I won, she couldn't attack me.

There was another lesson to be learned. Four years as a budget-balancing chief executive had cost me the left wing of the Democratic Party. I had always been a mainstream Democrat, but an analysis of voting patterns in my pre-1981 races indicates that I had also been palatable to the liberal wing of the Democratic Party. In 1981 that had proved to be no longer the case. Now, in 1982, that presented a problem in my one-on-one primary campaign against the more liberal-talking Mario Cuomo.

I wanted a ticket that represented mainstream Democrats across the State. I said I wanted, for Lieutenant Governor and Comptroller, candidates from the suburbs and Upstate. Lieutenant Governor was an easy choice: Alfred B. Del Bello. A class guy. Italian, to offset Mario's ethnic strength. From Westchester County. A former Mayor of Yonkers and then the Westchester County Executive. So then we had to find a candidate for Comptroller who would be from Upstate—that was a little more difficult. So we went through the possibilities, and the one we finally came up with was Raymond Gallagher, from Buffalo. He had been suggested by the Erie County leader, Joseph Crangle, and to our surprise he was also acceptable to Crangle's rival James D. Griffin, the Mayor of Buffalo. I asked LoCicero to check him out politically, and he came back and said he was okay.

So we call Gallagher when we are in Syracuse at the June nominating convention and we say we would like to meet with him. I'd met him a month or so before; I had ridden in a car with him between campaign stops in Buffalo. So Gallagher comes over to our hotel suite with Joe Crangle and we talk

*There I had referred to her as a "horror show" and a "disaster." I never retracted the substance of any of these remarks. I simply said I was sorry I had said them.

about it. I say, "Is there anything you want to tell us that will embarrass us at a later time unless we know about it now?"

He says, "No. Nothing embarrassing."

So we have the press conference announcing the ticket. Well, then the next day Wayne Barrett of *The Village Voice* stops me and says, "Can I ask you a question?" It is my policy not to talk to him unless there are other reporters around, because it is likely he will not be fair when he writes his story. But there were other reporters present, so I say, "Yes, Wayne."

He says, "Have you checked out Gallagher's record? Do you know his record?"

"Yes," I say.

"And his record is okay with you?" Barrett says.

Well, as I am saying "yes" I know that he must know something. But it is too late. Of course, Barrett doesn't ask me specifically—then he couldn't do his hatchet job. But we found out soon enough. It turned out Gallagher was opposed to abortion, gun control and the Equal Rights Amendment. And it was not nice of him not to tell us. And my political people were foolish not to have found that out.

So, of course, we bring Gallagher in and we talk about it. Then we go out and call the press in and try to put the best face on it. I say, "I got only seventy-five percent of the vote when I ran. He got seventy-seven percent. It is phenomenal what he did up in Buffalo in his State Senate race. And as it relates to his position on abortion, he is saying what Catholics say. What's wrong with that? Do you mean to say that no one who opposes abortion can ever run State-wide and represent the Democratic Party? That is ridiculous. And on gun control and the ERA—I set the policy. You should be glad he's the Comptroller and not in the State Senate, where he can vote on these items."

Then he got up and said, "I would never stop any Medicaid checks for abortion. I will not let my personal beliefs intrude upon my professional obligations as Comptroller."

The irony is that the Koch ticket made it through the primary—all of it but me, that is.

Shortly before the September primary, Carey endorsed me, but it didn't help. Cuomo's reaction to the Governor's endorsement was a swift and politically effective one. "I told him to lay off those PCBs,"* he said. The Lieutenant Governor was alluding in a sarcastic way to a statement Governor Carey had made in 1981. At that time a State office building in Binghamton had been found to be contaminated with PCBs, and Governor Carey had offered to publicly drink a glass of water from the building in an attempt to set the public's mind at ease. The statement had been one of those that Governor Carey had been given to making that enraged many people.

But now it was Carey's turn to be enraged. After spending almost the entire primary campaign as a neutral observer, he was, in the final act, declaring himself a major player.

After some negotiating, Carey endorsed me. Garth's feeling was that a Carey endorsement would hurt, but I wanted it anyway. I said to Carey, "It is an honor. History will remember you as one of the great Governors of the State of New York." And I said the same thing on Thursday, September 16, when he endorsed me at the St. Regis Hotel.

As we were leaving, Ken Auletta of the *Daily News* stopped the Governor and said, "Why don't you just come right out and say you don't like Mario and that is why you are doing this?"

The Governor said, "The reason I don't, Ken, is that it's not true. I do like him. Why don't *you* come out and admit that your anger is based on the fact that you were Howard Samuels' campaign manager in 1974 and I beat you?"

Auletta just laughed. And I laughed too. What the Governor was doing was what I constantly do with reporters: take them on.

As we walked out onto the street, the Governor said, "Ed, I have to tell you a little story. In 1974, when I was running against Samuels and Mario was running for Lieutenant Governor, he endorsed Samuels at the convention. I said to Mario, 'Why did you do that? Don't you know that Samuels is running against me and that he has already said that he wants Olivieri† for Lieutenant Governor?' And Mario said to me, 'I

*Polychlorinated biphenyls—a group of toxic chemical compounds.
†Anthony Olivieri, former State Assemblyman and City Council member and now deceased.

know that, but Samuels said he is really for me and that he will give me money for my campaign after the convention.' I told him then, 'Mario, how can you do that? He is treating you like a mop—putting you in a closet and buying you with a promise of money for your campaign.' "

And that was the last I heard from Carey until primary night.

On the morning of the primary, I called Garth at his apartment at 7 A.M. I said, "David, I let you sleep from six to seven A.M."

He laughed.

I said, "What did the tracking polls show last night?"

He said, "We're three points up."

I said, "Well, that's better than being three points down. We have done all that we could do. There are no regrets."

"You're right," he said. "Now we wait."

Then I went to the polls and voted. All the people I encountered were friendly and said they had voted for me—but that would be only a handful.

From there I met Dan Wolf, who seemed to sense defeat. He said, "Ed, now be sure that you are up and smiling all day. Otherwise, people will think that you are depressed and it will become the subject of conversations."

Before lunch I campaigned in Midtown and at Court Street in Brooklyn. And wherever I went, the crowds—whether Hispanic, white or black—were very responsive. The question was whether this was just the celebrity that comes from having been on television or whether it was the kind of affection that ultimately translates into votes.

At 6:15 P.M.. we all had dinner at Gracie Mansion—Bobbie Margolis, Dan Wolf, Bob Wagner, Victor Botnick and I. There was a very heavy feeling, a feeling that had started at lunch at India House. Victor said that the exit polls indicated the election would be very close. So we ate and we talked, and somehow the thought that I was not going to be the next Governor seemed to be looming before us. There was a big bus that the campaign had rented to bring everyone back from the Sheraton Centre Hotel. We stayed at Gracie Mansion as long as we could, and then my little group piled onto this large, empty bus and rode over to the hotel. And there, there were parties upstairs and lots of people who were certain that I was going to win in a landslide.

I had wanted to win big. I had wanted to eliminate the possibility of Mario's continuing to run on the Liberal Party line. By evening I had given up on that. But as we rode over to the hotel I still did not believe that I would lose. It is painful to think of it now. There we were in that hotel suite, captive to the various nonfunctioning television sets and radios and getting the results in dribs and drabs. It was then, when the first City returns came in, that I knew it was hopeless.

I tried to be stoical. I was sitting on a sofa with my brother and sister. There was at one point confusion as to conflicting reports out of Nassau County. I was calm as the news sorted itself out. In the end, the margin was 52 percent for Mario and 48 percent for me.

The following is the text of my September 23 concession speech.

First, don't shed a tear. It is better to win than to lose. But if we have done everything we can and the people decide otherwise, that is the nature of the democratic system, and so I have no regrets.

And I'm *still* the Mayor.

And that's not bad.

In fact, it's good.

Because I love New York City, and all the people in it. And tomorrow I'm going to go on working just as hard as I always have.

There are a few important points I have to make.

First, congratulations to Mario Cuomo.

Mario waged a good race, and so did we.

But the people spoke, and now Mario is the Democratic candidate for Governor.

And tonight I repeat what I said at the outset. I am supporting that Democratic candidate—Mario Cuomo.

And I urge all my supporters to do the same in November.

What's important to all of us is that we keep a Democrat in Albany, doing what's best for all the people of New York State.

That's why I wanted to go to Albany.

To make a difference.

It was a difficult decision for me to make.

I believed then and now that my experience as Mayor would have best served the people of New York State, and the people of the city I truly love, New York City.

I pledge to you and to Mario that I will use that experience to assist him in any way I can.

Because what's important now is that we elect him as our Governor.

I want to thank people across New York State who have helped me, especially the Labor Coalition. I know it wasn't easy for the Coalition.

One more thing.

Don't be disappointed for me.

I have spent seven months—seven very difficult months— trying to be the Governor of the State of New York. Even though I won't have that privilege, it gave me experience. I learned a lot. It will help me be a better Mayor.

So don't be upset. And do be happy for Mario. Because that's the way the Democratic Party will win in November.

Thank you, everybody.

22

New York: Coming Home

FOR ABOUT A MONTH following my primary defeat I was
depressed. First of all I blamed myself for not doing what I
thought had to be done. On the day I made my official
announcement, I had said to reporters who were commenting
that my victory was "a shoo-in" that I was not sanguine
because of what I referred to as the radical voter on the left.

And there were people besides myself whom I blamed. I
was angry with those who had talked me out of speaking
frankly about the one-issue voters. I was angry with those
who had run the nonmedia campaign. I believed that that had
not been done well. I wished that I had been my own
campaign manager. Undoubtedly I was unfair in my feelings
about those who had worked so hard. But I was desperately
trying to analyze why I had been defeated.

I have concluded that my defeat was overwhelmingly in the
City of New York, where I got 52 percent instead of the 60
percent that I had received in the 1981 Mayoral primary.
There the following factors had an impact, and probably in
this order:

First, I had been guilty of hubris in running at all when I
had just been elected Mayor with the largest margin any
Mayor had ever achieved—to wit, 75 percent of the vote.
And before that election, I had said that I never wanted to run
for anything other than reelection as Mayor. Indeed, I had
challenged Divine Providence by making that statement before the Western Wall in Jerusalem. When I returned from my
trip to Spain, and reporters were waiting to ask me if I was

going to run for Governor, one reporter reminded me of my promise before the Western Wall. And I had flippantly replied, "That is a matter between God and me, not between you and me." But in fact, it was a matter between me and the public. They felt betrayed. I had said I loved them and no one else. Then I told them that I no longer wanted to live with them, that I wanted to take a new lover in Albany. There were large numbers of people who approved of my record and preferred me to Mario Cuomo but decided to show me that I couldn't get away with what I was doing without suffering the consequences of having rejected them.

Secondly, I believe there was a group that voted against me because I had supported the Israelis' invasion of Lebanon. They were subsequently, and quite rightly, horrified by the Palestinian massacre. And they associated it with me.

Third, there was a group, although small in number, that didn't want to lose me in the City and voted against me for that reason. This group consisted not only of those who wanted me for myself, but of those who feared an administration under Carol Bellamy. And here I had only myself to blame, because she had been held in the highest regard before I referred to her as a "disaster" and "a horrow show." Those words came back to haunt me.

Then, in all candor, I don't believe that our media campaign adequately presented me as I am. It was a superb traditional media campaign talking solely of my record, which is a good one, but it did not allow me to talk about my philosophy, which is also a good one and is overwhelmingly supported by New Yorkers. So by default we allowed Mario Cuomo to preempt this meaningful area. And since he had no record of achievement, the philosophical area was very important.

And my field campaign was inadequate. Those in charge did not go throughout the State to seek volunteers and to check on those volunteers and the organizational people who were working for me. Instead, they sent me and my traveling team throughout the state on small airplanes to small events. They simply accepted the reports they received and were lulled and gulled by them. They berated me for having failed to use patronage, claiming that therefore they could not get volunteers from inside government to help. When I asked them why they didn't get the volunteers who had helped me over the years and who were not in government, they said they didn't exist anymore. I believe they did and do exist.

Having said all this privately, and with the passage of four weeks, I realized that I had not touched on one final aspect. It has to do with someone I am not fond of and who I don't think is fond of me but who is a good reporter, who mentioned it in one of her profiles during the campaign, in which she showed a marked bias in favor of Mario Cuomo. She said that I had not demonstrated a desire for the job. She said my heart wasn't in it.

My desire to be Governor was based almost solely on my belief that the State government was where the power would be in the future. It was not owing to any idea I would enjoy being in Albany or in the Governor's role. Indeed, I knew that I would not enjoy the job as much. Being the Mayor in New York allows me to talk to thousands of people and stand in line at movie theaters and restaurants. I can walk down the hall to talk to Tom Cuite and the members of the City Council and enjoy the sparring and infighting involved with all the other City officials. I enjoy having a first-rate, first-name relationship with fifty Commissioners and I am constantly sending them notes to credit them or spur them on. And I know that what I am doing in the appointment of Criminal and Family Court judges will have an impact for thirty years after I have left office, because those judges are for the most part automatically redesignated by succeeding Mayors. And I know that I have changed the way government works, and I can get things done without the glue of patronage and judgeships. Those are things that would not have been available to me in Albany. In my heart, I knew that I really belonged in New York City.

Being the Mayor of the City of New York has been a very special experience. I have a responsibility to more than 7 million people. And as I travel the neighborhoods and speak to thousands of people, I realize what a unique city this is and how lucky I am to be its Mayor.

There are 157 nations represented at the United Nations. The City of New York includes nearly two hundred different religions, races, national groups, ethnic backgrounds. And somehow or other we have learned to live with each other. It used to be said that New York City was a melting pot. It never was, and it isn't today. Our fathers and mothers and some of us, in order to be perceived as Americans, wanted to believe that we had lost our own racial or ethnic traditions and had become homogenized. That never happened. What in fact happens is that you gain respect for the traditions of others and you absorb some of those traditions, but you don't lose your own. Though in earlier times the immigrant groups were ashamed of their backgrounds and changed their names— and I now refer to Jews, Greeks, Italians and even some Irish who took American names in order to lose their identity—that doesn't happen today. Black is beautiful. Spanish is the language of the future. Women want to be astronauts and are. And Jews play golf. We suddenly have an appreciation of our own worth and our own traditions. We recognize that God made us whatever we are, and whatever we are—excluding the corrupt and the criminals—we are the best.

Yet how do you govern in a city where everyone thinks he or she is the best and can do it better than you? You do it by conveying that you are giving it everything you have, and you demonstrate that what you are doing is what they would be doing if they were in your place. You become their hand on the wheel of government. People want to touch you, praise you, harangue you, love you and hate you. And as Mayor, you must be able to accept it all and at the same time not become overwhelmed by the praise or overcome by the abuse.

I have as my shield ever before me the premise that public service is the noblest of professions if it is done honestly and done well. I know that in the private sector, no matter how much money you make (and it's nice to make money) you can't have the sense of satisfaction that comes at the highest levels of government from helping to improve the lives of millions of people. I know that every Mayor of New York since Fiorello LaGuardia has been measured by the public and has measured himself against the image of the Little Flower. He has created the standard. I am hopeful that at the end of my Mayoral career, whether that be another six or ten years, I will have left such a positive mark. I believe that I will, but only the historians will be able to make that judgment.

I believe that I was able to take a city on the edge of bankruptcy and make it bankable. I believe that I was able to lead a citizenry in total disarray, shaken by what had occurred in the financial debacle in 1975, without confidence in the government or themselves, and turn them around so that they now have confidence in themselves and faith in their government.

Few people have been given the opportunity given to me. I hope that I never cause people to regret their trust in me. Somehow or other, truly or falsely, we believe that if you are born in New York or come here to live, when you see yourself as a New Yorker you talk faster, you walk faster and you think faster. We want the rest of America to respect us and, if possible, even to love us. We know that there has been a love/hate relationship between the rest of America and the City of New York. I am of the belief that love is in the ascendancy. I hope so.

I am the Mayor of a city that has more Jews than live in Jerusalem, more Italians than live in Rome, more Irish than live in Dublin, more blacks than live in Nairobi and more Puerto Ricans than live in San Juan.

It is a tremendous responsibility, but there is no other job in the world that compares with it. Every day is new. Every day is dangerous. Every day is filled with excitement. Every day has the possibility of accomplishing some major success that will impact positively on the lives of the citizens of the City of New York. Every day I am both humbled and made even more proud than the day before.

Now, aside from the considerable business of running this city, it is on to the battle of the third term. Lately I have been saying, "Eight good years deserve four more."

23

The Last Word: Front Page
News—Top of the List

ON TUESDAY NIGHT, January 17, 1984, I was at Steve Ross'
house for dinner. There were about a dozen guests there,
among whom was Arthur Liman, who is one of the most able
attorneys in New York. When I walked in Arthur said, "One
of my associates at my law firm is reading your book—he
says it's first rate."

I said, "I don't understand how that can be. The book
hasn't been published yet."

He said, "There are copies of the galleys all over town."

Several weeks prior to that dinner, Bill Rauch had shown
me a little yellow book that was a bound paperback edition of
the unproofed galleys of *Mayor*. He said Simon and Schuster
was sending these bound galleys out to the reviewers for the
purpose of attracting attention to my book prior to its publication.
As soon as I saw those little yellow books I said to Bill: "Tell
them not to send those books around. Someone will give one
of them to a reporter and the book will leak." At that time
Mayor was not due to appear for four months.

Throughout dinner at Steve Ross' house I worried that
Simon and Schuster had gone ahead and sent out galleys and
that that was what Arthur Liman's associate had read. At
about 8 P.M., during dinner, Bill Rauch called. He said: "Ed,
I have just spoken to Sam Roberts of the *New York Times*.
The *Times* will have a story on your book tomorrow, and Sam

wants to get a quote from you about why you wrote the book.''

I said, ''I'm not calling Sam Roberts. Whatever he wants he can get out of the Foreword of the book. Does he have the whole book?''

Bill said, ''Apparently he has. The story is expected to be over six-hundred words, with line-by-line excerpts from the book.''

Then Bill said, ''I have also spoken to Bill Murphy from the Associated Press and others and I have been told that the *Village Voice* will also be doing a long piece on the book tomorrow. So it is starting.''

After speaking to Bill I was worried. I didn't want to be rude to my hosts and leave dinner to go out and get the papers at 10 P.M. when the *Times* comes out. But I must have looked pensive throughout the evening because I was asked by others at the dinner if there was anything wrong. I told them I had been told by my press secretary that both the *Times* and the *Voice* would be carrying comments the next day on my yet unpublished book.

Finally, at 11 P.M. I left the dinner and went to the *New York Times* offices on 43rd Street to buy the papers. The article that Sam Roberts wrote was quite fair and it carried an interesting headline: ''In New Book, Koch Says He Was 'Guilty of Hubris' in Running for Governor.''

The next morning Bill came over to Gracie Mansion at 6:30 A.M. and we rode down to Sheridan Square in the Village together to buy the *Village Voice*. I wasn't particularly concerned about what effect the *Voice*'s story would have except insofar as legitimate reporters occasionally use that weekly as a tip sheet. We knew that whatever the worst was that would be said about *Mayor*, it would be in the *Voice*. Instead of going to the gym as I normally would from 6:45 to 7:30 A.M., I went directly to my office at City Hall. Bill and I sat there and read the *Voice* piece which was quite long and sought to portray *Mayor* as a kiss-and-tell book. The front page of the *Voice* had my picture on it and then a scornful headline that read: ''Mayor Dearest.''

The article contained long quotes and sensationalized passages.

But what the *Voice* was unable to find, and what no other writer has been able to find to date in the entire book, is a substantial factual error.

Over the course of eight months of careful scrutiny, four episodes related by me became the subject of controversy as to their accuracy. First, the episode which occurred on January 15, 1978, in the Convent Avenue Baptist Church was disputed by Basil Paterson. I had written that the heckler in the balcony shouted: "Don't let him speak. Send the Jew back to the synagogue."

Basil Paterson chose to dispute that language. On television, Basil cited a *New York Times* account of the incident. In that account the *Times* reporter recounted that the heckler had shouted: "Let the black man speak first. We can't go into the synagogue and speak. The rabbi won't let you go into the synagogue and speak." My response to that was that the two reports of what occurred are not inconsistent. In fact, the reported accounts are each consistent with each other in their anti-Semitism. When asked about the heckler's statement as set forth in the *Times'* truncated version, Basil Paterson said on February 26, 1984: "I don't think I would interpret that as anti-Semitic, but you might consider it kind of a crude statement." Would it simply have been viewed as "a crude statement" if there had been a black person sitting in a synagogue awaiting his turn to speak and a member of the congregation had stood up and shouted: "Let the Jew speak first. We can't go into black churches and speak. Black ministers won't let us go into their churches and speak."? Had I ever been in such a synagogue and had such an incident occurred, I am certain I would not have sat by in silence. And it is that part of Basil Paterson's response that I find interesting. Nowhere has he disputed my assertion that he did not rise to speak out on my behalf. Indeed, never once that I can recall over the course of twelve months as my deputy mayor, did Basil Paterson defend this administration against the attacks of the racial demogogues. That is Basil's way. He is likable and charming, but if you are looking for someone who will stand up and do the right thing when doing so means that someone somewhere may get upset, then do not look to Basil. Look what he did on Jesse Jackson and Louis Farrakhan, for example. On May 4, 1984, the American Jewish Committee had its meeting and they invited Basil to speak. During the question and answer portion the issue of Jackson and his support of Farrakhan came up and Basil was asked if he, Basil, as a mayoral candidate, would repudiate Farrakhan's support. Basil's response was the predictable one: "I don't think it is appropriate for me to respond at this time," he said. Why not, Basil? Why wasn't it appropriate to comment? I'll tell you why. It wasn't appropriate because Basil's disposition requires him to sit on his hands whenever there are two sides to an issue. He thinks he can be everything to everybody. He has to be dragged into making decisions. Now, it does take strength to stand up against one's own constituency. But that is what leadership is all about. You have to stand up when there are wrongs being committed—even if it's in a church—even if it's one of your own who is perpetrating the injustices against someone else. Now, just to be clear: I know how the game is played. There is no doubt in my mind that were Basil to run for mayor in 1985, he would, at that time, repudiate Farrakhan's support. Why would he be free to do that then and not in May, 1984? Because in 1985 he will be given permission by his supporters in the black leadership to do so. They will give him a temporary waiver of "principles" so that he may do the politically expeditious thing.

The second disputed area was the account of the lunch at which Cy Vance conveyed to me that, after the 1980 presidential election, Jimmy Carter would sell out Israel. In my account, I wrote that I said at the lunch: "They [the Jews] believe that if he [Carter] is reelected he will sell them out.

"Vance nodded and said, 'He will.'"

At the lunch were three other people. Two recall the incident exactly as I reported it. The third recalled that I had posed the question and that Cy Vance had mouthed the word "yes" but had not uttered it. Cy Vance recalls it somewhat differently, and in a letter to Dr. M. T. Mehdi, President of the American-Arab Relations Committee, who asked him whether the incident occurred, Cy responded as follows:

"Mayor Koch asked me if I believed that President Carter would exert pressure on Israel in a second term to try to bring about a reduction of the Middle East problem. I told him that

I believed the President would." There is no doubt in my mind that Cy Vance recalls it that way, and there is no doubt in my mind that it happened exactly as I reported it. It is the best illustration of *Rashomon* the Japanese movie, which reported how different people participating in the same incident will recall it differently. There was no reason for me to tell Bill Safire, the *Times* reporter, anything but the truth as I recalled what had occurred and that is what I did. It is quite understandable that Cy Vance, the former Secretary of State, would recall it more diplomatically. And Bill Safire probably summed it up best when he said: "Okay, jesting Pilate, what is truth? I suspect that Mayor Koch remembers saying 'sell out' because that is his vernacular, and former Secretary of State Vance remembers the words 'put pressure on' because that is the diplomatic lexicon."* I believe in his head Cy Vance recalled the incident as he stated it and that in fact he either mouthed the affirmative to my question or said the "terrible" word "yes."

The third area of disagreement was perhaps the strangest. Shortly after *Mayor* was published, I was told that Charlie Rangel was saying that the lunch itself at Sweets on April 13, 1979 had never occurred. He said that he had left the restaurant early and before lunch. However, everyone who had been at that lunch, with the exception of Charlie apparently, remembered the lunch very clearly—and they remembered that Charlie had not only stayed throughout a leisurely lunch but that he had ridden back to City Hall with me and made phone calls in my office. It would have been difficult to forget that day. During lunch Charlie went to the telephone once, and when he returned he announced to us that his wife, Alma, and his children had been overcome by gas in their Washington, D.C. home. Myself and those with me, of course, expected Charlie to excuse himself and head for the airport. We all found it strange that Charlie would sit through a long lunch and then ride back to City Hall while his entire family was in a hospital in apparent peril in Washington. We could hardly have forgotten that day—and I find it difficult to imagine that Charlie did. Upon being reminded of the inci-

*See *New York Times*, February 20, 1984, p. 19.

dent by one of those at the lunch, Charlie gulped and said he was not going to pursue the matter further—and he hasn't.

Finally, Bella Abzug wrote a letter to the *New York Times Magazine* which had printed an excerpt from *Mayor* that involved her.

The excerpt the *Times* had chosen included the piece about my interview by Bella in which she expressed her distaste for my position in favor of jets for Israel. This was in 1968. In her letter to the *Times* Bella claimed she had never opposed jets for Israel. However, the record does not bear out her claim. A 1970 piece of campaign literature distributed by Howard Squadron's Congressional campaign committee quoted Bella as having said on March 26, 1970, at the Village Independent Democrats candidates' forum: "I would find it difficult to vote for planes for Israel." Moreover, as damning proof, let me cite the following open letter published in the *Village Voice*.

The Village Voice, September 28, 1972

Why I'm Not for Bella

Dear Sir:

We have all gone through some pain with the death of Bill Ryan, and the bitter succession fight over his seat. I was called at home by a supporter of Bella Abzug, asking for an endorsement, even before I had a chance to go to Ryan's wake.

Bella's politics are fine; the problem is her character, and in the end, I reluctantly think this disqualifies her from taking Ryan's seat. I have seen her call too many good people "cocksucker"—and worse. There is a limit to the personal viciousness permissable within the politics of change.

I was there when Bella said at the VID in 1970 she was against the jets for Israel. And then I watched her deny she ever said it. And finally I lied, and denied she ever said it, so that she might defeat Barry Farber. I am now ashamed of all that.

Bella is a divisive figure. She cannot represent the Irish working class of Inwood on the Ryan faction of the reform movement. She brings out the worst in people because humility and charity are not in her. You cannot disagree with Bella and have a human conversation.

Also, I think Bella is an invention of the media—pure Frankenstein.

But the fact is the people—the true repository of politics—don't like her. She defeated Barry Farber by the smallest margin any Democrat ever won the 19th C. D. She lost to Bill Ryan by 18,000 votes. And her book has not sold more than 5000 copies, at a time when a book by her colleague—Don Reigle—is a national best-seller.

In the end, the thing that is in Bella that let her decide to run against Bill Ryan in the first place, is the thing that has made politics such a miserable profession.

I hope that either Priscilla Ryan, Paul O'Dwyer, or Franz Leichter win the seat this Sunday. The issue is neither ideology nor sentiment. The issue is character, and the diminution of the politics of insult and ego.

—Jack Newfield
Manhattan

Believe me, Bella was saying in 1968 what she was saying in 1970.

In 1984, the *Voice*, not being able to attack *Mayor* on the basis of factual errors, was reduced to doing what it always does: attacking my personality. And that is what all my antagonists found themselves doing in their reviews of *Mayor* in the ensuing weeks. They didn't review the book. They reviewed me. The reaction to *Mayor* was similar to what the reaction is to many of the nonconformist actions I take. That is, those who like me thought it was terrific; those who are indifferent remain so; and my opponents attack me for having personality defects.

At 7:30 A.M. on January 18th, I called Michael Korda, my editor at Simon and Schuster. I said, "Michael, both the *Times* and the *Voice* have the galleys of my book and the *Voice* has sought to sensationalize it. We can't wait until April to bring the book out. We have to get it out as soon as possible."

He said he would go into the office and immediately have a meeting to determine where in production the book was and how soon they could get it into the bookstores. At 10:30 that morning, Michael called me back. He said he could have the books out by the end of January. The book was in fact delivered ten days later, three months ahead of the original publication date, a publishing miracle.

Now, that same morning I had a press conference scheduled with Diana Ross the singer to announce that she would be donating a quarter of a million dollars to the Parks Department for the purpose of refurbishing a playground in Central Park. Very few of the reporters in Room Nine had that morning actually seen copies of the galleys, other than what they had seen in the morning's papers, but they all wanted to ask questions about the excerpts. I said: "I will not answer questions on my book based on early drafts, unproofed galleys or purloined copies. When the book, in its final form, becomes available, I will answer questions then."

Notwithstanding my silence, *Mayor* was fast becoming a major news story and in fact, from whatever source during that ten-day period, Xeroxed copies of the galleys were being distributed throughout town. It was like a dissenter in the Soviet Union having his works appear in *samizdat*. And as reporters read those galleys and solicited responses from those people who had been mentioned in the book, pages and pages of news stories were appearing, and *Mayor* was becoming a major political book in the City of New York, without yet being on the shelves and available to the general public.

Several days before the book actually appeared I learned that Gay Talese would be reviewing *Mayor* for the Sunday *Times* Book Review section. Dan Wolf said: "You could not get a better book reviewer for this book. Talese is an inconoclast. He will understand intuitively what you are doing in your book. He wrote a book on the sex industry that was put down by some of his colleagues but it was a good book and it eventually prevailed over the naysayers."

Dan was exactly correct and when the review appeared it was clear that Talese had seen just the iconoclastic quality in *Mayor* that Dan had referred to in Talese's *Thy Neighbor's Wife*. In his review Talese wrote: "And now, suddenly, there is an even more remarkable event—a factual book by a politician *still in office* who exposes his colleagues, who cross-examines their motives, who penetrates their psyches, who reveals them in the raw. It is the perfect political book for 1984." Meanwhile, Max Lerner called *Mayor* a "frolic," and a monument to *toujour l'audace*: audacity always. And Talese's colleague at the *Times*, Russell Baker, described my

NEW YORK POST · METRO · TODAY'S RACING

THURSDAY, JANUARY 19, 1984 · **30** CENTS · ★★ · © 1984 News Group Publications Inc. · Vol. 183, No. 56

35 cents beyond 50-mile zone, except L.I · **AMERICA'S FASTEST-GROWING NEWSPAPER** · ABC AVERAGE SALES EXCEED · **960,000**

THE KOCH EXPLOSION

- **Red-hot book sets N.Y. afire**
- *Memoirs rip top pols around U.S.*
- **Stung biggies strike back at hizzoner**

Rigby's impression of author Ed hard at work on memoirs.

INSIDE: 5 pages of dynamite disclosures!

Page one of the January 19, 1984 edition of the New York Post, copyright © 1984 by News Group Publications, Inc. Reprinted by permission.

book as "a priceless service to the dismal art of politicans' literature."

Not all of their fellow reviewers agreed with them, however. The local reporters' reviews and commentaries were interesting only for their predictability. Those who had over the years attacked me as Mayor, attacked by book. Ken Auletta, in a column entitled: "*The Secret Life of Mayor Mitty*" said *Mayor* is "garbage and no fresh news . . . just the old news that the author was a hopeless narcissist.' Michael Kramer, a columnist for *New York* magazine, with whom I had been feuding since the gubernatorial campaign, referred to *Mayor* as "spleen-venting slurs." Frank Lombardi, a political writer for the *Daily News*, opined by way of a review: "If that's all there is to Edward I. Koch, hizzoner is a small man indeed." Andy Logan, a columnist for *The New Yorker*, who had loved Lindsay and who, in six years, had never found a single kind word for me, discerned in *Mayor* an author who is: "arrogant," "mean," "cold-hearted," and "self-deluded." And Arthur Schlesinger, Jr., the professor, in a review for the *New York Review of Books*, called me possessed of an "over-powering egotism"; and he said in my forthrightness, he found, "an instrument of aggression." In Professor Schlesinger's review, I, however, found intellectual deceit. How, when he had been a charter member of the "Dump Koch" committee in 1981,* could Dr. Schlesinger purport to write a fair review of *Mayor* without at least alerting his readers to his political biases? Didn't Schlesinger the reviewer betray Schlesinger the historian by not revealing the biases of Schlesinger the politician? When I was asked, I explained the heart of elitism is that the ethical conduct rules they wish to apply to other people don't apply to them. They can tell people how to be victims without having to be victims themselves. Moreover, the fact is there was a lot of envy involved with those who reviewed *Mayor* negatively.

This was, in many cases, their beat—politics in the City of New York, the fiscal crisis, the transit strike—and I scooped them. That is the heart of it, and I said so at the time.† On

---

*See *New York Times*, January 28, 1981, p. 83.

†See *New York Post*, Thursday, February 2, 1984, p. 9.

February 18, when it was first known that *Mayor* would appear at the top of the *New York Times* nonfiction bestseller list, I was interviewed by Leslie Bennets of the *Times*. She said: "How does it make you feel?" I said, "Amused. Can you imagine the heartbreak at the *Village Voice*? This book would never have been so well received had it not been for my enemies. Why, if my most hostile critics hadn't sought to sensationalize my book, it would have taken weeks before it became a No. 1 bestseller! I think I'm going to have the *Voice* cover bronzed, along with my baby shoes."

Since *Mayor* appeared, people from around the country have been writing to me in my capacity as mayor. They seem delighted to learn about New York City and that is helpful to the City. Public officials whom I have met, many of them mayors, have told me how much they like the book because they could identify with so many of the situations and for them it was a feeling of deja vu. My publisher has told me that there will now be many more books written by those still in public office and the test that will apply will be, have you met the standard of *Mayor* in terms of telling what happened as it happened? This is heady stuff but it will not go to my head because I am just a little mayor from a small town on the Hudson and I enjoy my job.

The book and this past eight months have been exhilarating with twenty-one weeks on the *New York Times* bestselling list. And they have made my job as mayor easier. Every honest politician knows his best issue is himself. I believe that many people in public life will now write books while they are still in office. I urge them to be themselves at their typewriters and to remember to tell the whole truth as they best recall it. It is the strength of the republic that the public should be informed.

I wasn't an author, but before I became mayor, I wasn't a mayor. Now I'm both—and it's fun reviewing the reviewers.

New York City
October 15, 1984

Afterword

I FIRST MET BILL RAUCH in 1977 when he interviewed me as a reporter representing the *Fire Island News*. He later came to work for me as my advance man—a position for which he was highly overqualified; his curriculum vitae includes a B.A. with honors from Harvard, where he was a member of the Porcellian Club, Harvard's most prestigious. Over the five years he has been in my administration, where he is now my press secretary, I have come to truly admire his intelligence, toughness, loyalty and gentle disposition. I asked Bill if he would on his own time sit with me on weekends when I was recording my thoughts, because I knew it would be difficult to sit alone and talk into the tape recorder. I preferred having the presence and warmth of another human being in the room when I was recording. And Bill, because of his good mind, would pose questions which would provoke me to provide a more comprehensive picture of the incidents I was recounting.

During our long association, he made one comment to me which may sound frivolous, but it is not for someone in public office. He said, "Never trust a reporter who has a nice smile." And he was right. The most guileful among the reporters, and this is not criticism on my part but simply a fact, are those who appear friendly and smile and seem to be supportive. They are the ones who will seek to gut you on every occasion. That is the nature of their business and the role that the Fourth Estate has taken for itself: the gutting of the politician in office.

In addition to simply being present and taking down my

thoughts and asking me the questions that expanded my comments and thoughts, Bill played an important role in putting the book together. After all, my recollections grew to a compilation covering nearly twenty-six years. Incidents in history tend to occur and recur, and comments made in one month are enlarged upon or changed six months later and are all part of the record. Bill went through the entire compendium and took my recollections at different times and put them together. Where there were inconsistencies, he asked me to resolve them or to provide my best recollection. His editing and research were key essentials in making the book meaningful. So while the thoughts and language are mine, the hopeful intelligence going into this book is both mine and his.

Index